£30.00

Cecilia Beaux

A MODERN PAINTER in the GILDED AGE

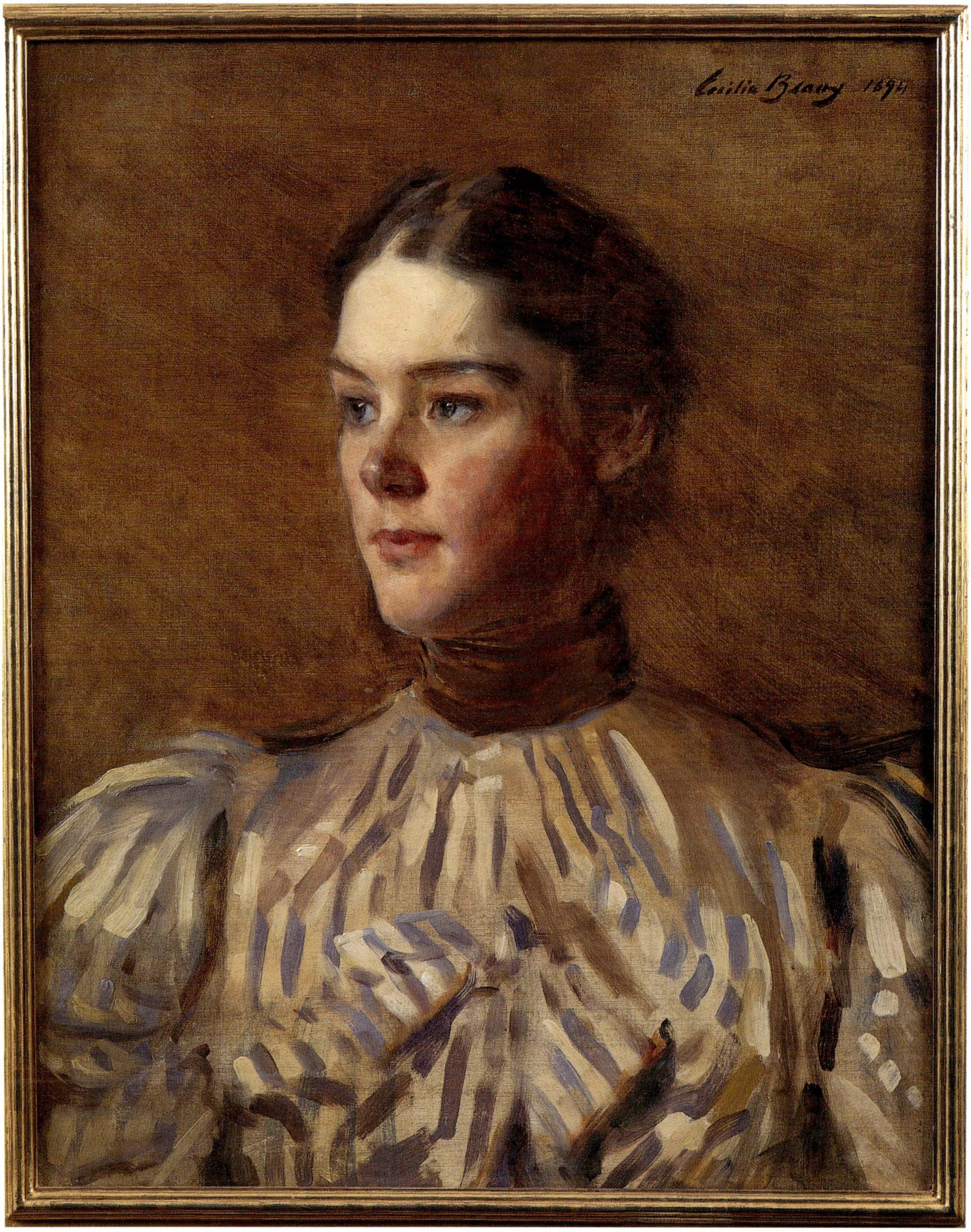
Cecilia Beaux 1894

Cecilia Beaux

A MODERN PAINTER in the GILDED AGE

ALICE A. CARTER

RIZZOLI
NEW YORK

To Kathryn Krall, Judith Belasco, and Ronald Nuse in memory of our childhood adventures in Philadelphia, Beach Haven, and Gloucester, Massachusetts

A.C.

first published in the United States of America in 2005
by Rizzoli International Publications, Inc.
300 Park Avenue South, New York, NY 10010
www.rizzoliusa.com

ISBN: 0-8478-2708-9
Library of Congress Control Number: 2005900675

Designed by Element group

Printed in China

1. FRONTIS: ***Self-Portrait.*** *1894. Oil on canvas, 25 x 20 in. National Academy of Design, New York*

Contents

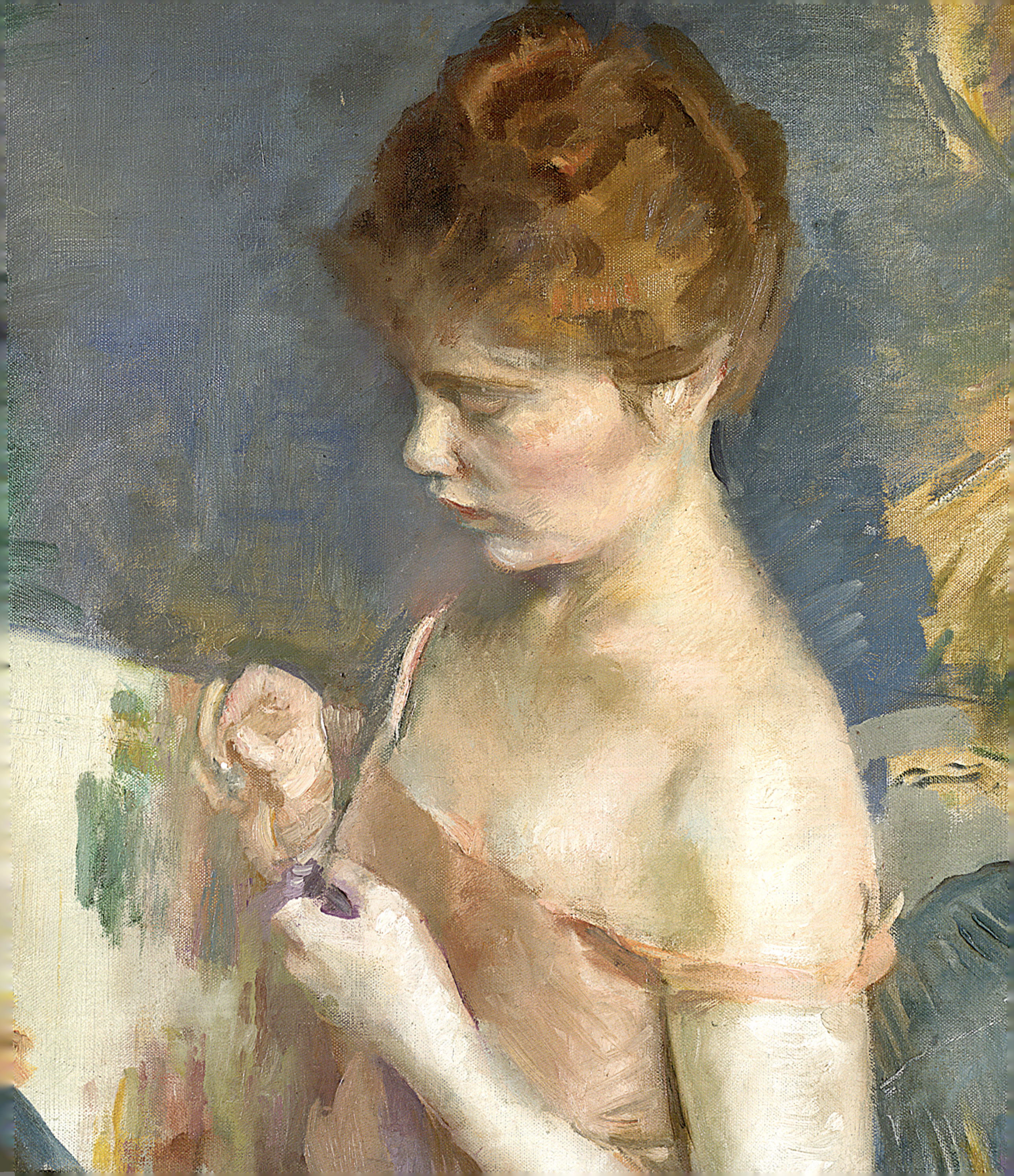

The Beaux Sisters

"Music is Love in search of a word."

—Sidney Lanier

The Symphony (1875)

If her life had been set to music, the theme for Cecilia Beaux's biography could have been Frédéric Chopin's *Heroic* Polonaise, a composition that stirred her soul, leaving her simultaneously thrilled and troubled. The bass octaves rumbled through the houses of her childhood with what she once described as "a prophetic significance and a deep note of warning."[1] Perhaps the family's well-polished Chickering reverberated with the piece on the very day Cecilia was born. Splendor and catastrophe wrapped together in seven minutes of piano virtuosity.[2]

The musician would have been Cecilia's eldest aunt, Eliza Leavitt—laboring over the complexity of Chopin's masterwork, while her sister labored to produce a new life. Eliza Leavitt was an extraordinary and dedicated musician. Thirty-one years old and unmarried, she could not have suspected that within a fortnight her time at the piano would be dramatically cut back. Much of the responsibility for this baby would fall on her slim shoulders.

Catastrophe came without warning. The child was healthy, and her arrival cause for celebration by the entire household: the young mother, Cecilia Leavitt Beaux; the father, Jean Adolphe Beaux; the aunts, musician Eliza and younger sister Emily; the maternal grandmother, Cecilia Kent Leavitt; and the newborn's two-and-one-half-year-old sister, Aimée Ernesta Beaux. It was May 1, 1855, Election Day in the newly consolidated city of Philadelphia.

Twelve days later Cecilia Leavitt Beaux was dead. The innovations of Joseph Lister concerning the use of antiseptics in medicine were still ten years away. Oliver Wendell Holmes's warnings about the contagious nature of puerperal fever (childbirth fever) went unheeded by doctors scandalized by the suggestion that they might bear some responsibility for the spread of contagion. Surgical instruments were not sterilized. Doctors routinely went from one patient to another, even to the autopsy room and back to their patients, without changing their jackets or thoroughly washing their hands.[3] In the 1850s infections were often passed from doctors and midwives to patients during home deliveries but were rampant in lying-in wards, where puerperal fever sometimes reached epidemic proportions, taking the lives of more than 20 percent of the patients.[4]

"What of those twelve first days of my life which were passed near or upon her breast, before the chill, and the devastating fever, and the end?" Cecilia Beaux wondered seventy-five years later.[5] Her mother's belongings were carefully folded and put away—cloaks, dresses, a few "exquisite" fans, and a white box with gold edging containing artifacts from her wedding: a veil, wreath, gloves, and slippers.

OPPOSITE: *Detail;* ***Dressing Dolls.*** *1928. Oil on canvas, 35 x 28 in. Private Collection. Photograph courtesy Spanierman Gallery Ltd.*

Jean Adolphe Beaux was overcome with grief. His wife was dead at thirty-three, and in her place was a newborn to whom her mother had given a single whispered legacy, her sister's name and her own, the music and the tragedy—Eliza-Cecilia. The name, a mother's final blessing, proved a curse to the father. Whatever fine characteristics Jean Adolphe Beaux may have possessed, fortitude and courage were not among them. He could not bear to hear his daughter called by his wife's name, and the family respected his wishes. Although she was to claim her birthright as an adult and sign her paintings "Cecilia Beaux," to her family, she was forever after "Leilie."

Thirty-eight-year-old Jean Adolphe Beaux, second son of Gabrielle and Jean Pierre Beaux, arrived in the United States in 1848 charged with the task of internationalizing the family business, J. P. Beaux & Co. Sewing Silks.[6] Against considerable odds and confounded by the English language, he did manage to open a factory. But his success was short-lived. "He was an idealist, not a successful businessman," wrote his fond daughter, Cecilia. "He never neglected his affairs, but it was not in his nature to—as the saying is—turn over money."[7] Nevertheless, at the start, the silk factory promised well. So well, that when the blue-eyed Frenchman began courting young Cecilia Kent Leavitt, her father John Wheeler Leavitt could find nothing amiss. Jean Adolphe Beaux's credentials were impeccable, and his prospects appeared to be excellent. The match seemed like salvation to the refined but embarrassingly impoverished Leavitt family. An engagement was approved.

Before their fiscal calamity, Cecilia Beaux's maternal grandparents, John Wheeler Leavitt and Cecilia Kent Leavitt, enjoyed the nineteenth-century version of the American dream. By all accounts, they were a perfect match. Both descended resplendently from established Puritan families. Cecilia Kent's father fought in the American Revolution. John Wheeler Leavitt could trace his own ancestry to a plucky nineteen-year-old runaway apprentice, who (although family legend sometimes put him on the *Mayflower*) probably arrived in Massachusetts in about 1628 and was one of the first settlers of the Massachusetts Bay Colony's Mattapan Plantation.[8]

The couple met in Brooklyn, New York, where Cecilia Kent was visiting her older sister and John Leavitt was starting up a dry-goods business with a cousin. They were married in 1820 and established a home on Dey Street in Lower Manhattan, then a modest middle-class neighborhood.[9] When the business flourished, John Leavitt built a luxurious home for his growing family on Barclay Street, across from the present site of the Woolworth Building, although by 1913 when that landmark was at last completed, the Leavitts and their eight children were long gone.

While their affluence lasted, the family made the most of their money and their position. John Leavitt built a gymnasium for the children that occupied the entire attic of the Barclay Street house. There was a bathroom, famous as the first of its kind in New York, with what Cecilia Beaux later described as "accessories" and water piped up to the second floor.[10] In addition to the house in the city, John Leavitt also maintained a country estate called Oakland on the Palisades that faced the Hudson River in Hoboken, New Jersey.

No expense was spared in educating the children, and the young Leavitts survived the perils of infancy to grow up in luxury. Tutors were hired to teach German and French. For mathematics, a Professor Gloubenskly and an intimidating Scotsman were engaged, and for music, Otto Dresel. Dresel's role in educating the Leavitt girls was legendary in the family. The tale passed down to Cecilia Beaux was that her grandfather, upon hearing that the twenty-two-year-old musician and protégé of Mendelssohn had recently arrived in the United States, immediately engaged him to give piano lessons to his daughters. Eliza credited to young Dresel (two years her junior) all her considerable skill, and her niece Cecilia was to speak often and with pride of "the immense advantage" of this brief connection.[11]

The Leavitt children studied hard, practiced tirelessly, and were a happy group who carried into adulthood memories of interesting conversation and much laughter. However, by 1845, when the children ranged in age from seven to twenty-three, there were signs that the idyll was about to end. John Leavitt's business, affected by changes in the Southern cotton industry, first declined and ultimately failed. In order to satisfy his creditors, everything was sold, including both homes. The family remained in the city but moved to a small house on Twenty-Third Street in what Cecilia Beaux described as a "rough suburb." Beleaguered by anxiety, John Leavitt's health declined.

Beaux credited her grandmother, the indomitable Cecilia Kent Leavitt, for stepping into the fray and salvaging the family honor if not their fortune. Although she had borne eight children in sixteen years and still had two under the age of ten at the time of the calamity, she summoned the resolve to maintain standards. The Leavitts might have been financially embarrassed, but they were not going to be socially humiliated. Even though the two eldest boys were both recent college graduates, according to Beaux, neither was of any help. The eldest, John, who as a boy had been "wept over and prayed over" by the family pastor for his refusal to subscribe to the Westminster Catechism, "lay all day on three chairs, eating nothing but dry bread and reading Swedenborg."[12] Samuel, the next in line who fared no better in his niece's estimation, was a "rivetted [sic] reformer" content to spend his life in poverty, dreaming of "impossible Utopias."[13] Acknowledging the impractical bent of her sons, Grandma Leavitt rallied her two oldest daughters for the challenges of genteel poverty.

At their mother's bidding, Cecilia and Eliza Leavitt set out to find work. The girls noticed an advertisement for a teacher of music and French, posted by the new residents of their beloved country home, Oakland; Cecilia, with the selfless resilience of the heroines in Victorian novels, applied. She landed the job and became a servant in the house where she had once enjoyed a childhood of privilege. Eliza, less dramatically but no less diligently, also worked tirelessly and established a pattern of industry that lasted the rest of her life. During her childhood, Cecilia Beaux remembered her Aunt Eliza, who sustained a long career as a music teacher, returning exhausted but undaunted from "long courses to inconvenient places with dripping skirts and wet gaiters."[14]

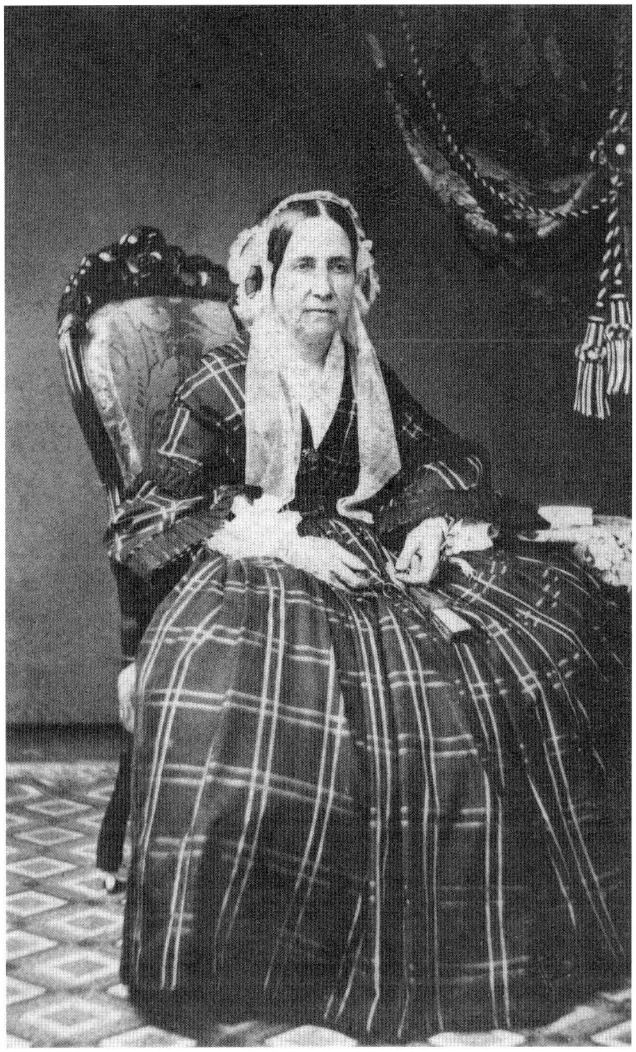

2. *Cecilia Beaux's grandmother, Cecilia Kent Leavitt, ca. 1850. Pennsylvania Academy of the Fine Arts*

Aware of the plight of the family, relatives stepped forward with offers of employment for the girls in Philadelphia, and it was there that the blue-eyed Frenchman from Avignon discovered his future bride. Although not a conventional beauty, young Cecilia Leavitt had a contagious exuberance. "She was not handsome," wrote her daughter Cecilia. "But her beautiful carriage and figure and her flashing smile were perhaps more effective than more regular charms."[15]

Cecilia Leavitt and Jean Adolphe Beaux were married in New York on April 3, 1850. The bride was exquisite, her head crowned with a wreath, her narrow feet encased in satin slippers, and her hands sheathed in lace-trimmed white kid gloves. When Cecilia appeared before him in her wedding dress, the love-struck Beaux (to whom the complexities of the English language remained forever elusive) was said to exclaim, "She is fit to give the hand to a King."[16]

Whatever she may have been fit for, Miss Leavitt gave her hand to an unpretentious and deeply religious French Huguenot who made no claim to nobility. Since the end of the eighteenth century, the Beaux family had been residents of the village of Mialet, a Huguenot refuge and the birthplace of Roland, leader of the Camisards, a guerrilla force that fought for Protestant rights during the reigns of Louis XIV and Louis XV. Mialet was home to several magnaneries (buildings designed for breeding silkworms), and like most of the local residents, the Beaux family worked in this trade.[17]

It was Cecilia Beaux, and not her diffident Papa, who promoted an extravagant familial pride in a royal ancestry dating back to the birth of Christ. Cecilia adopted the sixteen-pointed star of Bethlehem as her family crest and claimed the haunting town of Les Baux de Provence as the ancestral home of the Beaux family. According to local legend, Balthazar, one of the three Wise Men, married a shepherdess and built a chateau for her on the limestone cliff that dominates the village. By the eleventh century the rulers of Les Baux, who professed to be Balthazar's descendants and as such to have an authority that superceded that of the crown, held sovereignty by force of arms over more than seventy towns. In the thirteenth century the pugnacious Lords of Les Baux put down their weapons but continued to defy the monarchy. The town became home to tournaments, troubadours, and the profane Courts of Love, which directly challenged the authority of the church. Through the subsequent centuries, Les Baux, convinced of its divine mandate, was the thriving center of French Protestantism. And thus it remained until 1632, when Louis XIII and Cardinal Richelieu, fearing the strength of the Huguenots and finally willing to confront Balthazar's progeny, had the chateau destroyed.

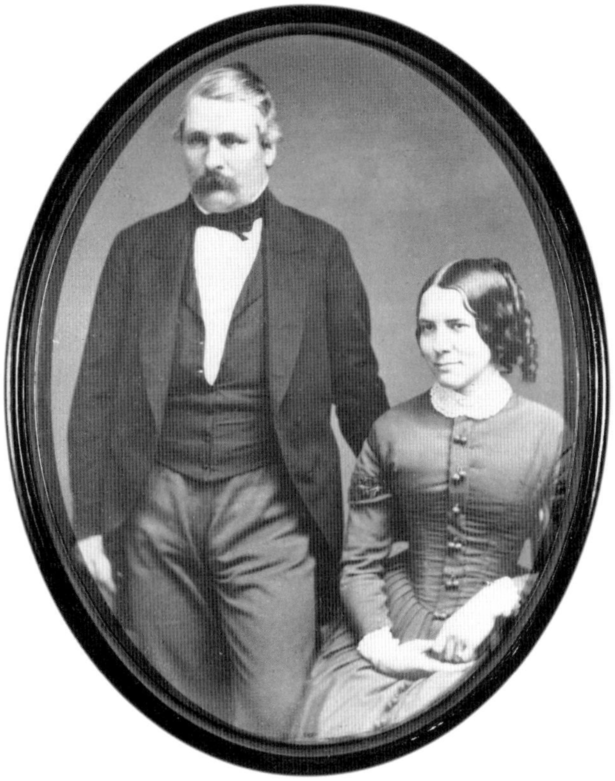

3. *Jean Adolphe Beaux and Cecilia Leavitt Beaux, ca. 1850. Pennsylvania Academy of the Fine Arts*

Throughout her life Cecilia Beaux delighted in this ancestral connection to France. "To Arles, to St. Remy,

Cecilia was wont to direct her thoughts," wrote her friend Thornton Oakley, " . . . and to that fantastic region of Les Baux, realm of her ancestors, where once were held the Courts of Love. . . . Hers too, was their battle-cry—*A l'Asard, Bautezar!*—which she would utter with all the fervor that is the spirit of Provence."[18] Cecilia Beaux's resolute spirit was indeed part of her heritage. But despite her defiant battle cry, best translated as "Spare no one, Balthazar!" there were those in her family who suspected that her determination owed more to the indomitable Leavitt women than any birthright from the Beaux family.[19] "To me at least it seems that Grandpa Beaux gave off an aura of piety, French Protestantism, and defeat, rather than poetry, light and gladness," wrote Cecilia Beaux's niece, Catherine Drinker Bowen. "I cannot help thinking it was the maternal example which inspired, rather than the rather sorry romantic from Avignon."[20]

Following the nuptials Jean Adolphe Beaux did his best to shoulder his domestic responsibilities, providing for his wife and her family, as Cecilia Beaux put it, "generously and delicately, as long as it was in his power to do so."[21] He took care of his concerns in Philadelphia and hired his father-in-law to manage a New York office for the family business, a job John Leavitt held until his death in 1852.[22] Cecilia, who throughout her life maintained an idealistic and forgiving attitude towards her father, claimed that the addition of Jean Adolphe Beaux to the family enabled her grandfather to die in peace, assured that his new son-in-law would take on the obligations of head of the household.

The young couple started a family immediately, but their joy in each other and in their first child, Alice Zepherine, born just ten months after the wedding, was soon tempered by tragedy: The baby died before her first birthday. John Leavitt's health declined and finally failed. Perhaps more than their shared faith in God, it was Cecilia Leavitt Beaux's legendary high spirits that sustained the couple during that difficult time, for they weathered it, and within a year welcomed another daughter, Aimée Ernesta.[23] By the time the Beauxs were anticipating the birth of their third child, the Leavitt women, as Grandpa Leavitt had hoped, regrouped around the successful J. P. Beaux & Co. Sewing Silks manufacturing plant and were comfortably and companionably relocated in Philadelphia.

The family survived the deaths of baby Alice and the patriarch John Leavitt with a certain amount of equanimity, but Cecilia Leavitt Beaux's untimely demise left them all anguished. "She was an adored being," wrote her daughter Cecilia, "and all through my childhood and youth, the friends who had worshipped her used to gaze long at me, in pity, and desiring to find traces in me of the beloved."[24] In the face of heartbreak, the Leavitts were brave; Jean Adolphe Beaux was not. Suddenly adrift in a foreign country, responsible to a family that was not his own, he simply parceled out his responsibilities and left. He entrusted the business to the care of his brother Edmund, his little daughters to the custody of their grieving aunts and brave grandmother, who within four years had lost a grandchild, husband, and daughter, and returned to France. "Simply decamped," wrote his granddaughter, " . . . fled back to France and stayed there for sixteen years. . . . He could not bear to hear his child called by her name—Cecilia, —couldn't bear indeed to live any longer in this country."[25]

With Beaux's defection, baby Leilie and her older sister, Aimée Ernesta (called Etta), became de facto orphans. From the time she was first aware of anything at all, it did not escape Leilie's notice that in some way, she was held responsible for the calamity. If she could have forgotten, her father, when he returned at last from his self-imposed exile, was quick to remind her. "Long afterwards," wrote Cecilia Beaux, "when I was a growing girl, watching me with saddened eyes, he said, 'You will never have shoulders like your mother.'"[26] Cecilia Beaux would spend the rest of her life trying to accomplish something truly extraordinary in order to compensate her grandmother, aunts, sister, and the father who condemned her by his absence, for their crushing loss.

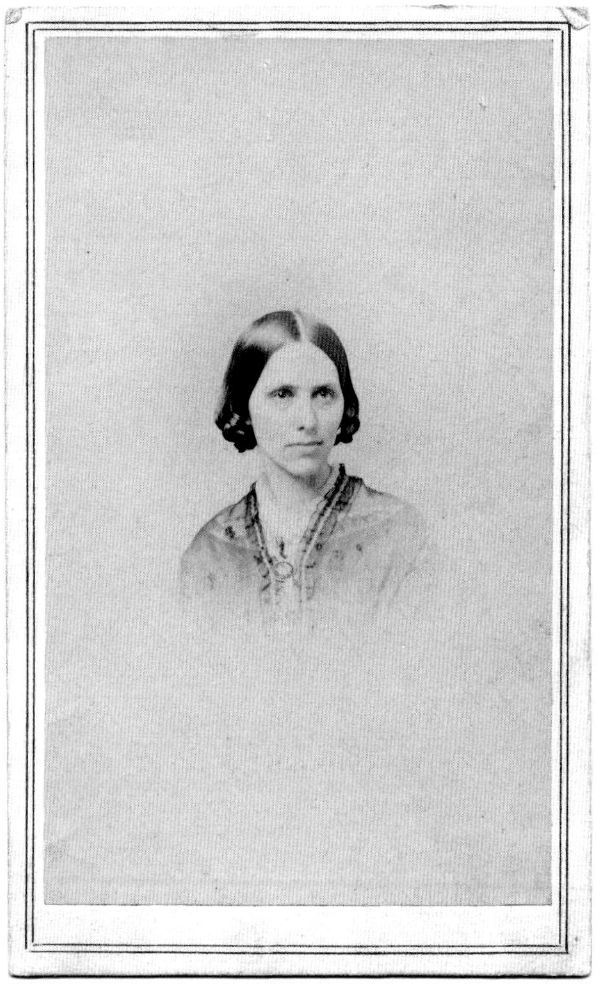

4. *J. E. McClees.* ***Eliza Leavitt.*** *n.d. Pennsylvania Academy of the Fine Arts*

Cecilia Beaux's first winter, the infamous season of 1856, was the coldest in living memory. The Delaware River froze in January. Despite the diligent work of the city iceboat and an ill-fated experiment to blast a shipping channel through the ice with gunpowder, the port remained closed until March. The financial disaster imposed on the city of Philadelphia by the severe weather did nothing to dampen the spirits of the inhabitants, who made the most of the situation and took to the ice. On January 26, an estimated 20,000 people were out on the river, "skating, promenading, flirting, or trafficking on its icy surface."[27] Inside the Leavitt house it was as warm as limited resources could allow, and Leilie and Etta, under the careful ministrations of the heartbroken but determined Grandma Leavitt, Aunt Eliza, and sixteen-year-old Aunt Emily survived and thrived.

While baby Leilie took her first steps, spoke her first words, and suffered her first illnesses, Jean Adolphe Beaux remained in France. Childhood was hazardous in mid-nineteenth-century America, as Beaux well knew, having lost his first daughter in infancy. In New York, Baltimore, and Philadelphia, close to 49 percent of the total mortality was among children under the age of five. Cholera and typhoid fever, often transmitted through contaminated water, were endemic. Raw sewage polluted the Schuylkill River, source of the city's drinking water. So much run-off from Laurel Hill Cemetery drained into the river that it was said that Philadelphians drank their own ancestors. Residents who survived in spite of the unsanitary conditions drolly attributed their strong constitutions to the immunizing effect of the perilous city water. Illustrator Joseph Pennell (ca. 1857–1926), a contemporary of Cecilia Beaux, once wrote an explanation of why Philadelphians of his generation were so healthy. "If you could stand Schuylkill water, you could stand anything."[28]

Typhoid and cholera were only two of the infectious diseases that stalked the young, and for most of these illnesses, there was no known cause and no known cure. Measles, pneumonia, bronchitis, diarrhea, influenza, tuberculosis, yellow fever, and diphtheria were common and often deadly. The family doctor usually treated childhood ailments, no matter how severe, at home. Children's Hospital of Philadelphia, the first pediatric hospital in the nation, opened its doors the year Leilie (Cecilia) was born but would only admit children suffering from noncontagious diseases or accidental injuries.[29] So the common upper-respiratory infections that attack small children must have struck fear in the heart of Grandma Leavitt and added to the

5. OPPOSITE: ***Dressing Dolls.*** *1928. Oil on canvas, 35 x 28 in. Private Collection. Photograph courtesy Spanierman Gallery Ltd.*

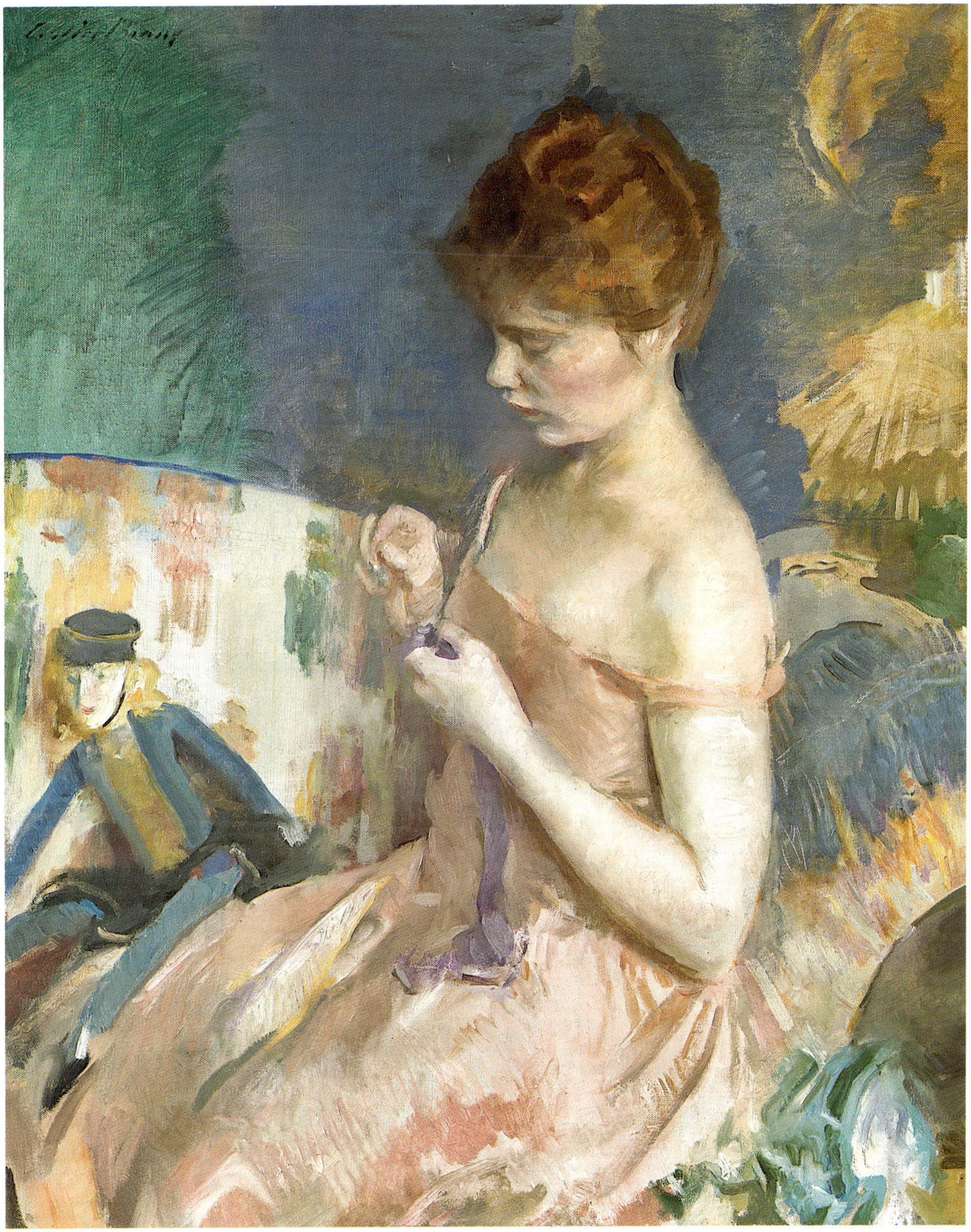

weight of the responsibility she felt for the abandoned Beaux children. Leilie's first memory was of her grandmother's love and concern. One sunny morning as she stood in her crib, she suddenly became aware of being awake and alone. Before she could cry out, a small, stout figure in black entered the room and in gratitude for the child's safe passage through the dangers of another night, recited a morning benediction, "I laid me down, I slept, and the Lord sustained me."[30]

Spring came at last. Elms, maples, and mulberries leafed out. Roses bloomed in backyards, and cats stretched and walked across the fences. Bells cast in Europe before the Revolution rang out the hours from the steeples of the old churches with such a sweet sound that years later, when the modern age made their timekeeping irrelevant and silenced them, people recalling their timbre were moved to tears. Quaker families in traditional dress carried large woven baskets to the Second Street Market to purchase groceries. But although William Penn would have recognized the city he founded and perhaps nodded with approval, Philadelphia was changing—modernizing.

Plans were proceeding to upgrade the city transportation system with the latest innovation: the horse-drawn streetcar. Lightweight and fast, a car loaded with twenty-five passengers could easily be pulled by two horses along iron rails at the unheard-of speed of eight miles an hour.[31] Once introduced, the cars quickly replaced the back-wrenching omnibuses that plied their torturous course over miles of cobblestone streets.[32] The city's architecture was changing too. New buildings were generally larger and less homogeneous. The impressive, gothic New Masonic Hall, dedicated on September 15, 1856, cost an unprecedented $185,328 and looked decidedly Victorian amid the stately colonial homes, brick meetinghouses, and Greek revival masterpieces of the architects John Haviland and William Strickland.

There were also less obvious changes, just as wondrous in their time. The use of chloroform to minimize the pain of surgical operations was a new and welcome innovation. Express carriages that delivered heavy parcels around the city were new, as were envelopes, public restaurants, ready-made clothes, and penny newspapers. French goods were popular, and there were numerous wholesale silk businesses vending cloth and ribbon from France.[33] Although by 1856 Philadelphia had fallen behind New York as the major center of American commerce, it was still a flourishing manufacturing town with a thriving textile industry that employed about 19 percent of the city's total work force.[34] In 1850, 284 textile firms existed in the city; by the end of the decade the number had nearly tripled.[35]

Jean Adolphe Beaux returned to Philadelphia in 1857 to two healthy daughters aged two and five, a growing city, and a prosperous business. He moved into the modest three-story brick Leavitt home on Locust Street and stayed for two years. He struggled to befriend his children but made little impression on the youngest, whose early memories centered on the benevolence of Grandma Leavitt, Aunt Eliza, and Aunt Emily. Her older sister Etta's recollections were more specific: Etta would later remember her father's artistic ability, his devotion to the French Collegiate Church, and his eccentricities.

To amuse his children, Papa Beaux would take out a slate and draw. His natural facility impressed Etta, whose imagination was sparked by the whimsical charm of his sketches of "wonderful animals doing amazing things."[36] He taught the little girls the hymns he sang at the French Collegiate Church, where he worshipped among other similarly lonely French exiles—simple melodies that the two sisters would sing in harmony throughout their lives, Etta on soprano and Leilie on alto.

Du Rocher du Jacob,
Toute l'oeuvre est parfaite
Ce que sa bouche a dit,
Sa main l'accomplira.
Alleluia, Alleluia.[37]

While generous in acknowledging her father's good qualities, in a candid moment many years later, Etta confessed to one of her daughters, "We didn't love Papa very much, he was so foreign. We thought him *peculiar*. He roasted the chickens on a spit over the fire, he said they weren't fit to eat any other way."[38]

Eventually, Papa Beaux's attempts to win over his children, provide for the family, and run his business proved futile. J. P. Beaux & Co. Sewing Silks was struggling. Rumors of Southern secession, along with fears that the market for textiles might be compromised by political unrest in the South, may have contributed to the decline of the establishment. The family saved a scrap of lined blue paper inscribed in Jean Adolphe Beaux's artistic script and written in his broken English—a notice to his employees urging them to stop working early once a week and give thanks that they were employed. "The exercises which will consist in a prayer," he wrote, "will take only a portion of the time allowed, but still those who will think them not agreeable with their feelings will be at liberty to retire."[39] Perhaps the employees did gather, did pray.

Nevertheless the business failed. Jean Adolphe Beaux returned to France in 1861, and this time he stayed there for twelve years. His granddaughter speculated that although his departure left the Leavitt women with a very uncertain financial future, they might have been relieved; "One less mouth to feed and the chickens roasting neatly in the oven."[40]

Perhaps it was fortunate that Leilie had no early memories of her father. The gap gave her room to create a legend that served her well. No matter what her father accomplished or failed to accomplish, she decided that he had given her an extraordinary gift. In the second half of the nineteenth century, France was the uncontested center of Western art. Students from all over the world flocked to Paris for instruction and inspiration. Most of the American artists who would make a significant mark in the field of portraiture in the late nineteenth and early twentieth centuries studied in France: John Singer Sargent (1856–1925); James Abbott McNeill Whistler (1834–1903); Thomas Eakins (1844–1916); Cecilia Beaux's teacher, William Sartain (1843–1924); and her chief competitor for the title of most influential female artist, Mary Cassatt (1844–1926). In time Cecilia Beaux would also make the prerequisite pilgrimage and study in Paris. But she had credentials that gave her a lifetime of confidence and comfort in the face of sometimes overwhelming obstacles—credentials her contemporaries could never hope to attain through either artist alliances or individual genius. Papa never realized "the priceless heritage we received from him at birth," she wrote in her autobiography.[41] Cecilia Beaux didn't just study in France; she was French.

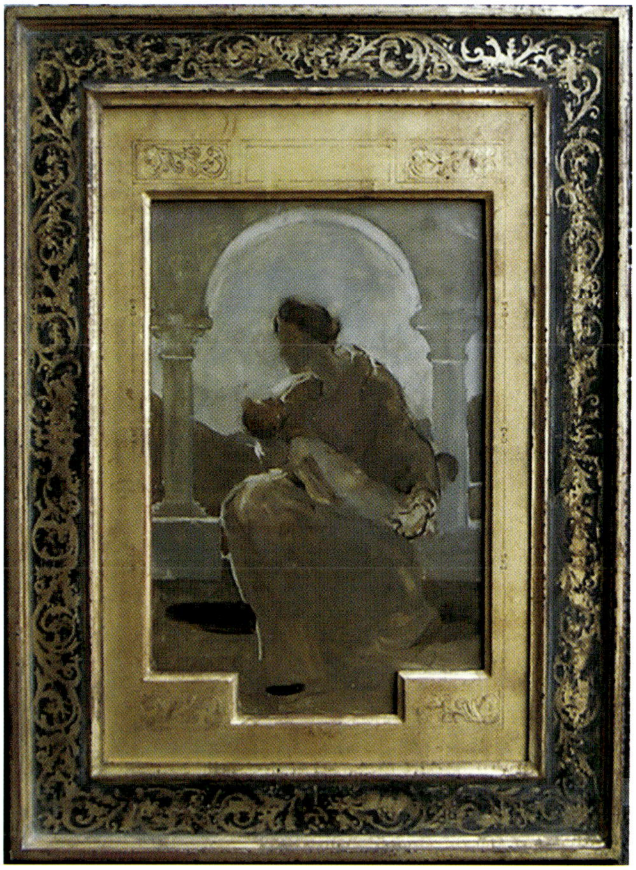

*6. **Madonna.** ca. 1900. Oil on paper, 16 3/8 x 10 3/4 in. Private Collection. Courtesy of Alfred J. Walker Fine Art, Boston*

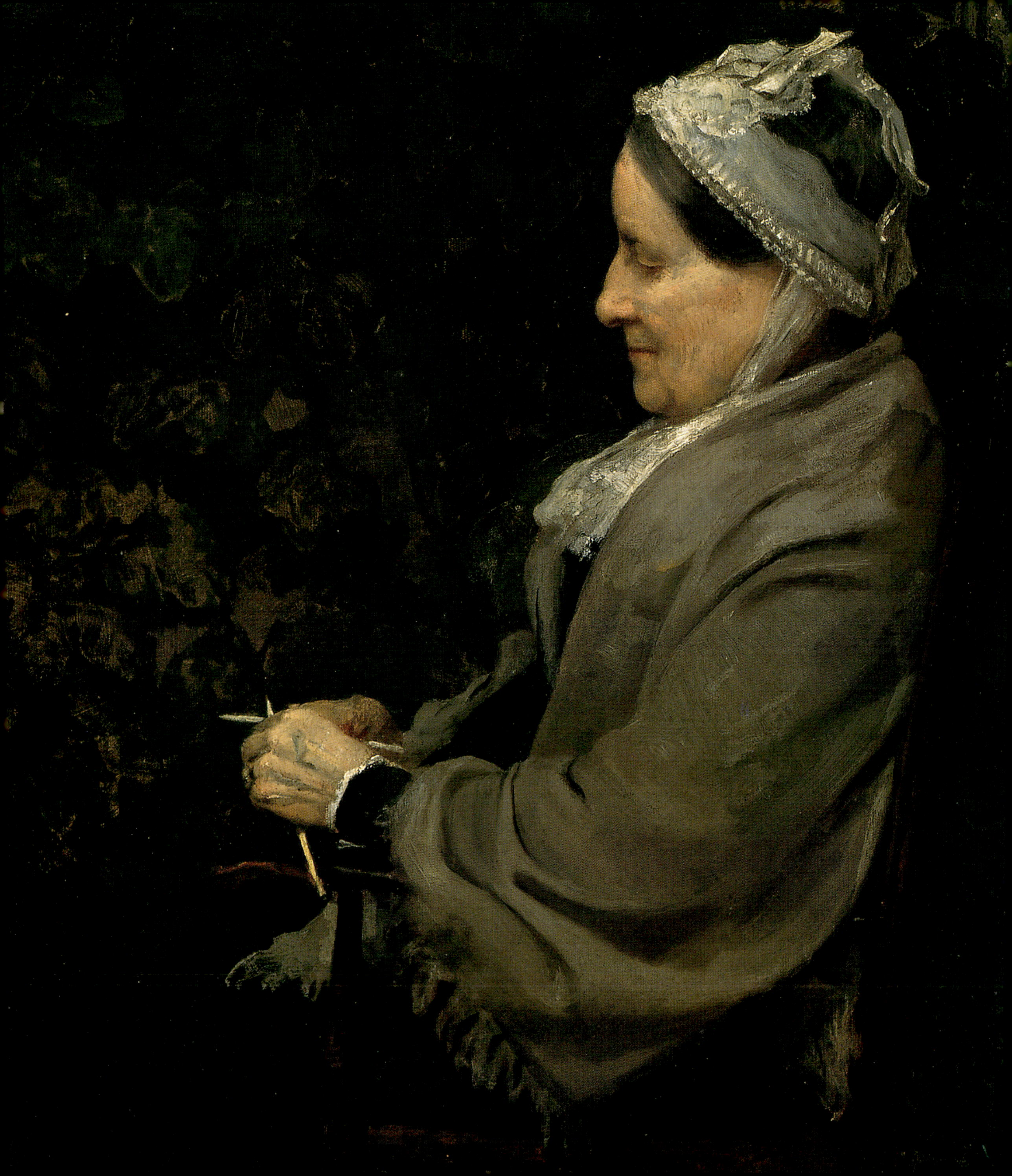

West Philadelphia

"Oh, sacrament of summer days
Oh, last communion in the haze,
Permit a child to join"

—Emily Dickinson

The collapse of J. P. Beaux & Co. Sewing Silks, coupled with the defection of Papa Beaux, plunged the Leavitt family into financial difficulties. Beaux sent money from France but never enough. Once again, Grandma Leavitt looked to her grown children for help. All three of her boys were employed and living in Philadelphia. The two eldest Leavitt sons, John and Samuel, whose early penchant for philanthropy had been tempered by a desire to put something more substantial on the table than dry bread, were employed. John worked in a rubber goods company;[42] Samuel and the youngest Leavitt son, Charles, had started a business partnership as coal dealers.[43]

Eliza contributed to the family finances by teaching music and assumed much of the responsibility for childcare and housework at a time when domestic husbandry was a daunting task. "In our house," Cecilia Beaux recalled, "much had to be done in the family that, in happier circumstances, would have been put out or done by servants."[44] There were gas lamps to maintain, window blinds to clean with lye, furniture to polish, groceries to purchase, food to prepare, heavy straw mattresses to turn, clothes to wash and press—a complex task in the era of the petticoat and hoop skirt—and sewing to complete. Ready-made clothes were a luxury, and the Leavitt women sewed their own garments as well as those of the Beaux sisters. Aunt Emily "put in thousands of fine stitches in delicate cambric, so that her youngest niece might be suitably arrayed," Beaux wrote, fondly remembering not only the garment, but also "the sweetness of the act that produced it."[45]

Sewing was an essential task in the household and, as such, one of the first introduced to Leilie. The silver thimble presented to her by Grandma Leavitt on her third birthday was worn out before it was outgrown. The Beaux sisters practiced their skills by mending sheets, making dishtowels, and sewing a complete wardrobe for their dolls—dresses, linens, even a "full line of underclothes."[46] Well into the twentieth century, when ready-to-wear outfits were widely available and her financial success made price no object, Cecilia Beaux continued to design and sew many of her own clothes with what her sister Etta described as the skill of a French dressmaker.[47]

Aunt Emily often supervised the girl's sewing lessons. Every stitch had to be perfect, Etta recalled, "Otherwise Aunt Emily made us rip it out. But Aunt Emily was amusing. She made us laugh. There was something contagious about Aunt Emily."[48] It was not long before Emily's vivacious spirit was noticed outside the family. Charming and attractive, with shining brown hair, dark eyes, and a disarming wit, it was hardly surprising when a fitting suitor appeared—a young man as determined and extraordinary as the

OPPOSITE: *Detail; **Mrs. John Wheeler Leavitt**. 1885. Oil on canvas, 45 1/2 x 34 in. Westmoreland Museum of American Art*

enterprising Leavitt women. The term "avuncular" could have been coined for the engaging William Foster Biddle, whom Cecilia Beaux later described as "after my grandmother, the strongest and most beneficent influence in my life."[49] Biddle, who was twenty-five years old when he and Emily married, took the little Beaux sisters into his heart. For the next fifty years he cared for his nieces-in-law with the consistent attention that neither the Leavitt uncles nor the girls' absent father had the strength to provide.

Trained as an engineer at the University of Pennsylvania, William Foster Biddle graduated in 1852 and held positions with several companies during the expansion of the railroads. When he met Emily Leavitt just prior to the outbreak of the Civil War, he was working as an engineering and transportation advisor to General George B. McClellan. A Quaker by heritage, Biddle nevertheless served under McClellan as an aide-de-camp, achieving the rank of Captain and participating in every battle of the Army of the Potomac until McClellan was relieved of his command after the battle of Antietam.

Eventually, Biddle was able to stabilize the family finances, but during the war years, the Leavitts struggled. With resolve and without protest, the family moved to more affordable housing at 1510 Lombard—a simple brick rowhouse.[50] Grandma Leavitt weathered the financial and emotional upheavals of the Civil War and managed the household so effectively that the two little children recalled no privation. Aunt Eliza and Aunt Emily were responsible for the girls' schooling, but it was Grandma Leavitt who supervised. She had an educational philosophy that her granddaughter Cecilia embraced and used as the framework on which to found her subsequent success: "everything undertaken must be completed, conquered."[51] This stricture was applied equally to housework, handwork, academic instruction, and artistic pursuits. Grandma Leavitt offered the Beaux girls a pragmatic education befitting their social class. Her curriculum was designed to furnish her granddaughters with the expertise to manage a household, the accomplishments to attract a suitable husband, and the skills to find appropriate work should circumstances dictate that they seek employment.

Although most parents hoped that their daughters' happiness and financial independence would be secured by an appropriate marriage, Grandma Leavitt was not naïve. By mid-century it was clear that many young women would not be wives and mothers. There were more women of marriageable age than prospective husbands. The shortage of men that became apparent in the Gold Rush years, as young speculators headed West, was greatly exacerbated by the appalling carnage of the Civil War, which claimed more than 620,000 lives. Poor women with few skills and little education secured an income where they could, either at home, by taking in day work such as sewing, or by seeking employment outside the home as domestic servants or factory workers. The careers deemed suitable for middle-class women were those that were either an extension of family responsibilities, such as teaching, or those that grew out of avocations originally intended to give an edge in the competitive marriage market, such as art and music. Girls like Leilie and Etta, whose family had standards if not ready cash, were usually educated at home to be skilled homemakers, accomplished amateur artists, and, if fate smiled on them and offered the preferred choice, charming wives and caring mothers.

While Philadelphians endured the war, sent their sons into battle, opened hospitals for the sick and wounded, manufactured everything from wagons to weapons, celebrated victories, and buried their dead, the girls stayed busy at home. "My Dear Papa," wrote eight-year-old Leilie in 1863, "I know that it is a very long time since I have written to you and I am very very sorry but the days and weeks passed away so quickly and I did not do it."[52] Aunt Emily, who also wrote to Beaux, presumably at more regular intervals, reported that the country was devastated by war. But if the hostilities made any impression on the two little girls, it was not evident in the autobiography that Cecilia Beaux carefully constructed many years later. Such recollections had no place in the story she would tell of her life. As an adult, Beaux—who looked much younger than her years and according to her sister, still had "French Roses in her cheeks" at age forty—was evasive concerning her age, sometimes shaving off eight years and often omitting her birth date entirely from biographical listings.[53] Her niece, writer Catherine Drinker Bowen, recalled that at the age of seventy-six Beaux "looked a handsome sixty" and that nobody ever mentioned her age.[54]

The war did affect the adults in the family. Although business thrived in Philadelphia throughout the war years, prices were inflated, and even after their move to more affordable housing, there was strict economy in the household. Nevertheless, the Leavitt women remained optimistic and entertained the hope that Jean Adolphe Beaux would return, if not to alleviate all their pressing financial worries, at least to lighten the burden by reclaiming his daughters. In 1863 Emily penned an encouraging letter. "We expect you to leave all rheumatisms in France and come home to us quite rejuvenated."[55] She had reasons for her optimism. The war news was encouraging, and with the defeat of the Southern troops at Gettysburg, the threat of invasion was lifted from the city's residents, who felt secure for the first time in two years. Still, Beaux did not return, did not write often, and did not send sufficient funds. "My Dear Mr. Beaux," wrote Emily, "Yours of 31st October gave us much pleasure for it became quite an anxious question, 'Why do we not hear from Mr. Beaux . . . the cost of everything is three times increased and even you could not go to market with $2.50—we do not indulge in luxuries—have had turkey only on Thanksgiving day."[56]

Beaux did not come home, but genial William Biddle did, and it was Uncle Will, not Papa Beaux, who claimed the girls. When his term of service ended, Biddle took a job as superintendent of the Freedom Iron Works, a substantial responsibility for the thirty-

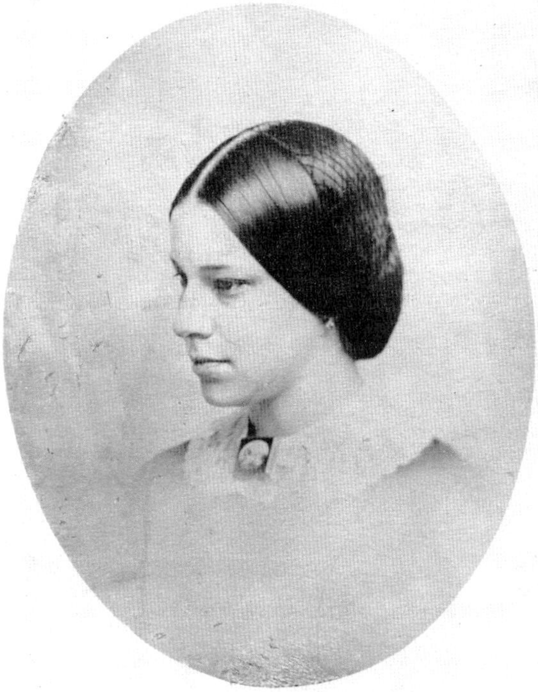

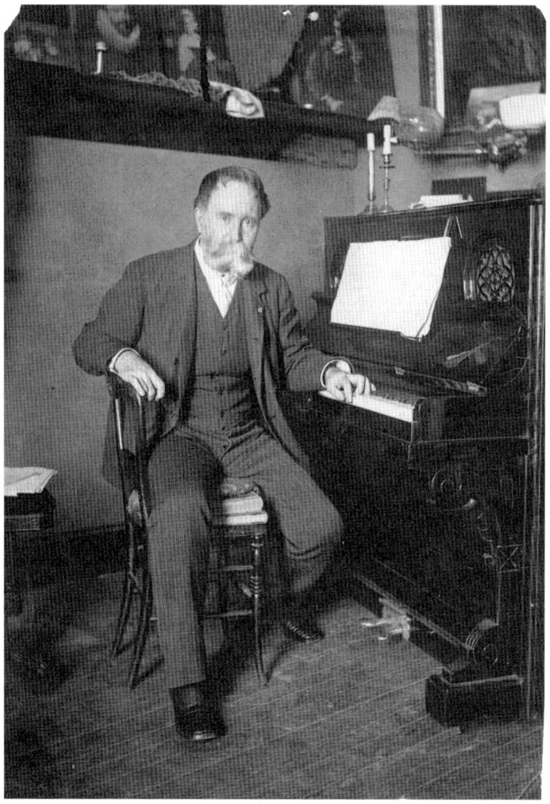

7. TOP RIGHT: *Peter A. Juley and Son.* ***Emily Leavitt Biddle.*** *n.d. Pennsylvania Academy of the Fine Arts*

8. BOTTOM RIGHT: ***William Foster Biddle,*** *ca. 1890. Pennsylvania Academy of the Fine Arts*

year-old engineer. The company was located in the central Pennsylvania town of Lewistown, where the demand for iron fed the regional economy. The local blast furnace consumed more than 360 acres of forest annually to produce the pig iron needed for the production of the high-quality wheels and axles Freedom supplied to the thriving railroad industry.[57] The girls spent the winter of 1864 with Aunt Emily and Uncle Will in Lewistown. Their large, rambling house tucked under a mountain and surrounded by a wild garden presented a considerable change for two girls raised in Grandma's spic-and-span city residence. It was a quiet season, with no extended family, no neighbors, and few visitors. Uncle Will spent long days at the ironworks, and the old house was empty except for Aunt Emily and the two girls. Mornings were occupied with lessons, but there were many hours left for other diversions. The house was sparsely furnished but fortunately included the one item essential to everyone's happiness—a piano.

Music was central to the life of the Leavitt family. Although Aunt Eliza was the principal instrumentalist, Emily sang and played the piano proficiently. But Uncle Will was the dedicated musician who so loved the art form that he bequeathed to his nieces an enduring enthusiasm for music. In later years his passion for music was passed down to Etta's six remarkable children, who in time would have a significant impact on the cultural life of Philadelphia.

William Biddle started playing the piano at the instigation of his mother, Hetty Foster Biddle, when he was very young. His training began inauspiciously, as his love of music was not innate and required strong encouragement. An agreement was drawn up between the child and his mother:

> H. F. Biddle promises to pay her son William on the first day of July 1840 the sum of $3.00 for half an hour's faithful practicing on the piano every day for six months beginning on the first day of May.

Evidently, William practiced, becoming expert enough by the time he joined the Leavitt family to sight-read difficult music with no stumbling or repetition. It was Uncle Will who introduced his niece to the "rhythmic passion" of the Chopin Polonaise, playing the complex bass octaves over and over until the child's "small heart actually seemed to experience an ecstatic growth" and bounded in her breast.[58]

Later Cecilia Beaux acknowledged the advantage of growing up in a household of musicians. "They understood perfectly the spirit and necessities of an artist's life," she wrote.[59] The musical atmosphere in the Leavitts' home affected Leilie at an early age, as she lay face down on the parlor sofa or on the rug under the piano, where the sound was thunderous, and the music flowed around her "like a cataract."[60] Emily gave her music lessons and Leilie was a compliant student who learned Schumann's "The Happy Farmer" without complaint. But she had heard enough of the accomplished playing of Eliza and the competence of Emily and Uncle Will to be dissatisfied with her own efforts.

Although she would forsake the piano while still a child, Leilie did not abandon music completely. Etta, whose eyes were deemed too weak to read musical notation, was encouraged to develop her vocal talents, and Leilie joined her. The girls sang at every opportunity, during chores and at play, their young voices rising in close harmony as they traded soprano and alto parts. During the winter at Lewistown, Emily formulated an ambitious diversion to encourage her nieces' aptitude. As a surprise for Uncle Will, she organized a trio, set a performance date, and chose a sufficiently challenging piece, Mendelssohn's "Elijah"—not the entire oratorio, but all the parts that could be satisfactorily performed by a soprano (Leilie), contralto (Etta), and tenor (Emily). There is no record of how the performance was received, but it is not difficult to imagine the scene: The handsome William Biddle, tired after a long day at the ironworks, sitting by the flickering fire while the winter winds blew over the shale-covered mountain, watching his lovely wife and two young nieces sing the haunting melodies.

Lift thine eyes, O lift thine eyes to the mountains
Whence cometh, whence cometh, whence
cometh help.[61]

Leilie was enchanted with Mendelssohn's composition and relished the companionship of the endeavor. All through her childhood and into her twenties, she continued to sing at home accompanied by her friends and family; "Elijah" with the addition of a bass part and as many as eight other singers, English madrigals, German quartets, duets, and evening hymns every Sunday. Both girls took voice lessons, but although Leilie practiced diligently and had "as much voice as the average child," she had no expectation of a musical career.[62]

When spring came the Beaux sisters returned to the care of their grandmother and Aunt Eliza, who had moved yet again in search of inexpensive housing. This time the family relocated to the edge of the West Philadelphia suburbs, an area just opening up to development. The property was close enough to the new horse-car line on the Chestnut Street bridge to allow access to Center City, but far enough away to shelter the children from the demoralizing effects of the war.[63] In February President Lincoln had increased his draft order to 500,000 men, of whom Philadelphia's share was more than 13,000.[64] Citizens were encouraged to volunteer, and many heeded the call, but by 1864 everyone in the city understood the consequences of war. Philadelphia was a medical center for the Union Army. Although military hospitals in the city had 10,000 beds, twenty-two civilian hospitals were needed to accommodate the overflow of sick and wounded. While the Beaux girls were delighting in the new house with its ramshackle garden and small stream, Philadelphians were dealing with the casualties from Grant's Wilderness Campaign. In a single week in May, 1864, 2,478 wounded soldiers were treated in the city.[65]

That same month, the Great Central Fair of the Sanitary Commission opened in Logan Square in downtown Philadelphia. The fair, which included a display of military arms and trophies, an exhibit of manufactured goods, a horticultural exhibition, and an immense art gallery 500 feet in length, netted more than one million dollars for the relief and care of war casualties and their families. More than 15,000 people attended the opening ceremonies.[66] On the day President Lincoln arrived from Washington with his wife, the crowd was so large that he had difficulty passing through the buildings. In Lincoln's honor, the orator Edward Everett delivered an address exuding, "Why this picture gallery excels anything ever seen here before, and everything that is scanned excites an intellectual curiosity and wonder."[67]

Perhaps the Leavitts took the horse-cars into the city to see the fair—just about everyone else did. The popular fine arts gallery, which housed more than one thousand European and American paintings, watercolors, and sculptures, was the largest art exhibition ever assembled in the United States. Nine-year-old Leilie may have had her first introduction to painting there—may have stood looking in wonder at the canvases hanging cheek by jowl in the bunting-draped hall, tilted invitingly toward the viewer. Beaux recalled that as a child she had seen the huge panoramic canvas *Rocky Mountains* by Albert Bierstadt (1830–1902). The painting occupied a position of honor in the center of the fair's great hall. And although Beaux, who had her coy reasons, claimed to have viewed Bierstadt's masterpiece in different circumstances, the colossal canvas made an indelible impression. "Where is the picture now?" she wondered in 1930, when the remarkable *Rocky Mountains* was decidedly *démodé*. "Its green was fresh then and its shadows no darker than the unrelated truth."[68] It might have pleased her to know that, although she feared the canvas would be tucked away "sickened and polished in a brown-grey limbo,"[69] it now resides in the permanent collection of The Metropolitan Museum of Art in New York. If Cecilia Beaux had indeed visited the fair, she would not have been able to admit it. Having pushed her birth date forward, according to her amended biography, she would have been too young to remember.

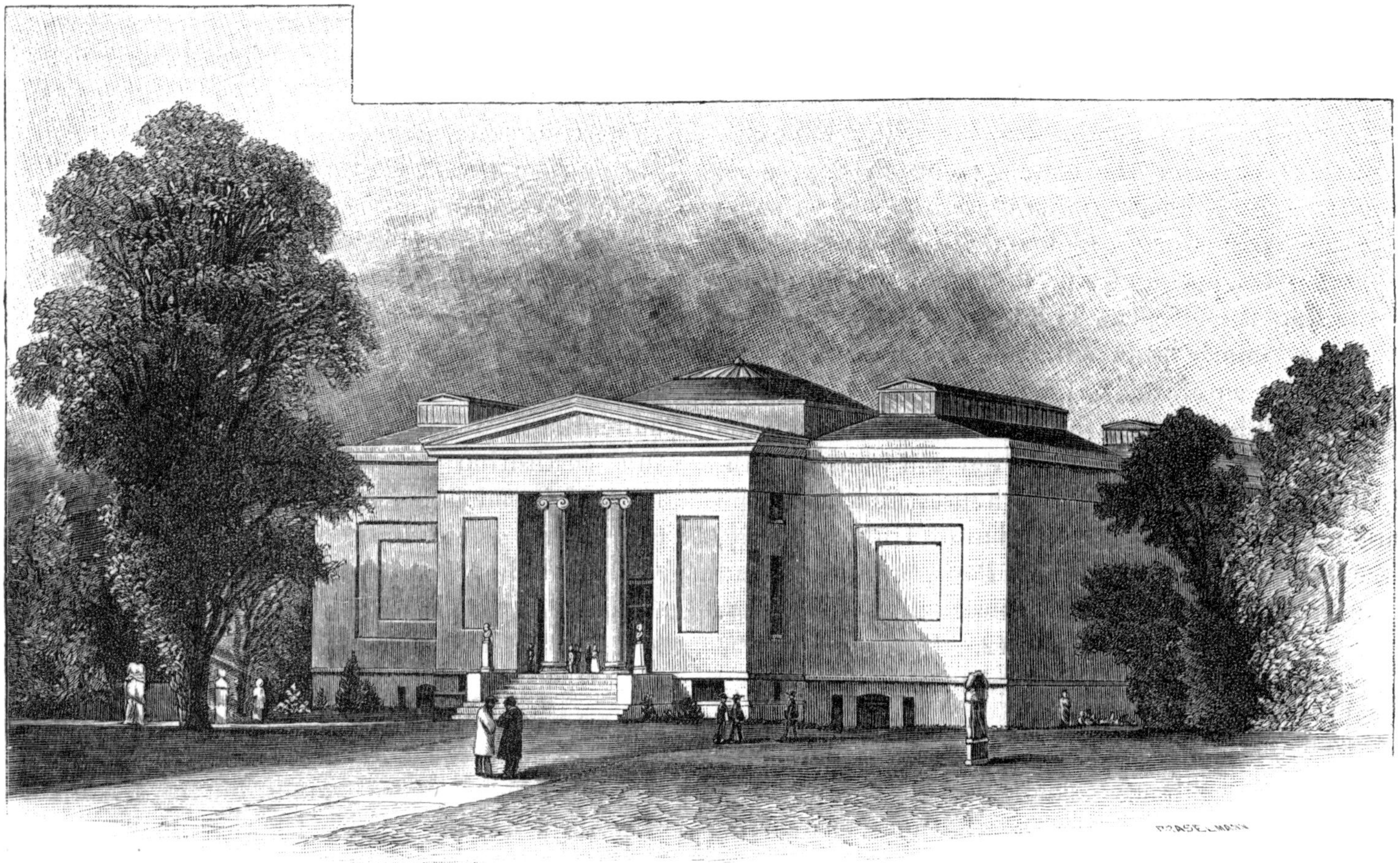

OLD PENNSYLVANIA ACADEMY OF THE FINE ARTS.

Nevertheless, she did acknowledge that her aunts took her to "what picture galleries and special exhibitions there were."[70]

The foremost "picture gallery" in Philadelphia was The Pennsylvania Academy of the Fine Arts, located at the time in a stately building at Tenth and Chestnut Streets. And it was there that as a young girl, Cecilia Beaux first "consciously observed" a painting. The canvas was the enormous *Death on a Pale Horse* (1817) by Benjamin West (1738–1820). Leilie lay on the floor to study the picture. Later she would maintain that she was unimpressed, that she knew her Bible, had read the book of Revelations, and regarded the massive canvas as an illustration, and "not a very impressive one."[71] By the time Beaux recorded her thoughts on the subject, it was considered unsophisticated to like the painting. The canvas was too romantic, too sublime to survive the Victorian era with respectable reviews, let alone find an appreciative twentieth-century audience.

Nonetheless, when Eliza and Emily found Leilie stretched out in front of the canvas, they had to pull her to her feet. How could she not be fascinated with West's painting? Perhaps she had heard about the artist, heard the familiar story of how he learned to paint from the local Indians, made his first paintbrush using hair from the tail of his cat. Starting from this inauspicious beginning and against considerable odds, he set out from Philadelphia to earn an international reputation in Europe as the American Raphael. The canvas itself had a fascinating history. In 1845 a fire broke out at the Academy. Volunteer firemen, hearing the alarm, left their businesses and made the dash through the city on a horse-drawn fire truck. They arrived at the scene in time to cut the massive canvas, its margins already blistering, out of the heavy frame and carry it to safety while their comrades deluged them with water so they could withstand the heat.[72] Leilie, who claimed to have registered "no recorded sensation, though a perfect recollection," while gazing at the painting, may have recognized something autobiographical in the picture's central theme. Death astride his terrible steed strikes down a family. The father raises a hand in futile defense of a child who clings to the dead mother and helpless baby.

The Pennsylvania Academy of the Fine Arts was the city's public gallery, but there were also several notable private collections, and with the proper introductions, it was possible to visit on certain days. Uncle Will Biddle probably had no trouble with proper introductions, as his social connections were impressive. A descendent of six generations of distinguished ancestors, his relatives had been making their mark on Philadelphia since the time of William Penn. Great-great-grandfather Owen Biddle was an associate of Benjamin Franklin and was at the State House for the reading of the Declaration of Independence in 1776. He was an active member of the Committee of Safety, an organization of patriotic citizens charged with the task of planning the city's defenses in the event of a British invasion.[73] Subsequent generations in Uncle Will's direct line were solid citizens who referred to themselves as "the Quaker Biddles," to distinguish themselves from their more fashionable and financially successful cousins who became politicians, professionals, bankers, and powerful merchants.[74] Still, Uncle Will's relatively modest means did not inhibit his access to the best the city had to offer. His family credentials were impeccable, and in Philadelphia it was not personal wealth but family background that counted. Many of the city's well-heeled citizens envied Uncle Will's pedigree. Well into the twentieth century it was not uncommon to hear Philadelphia Episcopalians and Presbyterians call each other "thee" and "thou," implying, if not a direct ancestral link, at least an affinity to the city's revered Quaker progenitors.

Uncle Will had a card for admission to the private gallery of Mr. William C. Gibson, an avid collector of contemporary art. Biddle, who brought home the latest music and once publicly debated the *New York Tribune*'s critic, Henry Krehbiel, on the pretentiousness of grand opera, shared Gibson's appreciation for

9. OPPOSITE: *"Old Pennsylvania Academy of the Fine Arts," from* History of Philadelphia: 1609–1884, *by J. Thomas Scharf and Thompson Westcott (L. H. Everts & Co., 1884)*

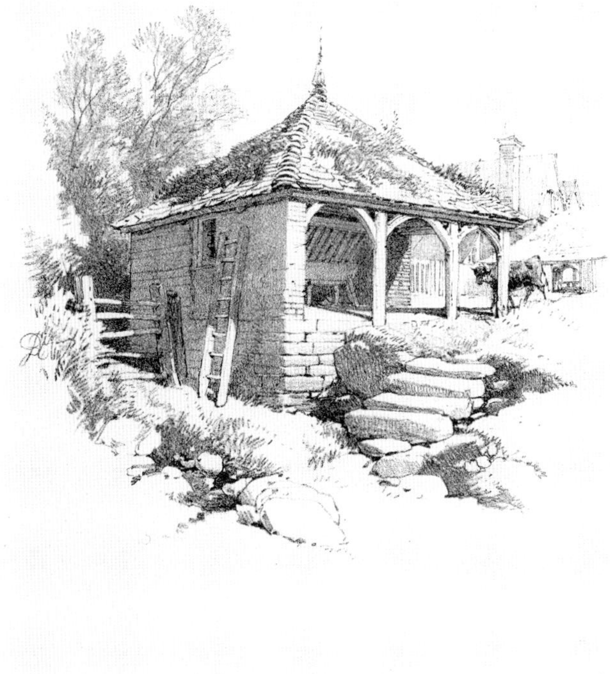

Lesson 114.

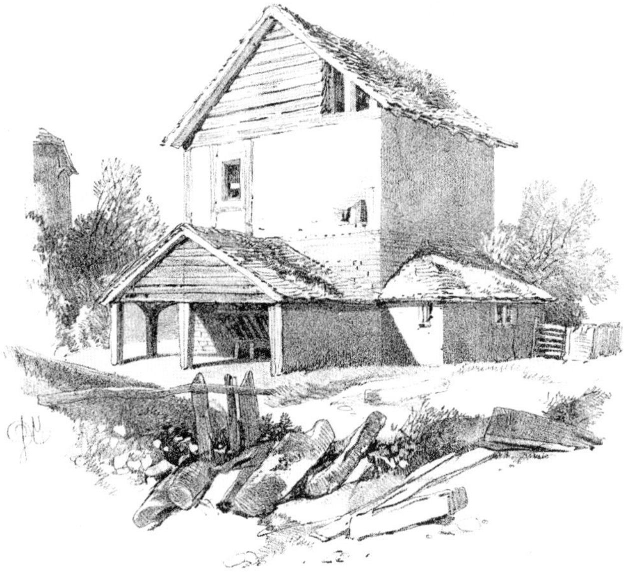

Lesson 115.

artistic innovation.[75] One cold winter day, after a long ride in the horse-cars, Leilie arrived with her uncle in front of Gibson's fashionable residence on Walnut Street, walked past the bleak granite-covered exterior, and entered the warm glow of an atrium complete with captive birds, exotic plants, and a world of art she would one day make her own. Perhaps because she was several years older than she had been when she visited the Academy, or perhaps because the artwork was contemporary, mostly small, and therefore accessible, Leilie relished the experience. Jean-François Millet's (1814–1875) masterwork, *The Angelus*, was on loan to the gallery. Hanging opposite a replica of Alexandre Cabanel's (1823–1889) opulent *Birth of Venus* whose naked protagonist stretched on foaming surf flanked by five fat cherubs, Millet's austere portrayal of devout French peasants pausing for their evening prayers presented a striking contrast. The romantic dignity of Millet's canvas, Cecilia Beaux recalled, "made the paintings near it look common."[76]

Leilie wandered enchanted through the sunlit space. A vigorously rendered head of a young man painted by Thomas Couture (1815–1879) caught her eye and was her initial and unforgettable introduction to the power of portraiture. But it was the paintings that revealed the people and landscapes of France, *The Angelus*, a bright portrait of a young French woman by Giovanni Boldini (1842–1931), *Great Oak at Ornan* by Courbet (1819–1877), and the "polished sweetness" of paintings by Hughes Merle (1823–1881) and Adolphe William Bouguereau (1825–1905) that thrilled her, drawing her into their narrative until she felt an atavistic pull towards the land of her ancestors. "My embryonic sense took hold once and for all, of something that was mine, and that nothing would cheat me of some day," she recalled.[77] The trip to the Gibson collection did not inspire Cecilia Beaux to ponder a career in art. "I did not see myself as having any possible relation or participation in what I saw around me," she wrote.[78] Although the experience did not awaken her artistic ambitions, from that time forward Leilie was determined to see France.

The excursions to galleries and exhibitions promoted Leilie's awareness of art, which revealed itself early and

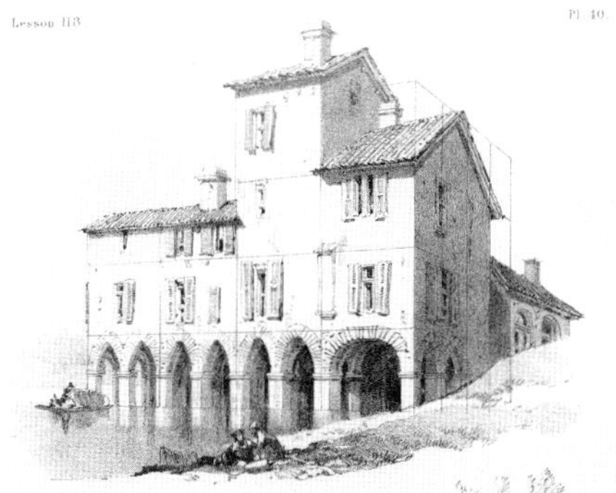

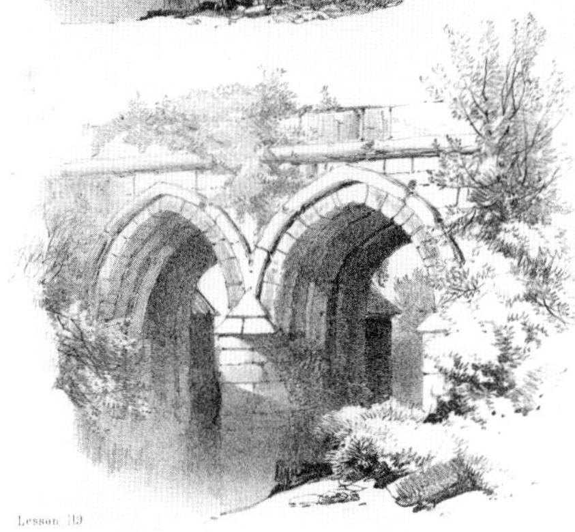

10-12. LEFT TO RIGHT: *J. D. Harding. "Lesson 114, A Cattle Shed"; "Lesson 115, Farm-Buildings at Penshurst"; "Lesson 119, Buildings at Puzzano, Lago Maggiore"; from* Lessons on Art *by J. D. Harding (W. Kent & Co.)*

was encouraged at home. Years earlier her delighted family had gathered around a freckle-faced, tousle-headed three-year-old with a wooden slate, exclaiming in wonder and admiration, "Leilie has drawn the organ-grinder!"[79] Perhaps this scene bespeaks the family's eagerness to find some spark of talent as compensation for their loss; perhaps it tells us more. But certainly, although music was the principal art form embraced by the family, it was not the only one. Remarkable Eliza, the professional-caliber musician, was also an accomplished artist who painted florals in watercolor, designed her own embroidery patterns, and was rarely without her sketchbook. On every outing, on summer holidays when the Leavitts escaped the stifling Philadelphia heat and fled to family in Connecticut or central Pennsylvania, Eliza drew with expertise. One of her surviving landscapes shows her skill, revealing a knowledge of perspective both mechanical and atmospheric as well as a keen sense of design. Of course she had benefited from the best instruction during her early years, when the Leavitts were among New York's elite.

Papa Beaux also had an affinity for art, and the desire to establish a connection between herself and her absent parent may have motivated Leilie's interest. But unlike Aunt Eliza, Papa Beaux had never taken art lessons and had evidently developed his ability on his own. Etta considered her father's aptitude innate, his birthright as a Frenchman. "Our father came from the South of France, the land of art and romance where it is almost Italy," she wrote. "I always felt that he could have been an artist. He could draw without lessons, without knowing it—which was a thing my distinguished sister never dreamed of doing."[80]

Etta was right about her sister. In fact, Leilie never dreamed of becoming an artist at all, lessons notwithstanding. "How could I dream of being an artist? I never did,"[81] she wrote. Her ambitions were of a different order. "If I had dreams, they were of poetry, or of houses, not fairy palaces, but very real abodes; such, indeed, as would have been exactly right for our family if we, that is our means, had permitted . . . and in these appropriate surroundings the ladies of my family moved or sat, in soft, rich, silk dresses and lace."[82] The ladies in Leilie's family, who had seen too much hardship and war to expect anything positive to happen except through diligence, did not wait for their young charge to develop a natural talent on her own. They believed in hard work and proper instruction.

One day in 1868, when Leilie was thirteen years old, Aunt Eliza returned from the city with a package of lithographs by the English artist James Duffield Harding (1797–1863). Harding was a painter whose expert landscapes in watercolor and oil were widely admired. The son of a drawing master, he carried on the family tradition, becoming a noted teacher whose most famous student was the artist and critic John Ruskin (1819–1900). Harding, who wrote several popular drawing manuals and published lithographs for students to copy, shared the Leavitts' opinion that art should be taught. In the preface to his famous *Lessons on Art*, published in 1866, he wrote, "The power to draw, or to appreciate Art and Nature, is, and must be, the result of education."[83] Leilie was about to be educated.

After setting out a well-sharpened, hard lead pencil, a knife to keep the point, an eraser to correct errors, and a sheet of fine white drawing paper, Eliza called in her young niece and suggested that she copy one of the Harding lithographs. Leilie was enthusiastic and proud to have the drawings in her possession. "Harding was a true artist," she wrote. "Every touch had quality and charm."[84] The drawing took shape beneath her hand, a small hut flanked by a tree, perfectly placed, exactly copied, and in proportion. Aunt Eliza was delighted. Leilie was not. Accustomed to a certain standard of excellence, the stitches perfect, the notes played with no stumbling or repetition, she realized that although the shapes were correct, the quality of the line was all wrong. Too shy to say anything to her aunt, Leilie persevered with her joyless task and "remained alive to this early disappointment."[85] In subsequent years she would realize the futility of trying to duplicate a printed line with a pencil. "Later," she wrote, "I was to know more of lithography."[86]

Leilie's drawing lessons were among the last she undertook at home. At thirteen she was a healthy, agreeable girl with fair skin, her father's arresting blue eyes, and very thick, tawny hair, which Aunt Eliza brushed for more than an hour every day and then plaited into two tight braids. She recalled being languid and feeling unoccupied, although her family made sure that she was busy. Under their tutelage she had learned to sew, cook, clean house, spell, take dictation, speak French, sing, and draw. She committed to memory poetry, long passages of the Bible, and the Westminster Shorter Catechism—all 107 questions.

Religion was important to the family. The Woodland Presbyterian Church, where Grandma Leavitt was a charter member, was their spiritual and social center, but the girl's religious training was handled with subtlety. No doubt Grandma's experience with her eldest son, whose mandatory instruction turned him away from the family's preferred church, caused her to employ more judicious methods. "The example I watched silently was in my grandmother's evident relation to something far from the little and big matters of living and housekeeping,"[87] Beaux recalled. Specifically, there was Grandma's daily hiatus. Every evening at six o'clock she retreated to her room and closed the door. Leilie was told she was "being quiet." Perhaps Grandma sat down relieved and exhausted in her favorite chair, unpinned her lace cap from her perfectly coiffed hair, kicked off her well-polished shoes, and put her swollen feet up on the adjacent table. Leilie presumed that she prayed. Perhaps she prayed for strength. By the time Leilie was born, Grandma Leavitt had been raising children with uninterrupted concentration for thirty-three years.

The girls tried not to tax Grandma's strength. "We loved Grandma very much," Etta told her youngest daughter. "We would have no more disobeyed her than—Oh my!"[88] Obediently, Leilie attended church and said her prayers with regularity but no particular conviction. Perhaps Grandma Leavitt sensed her ambivalence. In 1864, just before the Beaux sisters left for Lewistown, Leilie was presented with a gift—her mother's inscribed Bible. Grandma added the child's name and the date. The slim volume with fine type and tissue-thin pages became Leilie's most treasured possession, her only tangible remnant of the mother she never knew. Soon afterwards, one cold afternoon in Lewistown while wandering alone in the frozen yard, Leilie recalled a beloved passage from Mendelssohn's "Elijah"—"If with all your hearts ye truly seek me." She suddenly felt God revealed to her "in a flood of rapture, recognition, and love."[89] Although this life-changing epiphany convinced her of the existence of God, Cecilia Beaux, who would work in a field rife with cynics and skeptics, would take her cue from Grandma Leavitt and keep her faith private.

13. OPPOSITE: ***Mrs. John Wheeler Leavitt.*** *1885. Oil on canvas, 45 1/2 x 34 in. The Westmoreland Museum of American Art*

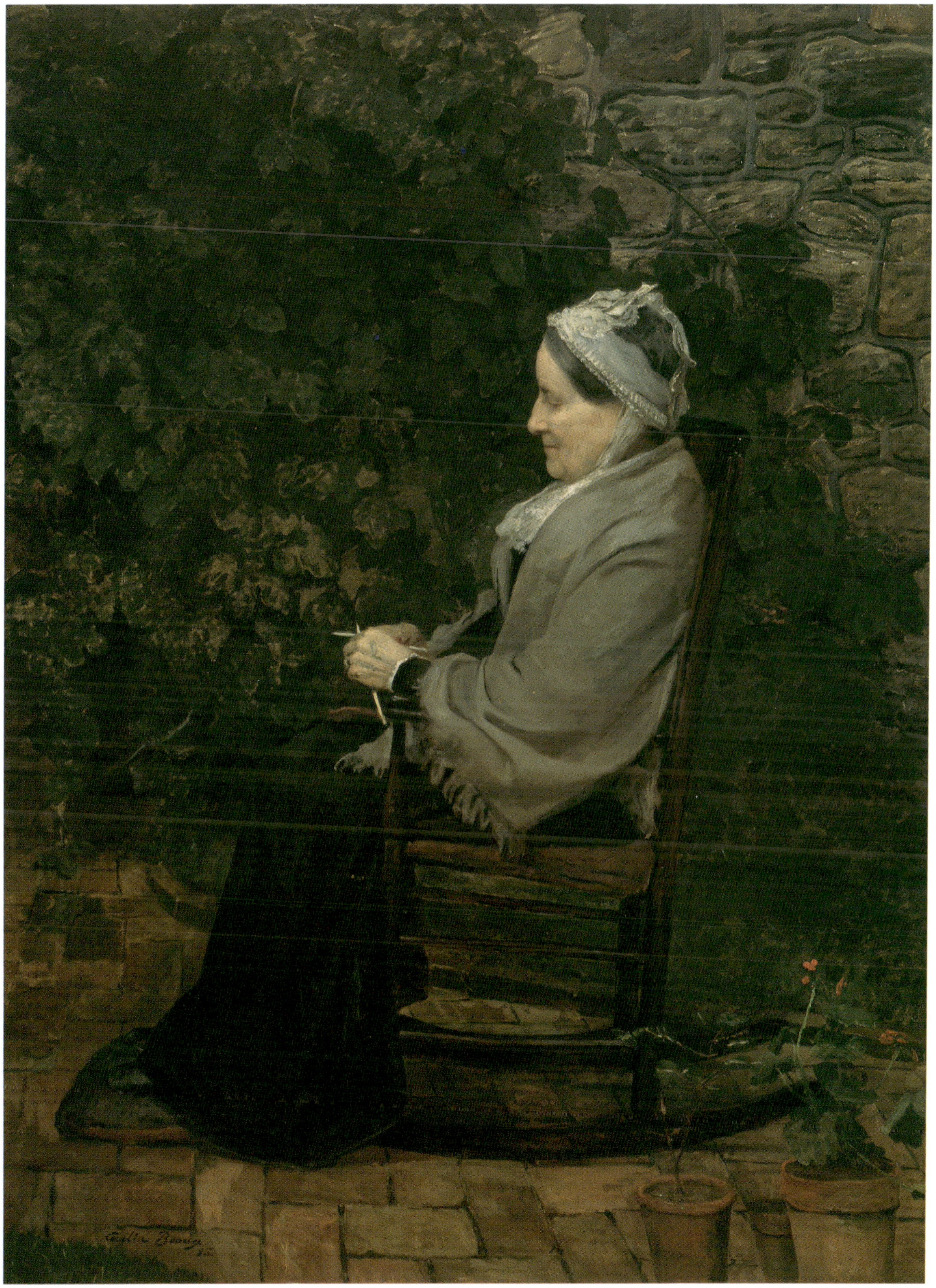

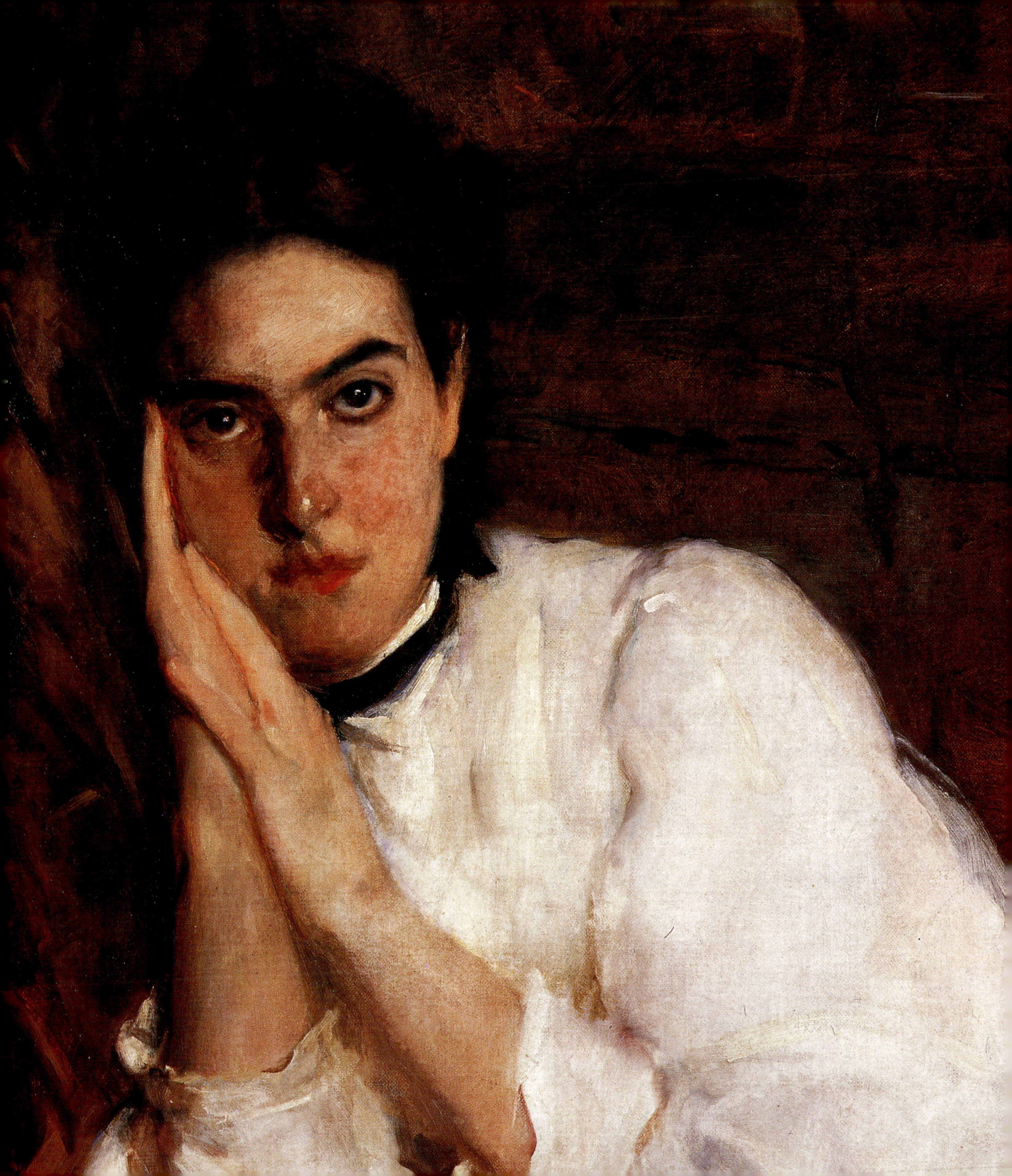

A Fashionable Education

"I feel thankful that my childhood and youth were not stuffed, gorged, with a multifarious fodder that deadened all appetite."

—Cecilia Beaux, *1930*

Leilie spent her first fourteen years in the protective circle of the extended Leavitt family, whose unconditional love mitigated most difficulties. There were certainly traumas and disappointments, but few were serious. A brush with death at the age of three, when she fell into an open cistern, was barely recalled; the death of a playmate, vaguely understood; and a summer holiday spent in central Pennsylvania sleeping on an uncomfortable husk mattress and dealing with rowdy, ill-mannered cousins, largely alleviated by the beauty of the countryside and the companionship of Aunt Eliza.

Only one incident marred the peaceful fabric of Leilie's early life. It involved two of her uncles, responsible Charles and philanthropic, impractical Samuel, who were grown men at the time and should have known better. One bitterly cold evening they crept into the bedroom Leilie and Etta shared, located the girls' precious dolls, snatched the toys from their warm quilts, and hung them by the neck and feet from the gas jets and door handles. The children discovered the outrage in the morning and were devastated, especially Leilie, whose passion for taking proper care of her "children" bordered on the obsessive and was well known in the family. Although the uncles were chastised by Grandma Leavitt and were properly chagrined, Leilie never forgave them. Sixty-two years later, when both men were in their graves, Cecilia Beaux recorded the incident bitterly in her autobiography, explaining that from that day forward she had "never really trusted the ethical principles of professional philanthropists."[90] For Beaux, strength of character was expressed through achievement. Throughout her life she sustained the belief that underachievers evidenced a moral turpitude and an odious resemblance to her careless Uncle Samuel, who not only traumatized his young nieces, but in the face of financial crisis, was unable to support the extended family. Aside from that one episode, Leilie appears to have breezed through her childhood and emerged, by her own account, as "both a realist and a perfectionist, pursued by an uncompromising passion for carrying through."[91]

In 1869, when Leilie turned fourteen, she began keeping a diary, a practice she maintained for the rest of her life, rating each day as "a good day," or "a bad day," and on occasion, even "a stupid day." Following her revelation in Lewistown, she remained devout, but having no desire to reveal the depth of her religious feelings, decided to express her devotion to God through flawless behavior. This decision was not easy to uphold, especially for a teenage perfectionist who felt compelled to justify her existence and to be someone extraordinary. She confessed in her diary, "Why is it harder for some people to be good than others, a great deal harder? Some people seem to be naturally good like Etta. . . . Sometimes it seems to me as if I

OPPOSITE: *Detail;* ***The Dreamer.*** *1894. Oil on canvas, 32 1/4 x 24 1/2 in. Collection of the Butler Institute of American Art, Youngstown, Ohio*

were tied down in a spiritual way to a string of a certain length. I get on very well at first and feel so free and happy, feel as if I was getting better, when suddenly I come to the end of my string and am thrown back to the old place again."[92]

In the fall of that same year, it was decided that Leilie should pursue her studies at a private school for girls in downtown Philadelphia. The proper institution had already been selected, as Etta had preceded her in this first foray outside the family circle. Looking back, Cecilia Beaux was certain that her alma mater, the Misses Lyman School, was the best and most exclusive in the city. But in fact, as Leilie walked with trepidation up the white marble steps for her first day of class, another institution for young ladies, The Agnes Irwin School, was beginning its inaugural year. And it was Miss Irwin's school in the fashionable Rittenhouse Square neighborhood that quickly became the preferred choice for the daughters of Philadelphia's elite.[93] Nevertheless, the Misses Lyman School was one of a number of respectable local academies for girls and probably a good choice for the Beaux sisters because the students, who ranged in age from ten to eighteen, came from a variety of backgrounds.

The school was located at 226 South Broad Street in the large brick and marble home of the principals, the Lyman sisters. Promptly at nine in the morning, Leilie joined her classmates seated at desks in the front parlor where they awaited Miss Catherine Lyman's entrance. A woman of medium size with neatly coiffed gray hair and sporting a lace-trimmed light gray poplin dress with a short train, Miss Lyman glided regally into the silent room. The other girls, familiar with the routine, rose from their chairs to kneel for the morning prayers, which Miss Lyman read in a rich, deep voice. The drama of the ceremony enthralled Leilie, who suddenly found herself in a new world. For fourteen years her life had centered on her relatives, and their ideas and habits were the only ones she knew. She was acquainted with very few young people, and those she did know were members of her family. So for Leilie, the Misses Lyman School was to present a "drama of unforgettable vividness":[94] "How far the Miss Lymans were from perceiving that their school for young ladies had, to one of them, at least, all the fascinating appeal of an original and perfectly set play."[95]

For the first and probably the only time in her life, Leilie did not—in fact, could not—strive for excellence. In many instances she was simply outclassed and overwhelmed. Some of the girls seemed unimaginably beautiful, with tiny feet shod in high-buttoned white kid boots. Others were from the best downtown addresses, houses that awed Leilie when she visited, with their high ceilings, rich damask curtains, palatial rooms, and soft, carpeted stairs. Her classmates were not required to help with household chores or to make their own clothes. In their affluent homes, there were servants to do the cleaning and a seamstress who sewed all day long in a remote upstairs room, fashioning everything from tulle ball gowns to the plain woolen dresses that all the girls wore to school, regardless of their family's wealth or social prominence.

Leilie made friends among these fascinating girls whose lives were so different from her own. A few of those friendships were evidently naïvely romantic—her first brushes with love, experiences she would later neither condemn nor deny. "The 'heart interest' of the place was keen, absorbing, and almost painful in its intensity, and not exactly to be called a school-girl infatuation," Beaux recalled in her autobiography. "But whether hidden, manifested, or in abeyance to the 'code' of the period, such seizures lie too near the roots of humanity to be at the command or denial of any age. They continue; hearts remain the same."[96]

Leilie's academic achievements were not impressive. In Latin and Arithmetic she was a beginner and was placed with the little girls in pinafores under the care of the younger Lyman sister. In most of her other classes she was an average student, assigned accordingly with girls of her own age. In French and Natural History, two subjects stressed at home, she was honored with inclusion in the top group. Although her proficiency in

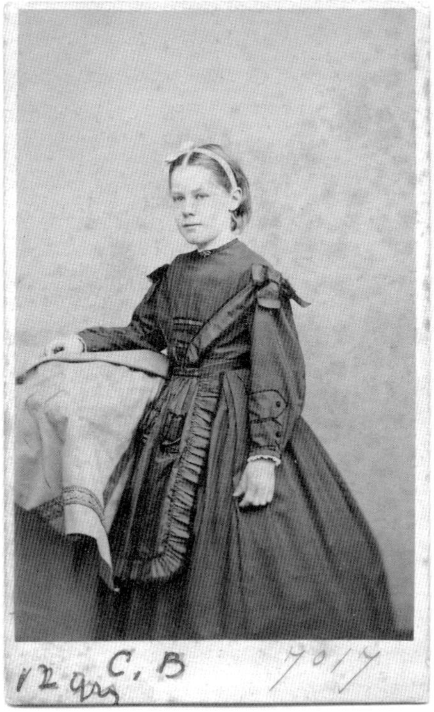

14. O. H. Willard. **Cecilia Beaux at age twelve**, ca. 1867. *Pennsylvania Academy of the Fine Arts*

English Composition eventually resulted in her promotion in that subject, by her own admission she never really concentrated on her studies. The spectacle of the school, the teachers, the girls, the gossip, and the romance were simply too distracting. Monthly reports were issued, and Leilie's were not what she would have hoped. "My reports were not bad, but they were not very good," she recalled. "And I fear they rather saddened those at home who were making real sacrifices for my education."[97]

Leilie and Etta's only distinction at the Lyman School was in writing rhymed verse; an extracurricular activity in demand when each term ended and the girls exchanged gifts of folded paper fans inscribed with sentimental or humorous poetry. "Rhymed verse flowed from us almost as easily as speech," Beaux recalled.[98] She credited this ability to their provincial blood, the legacy of her inattentive father who still resided in France and apparently was only doling out genetic favors. More likely, the girls' ear for language was the result of Grandma Leavitt's devotion. Throughout their childhood every difficult household chore—the mending of sheets, the endless dusting, and the waxing of the old, heavy furniture—was accompanied by Grandma's loud reading: Sir Walter Scott's novels and poems, Longfellow's poems, the Psalms and long chapters of the Bible, as well as the girls' favorite, John Bunyan's *The Pilgrim's Progress*. When Grandma Leavitt brought out that book, her delighted granddaughters would recite in unison, "As I walked through the wilderness of this world, I lighted on a certain place where was a den, and laid me down in that place to sleep; and as I slept, I dreamed a dream. . . . "[99]

The art class at the Misses Lyman School was popular but required an additional fee, which Leilie's family could not afford. It was just as well, as the class was the only one in the curriculum that she regarded with contempt. Drawing instruction took place in one of the upstairs rooms where Leilie never had occasion to venture. But she did watch her classmates gaily descend the stairs with dirty hands and smudged aprons, their loose charcoal renderings held high over their heads. "This was my first sight of students' work and it was indeed revolting. I would have had to be dragged to the class in irons if it had been my fate to go."[100]

In June of 1871, when she turned sixteen, her family decided on a different course. Although she belittled the drawing classes at school, Leilie continued with her art lessons at home, and the results were encouraging. It was Uncle Will Biddle—perhaps after reviewing her monthly reports with consternation—who determined that his niece would be best served by quitting school and pursuing her interest in art. Leilie, who did not object to Uncle Will's decision, nevertheless wondered how her modest success at home could be parlayed into a calling. "The gulf between me and such an ambition was just too great. I could not see across it," she explained.[101]

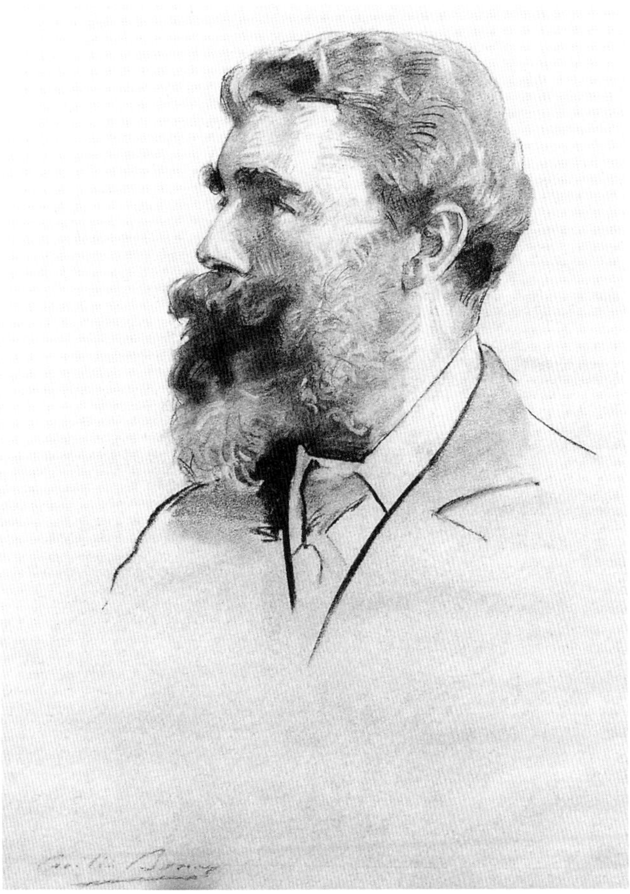

15. ***Thomas Allibone Janvier.*** *n.d. Charcoal on paper, 19½ x 13¼ in. The Century Association, New York*

Although Leilie loved the paintings in the local galleries, she had no idea how they were produced, having never seen a palette, canvas, or paints. At sixteen she was a tall, attractive young woman with a "quick step and a pretty figure."[102] Certainly, her Uncle Will assumed she would eventually marry. So he was probably not as concerned about promoting a career for his niece as he was about keeping her safe and sufficiently occupied until the right man came along. Leilie's trepidation concerning a future occupation did not deter his enthusiasm for finding her one. Like everyone else in the immediate family, once he set his mind on something, he followed through.

The popular classes at the Pennsylvania Academy of the Fine Arts had outgrown their old quarters and were suspended while a new museum and school was built at the corner of Broad and Cherry Streets in the heart of the city. It was to be a grand building, designed by architects Frank Furness (1839–1912) and George Hewitt (1841–1916) with all the latest amenities. During the construction, which would take six years, the Academy's instructor, the painter Christian Schussele, continued to teach on a limited basis in his home. But his classes for serious professionals were not suitable for sixteen-year-old Leilie.

The resourceful Will Biddle knew of an appropriate, qualified instructor, happily a member of his own family. Catharine Ann Drinker, whom he called "Cousin Kate," was the niece of his aunt, Sally Drinker Biddle. Kate, who was thirty when she was introduced to Leilie, had lived a life of adventure outside her new pupil's circumscribed upbringing and had much to offer the young girl. Cousin Kate was the daughter of Sandwith Drinker, a sea captain who endured the early nineteenth-century perils of his occupation with aplomb, once quelling a disturbance on the deck of one of his ships in his silk pajamas. After surviving near-mutinies, storms, and an attack by pirates, he wrote in his diary, "How I do detest the ocean, a ship, and everything connected with them."[103] In 1849 Captain Drinker saved enough money to do something he considered less detestable and started a shipping business in Macao, China. Established and no longer in fear of his life, he sent for his family in America—his wife Susanna, his son Morton, and his daughter Kate.[104]

Captain Drinker's business prospered, and the family lived a dazzling life in China's international community. Commodore Perry and Consul General Townsend Harris were family friends and stayed at the Drinkers' house when they came to Macao. Kate benefited from lessons with expert tutors, studied Chinese art, learned mathematics, and became fluent in French.[105] The leading Hong Kong merchants hosted fifty-course dinners and lavish receptions. Kate was no beauty even as a child, but she had admirers. When she was only ten years old, a Chinese merchant prince, purportedly one of the most powerful in the country, proposed a marriage between Kate and his son. The incident caused Sandwith Drinker some anxiety. Foreigners were tolerated in China, but not trusted, so Drinker's refusal on behalf of his young daughter necessitated considerable diplomacy.[106]

Drinker must have been an adroit diplomat. The family's social life flourished right through the violence and suspicion generated by the mid-century opium wars, although their business interests proved vulnerable. Three of Drinker's ships were sabotaged. In the most startling incident, eleven European passengers on one of his vessels were seized by the Chinese and beheaded.[107] In January 1857, Drinker—perhaps to celebrate the new year—decided to host a breakfast for the officers of European vessels in the harbor. The meal was not a success. The Chinese chef aiming to take down the odious foreigners single-handedly, baked arsenic into the bread. Discovering the plot, Drinker sent a doctor to administer an emetic to all his guests but in his excitement, neglected to treat himself. Although the exact cause of his death on January eighteenth was never determined, he suffered greatly from the poisoning and never recovered his health.[108]

After her husband's death, friends raised $12,000 to send Susanna Drinker and her family home.[109] In 1858 Mrs. Drinker boarded the *Storm King* with three of her four children—Kate, by then sixteen, and her two younger siblings born in China, Henry and Elizabeth. The Drinkers' oldest son, Morton, had been sent back to the United States to attend school before the catastrophe unfolded. The voyage home was an adventure beyond belief. They were becalmed for three weeks in the China Sea. Six-year-old Henry, who even as a child was not prone to hyperbole, later remembered passing part of the time watching poisonous sea snakes churn up the water. Periodically members of the crew would row out in a launch and tow the vessel from its own filth. Their perpetually intoxicated captain menaced Kate with his knife. Retaining her composure, she commanded he lay down the weapon; miraculously, he complied. By the time the wind kicked up, the captain was so incapacitated that he had to be locked in irons, and Kate, who had been taught to navigate by her father and was the only person on board qualified for the job, set their course for home and was somehow able to guide the ship around Cape Horn.

When the journey ended, the family settled in Baltimore with their lives intact, but their finances ruined. Kate took art lessons at the Maryland Institute, hoping to launch a viable career in commercial art. Susanna established a school, Mrs. Drinker's Academy for Young Ladies.[110] However, their troubles were not over. Within four years Susanna Drinker was dead from the complications of a uterine tumor, and Kate, just out of her teens, was left to manage the family and the school on her own.

Perhaps Mrs. Drinker's Academy failed under Kate's inexperienced management, or perhaps the war intervened. But by 1865 the school was closed and Kate had moved her sister, brother, and maternal grandmother Shober to Philadelphia, where relatives helped them find a tiny house on Pine Street. Still determined to establish an art career, Kate enrolled in the Pennsylvania Academy of the Fine Arts.[111] Only six years later, when her cousin Will Biddle took his niece to her studio, indomitable Kate—whom fate had honed to an even stronger metal than the Leavitt women—was an art teacher at Miss Sanford's School and a well-established painter of academic subjects.

Kate Drinker's studio was on the top floor of an old house at Fifth and Walnut Streets, close to the leafy oasis of Independence Hall. The studio was a typical nineteenth-century atelier with all the predictable accoutrements. But to Leilie it presented a new and fascinating world. "I am glad that the studio was typical and traditional, and not to be confused with any ordinary or domestic scene, for it was the first studio I ever entered," she recalled. "On its threshold everyday existence dropped completely out of sight. . . . "[112] Kate's studio functioned as both a workplace and a showplace. She was a busy professional who sold her pictures, so visitors and clients came to soak up the atmosphere. There were artifacts from China, dark Eastern furniture, and a large gold Buddha that sat heavily in a corner. The day Leilie arrived, Kate's lay figure (studio mannequin) was clothed for a Biblical painting in progress, *Daniel at Prayer*. Heavy drapes blocked all the windows, so that the only illumination came from a single skylight emitting dust-flecked rays that brightened the room like a benediction.

Kate selected suitable lithographs for her apprentice to copy, a series of studies of Greek sculpture produced for instructional purposes by the French artist Bernard-Romaine Julien, who made a living publishing drawing manuals for students.[113] Kate also supplied Conté crayons, yellow paper, and an easel placed at the edge of the room, facing the wall, where the light would fall from above and behind, eliminating any distracting shadows. Leilie copied the studies carefully. The subtle gray of the paper combined with the soft, sweeping quality of the lithographic crayon impressed her. "The subjects were beautiful, and I knew it and adored them," she remembered.[114]

Leilie worked diligently, making sure all the proportions were perfect, but frustration soon set in. Her dilemma was familiar, the same one that had plagued her when she copied the Harding drawings. Her work looked ugly, the crayon gritty and hard. A tentative fingertip stroking the line into a subtle fade failed to produce anything close to the desired effect. Having no idea how the lithographs were produced, she assumed that some fault of her own prevented her drawings from capturing the refinement she admired. Verging on tears, Leilie could voice no explanation for her disappointment, and Kate, who at the same age had navigated a vessel through treacherous waters and thought the drawings looked fine, probably wondered what could possibly be wrong with her new student.

Leilie studied with Catharine Drinker for a year. In that short time she changed from an emotional teenager capable of weeping over a flawed drawing to a young woman with resolve and, in the wake of her experience at the Lyman School, a renewed sense of confidence in her ability to excel. When the light faded in the studio, she often postponed the forty-minute horse-car ride to West Philadelphia and spent the evening with her teacher. On several occasions she accompanied Kate to the sumptuous home of print collector John S. Phillips. Phillips's collection consisted of more than 50,000 works of art, catalogued chronologically and stored in handmade cases according to schools. Highlights of his holdings included prints by Daniel Hopfer (1470–1536), an etcher from Augsburg, Germany, who revolutionized publishing in 1493 as the first artist to use etching in the printing process. Works by the premier English line engravers, William Sharp (1749–1824) and William Woolette (1735– 1785), who was well known in Philadelphia for his engraving of Benjamin West's *Death of General Wolfe*, were also represented. A group of priceless sixteenth-century woodcuts, the first to reproduce accurately the look of brush strokes, was among the most treasured works in Phillips's collection.[115]

Leilie studied the pieces, beginning at last to unravel the confounding mysteries of the printing process. But although the artwork was impressive, the collector fascinated her more. Mr. Phillips was nearing the end of his life when Leilie met him, and to her young eyes, he looked like Father Time. Yet as he discussed his collection, the years dropped away, and his dark eyes shone, still passionate about the artwork he had compiled, catalogued, and mounted, unaided, for thirty years. After viewing the prints, the group settled in the parlor, where the maid offered Madeira and queen's cakes. It was then that Leilie noticed the old man's hand shaking—not from age but from the emotion of revisiting his beloved collection. Even at sixteen, she understood. She was shaking too, and for the rest of her life she felt a connection to the kind old man who introduced her to printmaking and shared her growing enthusiasm for art. Phillips must have felt the bond too, the passing of a torch from one generation to another. The last time they saw one another he put his arms around Kate and Leilie, gazed into their eyes, and recognizing kindred spirits looked from one to the other and said, "My fine friend, my fair friend."[116]

These excursions were a rare treat. More often, after a long day in the studio, Leilie went to Kate's house on Pine Street. There she climbed the stairs to the third-floor study, where a library of books, among them *Alice in Wonderland*, *The Bab Ballads*, and Edward Lear's charming drawings and nonsense verse, all new at the time, captured her imagination. Kate's collection also included more adult offerings, and Uncle Will, noting this, did not always approve of the influence his sophisticated cousin wielded over his sheltered niece. He was shocked when Leilie brought home Samuel Richardson's monumental and daring novel *Clarissa*. Looking back, Cecilia Beaux could not recall whether she actually read the book, trembled through the long seduction, hated the rakish villain, or abhorred the rape. She did remember her uncle's disapproval and the novel's quick return to Kate.

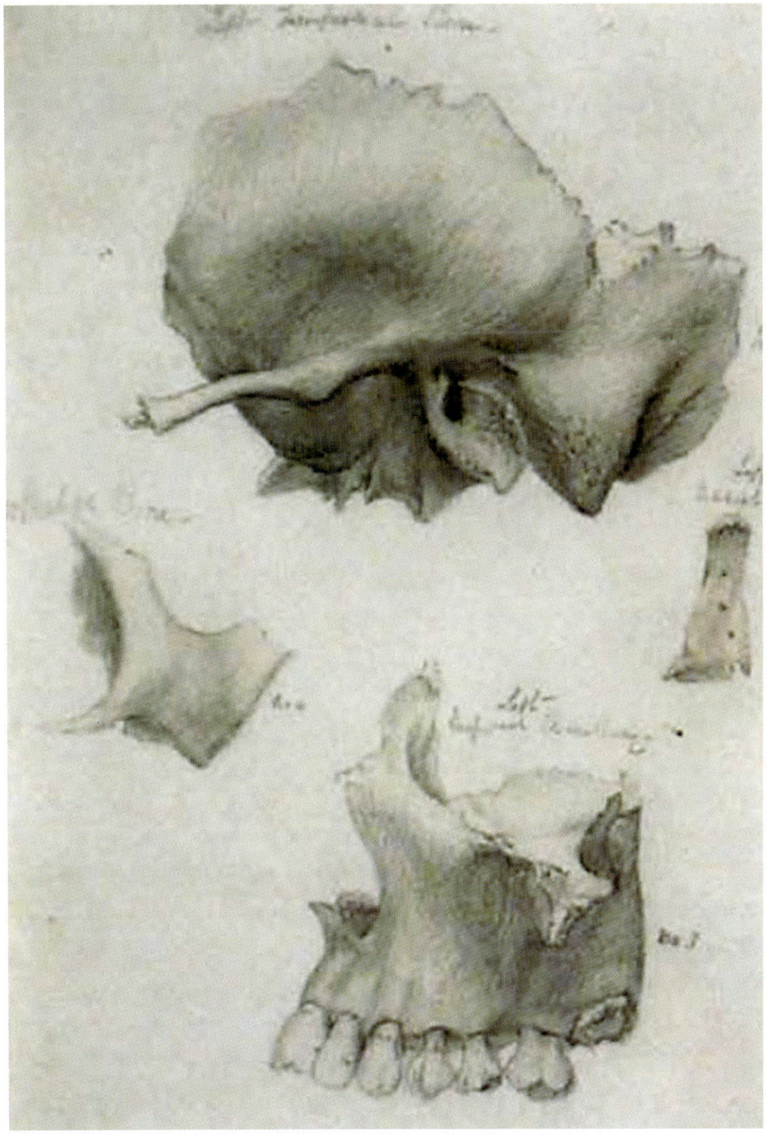

16. ***Left Temporal Bone.*** *1873. Graphite on paper, 7 x 5 in. Courtesy of Alfred J. Walker Fine Art, Boston*

The cast of characters at the Drinkers' Pine Street house proved as interesting as the library. Kate's eighty-six-year-old Grandma Shober, whom Beaux fondly described as "a sprite in full Quaker dress," was a tiny lady who was opinionated, domineering, and entertaining. She seemed to understand Leilie and quickly adopted her into the Drinker family.[117] Grandma Shober was the first person to call Leilie "Bo," a name she loved and encouraged her friends to adopt. The moniker carried no particular connotations, as it was neither her mother's name nor exactly her father's but something entirely her own. Leilie was also introduced to Henry Drinker, Kate's younger brother, the one who harbored such vivid recollections of their difficult voyage. Henry had survived and thrived despite his traumatic childhood. A new graduate from Lehigh University with a degree in Mining Engineering, he took more than a passing interest in his sister's young apprentice. However, Leilie, who was not indifferent to the attentions of young men, had her eye on someone else.

Thomas Allibone Janvier, who at twenty-two was already on his way to establishing himself as a writer, was a frequent guest at the Drinkers. His promise, evident even as he began his career as a fledgling journalist, would be fulfilled in later years when he became one of

America's most respected authors. Sixteen-year-old Leilie may not have been particularly impressed by Janvier's potential as a writer, yet she did notice his extraordinary good looks. He was, she remembered, "handsome as a troubadour."[118] If Leilie wondered why Janvier spent so much time at the Drinkers, she never asked and was completely surprised when Kate and Thomas announced their engagement. "In my ignorance of life," Beaux wrote, "I thought that only youth had a right to love. I never suspected that her young friend was the fiancé of my instructress. There are powers more potent than the freshness of youth."[119] Cecilia Beaux would go on to develop her own powers and, as her youth faded, to find strength in Kate's example.

Janvier's physical attributes must have presented a striking contrast to Kate's homeliness. Kate was a small woman and, at thirty, full of energy. But despite her vitality and obvious intelligence, she was so unattractive that in later years her sister-in-law would worry with every pregnancy that the new baby might take after Aunt Kate. Despite Kate's urbane background and artistic training, she had no sense of fashion, and her dowdy clothes did nothing to improve her appearance. "No matter how styles changed," the Drinker's youngest child, Catherine Drinker Bowen later wrote, "Kate remained one lap behind. When women wore plain sailor hats, hers had flowers; if their stockings were beige, hers stayed black. Nevertheless, as a spinster in her thirties, she captivated Thomas Janvier, eight years her junior and a fascinator if one ever lived—caught him, married him, and outlived him by some ten years."[120]

As their year together ended, Kate recommended that her protégé attend art school. Leilie welcomed the opportunity, and Uncle Will, who may have been glad to direct his niece away from Kate's growing influence, lent both financial and moral support to the new venture. The Philadelphia School of Design for Women, an all-female academy founded in 1844, maintained a fine reputation for providing training in practical and commercial art. But at the time the student body consisted of older women whose careers and lives had been disrupted by five years of war. Theodore Knauff, the author of a 1922 school history, wrote that in the late 1860s and early 1870s " . . . women of mature age had flocked to the school to get a training to fit them for self support which they had missed in their earlier life."[121]

Fortunately Kate knew of a school offering separate classes for men and women founded to fill the void left by the closure of the Pennsylvania Academy. The student body was young and the curriculum sound, so the institution seemed to be a good choice for Leilie. The director was Francis Adolf Van der Wielen, a twenty-five-year-old Dutch artist whose deteriorating eyesight threatened his career. Teaching was to be his salvation, a chance to earn a living and to pass on the knowledge he had acquired during his student days at the venerable Antwerp Academy of the Arts, an institu-

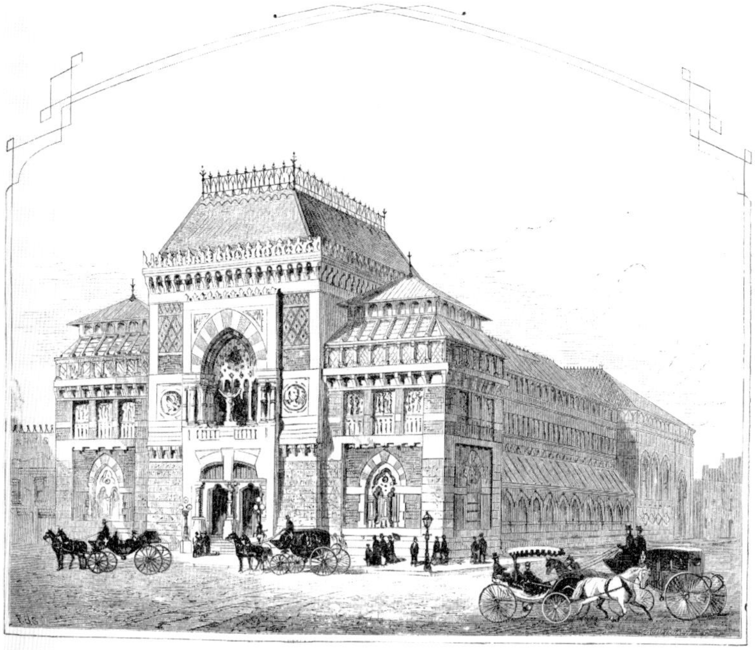

17. ***"Pennsylvania Academy of Fine Arts,"*** *from* History of Philadelphia: 1609–1884 *by J. Thomas Scharf and Thompson Westcott (L. H. Everts & Co., 1884)*

tion that had been training painters since 1663.[122] When Leilie, on the arm of Uncle Will, climbed the stairs to the school's two light-filled rooms, she stepped into a 206-year-old tradition of disciplined European artistic training.

The rooms were freshly painted, filled with plaster casts and easels, and populated by other young girls of Leilie's age and a few older women. Years later Cecilia Beaux remembered Van der Wielen as a good-looking yet somber young man with a ruddy complexion, a mass of auburn hair, a full beard, and a strong accent. When he asked his new pupil if she had ever "enlairrchet" anything, she had no idea what he was talking about and said no just to be safe. Her first assignment was to "enlarge" something, a skill that really was new to her—to take a small lithograph of a bearded old man, gird it out in squares, and make a life-sized drawing.

With the introductions made and the lesson decided on, Uncle Will took his leave. "I felt quite lost when my guardian and protector left me and had small confidence in my ability to succeed with what was required,"[123] Beaux recalled. Nevertheless, as she began her assignment she took pleasure in the task. Her tools, for once, fit the style of the drawing she was to copy. The enlargement was successfully completed in a day or two and was shown to Mr. Van der Wielen, who approved it and permitted her, Beaux recalled, like Alice in Wonderland, to pass to the next square.

Although she longed to draw with the other women who were dutifully copying the plaster casts—an activity known as "drawing from the Antique"—Van der Wielen required one more test of Leilie's proficiency before she could join them. Plaster cylinders, spheres, squares, and rectangles were arranged on a table for her to draw. Although very little instruction was given, Leilie had enough experience to know what was required, a mastery of perspective and value—two of the most difficult lessons in art, problems that challenge every artist, no matter how accomplished. Although repelled by the machine-made shapes, which Beaux in retrospect remembered as ugly and akin to Cubism, a form of artistic expression she would come to loathe, she warmed to the task and eventually understood its importance. "I had been taught by this exercise, if I chose to apply it, every rule of linear and aerial perspective," she recalled.[124] With her second test successfully completed, Leilie was promoted to the "Antique," where she joined her new companions.

Mr. Van der Wielen's male students developed their skills beyond the somewhat tedious chore of copying plaster casts and progressed through a curriculum that included training in still life, anatomy, and life drawing. However, education for the women stopped with the "Antique."[125] In 1872 drawing from a nude model was considered improper for young ladies even in all female classes. Before the closure of the Pennsylvania Academy, the question of a women's life class had been a contentious one. In fact, any interest in studying the nude body was suspect as potentially prurient and, as such, hardly a respectable activity for a lady. For years women were barred from drawing in the Academy's sculpture gallery, because many of the casts were either nude or partially draped. Finally in 1844 the Academy's Board of Directors passed a landmark resolution: Women received the exclusive use of the sculpture gallery from 10 to 11 A.M. on Monday, Wednesday, and Friday for three months out of the year. This segregated system lasted for twelve years, until a more practical arrangement was initiated that allowed men and women to use the galleries at the same time. The Greek and Roman gods and warriors, the *Apollo Belvedere, Laocoön, Fighting Gladiator,* and others that displayed more than was deemed proper were fitted with fig leaves, so the sight of their plaster of Paris manhood would not cause the ladies any embarrassment in the company of their male colleagues.[126]

If exposure to undraped statuary was so controversial, it is no wonder that the introduction of actual life classes for women took another twelve years. When the classes were finally initiated in response to numerous requests from the Academy's serious female students, the women were segregated and only female models were hired to pose. Still, the thought that a respectable lady might have any interest in the human body was repugnant. This was an era when women didn't discuss anything corporal, when they called their underwear "unmentionables." Middle- and upper-class Victorians considered the purity of their wives and daughters a sign of moral and intellectual superiority. The rabble of disadvantaged immigrants, freed slaves, and the unsightly poor were suspected of having lower ethical standards, and it was comforting for those who were affluent to suppose that the deprivations of the poor were the well-deserved result of a dissolute lifestyle. Lower-class women were thought to be promiscuous, and indeed the women who posed for the life-drawing classes did so because they needed money. At the time nearly all of these models were prostitutes, and the idea that a decent woman would spend hours studying the body of someone so despoiled was scandalous. Nevertheless, in 1868 thirteen brave female artists who were serious about their profession risked censure and signed up for the first women's life class at the Pennsylvania Academy of the Fine Arts. Not surprising, Catharine Drinker was among these pioneers.

European schools were even more segregated than their American counterparts, and Van der Wielen, without the clout of an institution like the Pennsylvania Academy behind him, apparently decided to offer his female students what was considered appropriate and risk no more. Leilie, who had made great strides during her year of study with Kate, mastered the school's curriculum for ladies easily and was one of the top students. Each morning Van der Wielen offered criticism and lectured on perspective, presenting both mechanical and visual examples. The mechanics of perspective were demonstrated on the classroom blackboard, where he drew the horizon line, selected a vanishing point, and constructed long lines of retreating objects. Visual acuity was sharpened by close observation. Holding a plaster block aloft, he would turn it slowly, asking his amused students, "How more you see on this side, how less you see on *that*?"[127]

After lunch the teacher took his leave and did not return. The women were free to stay all day and draw if they liked. Leilie stayed and made friends with the most accomplished artist in her class, a woman of twenty-four newly engaged to a young physician. The doctor had presented his fiancée with an unusual gift—a complete set of the bones of the skull. Every afternoon Leilie's friend brought out this treasure, carefully unwrapped all the pieces, and set them on a sheet of white paper in good light so that the two women could copy them. Leilie made drawings of the entire collection: the ivory clarity of the bones of the cranium, the delicate power of the facial bones, the translucent perfection of the double-winged sphenoid.

This exercise was as close as she would get to drawing from life. In contrast to the dusty casts, the bones were stunning, and to Leilie, whose unwavering faith opened her mind to such thoughts, they seemed to have been constructed by the hand of a master. This happy accident, the rather strange gift of the young physician to his fiancée and Leilie's presence in the class at precisely the right time, was the kind of coincidence that led Beaux to question whether her career in portraiture was preordained, "a momentary access from the stars."[128] Certainly the opportunity was useful and extraordinarily fortunate. As a result of her study of the skull bones, Beaux wrote, "I always saw the structure under the surface."[129] Her paintings prove the point. Behind the skillful brushwork and depth of feeling that distinguish the Grand Manner portraits for which Cecilia Beaux would later become famous was the masterfully constructed human head, drawn with solidity and anatomical accuracy.

18. OPPOSITE: ***The Dreamer.*** *1894. Oil on canvas, 32 1/4 x 24 1/2 in. Collection of the Butler Institute of American Art, Youngstown, Ohio*

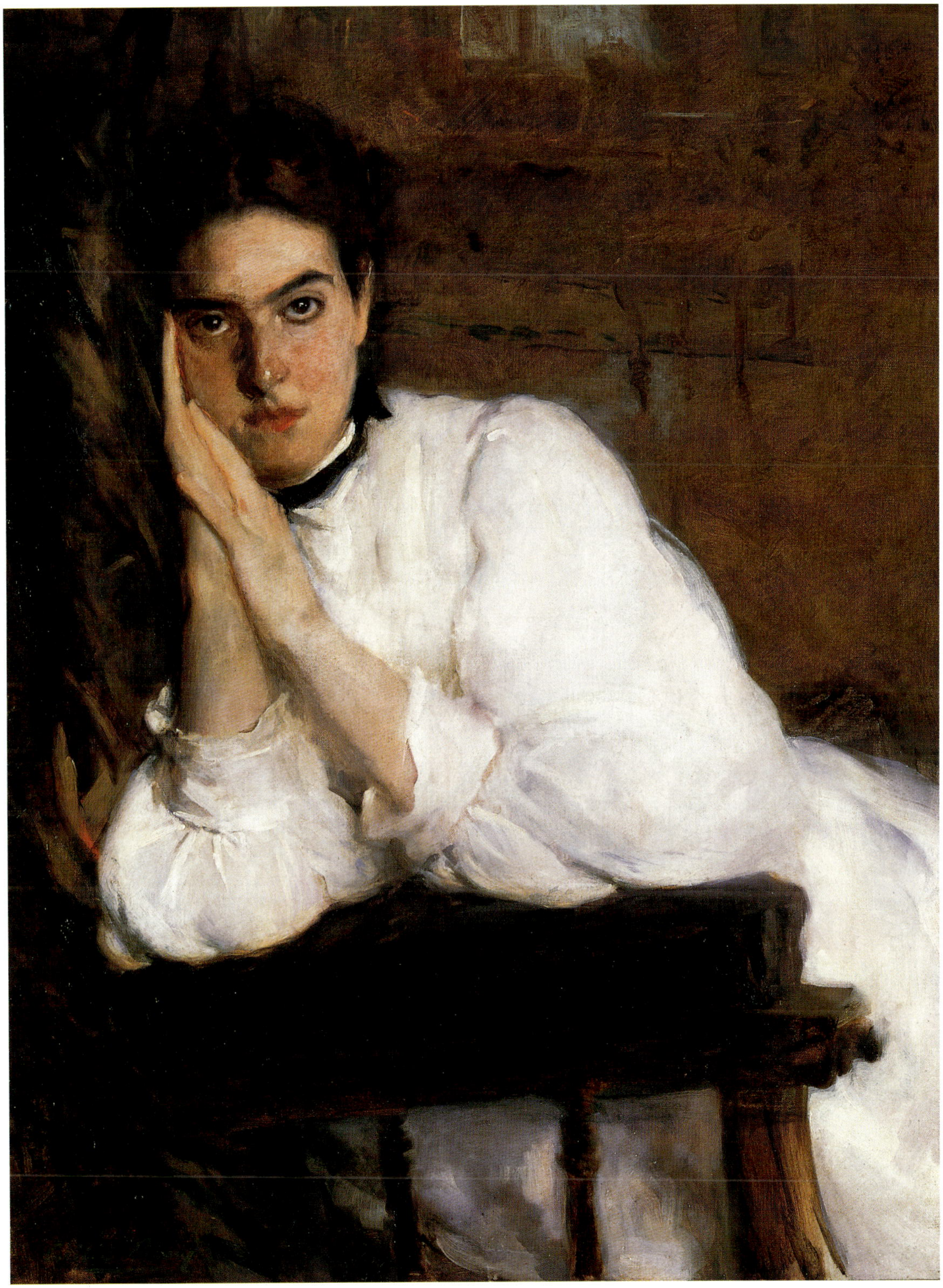

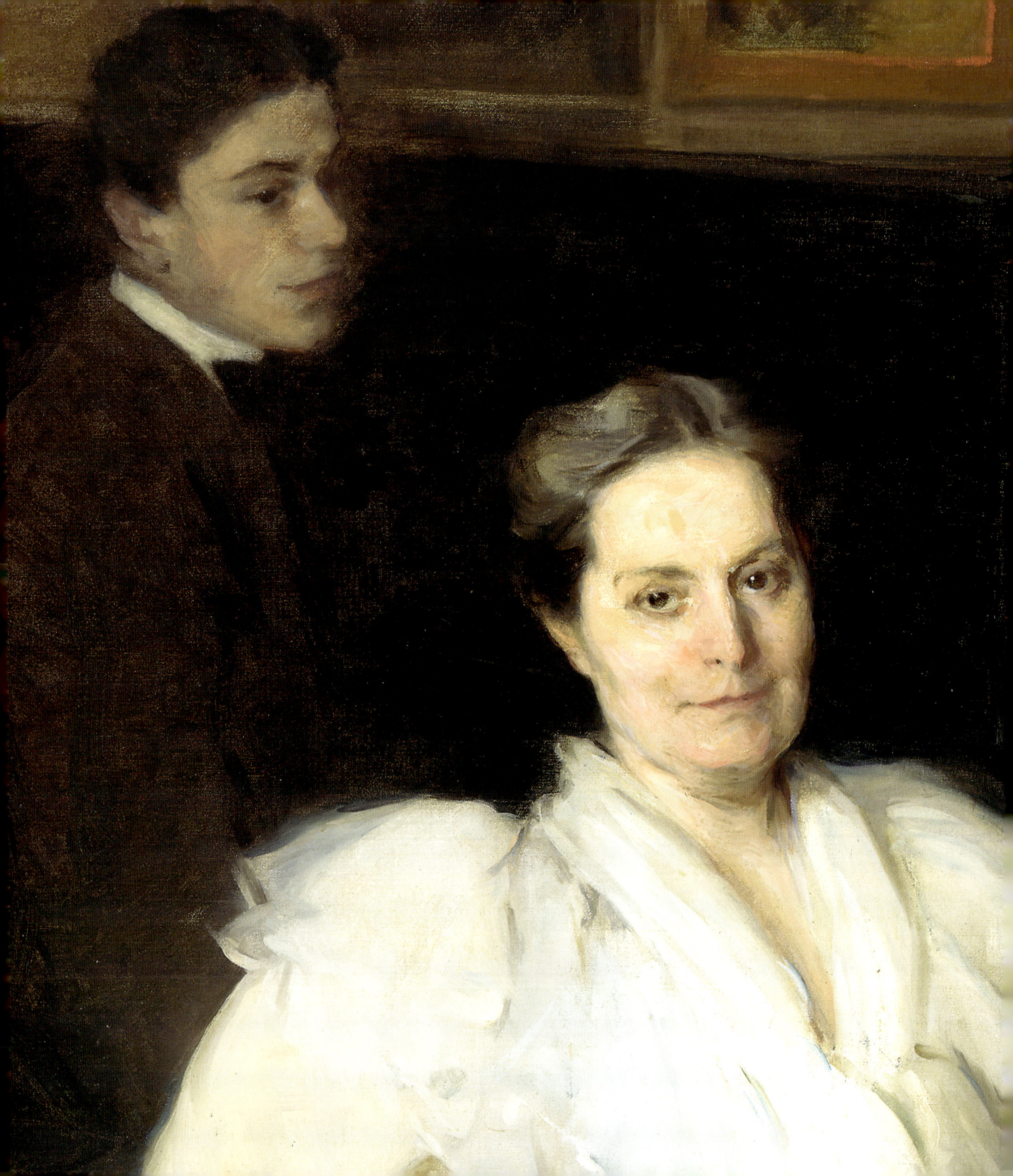

The Academy

"Fine art is that in which the hand, the head, and the heart of man go together."
—John Ruskin *(1819-1900)*

In 1872, while Leilie was attending the Van der Wielen School, Jean Adolphe Beaux returned from France; either he was not invited to rejoin the Leavitt family or he chose not to. He set up residence at 319 Garden Street, got a job as a clerk, and apparently yielded to William Foster Biddle in all matters concerning his daughters. At the time, Grandma Leavitt, Uncle Will, Aunt Emily, Aunt Eliza, Etta, and Leilie were in the process of moving again. For Etta and Leilie, this would be the eighth move of their unsettled childhoods. After years of struggle, their economic woes had ended. William Biddle was established in a prestigious job as the vice president of the Lehigh Coal and Navigation Company. With his finances secure, he was able to provide his wife and in-laws with a spacious house capped by a distinctive mansard roof at 4305 Spruce Street in the West Philadelphia horse-car suburb that the family loved.

After Jean Adolphe Beaux's return to Philadelphia, Leilie's relationship with him seems to have been tender, yet distant. In her autobiography she mentioned his thoughtful birthday gift to her—an anthology of Keats's poetry. In her diary she recorded an unsuccessful attempt to make him a cravat.[130] Papa Beaux reestablished his affiliation with the French Collegiate Church in Philadelphia, and after his homecoming, religion took an even more profound hold on him. Although he visited his daughters on Sundays and apparently attended Woodland Presbyterian Church with them, he also encouraged them to accompany him to the simple services at his church, where he was respected and was put in charge of selecting the hymns. Cecilia Beaux remembered the congregation as a rather sad group of homesick exiles from France—poor, obscure people, who took what comfort they could in their shared faith. Within this humble group, Jean Adolphe Beaux found community and solace. His daughters were sympathetic. They loved their Papa, although his disregard of the social standards that were so important to the Leavitts sometimes embarrassed them. "Fine sermon & whole service very edifying, but Papa's pants were split," Leilie wrote in her diary on Thanksgiving day, 1875. "I had sewed them before going to church and was in continued fear that they would split again."[131] It is difficult to imagine William Foster Biddle, who enjoyed the constant attention and admiration of the five women in his household, showing up to church in torn trousers.

Because her school was closed for the season, Leilie stayed at home during the sweltering summer of 1872, the hottest on record. The heat proved a trial even for stoic Philadelphians, who expected miserable weather in the summer. Charitable societies sent poor children to the country and to the seashore in July and August for relief; their benevolence was thought to have saved

OPPOSITE: *Detail;* ***Mother and Son.*** *1896. Oil on canvas, 57 1/4 x 40 in. Courtesy Christie's Images*

many lives. Nevertheless, the mortality rate in the city was abnormally high. In a single week in July, 746 deaths were recorded, many of them heat-related.[132]

By the time Leilie was once again making the trip to Center City, the airless summer had given way to a spectacular autumn. On September 28 of that same year, the citizens celebrated. Thousands turned out for the Fall Regatta on the Schuylkill River. The local favorite, Max Schmitt, who is immortalized in Thomas Eakins's painting, *The Champion Single Skulls*, won the main event by rowing the 3-mile course in 22 minutes, 30 seconds.[133] The heady mood, which came on the autumn breezes and was bolstered by Schmitt's dramatic victory on the river, was soon snuffed out as another disaster struck. On October 28, a strain of equine influenza was diagnosed; by the end of November, nearly every horse in the city was affected. The economic consequences were immediate and far-reaching. For more than a week, two of the passenger railway companies had to shut down completely. On busy Market Street, men and boys pulled the carts and wagons necessary to deliver goods and services.[134]

Somehow Leilie got to class and continued the dreary cast studies with the focused diligence and resolve that by the age of seventeen were fundamental to her character. "Let the girl student ask herself if she can help spending her days in the classroom, if she can keep away from the thoughts and sights she wishes to set down," Beaux wrote many years later.[135] Beaux maintained that the greatest strength of any female artist is "conscientious perseverance."[136]

How long Leilie might have persevered with the limited curriculum offered to the women, while being denied the full course of study enjoyed by the men, is open to conjecture. Perhaps she would have stayed at the school until Uncle Will determined enough was enough. After her second winter at Van der Wielen's, any decision that might have been forthcoming was avoided when the proprietor surrendered to the charms of one of his students and became Mr. Van der Wielen-Brown. Miss Brown's sizable fortune, Beaux recalled, "floated them away, far from the ennui of class exercises in drawing."[137] The defection of Mr. Van der Wielen closed a door on a chapter in Leilie's life, but opened one for the enterprising Catharine Drinker, who took over the management of the school.

Faced with the responsibility of running Van der Wielen's, Kate decided to resign her position at the Miss Sanford's School for girls, where she had been in charge of the drawing classes. Kate had a replacement in mind, Miss Eliza Cecilia Beaux. Leilie was eighteen years old when this first professional opportunity was offered, and she was eager to accept the position. As Beaux remembered, Miss Sanford ran a "thoroughgoing" institution of "high eminence."[138] Although Miss Sanford's school lacked the social prestige Beaux attributed to her alma mater, the Misses Lyman School, it maintained a reputation as a place where young ladies were groomed both morally and intellectually under the resolute eye of the vigilant proprietress, who looked on each of her students as a soul in need of salvation. "Her acceptance of me as Mrs. Janvier's successor must have come as near to being a compromise with her judgment as she ever permitted herself to allow," Beaux recalled with humor.[139]

Leilie's offer at Miss Sanford's School caused excitement at home. Their youngest family member was following in the footsteps of her mother and her aunts, who had all been honorably employed as teachers. Leilie restyled her simple hat into a bonnet, so that she would appear to be at least as old as the girls in her class. "She looked so much like a little girl that we were afraid they would laugh at her," Etta explained.[140] Leilie taught one day each week for two hours—one class for the little girls and another for the older ones. Kate left no instructions and no curriculum, so Leilie was on her own. Her major goal was to keep the girls working and quiet. Several of her charges seemed to have the potential for mischief, and sensing this, she regarded them with trepidation. Her fears proved unfounded. The children behaved, and Leilie's assignment at Miss Sanford's continued, and for a number of years it was her major source of income. "She got on splendidly," Etta remembered, "like she was a born teacher—she taught all the girls about her in a class while she was still studying herself."[141]

Leilie's studies did continue, but they were mainly self-directed. It would be several years before she would once again enroll in an official class. Certainly, her family thought her formal education was complete. In the 1870s it was uncommon for women to attend college. Vassar, the first comprehensive liberal arts college for women, was only seven years old at the time, and was still considered a revolutionary enterprise. There was much discussion in the popular ladies' magazines concerning what constituted a woman's "sphere," and the general consensus, Vassar notwithstanding, was that it was still in the home.[142] Women were considered morally superior to men and, as such, honor-bound to stay within the family circle and to assume the responsibility for nurturing the ethical principles of their husbands and children. Benjamin Silliman, Yale University's first professor of chemistry, summarized mid-century attitudes concerning education for woman. A large family and a happy husband were the best credentials for women, he once told an appreciative audience.[143] Although an appropriate degree might be "Mistress of the Arts," Silliman explained, a woman should be cautious about putting the "Arts" before her husband and strive for the most honored diploma of them all, "Mistress of the Hearts."[144]

The fact that Etta had gone no further in her education after she completed her studies at the Misses Lyman School was not unusual at a time when there were few opportunities for women, and only 1 percent of the total population attended college.[145] After leaving school, Etta did what was expected of her. She remained active in the Woodland Presbyterian Church, helped with the housework, took singing lessons, taught French lessons to her cousins, and waited for the right young man to come along. A humorous poem published in the popular magazine, *Godey's Lady's Book* poked fun at the common practice of sending a young girl off for an abbreviated education.

Placing a Daughter at School
I have brought my daughter to you to be taught everything

"Dear madam, I've called for the purpose
Of placing my daughter at school;
She's only thirteen, I assure you,
And remarkably easy to rule.
I'd have her learn painting and music,
Gymnastics and dancing, pray do,
Philosophy, grammar and logic,
You'll teach her to read, of course too.

"I wish her to learn every study
Mathematics are down on my plan,
But of figures she scarce has an inkling
Pray instruct her in those if you can.
I'd have her taught Spanish and Latin,
Including the language of France;
Never mind her very bad English,
Teach her that when you find a good chance.

"On the harp she must be proficient,
And play the guitar pretty soon,
And sing the latest opera music
Even though she can't turn a right tune.
You must see that her manners are finished,
That she moves with a Hebe-like grace;
For, though she is lame and one-sided
That's nothing to do with the case.

"Now to you I resign this young jewel,
And my words I would have you obey;
In six months return her dear madame,
Shining bright as an unclouded day.
She's no aptness, I grant you, for learning
And her memory oft seems to halt;
But remember, if she's not accomplished
It certainly will be your fault."[146]

Leilie's apprenticeship with Catharine Drinker and her subsequent work at Van der Wielen's were within the boundaries of what was considered an acceptable course of study for a young woman. Her art education fit in with the conventional view that certain accomplishments were of value to a wife and mother, and that employment in the arts was a satisfactory occupation for a woman unlucky enough to need one. The acquisition of a useful accomplishment was the goal Aunt Eliza had envisioned when she carried home the portfolio of Harding lithographs for her restless thirteen-year-old niece to copy. "My Aunt Eliza, Miss Leavitt, you know was an artist herself—both in music and painting to no small extent," Etta recalled. "It was her first intention that Cecilia should study to design or illustrate—never dreaming that she was truly gifted."[147] Leilie's true gifts were not immediately obvious, although the family did take note of her growing commitment to a career in art. When they moved to the new house, she set up a studio in the third-floor bedroom that the sisters shared. Etta, who later admitted that she and Leilie used to "fight dreadfully," yielded compliantly to the attendant inconveniences of living with an artist.[148] "We slept for some years under the shadow of all the heathen gods and goddesses, crayons of plaster castes [sic]," Etta cheerfully explained.[149]

In addition to her teaching duties at Miss Sanford's School, Leilie accepted private students, although the enterprise got off to a dubious start. Her first two pupils were a boy of twelve and a somewhat older girl. Curiously, Beaux, who was a beautiful young woman herself, wrote in her autobiography that her female student was entirely too attractive to be committed to her lessons. Her "golden tawny locks and dimples gave promise of abundant interests she might have in other directions, and quite soon, so that it seemed almost superfluous to provide her with other occupation or diversion," Beaux wrote coldly.[150]

While her students worked diligently at their lessons, Leilie "sat by" with a book, looking up occasionally to offer counsel or encouragement. It was under these circumstances that she discovered the complete works of John Milton, which she read spellbound while the children, whom she remembered as possessing no "perceptible degree of natural talent," tried their best to accomplish what was required.[151] In subsequent years Beaux took these private lessons seriously and by the time she was twenty she planned them carefully and rejoiced in her students' accomplishments.[152]

Leilie's job at Miss Sanford's school combined with her private teaching totaled only six hours a week, although transportation and class preparation must have added to her obligation. Still, there was ample time to seek other employment opportunities. In Grandma's house malingerers were not tolerated. "Although all sorts of intangibilities and uncertainties hovered about my existence, there was one rock bottom reality," Beaux explained. "I must become independent."[153] Towards this end, Uncle Will arranged for a tour of the lithographic company of Thomas S. Sinclair & Son. It was there that Leilie got her first introduction to the lithographic process, and in a rush of recognition "saw the beautiful quality of line I had always wondered at, fully accounted for."[154]

The owner of the establishment, Thomas Sinclair, had studied lithography in Edinburgh, Scotland, and by 1838 had established his own printing firm in Philadelphia.[155] Thirty-five years later, when Leilie visited, business was booming, and Thomas S. Sinclair & Son enjoyed a reputation as one of the finest printers in the city. The thriving enterprise—several floors of working printing presses containing huge stones five inches thick and up to two-and-a-half feet long—bustled with activity. Leilie might have been intimidated by the energy, noise, and sheer power of nineteenth-century technology had it not been for the reassuring presence of her solicitous uncle. "The son and manager of the firm was eager to take us about," Beaux remembered. "I always felt when with my uncle that I was appearing to the greatest advantage possible."[156]

The younger Mr. Sinclair, their guide on the tour of the printing plant, encouraged Leilie's interest in lithography and gave her a trial assignment. She was to copy a photograph of a young actress and transfer the drawing to the receptive gray surface of one of the stones. When Leilie finished her drawing, it was approved, paid for, and printed as an advertisement. The actress, whose likeness she had so carefully rendered, sent a complimentary note saying, "I'm pleased to death with the picture and everyone thinks it's lovely."[157] The gushing prose amused her family, but Leilie was flattered and tucked the note away to save among her treasures.

Leilie's career as an illustrator was launched by this early success. For a number of years she worked diligently in the field. However, as a young woman, living at home and working alone, her opportunities in the profession were limited, and she never progressed too far beyond copy work. The one other graduate of the Van der Wielen School who subsequently became famous was the illustrator Howard Pyle. As a regular contributor to the prestigious *Harper's Monthly Magazine*, the illustrator of more than one hundred books (including one by Thomas Janvier), and the author and illustrator of nineteen more, his works were widely admired and eventually reached an international audience. In a letter to his brother Theo written on September 11, 1882, Vincent Van Gogh asked, "Do you know an American magazine called *Harper's Monthly*? There are things in it which strike me dumb with admiration, including . . . sketches of a Quaker town in the olden days by Howard Pyle. I am full of new pleasure in those things, because I have hope of making things that have soul in them myself."[158]

Howard Pyle had profited from the rigorous curriculum offered to Van der Wielen's male students and emerged full of confidence in his abilities. This self-assurance led him to pursue challenging jobs unencumbered either by doubts or by the restrictions that hindered a proper young lady like Leilie, who convention dictated must be protected and chaperoned. So while young Pyle planned a research trip to Chincoteague and Assateague Islands on Virginia's Eastern Shore, Leilie worked industriously in a corner of the bedroom she shared with Etta. Pyle fulfilled his plans, visited the two picturesque islands, and made drawings of the local landscape, the annual pony roundup, and the subsequent auction. He wrote a manuscript to accompany his sketches and sent the completed project to *Scribner's* magazine, where it was published.[159] The opportunity was pivotal. Acting on encouragement from one of the magazine's editors, Pyle packed up his belongings, moved to New York, and headed towards a promising career.

The modest success of Leilie's first portrait led to new opportunities for her, too, but they were not on the order of those presented to Pyle. In 1874, when she was nineteen, she made a lithograph that was offered for sale—a drawing of two cats, draped over the back of a chair. Beaux's print was either a copy of a line engraving, published in the December 1873 issue of *St. Nicholas* magazine, or a copy of the photograph from which the line engraving was made. Most probably, Leilie worked from the photograph. In 1874 lithography was one of the cheapest ways to make multiple copies of photographs. Etta later wrote that her sister made a "crayon" of the cats. At the time, a "crayon" referred to the technique of drawing with pastels or charcoal directly on the surface of a pale photographic print. Either way, neither the concept nor the pose was original.[160]

The print was popular and earned some money for Leilie, and that was sufficient cause for celebration. Leilie presented a copy to her mentor, inscribed "To C. A. Drinker with the sincerest regards of E. C. Beaux."[161] Kate was obviously proud of her pupil. Thomas Janvier, likewise impressed, composed a short review of Leilie's print for the Philadelphia paper where he was employed as a journalist. "The lithograph which is Miss Beaux's first published work, is remarkable as showing perfect power over the stone, as well as force and delicacy in drawing," Janvier wrote enthusiastically.[162] When the stone was stolen and bootleg copies made and sold, the family was infuriated. "You ask about those cats," Etta

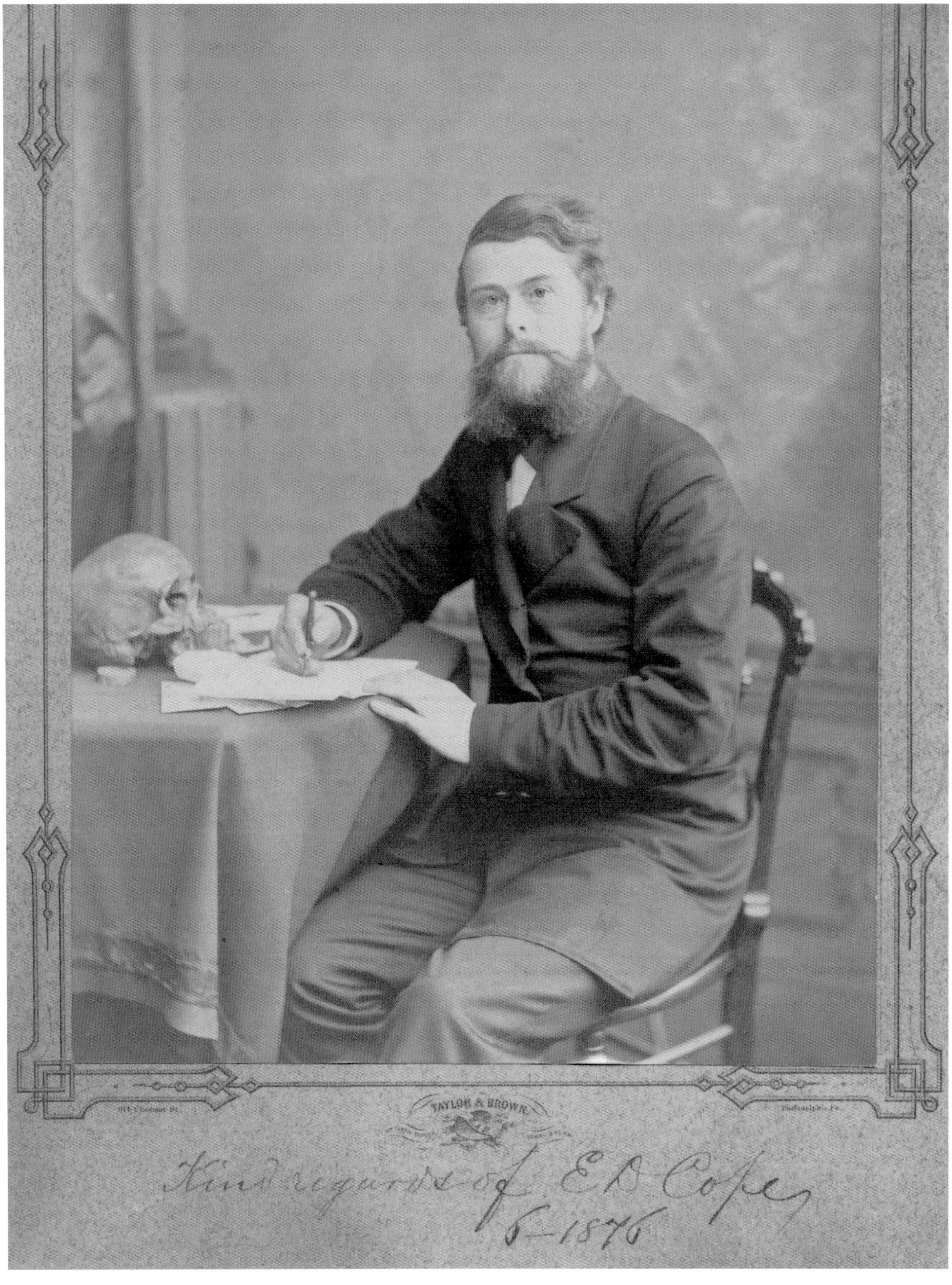
TAYLOR & BROWN
Kind regards of E D Cope
6-1876

wrote twenty-eight years later in response to a request for information about her sister. "First she made a crayon of them which is a wonder, so soft and furry. Then she made a lithographic copy of the crayon. There were 100 printed and they sold in no time. Having no copyright the stone was stolen and copied. . . . [S]he might have made a trip to Europe on those pussies."[163]

It was just as well that nineteen-year-old Leilie stayed at home. Later she was glad that when she finally did go to Europe, she had acquired the training and maturity to appreciate the experience. "Let me say that she doesn't believe in young girls going to Paris alone to study. She was past girlhood when she went," Etta wrote.[164] Leilie did dream of travel. She was still determined to see France, and although she may have been ambivalent about her father's presence in her life, she remained fascinated with his European heritage.

Cecilia Beaux later wrote that her grandmother strongly approved of the work and discipline inherent in her illustration career and "gallantly took part in the struggle." Grandma's contribution was predictable. Continuing the tradition established when Leilie was a small child with a worn thimble and an aversion to anything less than perfection, Grandma read aloud while Leilie worked. The book selected was Sismondi's *History of Southern Europe*. There was a sizable section devoted to Provence, and Leilie was eager to learn about the land of her ancestors. She listened with sustained interest to the story of Jaufré Rudel, a twelfth-century troubadour in love with the Lady of Tripoli, a woman he knew by reputation alone. On the long journey to see this paragon, Rudel was struck with a fatal illness. After hearing of her suitor's plight, the Lady rushed to his side—but too late. The unfortunate Rudel died in her arms. Leilie delighted in this romantic legend that typified the chronicles of the troubadours, whose stories and songs inevitably concerned love either absent or unrequited and always outside of marriage.

The illustration assignments and Grandma's accompanying reading continued through Leilie's twentieth year, when she received a commission that required aesthetic judgment as well as her usual measure of forbearance. The job entailed preparing several illustrations of fossils for *The Vertebrata of the Cretaceous Formations of the West*, a multivolume report sponsored by the U.S. Geological Survey. The author of this work was another of Uncle Will's intriguing relatives, the paleontologist Edward Drinker Cope. In the fall of 1875 Cope had come into a sizable inheritance. The bequest allowed him to fund the publication of research garnered from four summers of fossil hunting in what was still the Wild West. Cope had endured countless hardships during these expeditions; somewhere near Fort Bridger, Kansas, he had come close to death when he contracted a virus that left him with enormous carbuncles on his neck and what he described as "terrible visions and dreams."[165] The memories of his various deprivations were about to be mitigated by the publication of the report, which he hoped would secure his place in the annuals of science and give him a decided advantage over his archrival, paleontologist Othniel Marsh. For Cope, the project was momentous, and complete accuracy was imperative. One of the opening shots in the feud between Cope and Marsh was the result of an error Cope had made in 1869. While supervising the articulation of a plesiosaur skeleton, he made a miscalculation that would haunt him for the rest of his life: Somehow the animal's head was attached to the end of its tail instead of its rightful place atop the spinal column. Marsh caught the error, and Cope, in spite of the subsequent triumphs in his career, never recovered from the humiliation nor forgave Marsh for exposing the mistake.[166]

The plesiosaur debacle was still fresh in Cope's mind when he entrusted his precious fossil specimens to

19. OPPOSITE: ***Edward Drinker Cope.*** *1876. From a private collection courtesy of Maxilla and Mandible, Ltd., New York*

William Biddle's young niece. Leilie understood the importance of the commission and was apprehensive about her ability to complete the task with the required precision. All through October and November she sat by her bedroom window until the light faded in the afternoons, rendering each small hollow and protrusion to the exact scale of the original, while she dreamed of sunny Provence and the unsullied love of the troubadours. Leilie's experience with the bones of the skull at the Van der Wielen School gave her confidence. However, unlike the polished skull bones, some of Cope's fossils were embedded in rock and at first glance looked like small lumps of mud. In order to complete the drawings successfully, Leilie had to decide how to resolve the contradictions between what she actually observed and what she knew would show the relics to their best advantage. Although the job was rife with anxiety, Beaux came to appreciate the experience. "Nothing the fossils taught a neophyte in art ever had to be unlearned," she later admitted.[167]

The day Mr. Sinclair and Professor Cope came to check on her progress, Leilie was terrified that they might find errors in her work and confided in her diary that when she heard them at the doorstep, her hands grew "icy cold."[168] The meeting went well. Although Sinclair and Uncle Will had both warned her about Cope's taciturn personality, something about beautiful Leilie stayed his reserve. She found him to have "lovely manners, easy and refined."[169] Within a month the job was finished. In spite of the success of her previous interview, she worried that Cope would find fault with her work. "Woke with unpleasant feelings of suspense and trepidation on account of anticipated visit from Cope and Sin [Sinclair] at ten," Leilie wrote in her diary. "Dressed & fortified myself for them but felt pale when they drove up."[170] Cope sat down in front of Leilie's most recent drawing—the skull of an extinct camel—and after some reflection pointed to a bony projection. "What's this?" he asked. When she tried to explain, Cope laughed and said, "Well, Miss Beaux, if you can invent them, what need is there for us going way out West to find these specimens?"[171] Leilie, who in the wake of Cope's comment was probably no longer pale, admitted feeling "rather miserable" but quickly made the corrections and was rewarded later in the afternoon when a note containing $75 was delivered in payment for the drawings.

Despite the remuneration and the valuable lessons she learned from what she later referred to as "the stone age," Beaux was not inspired to pursue a career as a scientific illustrator. She wrote a poem describing her plight in what she later described as a "rebellious moment":

> Lost hope, lost courage, lost ambition
> What's left but shams of these to hide my
> true condition?
> Feigned peace and joy, feigned happy effort
> False tongue, proclaiming, "Art's my comfort."
> Nought's left but bones, and stones and duty
> that's not pleasure,
> But grinding, ceaseless toil, whose end's
> the measure
> Of the short web of life the fates have spun me.
> What's this . . . I've uttered words of treason.
> What's lost? My time, my daylight, and my reason.[172]

Beaux recalled that the long hours spent bending over the fossils and the anxiety about possible errors caused her body to rebel, as well as her spirit, and took a toll on her "solar plexus." To relieve that anxiety in the pit of her stomach, she tossed aside her drawing tools, lifted her heavy long skirts, flew down two flights of stairs and into the garden, where a run around the cherry tree helped to relieve the stress. Thus refreshed, Leilie returned to her work, followed through, and finished the task at hand. This feeling of trepidation, the note of warning that periodically eroded her confidence, was a reoccurring problem. When Beaux was an elderly woman at the end of her career, when her youthful doubts were dimmed by years of stunning success, she told her youngest niece, "In every picture I've painted there came a time when it was impossible to continue. There was a hill I couldn't climb. It's then when that pressure bears down on the solar plexus, that you must keep *on!*"[173]

During Beaux's "stone age," she never considered becoming a painter. "At this time and for long afterwards," she wrote, "I did not connect the work I was to do with *Art*, the high mystery, nor did I consider myself in any way an artist or even that I was ever to become one."[174] Although Leilie had no idea what her future held, she did know that it was possible for a local woman like herself to earn a respectable living as a painter. Catharine Drinker was busy and successful, and although Leilie did not admit to her ambitions, she did have them. Recording the events of a November Sunday in her diary, she confided, "An earnest sermon from Dr. C., but was inattentive and thinking about a picture I have in my mind and which I hope *some* day to depict."[175] It would be several more years before Leilie would strike out on her own to become the artist Cecilia Beaux. In the meantime, Leilie's "rock bottom reality" required that she earn her keep.

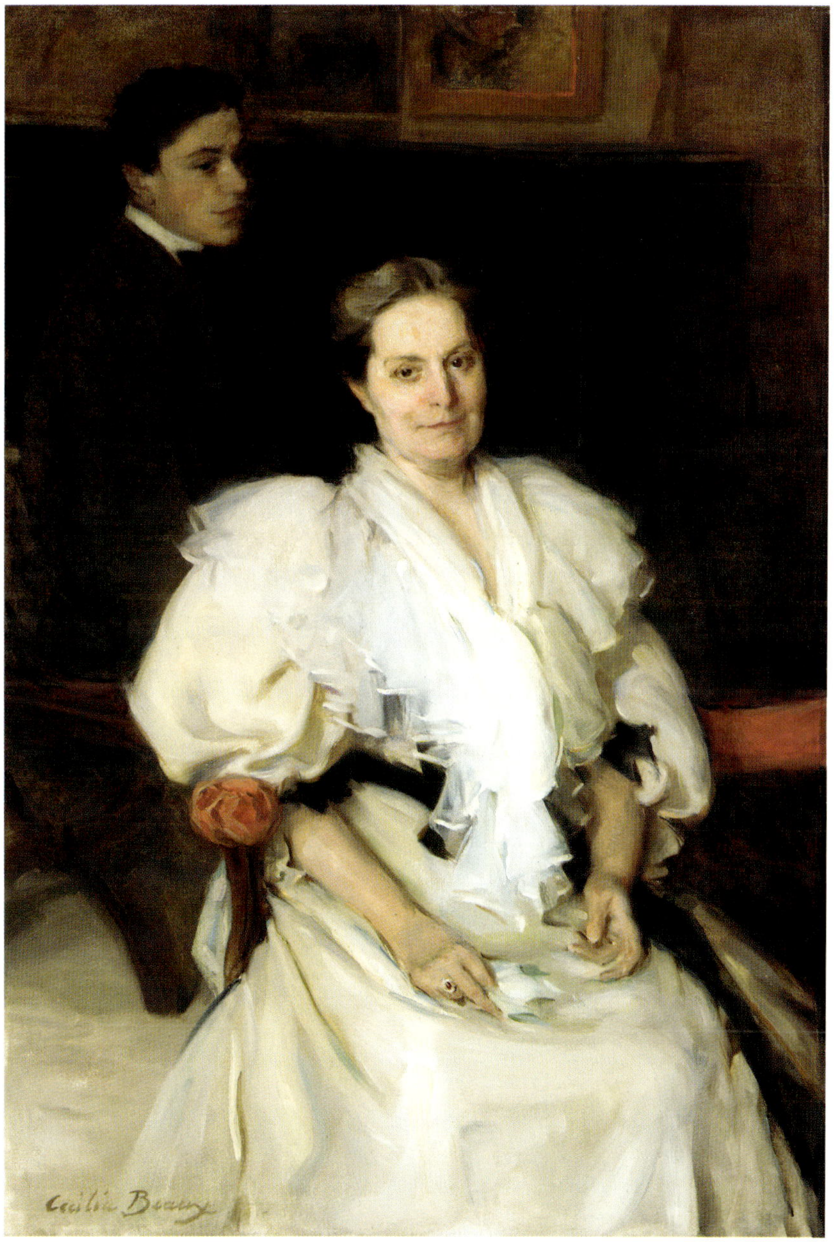

20. ***Mother and Son.*** *1896. Oil on canvas, 57¼ x 40 in. Courtesy Christie's Images*

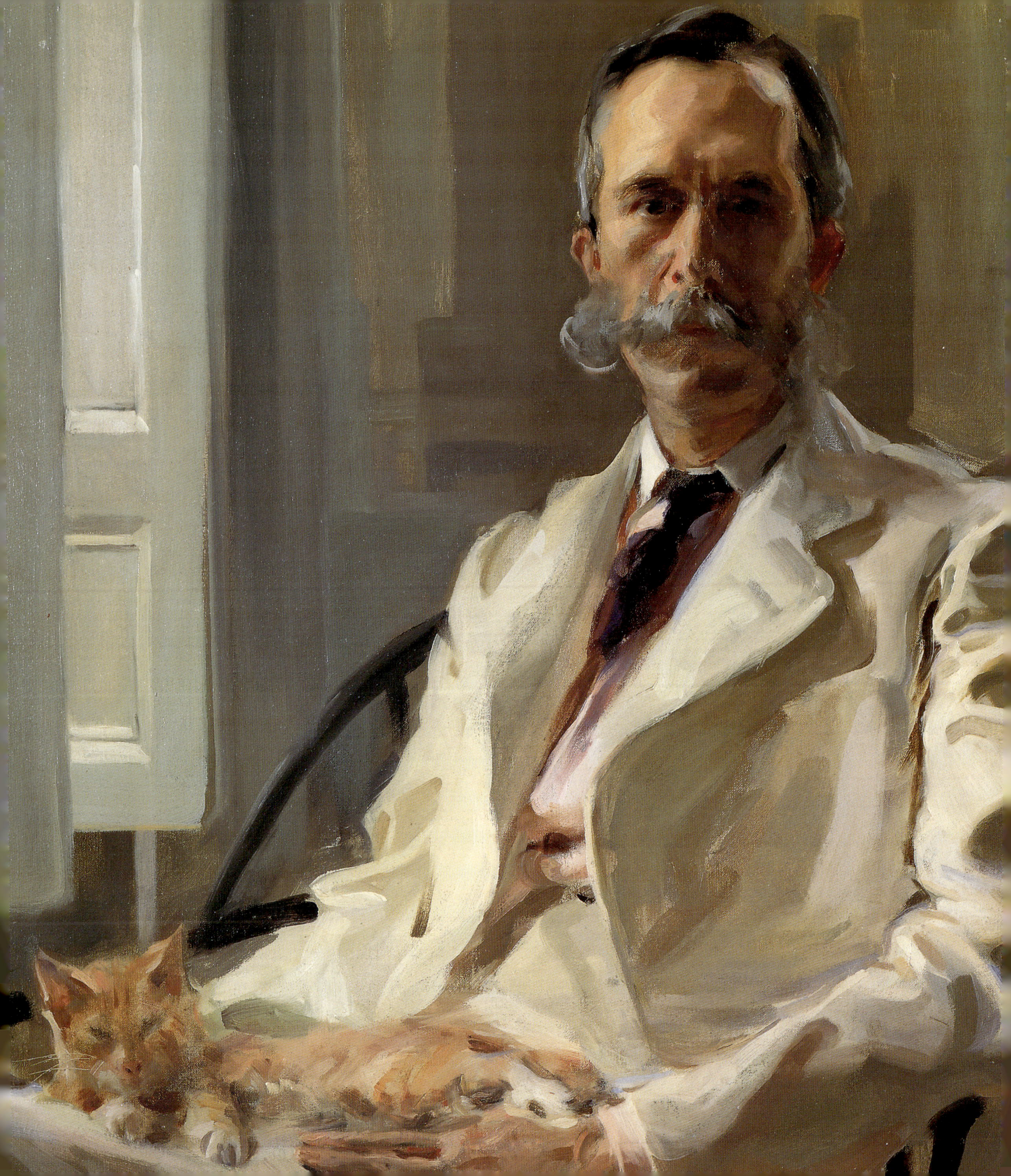

Studio on Chestnut Street

"I do not believe that great painting or sculpture or surgery will ever be done by women, yet enough good work is continually done by them to be well worth their doing, and as the population increases, and marriages are later and fewer, and the risk of losing fortunes greater; so increases the number of women who are or may be compelled at some time to support themselves, and figure painting is not now so dishonorable to them."

—THOMAS EAKINS, *September 11, 1886*

For three years—from the time she left the Van der Wielen School until 1875 when the Cope lithographs were completed—Leilie stayed close to home, tackled the commercial projects that came her way, and waited for her adult life to begin. "I got my work done," she recalled, "but there was not much time for meditation on the status or real value of it."[176] During this hiatus Leilie was busy and happy. In spite of Grandma's strictures concerning morality and hard work, the household was spirited and full of affection. One of Etta's friends, who after many years still harbored fond memories of Spruce Street, recalled, "It was exciting to go to that house. People loved it. A plain house, but those aunts were amazing. Beside them other women seemed like stuffed dolls."[177] It was unusual for a day to go by without someone stopping in either at teatime or after supper. In the evening music echoed through the rooms, wound its way up the stairs, and escaped onto the street. Uncle Will, Aunt Emily, or Aunt Eliza played the piano, and on many occasions family and friends formed a chorus. On the rare days when there were no visitors, Leilie noted in her diary, "Another stupid day, no company" or "No one came, tiresome day."[178]

Many of the callers, who showed up on what Leilie categorized as a "very pleasant day," were young men who came to see the Beaux sisters. Grandma Leavitt and both aunts encouraged this parade of eligible bachelors. The aunts helped the girls with their sewing, hemmed skirts, fashioned overskirts, and even altered their own clothes so that their nieces would look their best. Leilie understood that her family hoped she would marry. "The family opinion in these matters was obvious, but it was never forced upon the reserved young premiere in the cast,"[179] Beaux wrote. Nevertheless, what was expected was implicit. Leilie and Etta amenably entertained the young men, who appeared on their doorstep, walked them home from church, or met them at well-chaperoned socials, where the Beaux sisters showed themselves to their best advantage, their hands gloved and their hair bedecked in pale blue and red

OPPOSITE: *Detail; **Man with a Cat.** 1898. 48 x 34 5/8 in. Smithsonian American Art Museum, Washington, D.C.*

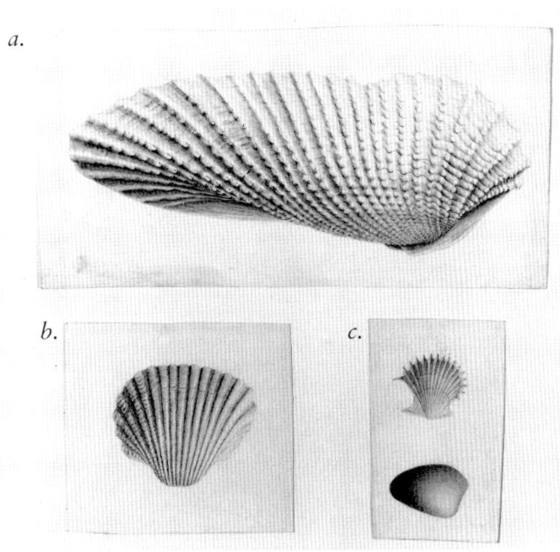

21. ***Shell Studies.*** *ca. 1875. Graphite and wash on off-white wove paper (a. 2 1/3 x 2 1/2, b. 2 7/16 x 1 1/2, c. 2 5/6 x 5 2/3 in.). Pennsylvania Academy of the Fine Arts*

ribbons. The handsome Thomas Janvier visited one November afternoon, prompting Leilie to record having "a jolly time."[180] Kate's brother Harry Drinker stopped by on an autumn evening when Leilie was out with her friends. Her ambivalence about his attentions had not changed. "Don't mind missing him," she wrote in her diary.[181] One young man asked permission to take her to church, and someone named Charlie invited her to a lecture at the Franklin Institute and walked her home, prompting her to write, "Charlie was lovely and I am stupid."[182]

During these heady years Leilie had a difficult time concentrating on anything other than her active social calendar. "I was not much alone," Beaux acknowledged later. "It was the time for love, and the little god was pretty constantly about."[183] But the whole process, the competition to catch a suitable husband, left Leilie confused and conflicted. Her diary alludes to a certain amount of heartbreak in the autumn of 1874, and in her autobiography she refers to a drama in November and a "sad heart." But it was all too much. The familiar feeling of trepidation, the deep note of warning, that pressure on the solar plexus that overtook her when she felt she just couldn't perform, prevented her from acquiescing to her assigned role. "There was a terrible standard of what love should be that held back the romantic heart," she wrote.[184] Nevertheless, Beaux later acknowledged that if her family had been firm, she would have complied: "If a stern voice had said, 'You are to marry this man. It is not yours to refuse. Come—, the doubter would have been thankful and would have obeyed."[185]

In August 1872 the magazine *Littell's Living Age* published an article reprinted from *Blackwood's Magazine* and quaintly titled "Old Maids." Leilie enjoyed *Littell's*, picked out relevant essays to share with her students, and listened while Grandma read interesting articles aloud. It would have been unusual if she had missed this particular piece, since it dealt with the decision to marry, a topic that interested her. The article in question suggested that women who chose not to marry were often more intelligent than women who settled for anything less than perfection. "The highest type of old maid has made no sacrifice," the writer argued. " . . . She is the woman who has never met her ideal and who has never been cunningly persuaded to accept something short of it."[186] Aunt Eliza, who never married, lived a full and interesting life. And although her Aunt Emily's life was similarly blessed, Leilie understood that Emily's happiness was not merely a result of her marital status but the consequence of a wise and considered decision. Aunt Emily had met and found her ideal in William Foster Biddle—an amazing man, intelligent, kind, hard working, well-connected, and unfailingly generous.

Uncle Will was the standard against which Leilie measured the unfortunate young men who competed for her attention. Had he been available to give Leilie advice while she was forming her opinions on such matters, he might have assured her that, all evidence to the contrary, he himself had a full measure of faults. However, William Biddle was not there to give advice or to be that stern voice she might have heeded urging her to marry. On October 28, 1875, he ate a hurried breakfast with his tearful family and boarded a ship for Venezuela, where he was to spend more than a year supervising the construction of a mine.[187]

"Fatality," Beaux once wrote, "is generally another name for misfortune, but Fate is an impartial agent, and may sometimes be caught in an act of beneficence."[188] Fate was about to take a benevolent hand in the career of Cecilia Beaux. And in consequence, Leilie did not have to make a conscious decision about her future. Her future came to her unbidden and at first scarcely perceived. On January 1, 1876, the city of Philadelphia ushered in the Centennial Year. On New Year's Eve people filled the streets. Cannons fired. The old bell on the State House rang out through the cold night, and Leilie reported in her diary that although she missed the great illuminations, she was awakened at midnight by all the noise. The festivities were the beginning of a celebration that would culminate on the tenth of May in the opening of the Great Centennial Exhibition. Although twelve years would pass before Leilie had an opportunity to travel, the world was about to come to her.

In her autobiography, where Cecilia Beaux assiduously avoided dating any event that might have revealed her age, she failed to mention attending the Centennial Exhibition. But of course she did. The exhibition grounds were not far from her house. During the previous year her family had gone several times to check on the progress of the buildings that were to occupy a 285-acre tract of Philadelphia's Fairmount Park—once hiring a carriage for the occasion and nearly getting "blown to pieces" by the winter wind.[189] The showpiece of the exhibition, conceived to function as a permanent art museum when the fair ended, was architect Hermann J. Schwarzmann's imposing Memorial Hall. For the run of the event, the huge granite building with its impressive glass and steel dome served as the exposition's art gallery. The Philadelphia engraver, John Sartain (1808–1897), chief of the Centennial's Bureau of Art, was so overwhelmed with applications for space that a separate Art Annex had to be constructed. On opening day 3,256 paintings, 627 pieces of sculpture, and 431 works of applied art from twenty nations were on display in the two buildings.[190]

Much of the artwork owed more to Victorian sentiment and morality than to artistic integrity. Nevertheless, there were some outstanding works on display, and Leilie had an opportunity to see canvases by two former presidents of the Royal Academy in London, Benjamin West and Sir Joshua Reynolds (1723–1792). *The Lock* by the English landscape painter John Constable (1776–1837) was exhibited along with the popular work of his countryman, Sir Lawrence Alma Tadema (1836–1912). The French artists Léon Bonnat (1833–1922), Carolus Duran (1838–1917), and Rosa Bonheur (1822–1899) also were represented in the exhibition. The American painter Albert Bierstadt, whose panoramic landscape of the Rocky Mountains impressed Leilie when she was a young girl, submitted *Western Kansas*. Emily Sartain, daughter of John Sartain, who organized the show, submitted a sentimental canvas titled *The Reproof* and was the only female artist to win a medal.[191]

Although she could not have known it at the time, Leilie's future was contained in the crowded buildings of the Great Centennial Exhibition. Among the paintings were works she admired, and among the nine million visitors were several who would become significant to her career. The American realist Thomas

22. *Cecilia Beaux and cousin Emma Leavitt reading in their Chestnut Street studio.* Pennsylvania Academy of the Fine Arts

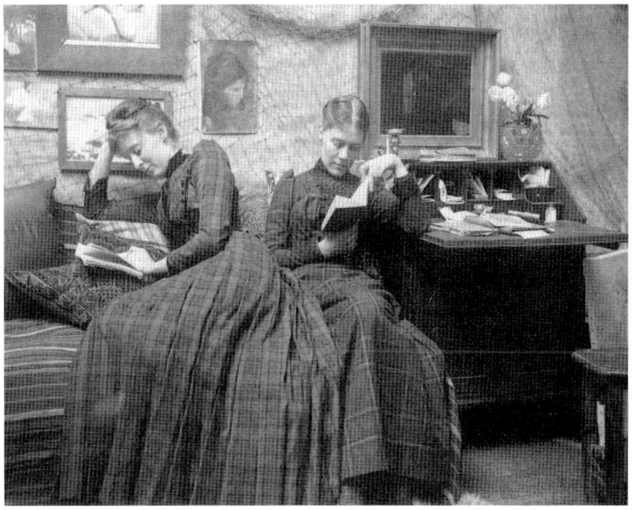

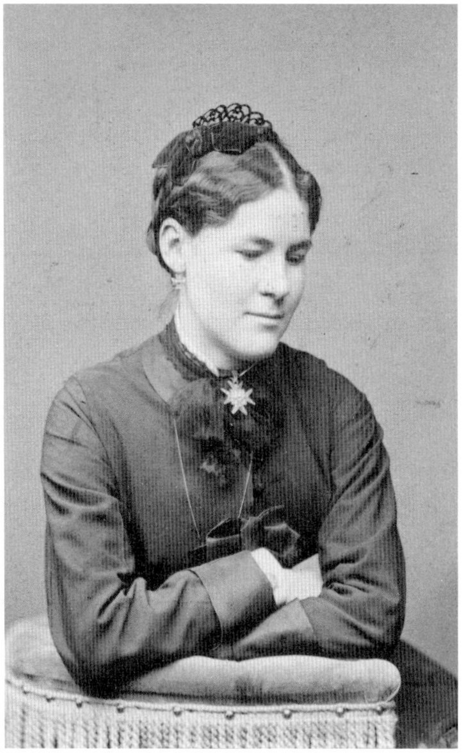

23. *Broadbent and Phillips.* **Cecilia Beaux's sister, Aimee Ernesta Beaux Drinker,** *date unknown. Pennsylvania Academy of the Fine Arts*

Eakins (1844–1916), who was to have a strong influence on her education, strode through the exhibition halls, his eyes brimming with tears. His own hope for artistic immortality hinged on public approval of his masterful painting, *The Gross Clinic*. Lambasted by critics for its bloody portrayal of a surgeon at work, it had been relegated to the United States Hospital Building and hung there in ignominy, far from the glamour of Memorial Hall. Later Beaux recalled that although Eakins's portrait of Dr. Gross came to be regarded as one of the greatest works ever produced by an American artist, it "horrified Philadelphia Exhibition-goers as a gory spectacle."[193] Eakins's friend, the painter William Merritt Chase (1849–1916), suffered no similar disappointment and attended the Centennial galleries in triumph. He had been awarded a medal, his first national recognition. Twenty-three years later it was Chase who proclaimed Cecilia Beaux to be "the greatest woman painter of modern times." Somewhere among the throngs of people another influential figure in Beaux's future viewed the artwork and enjoyed the festivities tucked under the protective arm of his anxious mother.[193] He was an unknown nineteen-year-old prodigy named John Singer Sargent (1856–1925). Beaux's subsequent work would be inspired by his amazing skill, and she would one day publish a sentimental eulogy acknowledging her debt to his brilliance.

The Centennial Exhibition was one of two momentous events that occurred in Leilie's life in 1876. The other was the reopening of the Pennsylvania Academy of the Fine Arts.[194] Although school records show that Beaux registered for classes there in 1876, 1877, and 1878, in her autobiography she stated that she never attended the school and that it was Uncle Will who made the decision on her behalf. "I would have turned toward the classrooms of the P.A.F.A., but my uncle, to whom I owed everything that my grandmother had not done for me, was steadfastly opposed to this. . . . Why should I be thrown into a rabble of untidy and indiscriminate art students and no one knew what influence?" Beaux wrote.[195] But, in actuality, despite her later denial which may have been motivated by a desire to distance herself from Eakins's subsequent notoriety, Leilie willingly climbed the polished steps and crossed the threshold into the vital artistic atmosphere of the Pennsylvania Academy of the Fine Arts, a progressive institution, light years away from the tiresome ladies' classes at the Van der Weilen School.

The fifty-two-year-old French artist Christian Schussele was still the instructor of record when the Academy reopened. But during the six-year closure of the school, his health had deteriorated. By 1876 the effects of a paralytic affliction that had plagued him for more than a decade were becoming increasingly apparent. Schussele had been an effective instructor before declining health compromised his energy. However, his renewed appointment presented a physical challenge he simply could not meet.[196] Thomas Eakins offered to assist. Although the visceral realism of his portrait of

Dr. Gross engendered serious criticism, Eakins was widely admired for the skill he had acquired during three years of European study at the École des Beaux-Arts in Paris. When he volunteered to help the ailing Schussele teach the evening life classes and offered his expertise as chief demonstrator in the anatomy class, the institution's Committee on Instruction readily agreed.[197]

Whether William Biddle was aware that his youngest niece had enrolled in classes at the Pennsylvania Academy or whether he was deep in the bowels of a Venezuelan mine and ignorant concerning events at home is unknown. What is apparent is that Leilie did attend the school and that her mentor, Catharine Drinker, accompanied her in this new endeavor. Leilie enrolled in the antique, costume, and portrait classes but studied with Christian Schussele and steered clear of Thomas Eakins and the ladies' life class. One of Leilie's colleagues, the illustrator Joseph Pennell, wrote a candid account of those days at the Academy, recalling that Schussele "was little and white and bald" and that the students made fun of him, attributing his ashen complexion to a habit of "eating the ends off tubes of white lead as a steady diet."[198] Poor Schussele, who circled the room stopping to sit next to each student to criticize their work, had to be helped to his feet before limping on to the next easel. The professor not only struggled to overcome his physical limitations but also struggled with the difficulties of the English language. Young Pennell, who was unsympathetic, quickly transferred his allegiance to Eakins and resented Schussele's unsupportive criticism. "Vy you dry do improve on der gast?" he asked his puzzled student.[199]

Eakins's criticism was more specific, and his teaching philosophy was more progressive. He disagreed with Schussele about the value of long study from the Antique and believed that students should make the

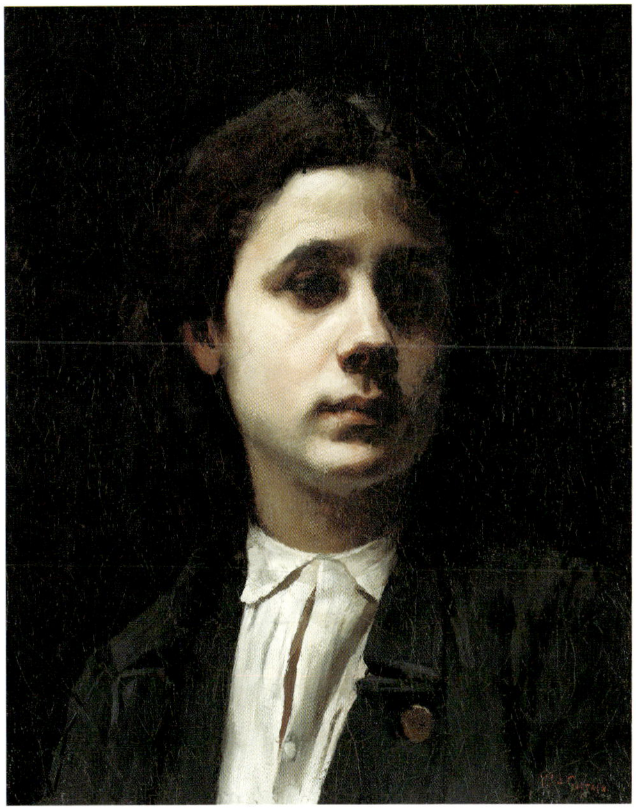

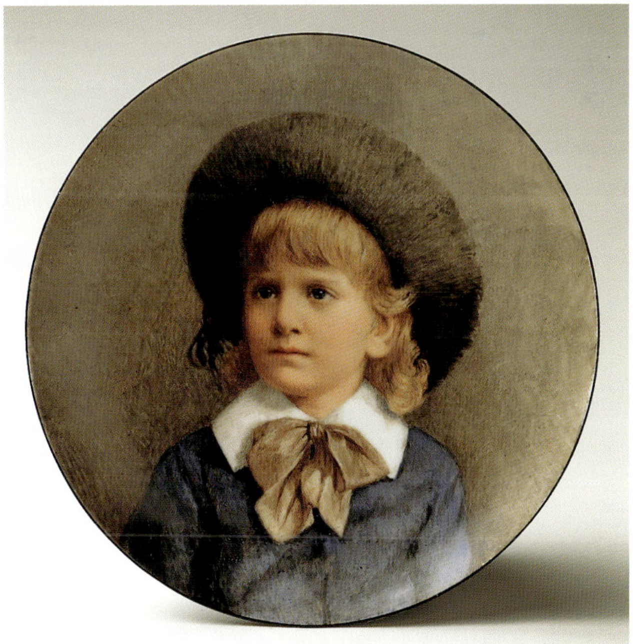

24. TOP RIGHT: *William Sartain.* ***The Young Musician.*** *ca. 1870. Oil on canvas, 18 x 14 13/16 in. Pennsylvania Academy of the Fine Arts*

25. BOTTOM RIGHT: ***Circular plaque with bust-length portrait of a boy.*** *1880. Porcelain plaque, 11 1/4 in. in diameter. The Metropolitan Museum of Art*

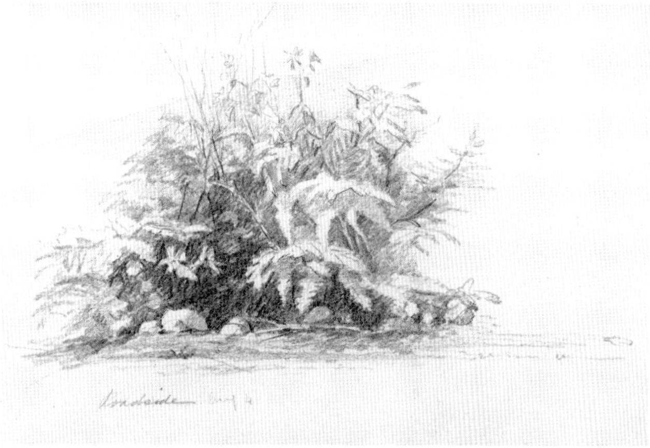

26. ***Sketchbook #2.*** *[Landscape study inscribed "Roadside, August 4"]. 1879–91. Graphite, pen, and white highlight on buff wove leaves, 5 3/4 x 9 1/4 in. Pennsylvania Academy of the Fine Arts*

transition to the life class quickly. "The Greeks did not study the antique: the 'Theseus' and 'Illyssus,' and the draped figures in the Parthenon pediment were modeled from life, undoubtedly," he told William Brownell in an interview for the September 1879 issue of *Scribner's Monthly Illustrated Magazine.*[200] Although Cecilia Beaux later wrote that she admired Eakins's teaching, in her three years at the Academy, she spent only one day in the life class and immediately retreated to the comfortable familiarity of the Antique.[201] Cecilia Beaux wrote that her uncle's "chivalrous and also Quaker soul . . . revolted against the life class and everything pertaining to it."[202] But perhaps it was Leilie who sensed something was amiss.

It was Eakins's contention that any serious art student should share his zealous enthusiasm for studying the nude. William Biddle and his niece were not the only people who disagreed. As the years passed the opposition to Eakins's teaching methods grew. A letter written to Academy president James L. Claghorn in 1882, probably from a concerned mother, expressed some of the common concerns about the life class. "Now Mr. Claghorn," she wrote. " . . . Does it pay, for a young lady of refined, godly household to be urged as the only way of obtaining a knowledge of true Art, to enter a class where every feeling of *maidenly* delicacy is violated, where she becomes so hardened to indelicate sights and words, so familiar with the persons of degraded women and the sight of male nudes, that *no possible* art can restore her lost treasure of *chaste and delicate thoughts!*"[203] Four years later reports concerning Eakins's behavior in the women's life class created a scandal that resulted in his dismissal from the Pennsylvania Academy.

Among the fifty-five students who joined Leilie and Catharine for that inaugural season were other accomplished female artists such as Susan Macdowell and Alice Barber.[204] Unlike Leilie, they quickly served the prerequisite time in the Antique class and moved on to the women's life class. Eight years later Susan Macdowell, a devoted supporter of Eakins's teaching philosophy and the class secretary, would become Mrs. Thomas Eakins. Alice Barber, who began her studies as one of Eakins's loyal allies, became a vocal critic, accusing her teacher of scandalous behavior that included encouraging the women in his coterie to pose in the nude, exposing himself to a female student, and lifting a loincloth from a male model in the women's life class.

27. OPPOSITE: ***Self-Portrait.*** *ca. 1880–85. Oil on canvas, 18 x 14 in. National Portrait Gallery, Smithsonian Institution, Washington, D.C.*

28. BELOW: ***Robert Redfield, May Whitlock, and Cecilia Beaux.*** *1885–86. Pennsylvania Academy of the Fine Arts*

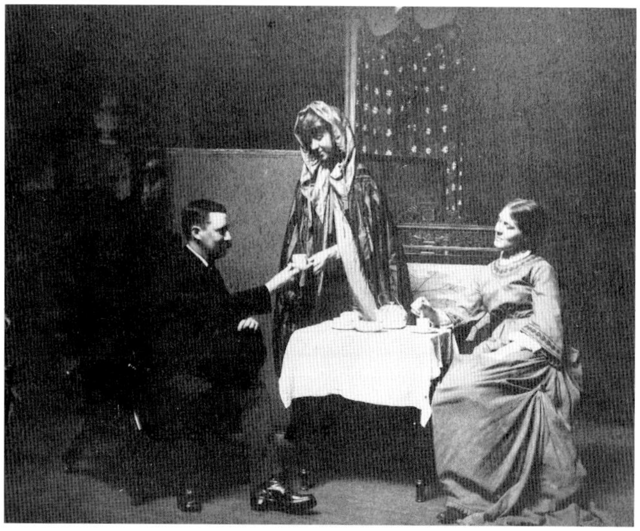

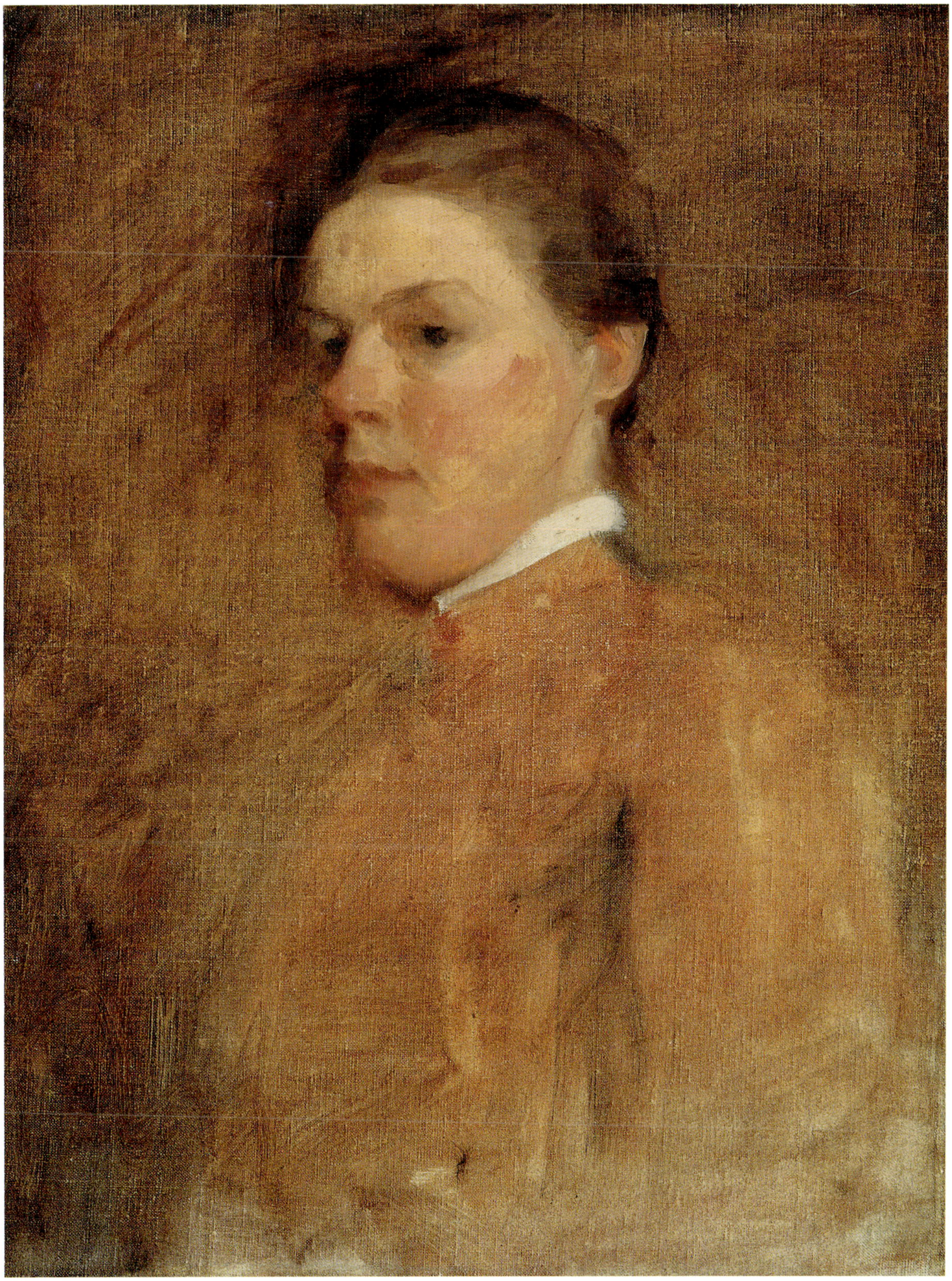

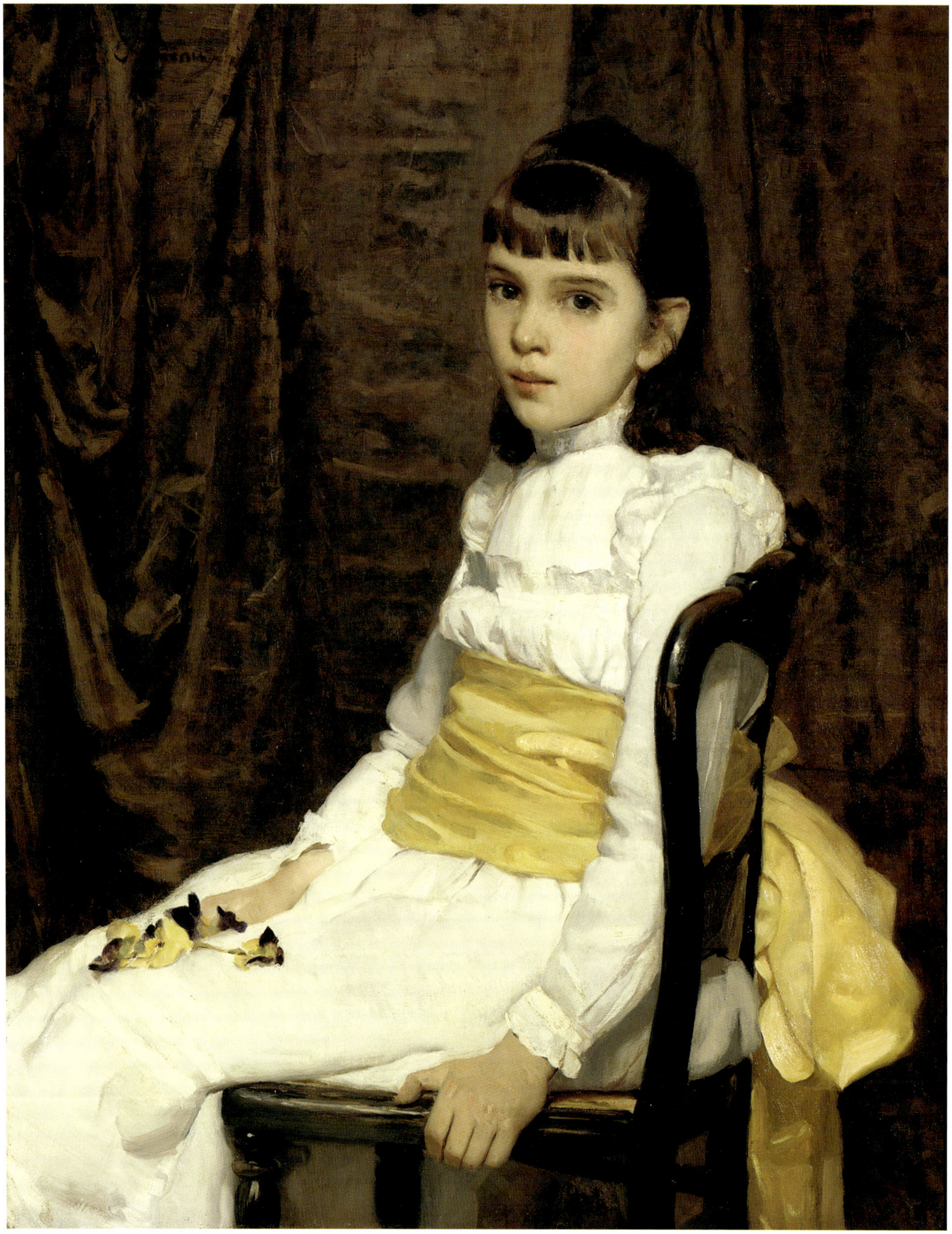

By the time Cecilia Beaux began recording her personal history, the scandal was more than fifty years old. Still, Beaux did not want anyone to believe that she was among the well-brought-up middle-class women who, in the thrall of the charismatic Mr. Eakins, stripped themselves of their Victorian reserve and posed in the nude like prostitutes. Beaux, who came to respect Eakins's skill and originality as a painter, wrote that she benefited from his teaching obliquely and absorbed his precepts from her classmates. "A curious instinct of self-preservation," she wrote, "kept me outside the magic circle."[205]

Even if Leilie did manage to avoid the notorious Mr. Eakins, the Pennsylvania Academy of the Fine Arts must have provided an extraordinary experience for a young woman who, concurrent with her studies at the Academy, taught Sunday School and wrote in her diary, "At the end of the day Christ will ask us what we have done." Inside the beautiful new building there was plenty to challenge both Leilie's sense of morality and Uncle Will's Quaker soul. The male students were boisterous and probably quite different from the proper young chaps who escorted the Beaux sisters home from church. The noxious odors of chemicals from the anatomy lab, cigarette smoke, and turpentine spread through the hallways and up the winding stairs. In the men's classes, which were unsupervised except for occasional visits from Schussele or Eakins, there were spontaneous processions, loud singing, and an uproar when the weekly pose was changed and the students pushed over rows of canvases, "butter side down."[206] The female models, who often wore masks to hide their identities, would sometimes faint from the heat, the smoke, and the difficulty of holding a pose. At lunchtime it was customary for the students to cross the street to the "pie foundry," where for five cents the pie of the day could be purchased. Another place offered bananas and crackers for the same price. Older students headed off to the "beer foundry." Those who could afford lunch shared with those who could not, and on days when everyone was flush and there was plenty of food, Pennell later recalled, "we shied the stuff all over the place."[207]

At some point during the time Leilie attended classes at the Academy, Uncle Will returned to take his place as the head of the household. And perhaps he was the one who made the decision that Leilie should not continue her studies at that particular institution. It is also possible that Leilie came to the same conclusion on her own. By 1878 Schussele's health problems had become incapacitating. Thomas Eakins was effectively managing the school and directing the curriculum toward the intensive study of the human body through drawing, painting, and a demanding program in anatomy and dissection modeled on the rigorous training offered to the city's medical students.

Changes in Leilie's personal life may also have convinced her that it was the right time to discontinue her studies. On September 26, 1878, intrepid Cousin Kate finally married her troubadour and became Mrs. Catharine Janvier. A year later on December 2, 1879, Leilie's beloved sister Etta walked down the aisle of the Woodland Presbyterian Church on the arm of Papa Beaux to be given in marriage to Catharine Janvier's younger brother, Henry Sturgis Drinker. Cecilia Beaux was twenty-four years old when Etta married, and although she looked much younger, by Victorian standards she was past the first blush of youth and certainly nearing a time of reckoning. After the marriages of her sister and her mentor, she must have wondered if her own options were diminishing. Beaux recorded her sister's marriage with expansive good will in her autobiography. "I watched my sister float away on the happiest of marriage destinies without a ripple to mar its certainty or one backward glance."[208] But perhaps Leilie was glancing backward. She did recall having doubts and remembered thinking, "Happy is she. Will I ever come to it?" Leilie had her chance with Henry Sturgis Dinker and had passed it by. Eighteen years later, in

29. OPPOSITE: ***A Little Girl.*** *1887. Oil on canvas, 36 x 29 3/16 in. Pennsylvania Academy of the Fine Arts*

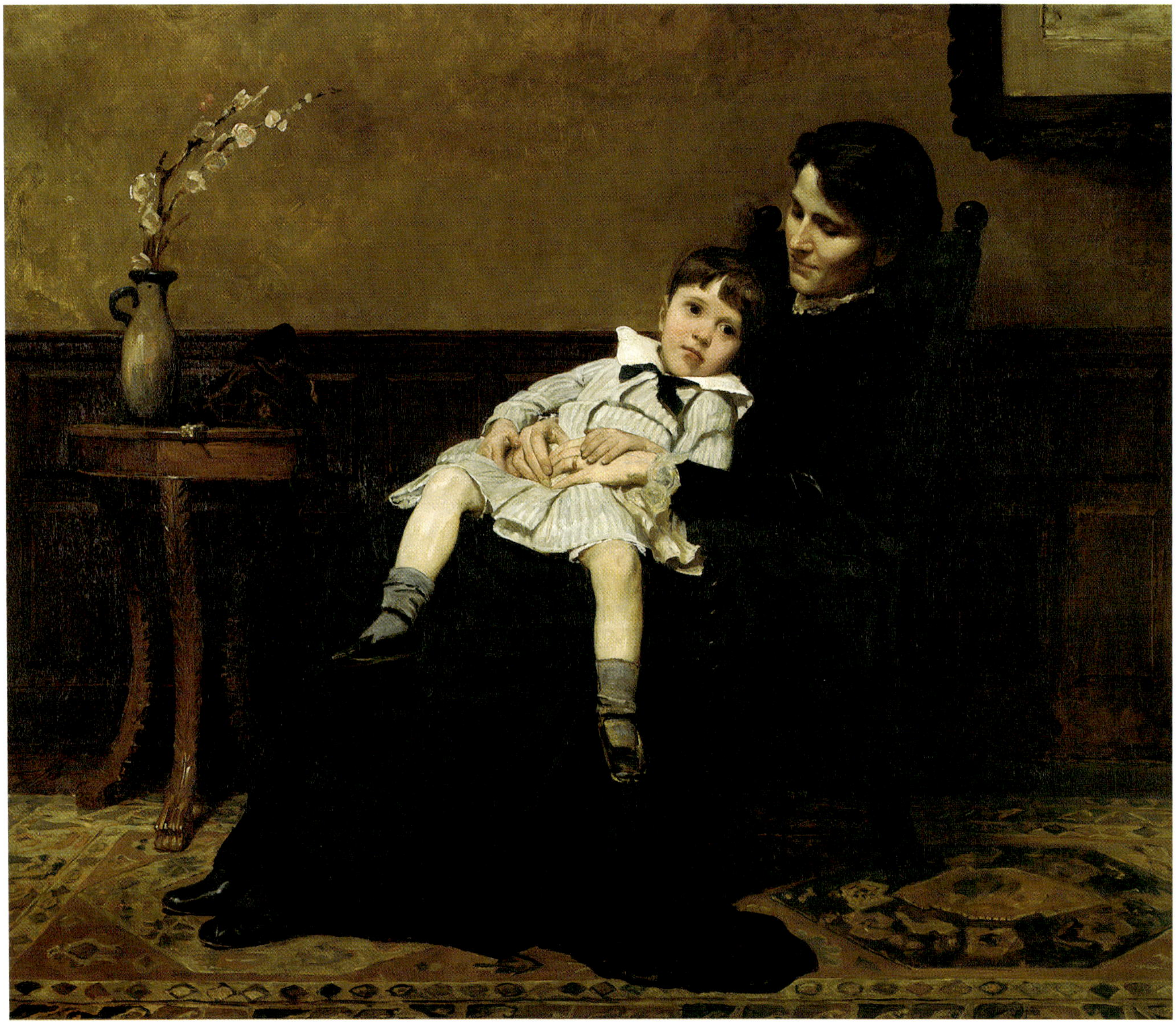

30. ABOVE: ***Les Derniers Jours d'Enfance.*** *1883–85. Oil on canvas, 46 x 54 in. Pennsylvania Academy of the Fine Arts*

31. OPPOSITE: ***Portrait of Howard and Mildred Colton.*** *1887. Oil on canvas, 55 9/10 x 42 in. Pennsylvania Academy of the Fine Arts*

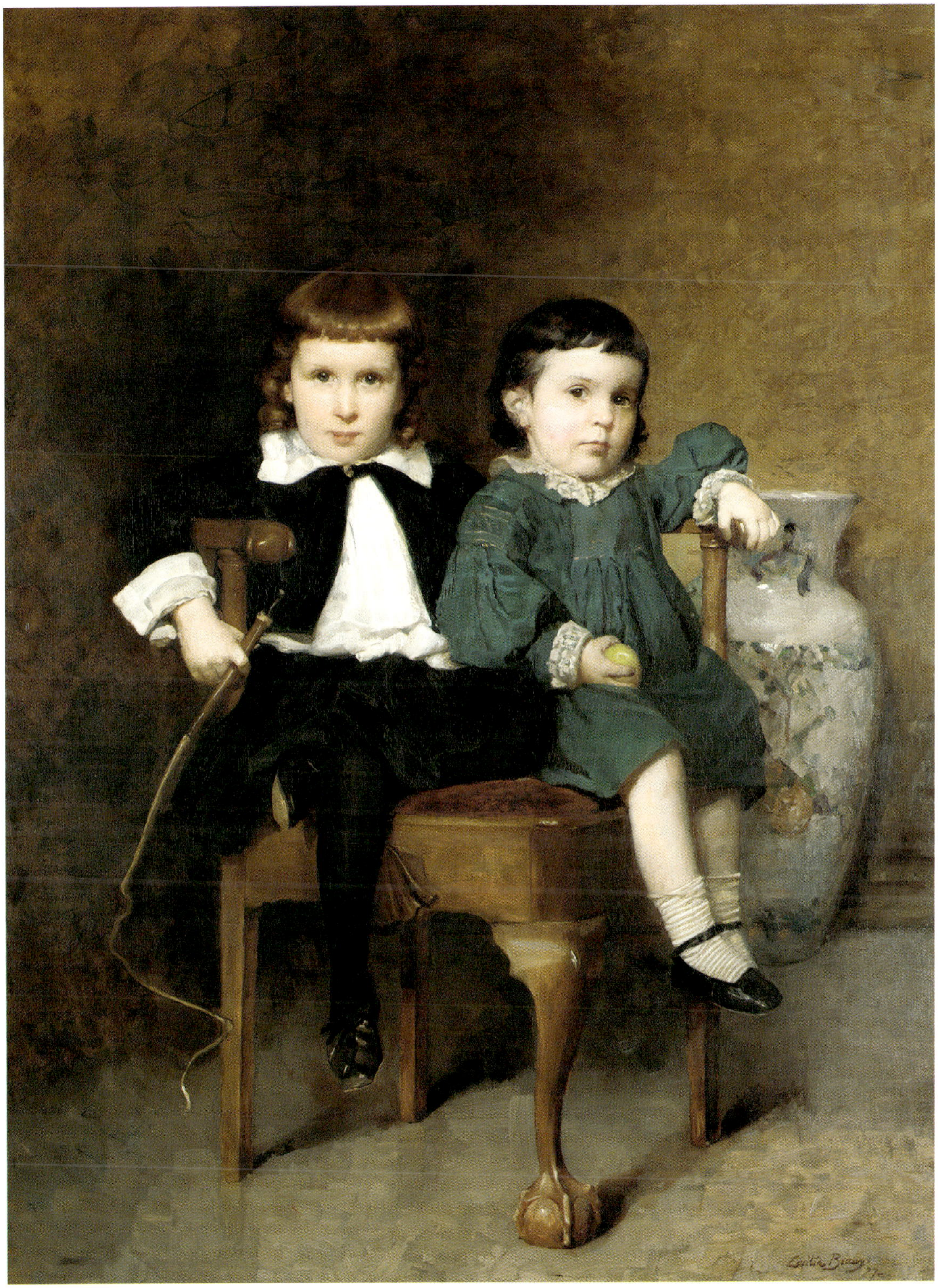

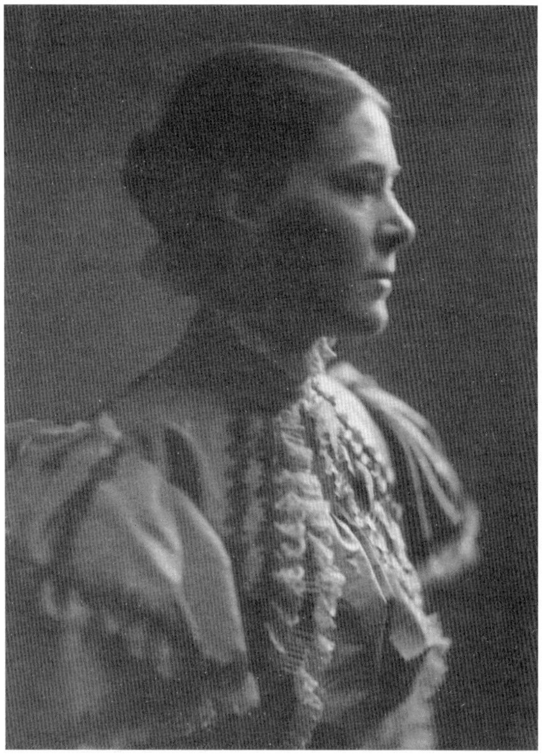

32. *Cecilia Beaux, 1885–90. Pennsylvania Academy of the Fine Arts*

1898, Beaux painted *Man with a Cat*, a luminous portrait of her brother-in-law. At the time, both of them were at the height of their success, Henry Drinker as a corporate lawyer, and Cecilia Beaux as an honored and established artist. The painting is among Beaux's best—the brush strokes free and masterful. Henry looks debonair, clad in a white summer suit. Seated by an open window, he meets the painter's gaze squarely but looks uneasy and nervously taps his leg with his hand as if eager to flee. The sleeping cat lying in his lap has trapped him in the chair.

When Etta was in her eighties, she told her youngest daughter Catherine Drinker Bowen that her husband had first proposed to Leilie. She refused him, Etta recalled, "She wouldn't marry anybody." Incredulous, Bowen asked her mother if she had ever been jealous, especially since the newlyweds moved in with the rest of the family immediately following the wedding and ten months later had their first child. "Jealous," Etta replied, "Of course not! Cecilia didn't want a husband, she had another life before her. And besides, she adored me and adored my children when they began to come."[209] Beaux wrote that following Etta's wedding she still expected to fulfill her family's expectations, find an ideal partner, and settle into comfortable domesticity. "I was by no means set against marriage and had no glimmering vision of another sort of future I might have," she explained in her autobiography.[210] Leilie continued to produce artwork and to contribute to the family finances, but she was still waiting for her future to catch up with her and not going out to seek it on her own.

In March 1879 Catharine Janvier suggested that Leilie take a course in china painting. At the time, decorating china was a popular diversion for female hobbyists and a source of income for professionals responding to a national craze for hand-painted porcelain. The interest was inspired by the work of a group of female art students from the McMiken School of Design in Cincinnati, Ohio. The students mounted a display of beautifully designed and crafted over-glaze china painting in the Cincinnati Room of the Women's Pavilion at the Centennial Exhibition.[211] Competing with the skillfully painted china were a number of creations of dubious distinction. One of the most popular works in the Pavilion was Caroline Brooke's *Iolanthe Dreaming*, a statue of a woman sculpted entirely in butter.[212] Many visitors bypassed the butter and went on to the porcelain, and the exhibit gained national attention when the work was lauded in the journal *The Art Amateur*. After the exhibition, *The Art Amateur* continued to promote the craft, fueling public interest by publishing patterns for china painting designed by expert professionals.[213]

Cecilia enrolled in a china painting course at the National Art Training School at Tenth and Walnut Streets. Her teacher there was the school's principal, French ceramist Camille Piton. Piton was the author of *China Painting in America*, a popular treatise on the subject capably translated into English by Catharine Janvier.[214] Because Piton concentrated on the mechanical process of applying paint to china rather than aesthetic considerations or the history of decorative arts, Leilie tailored the medium to her own interests. "My instructor said nothing to me of the legitimate field of this kind of work," Beaux complained, "and I at once began adapting it to portraiture."[215] Leilie completed a number of portraits on china and worked in the craft for at least seven years. Her likenesses were all based on photographs and some, like her crayon portraits, may have been worked directly on top of photographs. Leilie's art training, combined with her meticulous perfectionism, made her well-suited for the task, which required more accuracy than artistry. She located a kiln to fire the plates and climbed the many rickety stairs to the Arch Street studio of seventy-six-year-old Charles Francis Schreiber, a pioneering and highly regarded portrait photographer, who made the solar prints she used for reference.[216]

Beaux wrote that the results of her work were, "Alas, too successful. . . . I managed to get upon a large china plaque a nearly life-sized head of a child (background always different) that parents nearly wept over."[217] One of the surviving plates is smaller than the productions Beaux described. But it is easy to see why she was so popular as a china painter. The portrait, carefully rendered in oil on a twelve-and-a-half-inch porcelain plate, is a likeness of Clara Hoopes Atlee, one of her family's neighbors on Spruce Street.[218] Using a thirty-two-year-old daguerreotype, Leilie painted Mrs. Atlee as she appeared at the age of eight. The portrait is both expert and charming. Photographically based or not, it shows amazing promise. The long hours spent struggling to model the undefined forms of Cope's fossils had taught Leilie well, as she managed to keep all the modeling soft, as befits a portrait of a child, and to simultaneously maintain the solidity of the head. A photographic stiffness and a hard highlight on the chin are the only flaws marring an enchanting portrait.

Pennsylvania Academy records show that Leilie exhibited her porcelain plates during the 1880s in the institution's annual exhibitions. However, she later renounced the work and claimed no part in the American Aesthetic Movement that began following the Philadelphia Centennial and provided creative outlets for many women in the applied arts. "Without knowing why, I am glad to say that I greatly despised these productions, and would have been glad to hear that although they would never wash off, some of them had worn out their suspending wires and been dashed to pieces," Beaux wrote.[219] "This was the lowest depth I ever reached in commercial art, and although it was a period when youth and romance were in their first attendance on me, I remember it with gloom and record it with shame."[220]

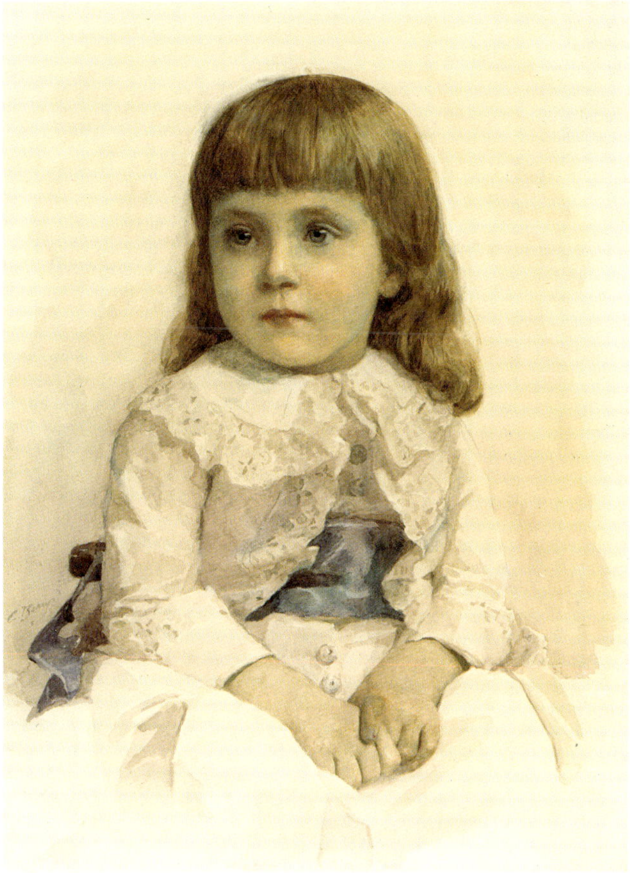

33. ***Edmund James Drifton Coxe.*** *1884. Watercolor on wove paper, 24 1/8 x 18 1/4 in. Pennsylvania Academy of the Fine Arts*

Concurrently with her career as a china painter, Leilie worked on a project that was a more accurate reflection of both her youth and her romantic heart. While laboring over the plates and plaques, she produced drawings based on the story of Elaine of Astolat. Elaine was the maiden of Arthurian legend who died of unrequited love for Sir Lancelot and arranged to be posthumously floated to Camelot in an open barge, her lifeless hand grasping a letter—a final declaration of devotion. Leilie's Elaine drawings have been lost, but exhibition records show that her very first entry into the Pennsylvania Academy's Annual Exhibition was not one of the plates but a crayon drawing of Elaine submitted to the 1879 show. Because Leilie's entry is listed as a "crayon," it is possible that this drawing, like others she produced in the late 1870s and early 1880s, was rendered over a photograph. The photographs in question would have probably been the Pre-Raphaelite-inspired work of Julia Margaret Cameron (1815–1879), an English photographer who contributed photographic illustrations—including several of Elaine—to an 1875 edition of Alfred Lord Tennyson's *Idylls of the King*.[221]

Leilie might have remained a competent copyist producing attractive portraits and romantic illustrations without any conscious effort on her part, but once again, her destiny found her. A wealthy classmate from the Lyman School, who was seriously committed to becoming a painter, rented a studio, organized a class, and hired Mr. William Sartain (1843–1924) to travel to Philadelphia from his home in New York and offer criticism twice a month.[222] When Leilie decided to join the group in 1881, she had no idea that the class would change her life. "Across all the intervening years," Beaux recalled, "it now seems to me that the record of this adventure should be written with a pen of fire. Time and experience have given it a poignancy, a significance, only dimly felt at the moment."[223]

Leilie's teacher, William Sartain, was the third and somewhat rebellious son of Philadelphia engraver John Sartain. In 1877, after eight years of study in Europe with the French realist Léon Bonnat, Sartain elected not to return to Philadelphia, where his influential father held sway over the artistic life of the city, but to make his own way in New York. Cecilia Beaux, who attributed much of her subsequent success to Sartain's teaching, never bothered to learn much about him. In her autobiography she failed to mention his connection with Bonnat and reported erroneously that he studied in Munich. Perhaps her lack of interest was the result of her ambivalence to Sartain's paintings. Leilie had not seen her teacher's work when she began her studies. When she did have occasion to look at Sartain's paintings, she was not impressed. In her autobiography she reduced her teacher's long career to "a few quiet sea-landscapes, some strong heads and small shadowy Oriental interiors."[224]

Sartain recalled that in the 1880s when Leilie was studying with him, "art students were practically now all under either myself or Thomas Eakins at the Academy." Although the two men were lifelong friends and had shared a studio in Paris during their student days, their teaching methods were diametrically opposed. Eakins's teaching philosophy was based on the principles he learned as a student in the atelier of Jean-Léon Gérôme (1824–1904), who had strong opinions on how to produce a painting. Sartain preferred Bonnat. When Sartain persuaded Eakins to join him in Bonnat's Montmarte studio, his friend stayed only a month. "I have given up on Bonnat," Eakins informed his father in a letter from Paris. "He is the most timid man I ever saw in my life & has trouble to join three words together. If you ask him the simplest question about what he thinks and the best way to do a thing, he won't tell you. He says do it just as you like."[225]

Although Beaux admired Eakins's work and had little regard for Sartain's, her opinions about their teaching styles were reversed. Leilie, who disapproved of Eakins's domineering manner and strongly held opinions, thrived under the gentle guidance of Sartain, whose style of teaching was modeled on the tolerant demeanor of his mentor. Like Bonnat, who taught such stylistically diverse artists as Toulouse Lautrec (1864–

1901) and George Braque (1882–1963), Sartain had no allegiance to any particular school or style of painting and let his students develop their own aesthetic. "What he gave us was simple and universal," Beaux recalled.[226] "His culture bore away all limitations of school and fashion."[227] Beaux studied with Sartain for two years. The class was loosely organized and met only three mornings a week, but there was enough time for Leilie to discover her own abilities and to begin working to perfect them.

In Sartain's informal class Leilie painted from the model for the first time, savoring the act of watching the image develop on the canvas and enjoying the quiet morning hours in the congenial companionship of her friends. When Sartain arrived every fortnight, she listened carefully to his criticisms and adopted many of his precepts. Like many Victorians, Sartain believed in phrenology and thought that the proportions of the head revealed much about the worth and character of an individual. Beaux adopted this opinion and never veered from it even when such thoughts were outmoded. "It was the set of the eyes that mattered, and the proportion of brow to cheek," Beaux's niece remembered. When one of her nephews brought his fiancée to meet Aunt Cecilia, Beaux immediately demanded that the young woman remove her hat and lift the hair so that the distance between the ears and the top of her head might be measured. "That's where one can tell if there's room for brains," she announced to her startled relatives.[228]

Although some of the information that passed from teacher to student in the hushed studio appears to have been outdated, much of Sartain's advice and counsel was timeless. Leilie learned how to handle painted values and how to put enough spirit into a portrait that a reviewer would one day comment that all her subjects looked like they had a nervous system.[229] Under the tutelage of William Sartain, Leilie's work took a huge step forward, and she gained a confidence in her ability that stayed with her for the rest of her life. Although she continued to accept commercial assignments for several more years, Leilie finally had a vision of what was possible: She would be a painter and a good one. The struggling young copyist, who felt pale when her client visited, faded into the distant past. Leilie turned what she later called "a very sharp corner," claimed her birthright, and began signing her paintings "Cecilia Beaux."

While Beaux was studying with Sartain, she painted several portraits of friends and family. Because her bedroom was not a suitable place for oil paints and solvents, in 1881, when she was twenty-six years old, she rented a studio with her cousin Emma Leavitt, an aspiring artist who had also trained as a china painter. The studio was located in the Presbyterian Board of Publications Building at 1334 Chestnut Street, and because the room was spacious, Cecilia suggested that her class meet there. As Sartain's responsibilities in New York made more demands on his time and his criticism became infrequent, the women hired a model themselves and continued to paint without instruction.

Renting the studio was a momentous occasion for Beaux; she was to launch her career within its dusky interior. The space was large and barren with gray walls, a high ceiling, and good, full light. Although later photographs show that the cousins eventually acquired all the necessary accessories and outfitted the room with the typical eclecticism of a nineteenth-century atelier, initially the place was sparsely furnished. There were six kitchen chairs and six easels for the benefit of the class and an etching press that functioned primarily as a hat rack, which Uncle Will had proudly obtained at an auction. The building housed a number of other artists, such as the portrait and landscape painter Isaac Williams (1817–1895), whom the younger tenants called "Old Williams"; the painter, and principal of the Philadelphia School of Industrial Arts, Liberty Tadd; H. R. Poore, who made his reputation painting pictures of sporting dogs; Stephen Parrish (1846–1938), father of Maxfield Parrish; and the illustrator Joseph Pennell.[230] Although Beaux acknowledged Stephen Parrish as her neighbor in the building, she failed to mention the other painters, perhaps because her introduction to their ranks provoked painful

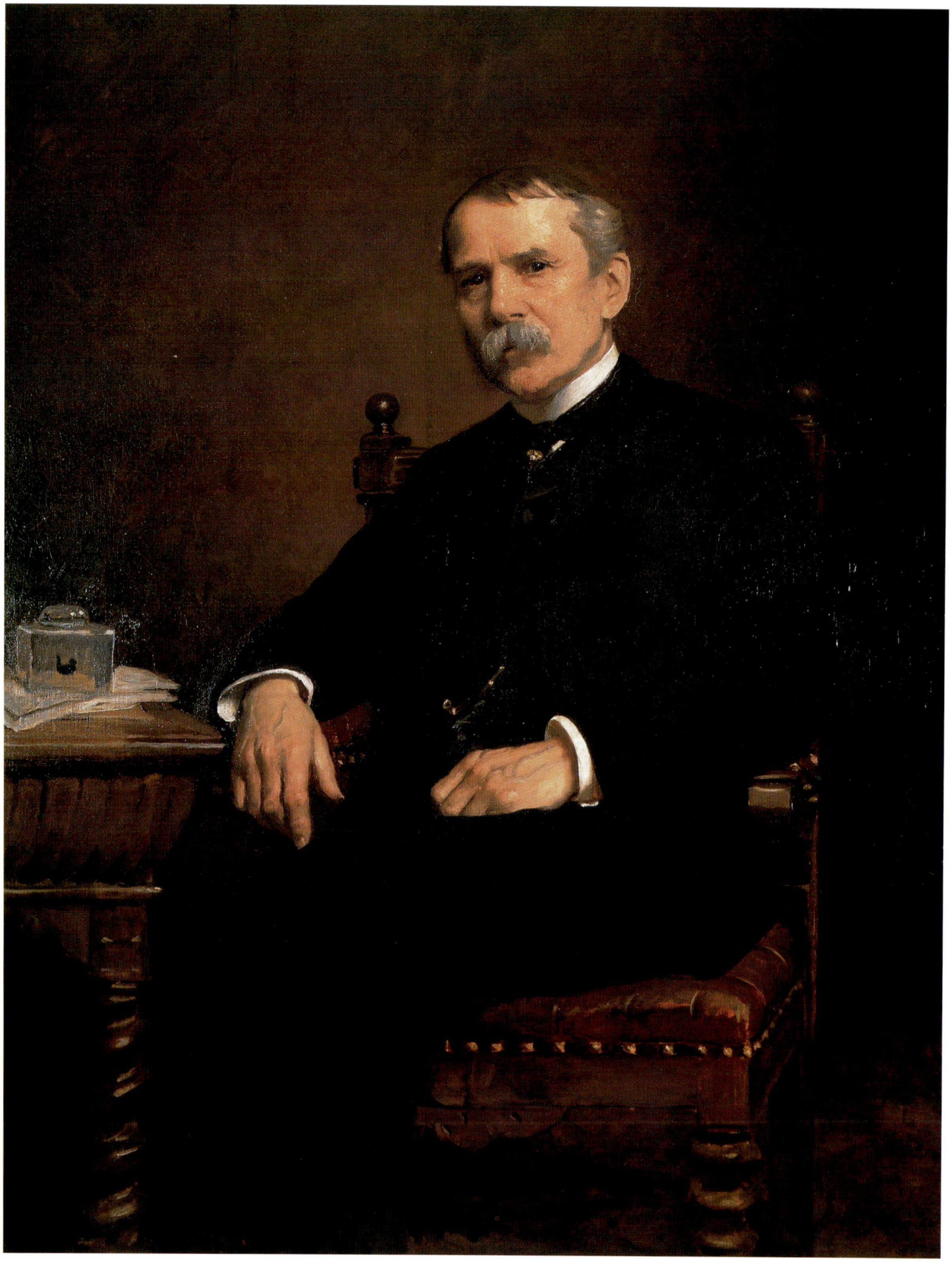

memories. Cantankerous Joseph Pennell, who at the time was not particularly fond of any of the artists in the building, wrote:

> . . . We hated more Cecilia Beaux, and most some arty females who had come in following her. . . . [W]e thought women had no business there, so we went in for revenge. One night, when we had swept up the studio and put in order the chairs, we took a tramp model's property pants and a coat, and stuffed them with papers, and a mask from somewhere and a hat, and gum shoes, and tied them all together; and as it grew dark, there were no lights on the upper flights of stairs, we carried out the gent and laid him, spread aboard, head down, at the bottom, and then we went home. And so no one ever found out, whether the man was murdered, or why Cecilia Beaux had a faint."[231]

Cecilia recovered from her faint and emerged more determined than ever. Even Pennell eventually conceded that following the incident she began to produce "her most interesting work."[232] By 1915 she had earned his respect, and when colleagues on the international art jury at the San Francisco Exposition failed to award Beaux the Grand Prize for painting, Pennell accused them of discrimination.[233] However, in those early days of her career, she must have felt the sting of his ridicule, and it very likely hardened her resolve. She completed a study of a friend, which was accepted, well placed, and, as Beaux put it, "considerably noticed" in an exhibition at the Pennsylvania Academy. Even so, Beaux must have realized that if she wanted her neighbors to take her seriously, she would have to end the class sessions at her studio. Emma Leavitt evidently moved out too, and Beaux had the place to herself. Sitting all alone in the extravagant space with five empty chairs and five abandoned easels, Beaux felt the need to accomplish something significant. She quickly went to work and soon envisioned an idea for a canvas that would prove her ability and professionalism.

Cecilia outlined the composition in her mind, and quickly transferred her idea in freely composed masses, lines, and color to a small piece of board. The painting was to be a double portrait of Etta with her firstborn son, three-year-old Henry Sandwith Drinker, whom the family called Harry, reclining on her lap—his small fingers gently resting on his mother's capable hands. Before she put brush to canvas, Cecilia conceived of a title for the painting. "Strangely enough," Beaux recalled, "the presiding dæmon spoke French in whispering the name of the proposed work, *Les Derniers Jours d'Enfance*."[234] Although Cecilia Beaux never mentioned it, critics noticed that Beaux's dæmon visualized a composition that was not entirely original, but owed a considerable debt to James Abbott McNeil Whistler's (1834–1903) famous *Arrangement in Gray and Black #1: Portrait of the Artist's Mother*, painted in 1871. Beaux's canvas was similar in subject matter, composition, and tone to Whistler's work, which she probably admired when it was exhibited at the Pennsylvania Academy in 1881. Nevertheless, it was a leap of faith for an unknown female artist, whose previous professional experience had been primarily as a copyist, to attempt to emulate the revered Mr. Whistler.

In order to create the painting, Cecilia had to convince her sister to pose. Etta was already busy enough with two young children and the care of her husband's Grandma Shober, who had declined considerably since her days with Cousin Kate and now needed to be watched with "tact and consistency."[235] The trip from the Drinkers' house on Irving Street to Cecilia's studio took an hour in the horse-cars, a significant journey for the young mother and her little boy. Once they arrived at 1334 Chestnut Street, there were eighty-four exhausting steps to climb to Cecilia's studio. But Etta was eager to cooperate. "A mother will do anything to have her child's portrait, and the same energy and confidence burned in my sister's veins as in mine," Beaux later wrote.[236] Like Whistler's mother, Etta was posed, seated, and dressed in black. The outfit Cecilia visualized

34. OPPOSITE: ***George C. A. Troutman.*** *1886. Oil on canvas, 48 1/8 x 38 1/4 in. Berry Hill Gallery, New York*

for her nephew was one he already owned, but Etta's costume had to be pieced together. Cecilia made one black satin sleeve with lace trim to cover the arm visible in the painting. Grandma Leavitt's black canton crêpe shawl was arranged on Etta's lap to serve as a skirt. There was an old steamer chair in a storeroom that Cecilia adapted for her use, but other props had to be brought from West Philadelphia and lugged up the many dark stairs—an heirloom table from the Drinkers and one of the Leavitts' best rugs.

Cecilia had never attempted to paint a full-length figure before, and her vision for this work required that she paint two figures. The large size of the painting (46 x 54 inches) also presented a challenge. At the start, trouble with the composition caused her to restretch the canvas twice. Realizing that she needed a horizontal mass behind the figures similar to the baseboard in Whistler's portrait, Beaux bought some paneling at a carpenter's shop, stained it a mahogany color, and placed it behind her models. Rambunctious Harry required frequent breaks, and when his portrait was completed, Cecilia, feeling sympathy for her sister, accepted the offer of another female artist to stand in for Etta and pose for the legs and feet. But in spite of all the difficulties, Cecilia was undaunted. Years later she wrote a letter to Thomas Janvier describing her career as a ladder she started to ascend as a teenager and never ceased to climb: "Some of the steps have been difficult and dangerously far apart, so that I have fallen through, but by strength of wrist and some pretty adroit kicking I have managed thus far to swing up onto the next rung."[237]

While Beaux was working on the canvas, she benefited from the practical help of William Sartain, who stopped by when he was in Philadelphia, and from the moral support of Stephen Parrish, who leased the studio down the hall. Beaux kept her door open so that she could step back and get a better view of the large canvas. Parrish never intruded, but sometimes as he passed by, he would wave his uplifted arms in approval and give an appreciative shout. Thus encouraged, she continued to work, while Philadelphia citizens went about their business unaware that a determined young woman, alone in a studio on Chestnut Street, was struggling with a painting that would bring their city international recognition. While Beaux worked, Mr. C. D. Fort, wearing lightweight shoes that he had fashioned out of cedar, tried to replicate a miracle and walked on the surface of the Delaware River from the Walnut Street Wharf to Ridgeway Park in two hours. On Front Street above Poplar, Mrs. Emily Bickel shot and killed her husband. The Philadelphia Athletics won the pennant of the American Baseball Association, and in Franklin Square, the romantic, flickering gaslights were replaced with the innovation of electricity.

By spring 1885, when Beaux was thirty years old, *Les Derniers Jours d'Enfance* was completed. A friend asked Thomas Anschutz (1851–1912), a protégé of Thomas Eakins and a rising star in the Philadelphia art world, to stop by and critique the painting. Beaux recalled that when Anschutz arrived in her studio he took his time, rubbed his chin and forehead, and regarded the canvas from every angle while she worried over his response. Finally, he turned, and pointing to little Harry's legs, inquired, "What did you think about when you were doing those legs?" Baffled, Cecilia sputtered, "Why, I thought of *them*."[238]

Anschutz's reaction did not deter Beaux, who was already deciding how she could kick her way up to the next rung on the ladder of her career. She sent her canvas to the American Art Association Prize Fund Exhibition in New York, and according to William Sartain, Beaux was in the running for a $2,000 prize.[239] Although the award eluded her, Beaux received a glowing review from the noted editor and critic Clarence Cook in the magazine *The Studio*, who wrote, "We shall hear more of this artist. Few figure-pieces have been painted lately here at all equal to this."[240] In the fall of that same year, Beaux submitted the portrait to the Annual Exhibition of the Pennsylvania Academy, where it hung on a corner panel in the large North Gallery and was awarded the Institution's Mary Smith Prize for the best painting by a female artist.

In later years Beaux could not recall what her family said about the portrait, the award, or the subsequent glowing reviews. She could not even remember what she thought about it herself. Later Beaux admitted that the painting had its virtues and had "lasted well." In retrospect the composition seemed naïve, but in the end, none of that mattered. *Les Derniers Jours d'Enfance* was a personal work as well as a public success—a heartfelt tribute to two orphaned girls, who began life as inseparable companions and were now embarking on very different destinies, Etta as a dedicated wife and mother and Cecilia as a committed artist.

While Beaux was working on *Les Derniers Jours d'Enfance*, she continued to accept commercial projects and to paint portraits. The years between 1885 and 1888 were productive ones during which she completed forty-one known likenesses.[241] Beaux's astonishing output may have been related to a fear of being classed with the many female painters who were not committed artists but merely biding time while acquiring an attractive accomplishment. Cecilia, who by 1885 had enjoyed some positive public notice and was filled with personal ambition, had no desire to be categorized with dilettantes.

When Stephen Parrish went to Europe and rented his studio to two young women, Beaux closed her door. In her autobiography she described her new neighbors with disdain. "They were not workers, and I then had my first view of art as an accomplishment to life."[242] Forty-six years later, following the publication of her book, Beaux received a letter from one of the young women in question, who had married and raised a family while enjoying a productive career as a portrait painter in Colorado. "I am still painting," she informed Beaux. "You should have heard my children's shouts of laughter when they read, 'They were not workers.'"[243]

Beaux's portraits from the late 1880s include watercolors of friends and family, crayon portraits, representations based on photographic reference, and several commemorative likenesses. One of her most successful works was a large oil portrait of her friend Ethel Page dressed as the mythological water nymph Undine. The canvas was not commissioned but painted for exhibition in Beaux's new and more favorably appointed studio in the nearby Baker Building.[244] Eager to repeat her triumph with *Les Derniers Jours d'Enfance*, Beaux sent *Ethel Page as Undine* to the 1886 American Art Association Prize Fund Exhibition in New York and again received notice from Mr. Cook in *The Studio*. Although Cook's review contained criticism concerning Beaux's handling of the costume, he declared that her work, while reminiscent of revered Philadelphia portrait painter Thomas Sully (1783–1872), actually surpassed his. "It recalls the late Mr. Sully's work," Cook wrote enthusiastically. "Though certainly Mr. Sully never painted so well as this."[245] When her painting was returned, Beaux entered it in the Pennsylvania Academy's annual exhibition, where she once again triumphed over her female peers and received the prestigious Mary Smith Prize.

These honors quickly enhanced Beaux's career. Within two years she went from a hopeful painter eager for a kind word from Thomas Anshutz to a respected professional. In 1887 she was invited to serve on the jury and hanging committee for the Pennsylvania Academy of the Fine Arts' 57th Annual Exhibition, a significant honor for any woman, especially one so new to painting. Yet the recognition was well deserved. Beaux's work showed spirit as well as skill. Before long the critical praise yielded financial rewards that translated into portrait commissions of prominent citizens, exactly the sort of work Thomas Eakins was hoping to garner when he completed noncommissioned portraits of Professor Benjamin Rand of Jefferson Medical College and the surgeon Samuel D. Gross.

Cecilia, whose likenesses and lifestyle were hardly controversial, had less trouble finding patrons than the notorious Mr. Eakins, although she greatly admired his work. "He need never have signed his pictures," she later wrote, "for the slightest of them can never be mistaken for the work of any other man."[246] Nevertheless, clients more interested in flattering likenesses than

Eakins's uncompromising realism found much merit in Beaux's vigorous work. In the mid-1880s she moved up the street to a new studio at 1524 Chestnut Street and completed portraits of Mr. George M. Troutman, the president of the Central National Bank, and of two respected clergymen, Reverend Chauncey Giles, pastor of the Swedenborgian Church, and eighty-four-year-old Reverend William W. Furness, the retired minister of Philadelphia's First Unitarian Church. Cecilia was proud of the Furness portrait and displayed it first in her Chestnut Street studio and subsequently at Earle's Gallery, where a reviewer from *The American* saw it and commented that "no one not coldly indifferent and insensible can study the work without being impressed by the attributes of benign, gracious, potent manliness it presents."[247] Beaux received $500 for the portrait—a very respectable price. At the time, Eakins charged similar fees and sold fewer paintings.[248]

The commissions, positive critical reviews, and recognition might have been enough for Cecilia Beaux. All the commotion was certainly more than she had ever expected. But happenstance again caused her life to take a turn. Her friend, artist Margaret Lesley Bush-Brown (1857–1944), who had studied in Paris and was about to return to the French capital, insisted on taking *Les Derniers Jours d'Enfance* back with her to submit to the 1887 Spring Salon.[249] In spite of Beaux's doubts and protestations, the canvas was removed from its stretchers, and Bush-Brown hauled it away to make its long journey. Once in Paris she restretched the canvas, strapped it precariously to the top of a cab, and took it to the studio of the revered French historical painter Jean-Paul Laurens (1838–1921). Laurens considered Beaux's canvas worthy and recommended that it be entered in the exhibition. Margaret Lesley Bush-Brown was evidently an extraordinarily loyal and selfless friend; she went to untold trouble on behalf of Beaux. After obtaining a suitable frame she filled out all the necessary forms, braved the crowds of hopeful artists standing in long lines for their paintings to be measured and registered, and waited for the verdict.

In the 1880s the annual art exhibition in Paris, called the Salon, held an unprecedented influence over the world of Western art. At a time when photography was still in its infancy and painting was the primary and most popular of the visual arts, the annual exhibition and competition held all the global drama and authority of present-day film festivals and major motion-picture award ceremonies.[250] Similar charges of favoritism and political intrigue surrounded the event. The awarding of the prizes was an occasion attended by both the artists and the international press. Success at the Salon translated into celebrity status, as well as commercial rewards for those fortunate enough either to be included in the exhibition or, even better, to be awarded a prize.

Beaux had little hope of a positive outcome. Although the huge exhibition included about 5,000 paintings, not all submitted work was accepted. Some of the paintings that did survive the jury were "skyed," hung so high in the vast exhibition halls that they were impossible to see. When Beaux received word that her painting would be included in the prestigious exhibition, she was astounded. "It had no allies," she explained. "I was no one's pupil, or protégée; it was the work of an unheard-of American."[251] No press notices were sent back to Philadelphia, although Beaux did hear that the painting was well placed on a center wall. When the exhibition ended, Bush-Brown shipped the canvas back to Philadelphia. "I sat endlessly before it, longing for some revelation of the scenes through which it had passed; the drive under the sky of Paris, the studio of the great French artist, where his eye had actually rested on it, and observed it," Beaux recalled. The French labels, the "A" for *admis*, and the number assigned to designate the painting's position on the wall were mysterious ciphers that stirred Cecilia's romantic heart and revived her childhood dream to visit her father's native land.

35. OPPOSITE: ***Man with a Cat.*** *1898. Oil on canvas, 48 x 34 5/8 in. Smithsonian American Art Museum, Washington, D.C.*

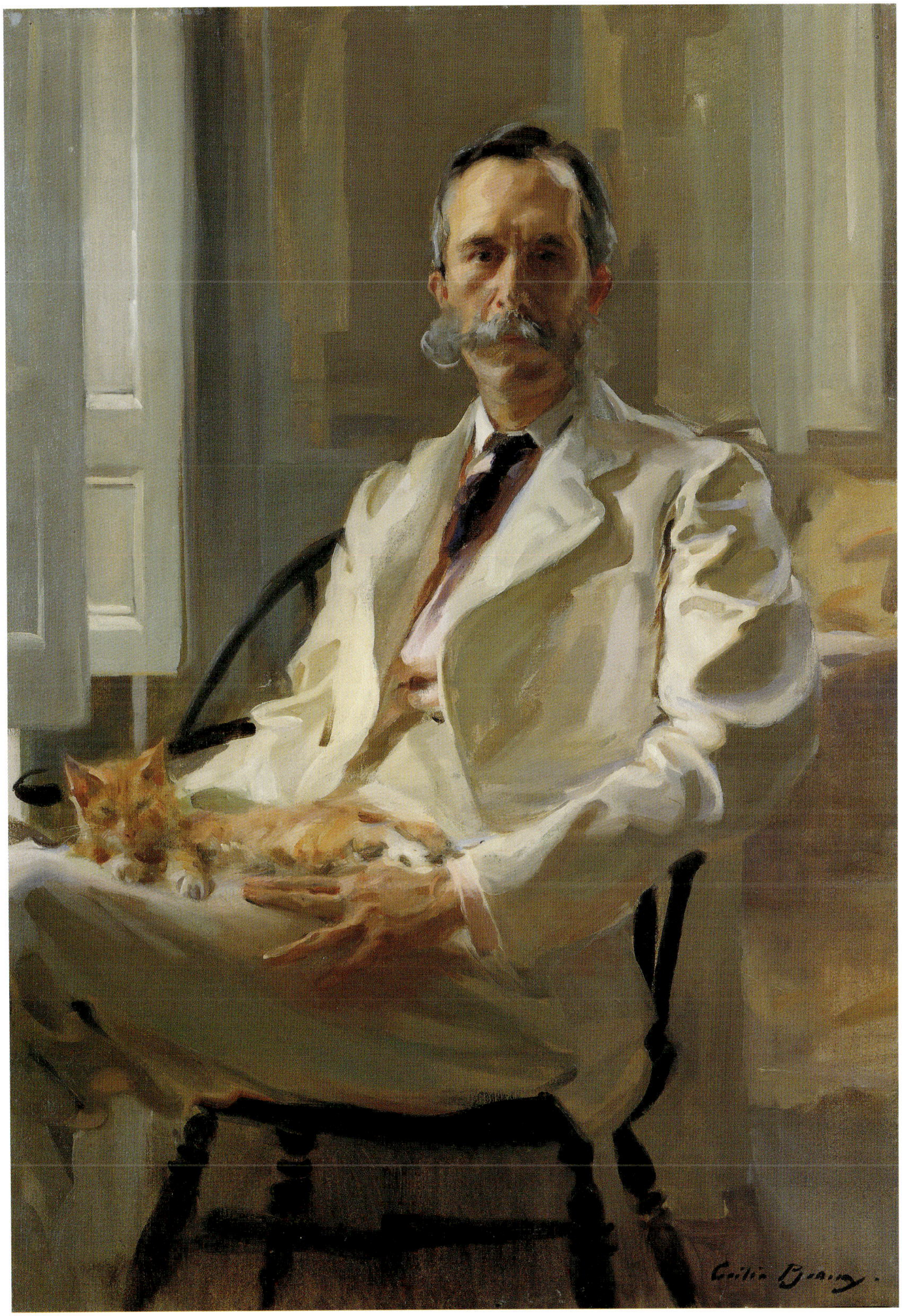

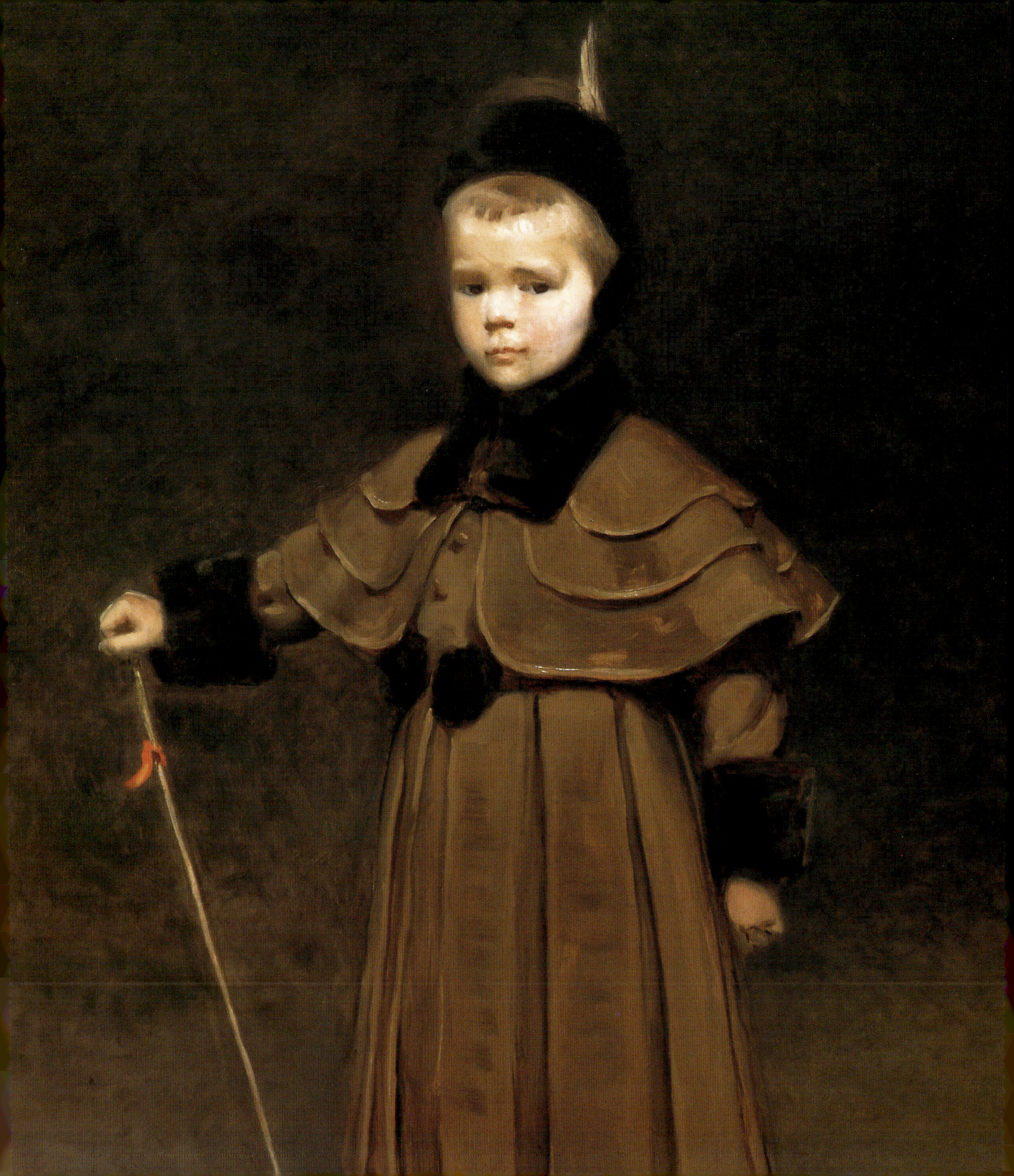

Paris, 1888

"Paris is a mighty schoolmaster, a grand enlightener of the provincial intellect."
—Mary Elizabeth Braddon *(1837–1915)*

On September 15, 1884, while Cecilia was working on *Les Derniers Jours d'Enfance*, Papa Beaux died in Philadelphia. In her autobiography, Beaux devoted a few lines to this pivotal event and admitted sadly that her father "had never been able to do for his daughters what he wished."[252] And with that simple eulogy, Jean Adolphe Beaux slipped quietly from the narrative of his daughters' lives. Cecilia Beaux's letters and diaries offer no nostalgic recollections of her father, who tried to return to his American family when it was probably too late for anything but polite acquaintance. However, something of Papa Beaux did remain with his younger daughter. Cecilia Beaux believed that her father's nationality was a birthright that both legitimized her need to accept art as her calling and explained her impassioned desire to see Paris for herself.

In spite of her recently acquired stature as a respected professional, Cecilia was determined to enroll in one of the French capital's revered art academies. For most American artists, rigorous European academic training—while not as essential as it had been before there were viable art schools in the United States—was still considered important for any artist wanting to compete in the international arena. "I had worked alone and fully believed that, in Paris, I would be among brilliant and advanced students, far ahead of a practically untaught American," Beaux wrote.[253] Aside from the technical training available in the city, the political benefits of studying with an influential teacher were far-reaching and a factor in admission to the Salons. Cecilia had been lucky with her first submission, but she was aware that in order to have subsequent work accepted she would not only have to perfect her skills but also establish significant alliances.

Beaux had saved enough money from her commissions to survive in Paris if she was frugal. But although she was thirty-two years old and mature enough to make a considered decision, convincing her family that an extended trip to the French capital was essential proved difficult. Aunt Eliza was so afraid that the adventure would come to a bad end that even after Cecilia had won her point and was irrevocably steaming toward Europe, she wrote bitterly, "You must know that the sting of parting this time is in the fear that you will be beguiled into making a wreck of your life and marring the peace of your family which may God forbid."[254] Grandma, similarly worried, advised, "Don't buy any startling clothes because they look stylish and 'So French!'" Uncle Will, who may have initially shared some of the same fears, proved easier to persuade; once convinced that Cecilia was

OPPOSITE: *Detail; **Cecil Kent Drinker.** 1891. Oil on canvas, 64 x 34½ in. Philadelphia Museum of Art*

resolute, he assumed his customary role as guardian, lent his financial support, and made all the complicated arrangements. He secured Cecilia's passport, letters of introduction and credit, and a January passage on the SS *Noordland*, bound for Antwerp. Uncle Will also located a suitable companion for his niece: Cecilia's cousin May Whitlock, an aspiring artist and intrepid traveler who was visiting Philadelphia from her home in Montana and apparently planning to go on to Boston, was persuaded to change her plans and join the adventure.

In spite of William Biddle's careful preparations, Cecilia left in a rout. She scandalized her grandmother and aunts by sailing away with her third-floor room in a mess, rubbish on the table, unpaid bills scattered about. "Aunt Emily and I spent part of the afternoon in your room, putting studio property in the closet and reducing chaos to some degree," Eliza wrote. "We did not like things one bit—but made it do as well as we could."[255] Cecilia's room was not the only thing she left in a mess. Her personal life was as tangled as her possessions, and she bestowed the resulting confusion on her family. Several days before she left, Cecilia sent a letter to her friend and fellow painter, Henry Thouron. "My Dear Friend," she wrote,

> You must not say any more—I understand. I have always known that there was a great gulf fixed and I knew you knew it—and I have let myself enjoy your friendship too much—feeling that I might do so—thinking that you understood—I could not help showing the pleasure I always felt—Oh, I could not help it. You think I am strong perhaps—but I am weak twice— I have been off my guard and I have done wrong—and I am punished. I cannot tell you—I cannot explain more than this. Try to be my friend still—I am going to keep your beautiful gift to prove how much I desire this—and for the roses I never thought there could be so much pain in such beauty and sweetness—
> We must not meet again to talk about this—if you knew all you would believe me. I want to bid you good-bye—but you must do what you think best. I am going to leave on Friday on the 1:20 train from the PRR Station—There may be other times—one or two.[256]

Poor Henry. Cecilia provided just enough encouragement for him to write several impassioned letters and to rush to the Pennsylvania Railroad Station in a snowstorm to see her off on the 1:20 pm train. He was too late. "Perhaps when Mr. Biddle is in the neighborhood of my studio, he may kindly tell me something of your departure, and you will make this little request for me."[257] Cecilia did make the request, and Uncle Will complied, cleaning up the mess of her broken romance while the aunts cleaned up her room.

Perhaps Beaux was in love with Henry Thouron. She saved his letters among her possessions, tucked in an envelope with a message for her heirs—"To be burned unopened."[258] Whatever Beaux felt for Henry, the obstacles to any permanent relationship were formidable. Thouron was poor, an unfortunate circumstance that her family would probably be willing to overlook, but he was also Catholic, a fact that in itself would have prevented any union. The Leavitts and Biddles would never have approved, and if that were not enough to dissuade her, the memory of Papa Beaux and his family of Protestant martyrs, who suffered religious persecution for 200 years would certainly have cooled her ardor. Professionally, Beaux was courageous. Personally, she was cautious and protective of her family and their deeply held values and prejudices. Henry Thouron was not the only man in Cecilia's life when she sailed for Paris. Two other suitors vied for her time, and any drawback to their attentions was apparently less obvious. As the *Noordland* plied its way across the tempestuous Atlantic, she sent no farewell letters but left them both with hope.

All the confidence that Cecilia felt about her adventure in Paris vanished as soon as the ship hit open water. "Why did no one tell me it was unbearable to go to sea? I wouldn't have done it. I could have easily been stopped," she wrote in a plaintive letter home.[259] For several days Cecilia was too ill to eat and subsisted on crackers and sips of champagne. When a storm generated a huge wave that reached the top of the mast, submerged the entire vessel (including the smokestack) terrifying everyone, she wrote, "I am so mad at the people . . . who said that January was as good a month as any. If I'd have known what it would be like I wouldn't have come—though if we ever do get safely over I shall not be sorry its [sic] done—but I'll never do it again."[260] Eventually the sea calmed and Beaux recovered completely. She and May, who had been invulnerable to the rough weather, made friends, roamed the decks, and set up chairs in the sun. On days when the wind was favorable, the engines were shut down, and the crew hoisted a large gray canvas sail. As soon as Beaux recovered enough to ponder her eventual voyage home, she asked the ship's chief officer when the best time would be to go to sea. "When your trunk is packed," he replied.[261]

Beaux's trunk for her present journey had been packed with plenty of warm clothes, her own and some of Etta's, as well as one of her favorite books, *Masters of Past Times*—a treatise on Dutch and Flemish painting by Eugene Fromentin. Cecilia also packed Henry Thouron's gift, the one she decided to keep—a set of monochrome drawings on oil boards that he had devotedly rendered from black-and-white photographs of the paintings Beaux hoped to copy at the Louvre. Henry's thoughtful present would enable Cecilia to skip the tedious work of composing and lighting her copies. She could paint directly over Thouron's drawings. Cecilia greatly valued this gift, if not the selflessness of the giver, who must have spent many hours transferring the complex compositions to the small boards.

When their ship finally completed the perilous crossing and docked in Antwerp, Cecilia and May got in a horse-drawn cab and took off through the narrow snow-dusted streets. They passed beautiful old walls, people in cloaks and wooden shoes, dogs pulling carts, and picturesque shrines on every corner. "We held each others hands and gasped," Cecilia wrote in a letter to her family.[262] That night there was no fire in their room, and the two cousins shared a bed encased in linen so soft and so cold that Beaux said that crawling under the sheets was like getting into vanilla ice cream. The next day, using Fromentin's book as a guide, they set off for the Antwerp Cathedral to pay homage to the

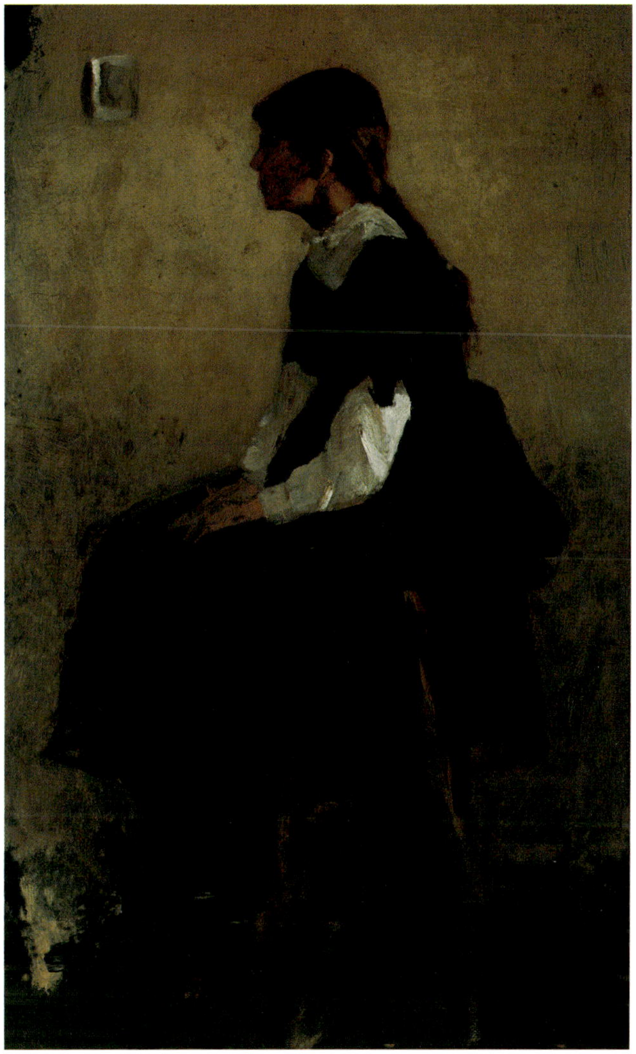

36. ***Seated Girl in a Long Black Dress.*** *ca. 1885. Oil on cardboard, 19⅝ x 12¼ in. Pennsylvania Academy of the Fine Arts*

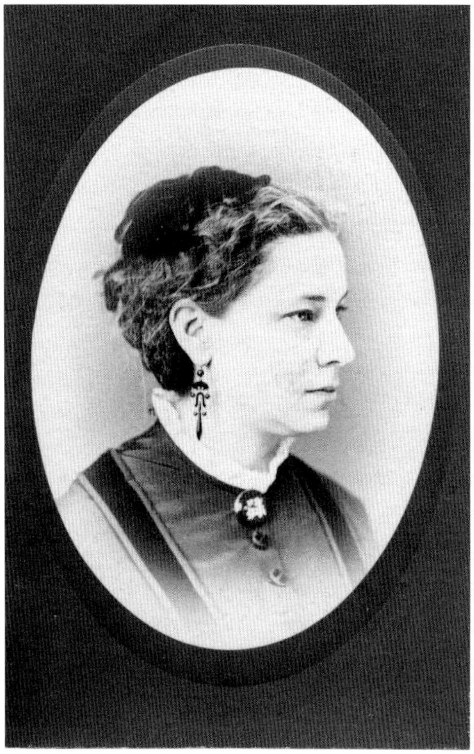

37. *Wenderoth, Taylor & Brown.* ***Eliza Leavitt, carte de visite,*** *ca. 1880. Pennsylvania Academy of the Fine Arts*

two great altarpieces painted by Peter Paul Rubens (1577–1640), *Elevation of the Cross* and *Descent from the Cross*. "There were those endless high arches over our heads, and a note or two of the organ playing—But there was no need of anything outside the pictures to move us," Cecilia wrote to her eager family. "I never expected to weep over any picture—but I did then. It was almost too much for me."[263]

The next day the cousins headed off by train to Paris, stopping in Brussels for another "feast of Rubens" at the museums. From Brussels to Paris they shared a second-class compartment with six good-natured Flemish women and two cheerful children, one a three-year-old toddler, who shocked them by drinking beer. Averting their eyes, they peered through frost-covered windows at the hard, frozen landscape until at last they arrived at the station. Cecilia had relatives in Paris, Grandma Leavitt's sister, Sarah Leavitt Austin, who was studying painting in the studio of Carolus Duran, and Sarah's grown children, Constance and Cecil. It was Cecil Austin, a medical student, who met the two travelers at the glacial Gare du Nord. They found lodgings at 12 rue Boccador, which proved sufficient and nothing more. The sheets were patched, May's bed was a slim cot, and a small, totally insufficient charcoal stove that the landlady rolled out at night provided the only heat. May caught cold immediately, and Cecilia worried about the damp, draughty accommodations. "It is bitter cold and I am hardly ever warm," she informed her worried family. "I am dreadfully afraid of chill-blains [sic] as many people have them."[264]

Cecilia, who credited her strong constitution to good circulation, never did get chilblain and remained healthy from the time she arrived in Paris in January until the sun finally broke through sometime in May, putting an end to her worries about the climate. The two cousins investigated a number of academies before deciding where to study, but they quickly made up their minds. On February 12, 1888, at six o'clock in the morning, they rose, dressed, and walked through the streets of Paris to present themselves promptly at eight at the best school for female artists in Paris, the Académie Julian. Cecilia and May, both of whom had limited funds, elected to attend the school only in the morning, as a half-day session was offered for a reduced price.

Rodolphe Julian founded the school in 1868, primarily as a preparatory academy for students attempting to pass the difficult entrance exams required for admission to the École des Beaux-Arts, the most prestigious art academy in Europe. Although Beaux believed that Julian had been a professional prizefighter, who had "never attempted to become an artist," in fact, he was a credible painter, who had studied with Alexandre Cabanel (1823–1889) and Leon Cogniet (1794–1880). Julian entered the grueling competition for the Prix de Rome (although he did not win), and in 1863 he exhibited two drawings and six paintings in the famous Salon des Refusés, a government-sanctioned exhibition of works rejected from the official Salon, which included paintings by Paul Cézanne (1839–1906), Camille Pissarro (1830–1903), Henri Fantin-Latour (1836–1904), and Edouard Manet (1832–1883), whose controversial painting, *Le Déjeuner sur L'Herbe*, shocked the press, the public, and French academicians with its defiance of standardized themes and methods. From 1865 through 1878, when he presumably became too busy with his academy, Julian's paintings were accepted in the official Salons.[265]

By the time Cecilia and May arrived in Europe, the Académie Julian was the largest art school in Paris, enrolling hundreds of students, both men and women, in seventeen separate ateliers scattered throughout the city.[266] The atelier Cecilia and May chose to attend was housed in a long attic at 28 rue de Faubourg near the Madeleine, within walking distance of their lodgings. There was no chance of Cecilia and May gaining a spot at the École des Beaux-Arts, as that institution did not accept female students until 1897. Even at Julian's, where women were encouraged to enroll, there were significant inequities. The fees were twice as much for women as for men, and while the instructors offered criticism at the men's studios twice a week, they arrived only once a week to help the women.[267] Even so, the school was considered progressive. Female art students, like their male colleagues, drew from live models. Women enrolled in Académie classes competed directly against their male classmates for monthly prizes and studied with the same teachers, established French masters such as Adolphe William Bouguereau (1825–1905) and Tony Robert-Fleury (1838–1912), who were there when the two cousins entered the school.

Nevertheless, Beaux was immediately disappointed —not by any specific problem with the management or instruction but with the skill of the student body. The brilliant classmates she dreamed of meeting when she decided to leave her home and make the long journey to Europe were not in evidence. She felt

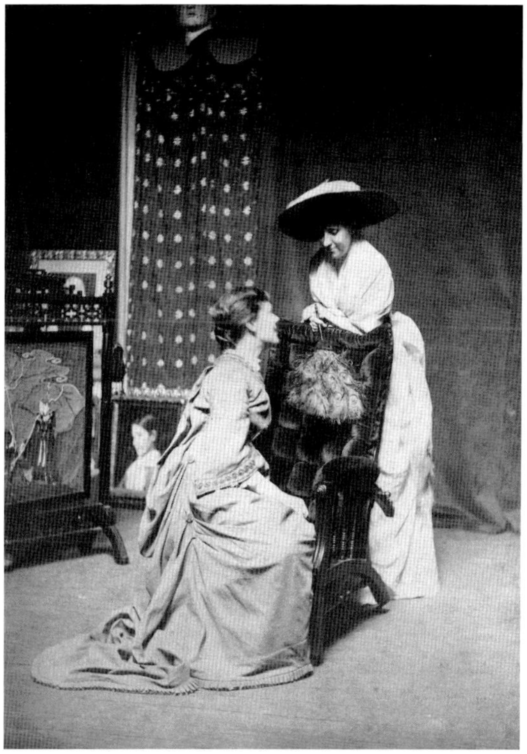

38. ***Cecilia Beaux (seated) with her cousin May Whitlock.*** *n.d.*
Pennsylvania Academy of the Fine Arts

deceived. "More even than on instruction, I had counted on an association of superiority," Beaux wrote. "I was to learn that the Académie Julien [sic] was a business enterprise, and could not be maintained for gifted students only."[268]

The majority of the women in Cecilia and May's class were English, although there were a few French students and some other Americans. Space was at a premium. Every Monday the artist who had produced the most successful drawing in a weekly competition was awarded the best seat. After the winner took her place, the other choice spots went to the earliest arrivals. The room was so overcrowded that the class monitor, called the *massière*, who was in charge of keeping order, had to be sure that each easel and chair was marked with a chalk boundary and that every student stayed within the confines of her allotted area.

On her first day at Julian's, after she had defined the periphery of her small space and wiped the chalk dust off her hands, she decided that although most of the other students were drawing, she would paint. In consequence, when Bouguereau arrived for his weekly critique, she was the only student working in oils. "We have really been face to face with the great man," she informed her family. "Looked a little apoplectic but nice and kind and like his pictures." Bouguereau was small in stature, probably under five foot three inches tall, but he loomed large in the eyes of his students. By 1888 he was established as one of the leaders of French Academic art and had garnered every available honor and decoration. His sentimental imagery, coupled with an amazing technical facility, translated into an international reputation and a strong market for his work. It was rumored among his students that he had made more than two million dollars from the sale of his paintings.[269] Whenever a teacher arrived for the weekly critique, all conversation was forbidden; but the appearance of M. Bouguereau must have quieted even the nervous rustle of long skirts.

Cecilia's painting was a portrait—head and shoulders with one arm raised. "I had worked on the face and it was bad," she confessed to her family. "I can and have done lots better—the being so near etc. was such a hindrance—as I expected it would be—but I had put the arm and shoulder in with a certain touch and freedom."[270] Cecilia's knowledge of French was rudimentary at the time, and when Bouguereau critiqued her painting, she admitted to missing many of the subtleties. However, a few key phrases such as *pas mal*, *une grande abilité*, and *je suis enchanté de voir*, convinced her that her teacher's initial comments were positive.[271] However, when Bouguereau proceeded to suggest that Cecilia was working in a formulaic manner rather than really observing the model, she could hardly feel triumphant. Even so, when the master left, the women, who had crowded around to hear the critique, informed her that she had received "a good many compliments."[272]

This first triumph established Cecilia's place in the class, which she defended in the weekly competitions, where her work often earned her the best spot on Monday mornings. However, even when one of her compositions was chosen by Julian to be *accrochée sur la mur* (hung on the wall), an honor that was fairly permanent, since once the work was selected it was never removed from its place of honor, she was not certain that her success justified the trip to Europe. Her family was worried. Grandma sent warnings about "time and money wasted," and Uncle Will wrote, "O Leilie Dear! The hole you left when you went out of our home seems to be getting larger instead of littler and the tears still come very close to the voice when we make our Sunday morning prayer for you. How long it seems since your going! And this is only the first little beginning of it all!"[273] Cecilia's achievements were further tempered by May's problems. When May's cold subsided, she developed a toothache that caused her to miss many days in the studio. Discouraged by her lack of progress, May left Julian's to enroll in a less demanding school.

These professional concerns did little to temper the enthusiasm of the two young women during their first month in Paris. Their Austin cousins and Florence Estes, a friend of Cecilia's from the Pennsylvania Academy, introduced them to the local community of young American artists. They attended "soirees," where they were served pink drinks and little cakes. In slippers and a borrowed dress, Cecilia danced the polka on a polished floor with a "typical handsome villain Frenchmen, glitteringly polite" with black hair, beard, olive complexion, embroidered shirt, and boutonnière. The exotic evenings included demonstrations of palm reading and hypnotism.

At Florence's tiny apartment on the rue de Vaugirard they were introduced to Alexander Harrison (1853–1930) and Charles "Shorty" Lasar (1856–1936), two prominent expatriate American artists who were living and working in Paris. Both men were alumni of the École des Beaux-Arts and former students of Jean-Léon Gérôme. Harrison, who arrived in France in 1879, showed his ability immediately, and at the age of twenty-seven he exhibited at the 1880 Salon. His Impressionist, plein-air landscapes found favor with each subsequent jury, and every spring when the exhibition opened, his paintings received favorable notices. Charles Lasar, who was three years younger, got a somewhat later start. However, in Gérôme's atelier, his ability as a draughtsman was legendary. Following his admission to the Salon of 1885, he too became an annual exhibitor. By 1888 Lasar was involved in a new venture and was running an art academy catering to the hopeful English-speaking female artists who flocked to Paris looking for instruction and dreaming of fame.

Cecilia Beaux realized that she had much in common with Harrison and Lasar and was eager to become acquainted. Like Beaux, both men were born in Pennsylvania, and although they had settled permanently in France, they still marketed their work in the United States and were frequent contributors to the Pennsylvania Academy's annual exhibitions, where Beaux had seen and admired their work. In 1887, when Beaux was on the jury, Harrison was awarded the Pennsylvania Academy's prestigious Temple Silver Medal.

The three young artists would have been on an equal footing in Philadelphia. They were all about to exhibit work in the Pennsylvania Academy's 58th Annual Exhibition, which was scheduled to open just two weeks after Florence's party. Even Uncle Will expected Beaux to enter a social circle that included Harrison and Lasar. After going to the Academy on varnishing day to help his absent niece by cleaning her entries with a raw potato and touching up the varnish, he sent her an enthusiastic description of Lasar's work and an endorsement of his character from a mutual friend. Beaux also anticipated a good reception, especially from Alexander Harrison. Florence had given her cause to hope for an offer of friendship. "She says Alex Harrison knows of me and says he said of me, 'Oh yes,

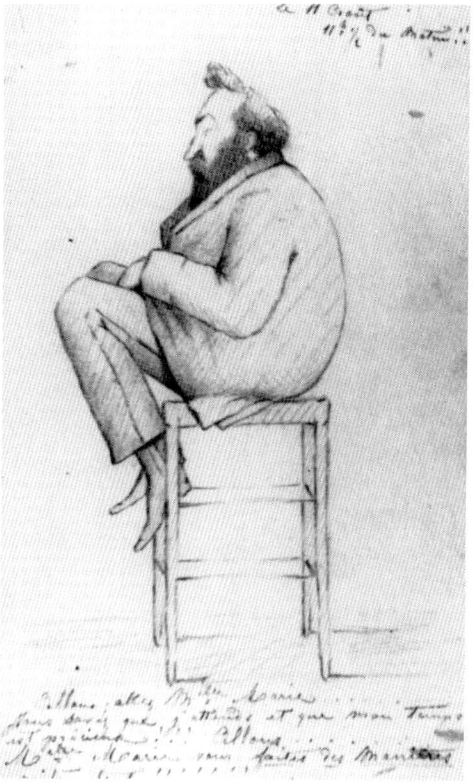

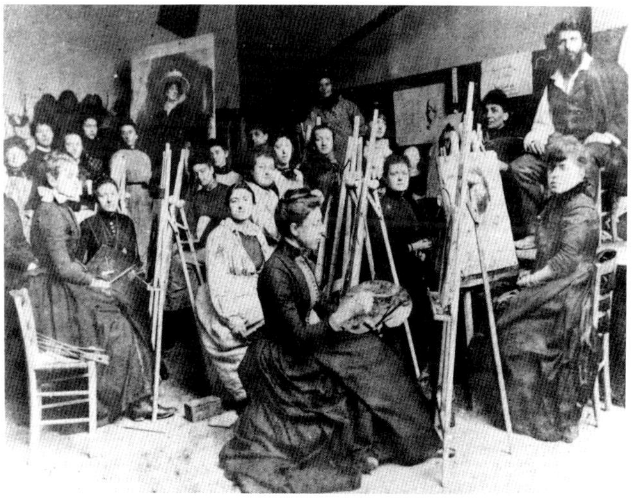

39. TOP: *Artist unknown.* ***M. Julian, August 11, 11:30 A.M.*** *Caricature from the album* Croquis de Mme Geraldi. *André Del Debbio Collection, Paris*

40. BOTTOM: ***Académie Julian at rue de Berri, Atelier with Students,*** *1889. André Del Debbio Collection, Paris*

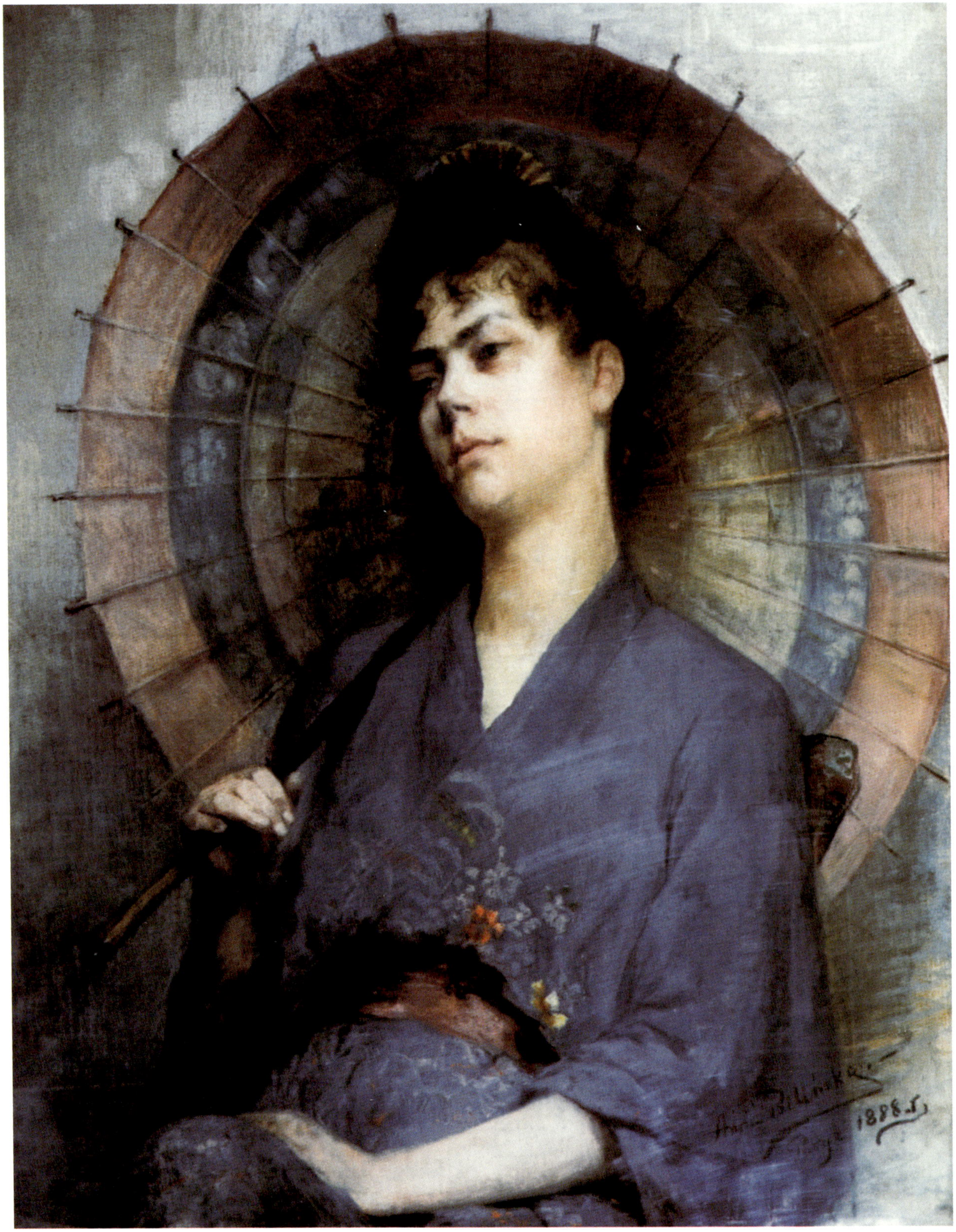

she is arrivée,' which don't [sic] mean arrived in Paris," Cecilia reported proudly.[274]

However, at the party, Beaux was disappointed. In Paris she was not an equal but a suppliant—one of the many hopeful young women on the outer fringe of the Paris art world, attending an obscure branch of the Académie Julian. An attractive young girl occupied Harrison's attentions, and Cecilia barely rated a cordial greeting. "None of us liked him—and we all felt that we have had a blow," she explained. "He is very tall, very handsome, and distinguished—dark hair and gray eyes, and long, dark moustache—And the worst cold, blasé expression. He looks at one as he would a horse—He has evidently two sides—one for Art into which all the weight and feeling of his nature flows—the small part that is left amuses itself coldly."[275]

Charles Lasar made a better impression, especially on May who was soon enrolled in his class. "We howled over Mr. Lazar [sic]" Beaux wrote, "—he was most comical—a funny little young man with intensely bright eyes, and dark hair standing around—and his legs about two feet long." Neither Harrison's manners nor Lasar's appearance dampened Beaux's desire to establish a friendship with these two young artists as she admired their work, and work was what brought her to Paris, not pleasant society. "My head is not turned by anything yet—and it is not going to be," she wrote emphatically, "But I am going to learn all I can from them."[276]

May and Cecilia worked at their separate ateliers through February and into March, braving the bitter winds that whirled down the broad boulevards blowing their long, woolen coats around their thin legs. It snowed constantly. The wet flakes never accumulated to cover the streets in sparkling white but fell in cascades from the gray sky to melt immediately on the wet pavements. At night, in what Cecilia called their "vulgar and uncomfortable pension," there was little warmth. "You poor frozen females," Uncle Will wrote. "We shiver and hug ourselves empathetically when we think of you in that icy room. . . . [B]etter be careful about that charcoal too, because when people die that way it's not at all becoming—color is *horrid*, so I'm told."[277] Cecilia and May were not asphyxiated by their stove, which was frequently borrowed by a neighbor who habitually forgot to return it.

41. OPPOSITE: *Anna Bilińska.* ***Woman with a Japanese Parasol.*** *1888. Pastel, 37 x 29 1/8 in. André Del Debbio Collection, Paris*

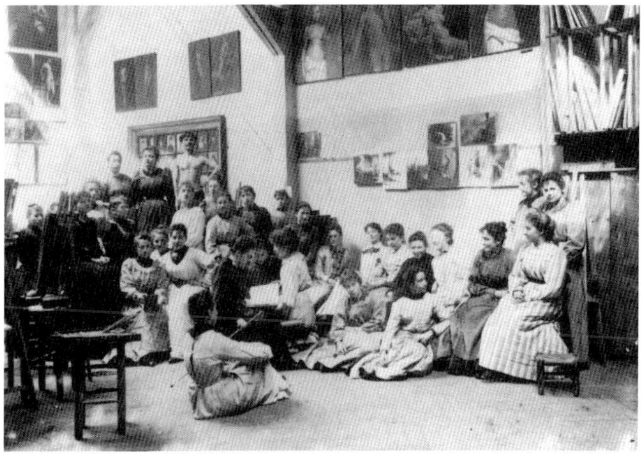

42. ***Académie Julian at Passage des Panoramas.*** *André Del Debbio Collection, Paris*

The instructor at the Académie Julian in March was Tony Robert-Fleury, a French painter of extraordinary skill whose large historical canvases brought him acclaim in the 1860s and 1870s. His most celebrated work, *The Last Day of Corinth*, won the Salon's coveted Medal of Honor in 1870. The year Cecilia arrived in Paris, Fleury was a youthful fifty-one and notably handsome, with gray eyes that Beaux later remembered, "smouldered with burnt out fires."[278] The fires, if they had burned at all, had probably been smothered by a bout of bronchitis from which the long-suffering artist was recovering. Nevertheless, he somewhat painfully negotiated the many stairs to the attic room where the eager women waited with their charcoal studies. Cecilia had given up trying to work in oils in the crowded studio and was drawing along with everyone else, so that when Fleury arrived, exhausted and probably not expecting too much, she knew she would not be able to dazzle him with her facility as a painter. Her drawing skill would have to speak for itself.

"Fleury is much less benign than Bouguereau and don't temper his severities," Beaux wrote. "I was one of the last, and pretty far back in a corner—and was scared stiff . . . when he left my neighbor and turned to my drawing."[279] Cecilia need not have been afraid. Her critique was a triumph. "*C'est bien, c'est bien,*" Fleury told her. He quoted French playwright Peirre Corneille, something to the effect of "a man's value showing in his first act."[280] Where had she studied? Beaux was proud to report that although she had painted a great deal, this experience at Julian's was her first in a life class. She was thrilled when Fleury noticed her name on the drawing and asked, "You are French too?"

Although Fleury's criticism of the other women in the class may have seemed severe to Beaux, his teaching methods were similar to Bouguereau's and were perhaps suggested by the business-minded Julian, who no doubt understood that paying customers must be encouraged. A positive comment, even if only the ubiquitous *pas mal*, was always presented before the instructor proposed areas for improvement. Beaux's drawing, although expert, still needed corrections. So after the praise, Fleury offered advice on keeping dark tones out of the light areas and suggested that the figure be constructed from within. But as he was leaving, Beaux wrote to her family, "he hinted of possibilities before me and as he rose said the nicest thing of all, 'we will do all we can to help you.'"[281]

Help was what Beaux desperately wanted—help and recognition in the undisputed capital of European art. "I want these men, Bouguereau and Fleury, to know me and recognize that I can do something," she told her relatives. Because she arrived in February, Beaux was too late to submit a painting to the 1888 spring Salon by the March 15 deadline, so there would be no opportunity to exhibit her work in the prestigious exhibition during her proposed year of study. Her one chance to gain distinction in that first winter in Paris was to enter a *concours* (competition) between her branch of Julian's at 28 rue de Faubourg St. Honoré and another of his nearby ateliers, a large studio known as The Passages (Atelier Passage des Panoramas). Beaux quickly discovered that the women who attended class at The Passages were much more accomplished than her own classmates, and she welcomed an opportunity to distinguish herself among equals.

Several of her competitors, the Polish artist Anna Bilińska (1857–1893), American Anna Klumpke

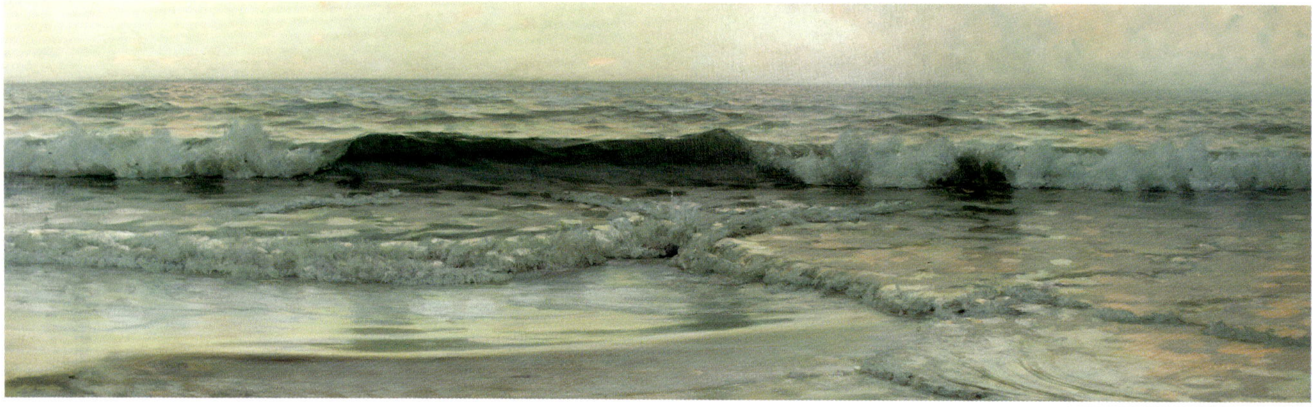

43. ABOVE: *Alexander Harrison.* ***The Wave.*** *ca. 1885. Oil on canvas, 39¼ x 118 in. Pennsylvania Academy of the Fine Arts*

44. OPPOSITE: ***Little Lamerche.*** *ca. 1900. Oil on canvas, 24 x 19 in. Fine Arts Museums of San Francisco*

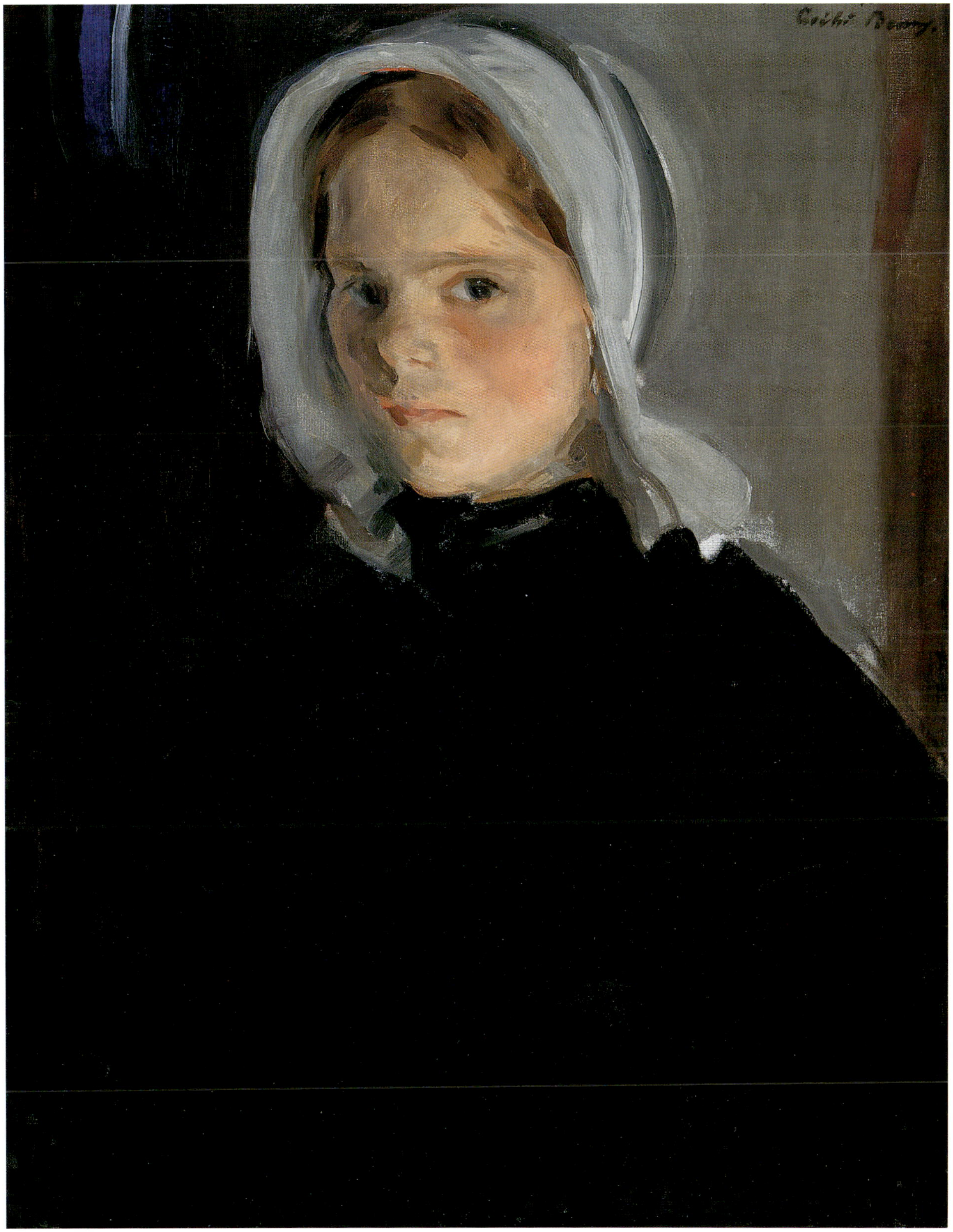

(1865–1912), and Amélie Beaury-Saurel (1848–1924), a Frenchwoman born in Barcelona, were amazingly skilled artists.[282] They had all studied at the Académie Julian for many years and understood the nature and time constraints of such competitions better than Beaux. Bilińska's pastel drawing from the *concours* has survived, so it is possible to see the pose presented to the contestants. The drawing portrays a pensive, dark-haired model in a blue, flowered kimono, holding a Japanese parasol that frames her face within its pattern of concentric circles. Although Bilińska's lyrical drawing is an obvious success, Beaux's painting did not progress well and she soon became disheartened.

> Here I am at this horrid *concours* . . . and such a nasty failure as I have made—I never did anything so badly—I was a fool to undertake to paint it. Bilińska and Klumpke are doing pastels—I don't like them, but they are better and more possible than mine. I have sunk into utter insignificance and have a good mind to stop altogether. Fancy a canvas as big as Ethel Page and doing it so to speak in ones lap—I who am used to twenty-five feet and a big looking glass—I haven't got one good thing in it—it's just a big coarse sign painting without body or bones.[283]

The competition turned out as Beaux expected. The other American, stout, quiet Anna Klumpke won the medal and a cash prize. Bilińska was second and got a medal too. Cecilia's painting was not even placed, and she wrote to her family that she was happy to let it "slide unnoticed into obscurity."[284]

Although Beaux had her discouragements as well as her triumphs at Julian's, one phase of her artistic training in Paris was always an unqualified success. Even on the bleakest of days, there was inspiration at the Louvre. There Beaux studied with the masters, carefully copying the paintings she loved on Henry Thouron's beautifully prepared panels. Sometimes she went to the museum on Saturday, when for two hours the drawing gallery opened, and the guards unfastened the small doors fitted over each frame to protect the artwork from the light. During this treasured time Cecilia would rush in with her sketchbook and copy the Raphael drawings. "Nothing could be more simple or more sufficient," she wrote.[285]

On her excursions to the Louvre, Beaux always had company. In fact, she never ventured out without a friend or suitable chaperone and behaved prudently. She attended church every Sunday, and her faith in the revelation she experienced as a child in Lewistown remained unchanged by bawdy Paris. Even if Cecilia had been tempted to stray from the narrow parameters of conduct and morality intrinsic to her character and upbringing, it would have been swiftly reported. When condescending Cousin Cecil, whom Uncle Will nicknamed "His Own Majesty," sent a letter to Philadelphia questioning Cecilia's decision to attend Vernissage (varnishing day) at the Salon as the guest of Philadelphia painter Clifford Grayson, she quickly defended herself.[286] "You really need not be worried about any indiscretions of ours. We have almost no temptations . . . and we are not going to do anything imprudent anyway."[287] Even so, there were frequent admonitions from home concerning what Aunt Eliza called the wicked city of Paris. "Remember," Eliza warned, "You are first of all a Christian—then a woman and last of all an Artist."[288]

Spring came to Paris in April and transformed the bleak city into a place of extraordinary beauty. Gardens bloomed in profusion. Beds of tulips and hyacinths became bright swatches in a landscape of imposing fountains and trees in early leaf. Lilacs, rhododendrons, and acacias bloomed. The Champs Élysées was filled with open carriages. Children drove miniature coaches pulled by goats. Waiters brought little round tables out to the street, and their customers sat for hours, smoking cigarettes, drinking wine, and watching the passing parade. Even Cecilia and May's ugly pension on the rue Boccador was transformed by the season. The menacing gray waters of the Seine, which flowed near their lodgings, became a sparkling blue ribbon spanned by picturesque stone bridges and flanked by rows of horse chestnut trees in full bloom. According to Cecilia, the only blemish on the beautiful landscape was the half-built Tour Eiffel rising over the city as the centerpiece of the 1889 Universal Exposition, which she considered "a hideous blot."

In nineteenth-century Paris the opening of the spring Salon was as much a part of the season as the warm breezes and the scent of lilacs in the air. Vernissage at the imposing Palais de l'Industrie coincided with Cecilia's birthday, and she attended, chaperoned no doubt, although evidently not by Grayson. There was no party in Cecilia's honor to mark the passing of another year. She preferred to ignore her birthday, although she did acknowledge the greetings of her family, who never understood her reluctance to celebrate. On May 1, 1888, she was thirty-three years old—the same age her mother had been on the day one life was traded for another, and Cecilia Beaux began the long journey that eventually led her to a bright spring day in Paris.

In her autobiography Beaux recalled the Salon and not the bittersweet anniversary. "To Vernissage flocked the élite of Paris, the aristocracy of Society, of the Stage, of Music, and Literature, as well as of the Plastic Arts," she wrote.[289] But although Beaux delighted in the spectacle and listened eagerly to the heated discussions that the work engendered, she readily acknowledged that she had no part in any of it. "The world of Art in Paris was in no wise opened to me, and in fact was too far out of sight to even be longed for," she admitted.[290] Beaux was familiar with many of the exhibitors through their paintings, but she was unable to recognize them. Later she suspected that she may have seen the venerated muralist Puvis de Chavannes (1824–1898) in his black silk cap, or the painters Jean-Paul Laurens (1838–1921) and Jean-Francois Raffaelli (1850–1924), or perhaps even the esteemed Pierre Auguste Renoir (1841–1919). The one celebrity she did recognize was a faded beauty surrounded by a throng of admirers—the actress Sarah

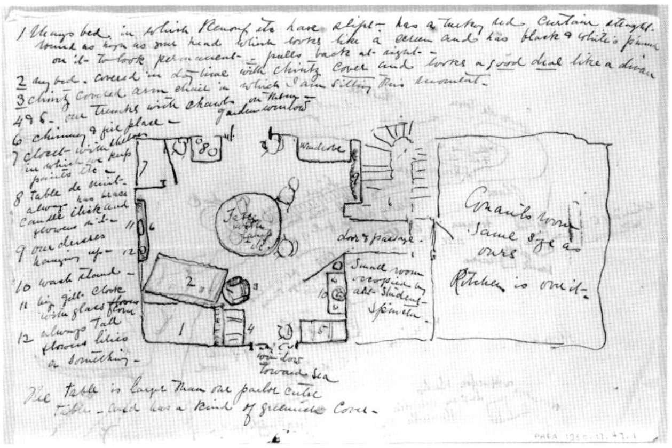

45. ***Sketch of Concarneau House.*** *1888. Brown ink on cream wove paper, 5 1/2 x 8 1/2 in. Pennsylvania Academy of the Fine Arts*

Bernhardt in a black lace dress enhanced by a bodice made entirely of fresh violets.

The pageantry of the 1888 Salon and the miracle of spring lifted the spirit of the city. "Every French heart bounded with the hour's happiness and I knew that my heart was French, too," she recalled.[291] Unfortunately, Cecilia's was not the only heart bounding. The season brought with it the second of her three suitors, Reverend Leonard Woolsey Bacon. Dr. Bacon was a respected minister, a nationally known commentator on religious and secular topics, and the author of two books; he was also a widower with eleven children. Cecilia's family greatly admired Dr. Bacon, and Etta was friendly with his daughters. After the death of his beloved wife, Susan, he waited the prerequisite year and then sailed hopefully to Paris to spend the anniversary of her death with the woman he hoped would be her successor.

News of Dr. Bacon's impending arrival did not fill Cecilia with joy. She wrote to Etta that she feared he would have all sorts of extraordinary plans. "I dread him," she confided.[292] Dr. Bacon was not a handsome man. Tall and spare with thinning hair, his long, dour face was punctuated by a drooping moustache and framed by bushy mutton-chop sideburns. When he arrived in Paris, Cecilia reported that he looked

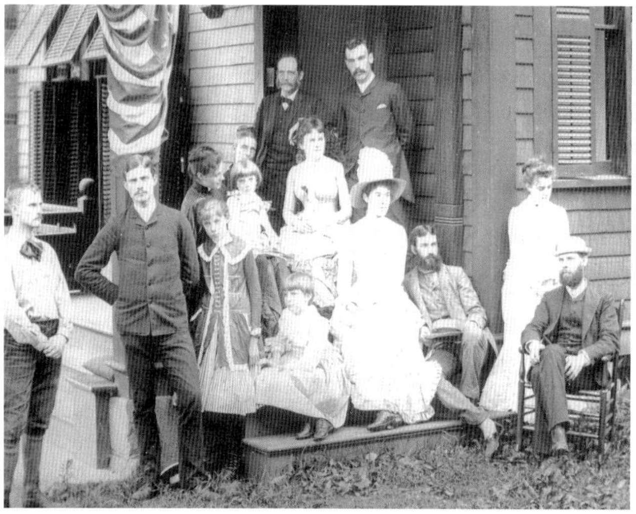

46. ***Leonard Woolsey Bacon** (standing in back; left)* ***and family,*** *ca. 1886. Courtesy of Jack B. Bacon*

haggard. Nevertheless, Dr. Bacon courted Beaux with considerable energy. "I was quite relieved when Dr. Bacon's week was over," she told Etta. "None of them liked him, and he didn't appear to advantage—I was sorry for him. I don't think he meant to be too nice to me, but he was, and they all thought him a rebounding widower which utterly disgusted me of course—the trouble is he does too much of what he feels like doing and is a good deal of an egotist. I'm afraid he thought I was frigid."[293]

Cecilia was evidently not cold enough to dampen the Reverend's ardor. When he arrived back in Philadelphia, he stopped Aunt Emily at the front gate and "flabbergasted" her by asking if she thought he had any chance with Cecilia. Emily, who was scandalized that such a conversation could take place outside the dignity of a formal proposal, rushed into the house in a state, "hands and feet cold, head hot," Uncle Will reported. William Biddle thought it was amusing that Dr. Bacon supposed that his Leilie would want to raise his three young children who were still living at home or funnier still, be a thirty-three-year-old grandmother to Bacon's grandchildren. Nevertheless, Uncle Will was as shocked by the garden-gate conversation as Emily. "How a man so little capable of self-restraint and self-denial with so little spirituality about his everyday life could feel himself a true minister of Christ and Christ's teaching is a mystery to me," he informed Cecilia.[294] Dr. Bacon did not suffer from Cecilia's rejection for very long. In 1890, he married Letitia Wilson Jordan of Philadelphia and fathered three more children.[295]

The Académie Julian closed for the summer on June 2, and after Dr. Bacon left the city, Cecilia and May made plans to leave, too. Their friend Lucy Scarborough Conant (1867–1921), a young American artist studying in Paris, was heading for the coast of Brittany accompanied by her mother. The Conants planned to spend the summer in the picturesque, medieval fishing village of Concarneau, where Alexander Harrison had rented a studio and Charles Lasar was teaching a summer class. When the Conants invited Cecilia and May to join them, the two cousins accepted, packed their bags, and headed off for a working holiday.

The four women took a train to the coast and, eschewing the popular Voyagers Hotel, rented second-floor rooms in the picturesque but primitive home of Madame and Monsieur Valdinaire, Concarneau's only florists. The Valdinaires' house and approximately an acre of flowerbeds were entirely enclosed by a high stone wall. Beaux's new landlords occupied the first floor and lived comfortably with a flock of chickens and a goat, who evidently enjoyed spending a good part of the day indoors. Upstairs in the women's rooms, things were spare but tidy. Beaux recalled that Papa Valdinaire cheerfully tacked wallpaper over the lath and plaster walls, sealing in cobwebs and spiders and brightening the atmosphere considerably. The windows were refurbished with white lace and chintz curtains, the furniture was adequate, and there were always flowers from the gardens to adorn the mantel and the nightstand.

Cecilia planned to paint in the garden. Initially, she thought she would attempt a portrait of a neighborhood Breton girl who wore the traditional lace headdress known as a *coiffe*. But when she walked down the road to request permission from the young woman's parents, she was rebuffed. "We found that the people, especially the country folk, did not really like '*les artistes*,'" she recalled.[296] Perhaps it was not Beaux's profession that bothered the local residents but her nationality. Although artists from all over the world flocked to Brittany to paint, a sizable number who made Concarneau their summer headquarters were Americans eager to experiment with Impressionist plein-air painting, a style of work still considered avant-garde in the United States. In 1886 an exhibition of 300 Impressionist paintings organized by the art dealer Paul Durand-Ruel opened in New York and inspired a generation of American artists to travel to the French countryside for inspiration.

Beaux tried plein-air painting. She tramped determinedly along the seaside paths, searching out appropriate subjects for landscapes and attempting small, experimental studies. When she eventually located willing models, Beaux struggled to apply Impressionist techniques to portraiture. However, nothing seemed to work. Her plans to paint outdoors were foiled by the changeable weather. There were days of rain followed by short periods of sun when Beaux would rush out and try to locate her models. "I am feeling a good deal discouraged about painting—although I work all day—not taking a nap in the afternoon I don't seem to accomplish anything in particular," she confided to her family. "It is so hard to find the same model for continuous and uninterrupted work."[297] Beaux soon realized that if she wanted a consistently available model, she would have to paint someone in her own household, and since Lucy and May were both working on their own canvases, Mrs. Conant was the only logical choice. She was ready to pose for Beaux on a moment's notice—whenever the sun broke through the overcast.

In Concarneau, away from the politics of the Parisian art world and the isolating female academies, Beaux established a more collegial relationship with "Shorty" Lasar and Alexander Harrison. The American artists socialized with one another and Beaux, May, and Lucy Conant became part of a lively group that included Harrison, Lasar, Florence Estes, the landscape painter Howard Russell Butler (1856–1934), and the painter and critic Arthur Hoeber (1854–1915). In the pleasant camaraderie of the seaside resort, where the artists often went out painting in a group, Beaux completely reversed her opinion of Alexander Harrison. "Mr. Harrison is the biggest and swellest of all," she informed her family. "I like him better than I did in Paris and there certainly is a good deal to him—hav'nt [sic] seen his studio yet but they say he has made some lovely *pochades* (sketches).[298]

It was not long before Beaux visited Harrison's studio, and both Harrison and Lasar returned the favor and called on Cecilia. Lasar advocated strictures for composition and color that most of his female students embraced like a lifeline—preferring technical advice to the vague *pas trop mal* they heard so often from the French masters. But although Beaux listened with interest, her own approach was more intuitive than technical, and she had enough confidence to understand that Lasar's method was not the only one. "You never saw anything so scientific as Mr. Lasar," she wrote to Uncle Will. "It is splendid for a teacher but I'm afraid it will be the ruin of him as a painter."[299]

Harrison's criticism was usually more useful, although chauvinistic and patronizing, which at the time troubled no one. Cecilia was thrilled when she was told that Harrison was so optimistic about her prospects that he declared, "She puts brains in her work, and that is what few women do—I can tell you."[300] When Harrison paid Cecilia the compliment of asking if she would like to paint his portrait, she wrote to her family, "I couldn't contain a small screech."[301] Harrison found the time to pose, and Beaux, who evidently calmed down enough to paint the portrait, felt honored to be given the opportunity. Although she was unsure of the result (and indeed the lower section of the canvas was never completed), she created a strong painting that showed the value of her summer working outdoors. Her palette lightened considerably, and her brushwork displayed a facility and confidence absent from the expert but careful work she completed in Philadelphia.

The "association of superiority" that Beaux established with Lasar and Harrison was what she had hoped for when she braved the rough waters of the North Atlantic to study in Europe. That summer in Concarneau she finally realized her aspirations and became a member of a vibrant community of serious, professional artists. No matter how harsh their criticism, it was clear that neither Lasar nor Harrison regarded her as another female amateur biding time while waiting for a marriage proposal. Cecilia was not about to disappoint them. By August she had made some pivotal decisions, which she began gradually to share with Uncle Will. "People do seem to me more interesting than anything else in the world and that is the bottom of my success in heads," she wrote. "But depending on them for all one's happiness is different—and you must remember that art is more like a person than an idea to me—a real friend." During those summer months in Concarneau, Cecilia decided that art, not marriage, would define her life. Her choice was neither easily decided nor painlessly dispatched. It necessitated resolving her relationship with the last and most fitting of her three suitors—a young man who had offered a proposal of marriage and was waiting patiently for a reply.

Edwin Swift Balch was the wealthy and well-connected son of a prominent Philadelphia attorney, Thomas Balch. His family traveled widely, and he had been educated in Germany and France before returning to the United States to attend Fay's School in Newport, Rhode Island. In 1875, he entered Princeton University and studied there briefly. "In 1875 I entered the class of '78 at Princeton as a sophomore," Balch later recalled. "I stayed there till spring, when one Sunday Dr. McCosh spoke in chapel about 'elephants and other natural products of the soil' which made me smile. He objected to my smiling and as a result I left Princeton and entered Harvard that fall as a Junior."[302] Perhaps Balch endured the inevitable gaffes of the Harvard faculty with equanimity, or perhaps Harvard better endured Balch, who cultivated a self-deprecating humor, because he graduated from the institution without incident and subsequently returned to Philadelphia to study law. Balch was admitted to the bar in May 1881 but later acknowledged, "I practiced law for a couple of years but did not like it." So instead of spending his days in an office, Balch lived the adventurous and creative life of a gentleman with the means to indulge an insatiable curiosity for both art and nature. He pursued these duel interests with skill and considerable devotion. For a time he took up painting and studied at the Pennsylvania Academy of the Fine Arts with Thomas Eakins and Thomas Hovenden.[303] By 1887 Balch was leasing a workspace at 1520 Chestnut Street. Although he was a distant relative of Catharine Drinker and may have met Cecilia through the family, it was probably the proximity of their studios that precipitated a friendship between the two young artists.[304] For the next five years, between 1887 and 1891, Balch dedicated himself to his profession and was a regular exhibitor at the Pennsylvania Academy. His best showing came in 1891, when three of his paintings were accepted in the annual exhibition.

One can only imagine what Cecilia Beaux's life might have held if she had decided to marry the energetic and entertaining Mr. Balch. If she suspected that assuming the duties of a wife would curtail her career, she was probably right. In the nineteenth century, when marriage was as demanding and time consuming as gaining success as a painter, combining the two separate spheres was practically impossible. Most of Beaux's female contemporaries in art remained single, with the notable exception of Berthe Morisot (1841–1895), who exhibited with the Impressionists and at the age of thirty-three married the brother of Édouard Manet. Painful as her decision was, Beaux faced it squarely and wrote first to Edwin Balch and then to Uncle Will, who obviously expected that after Cecilia returned from her year in France she would become Mrs. Edwin Balch.

> And now prepare your dear mind for the real and serious thing I have to say—You will not perhaps believe the struggle that it costs me—because I know this is the real end—It is all over between me and Mr. Balch—It is not his fault—but I believe now that he is reconciled to it—He speaks of it as "the break which I foresaw" and at the end—"I have written more but torn it up as it is silly to reproach you." He will never know how much I cared for him and do still. What I admired in him, what attracted me, and what I really loved—time and distance could not, and have not changed—but what was not satisfied has grown more imperative and for the first time I know that it will not do—I have expanded here and could not get into the place I might have got before—though even then I should have had to stifle something—You will say that I ought to have known this before—that if I had listened to reason I should have saved many people much pain—to which I can only say that no one but myself can know how I clung to what I found in him—I know that it was selfish, but I hoped to make up for it—Of one thing I feel sure that he does not suffer now more than I—and he has as regards this side of his life, a much more hopeful future than I—All the same I ought to have known before. I ought to have made the sacrifice and taken the risk of losing. Do not think I am not paying for it—That is all—.[305]

When news of Cecilia's decision reached Philadelphia, her family was supportive. "I confess to being taken by surprise," Uncle Will wrote. "Because we had all been so industriously preparing for and reconciling ourselves to the other thing. . . . I am sorry for him—but do not think his life will suffer."[306]

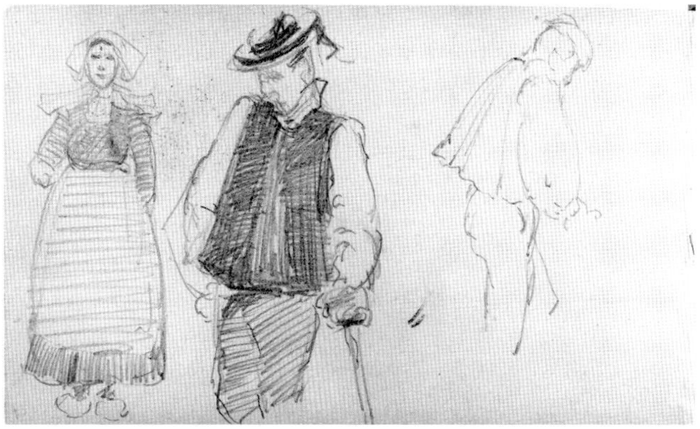

47. ***Sketchbook #3 (Concarneau)*** *[Breton Man and Woman in Native Dress]. 1888. Graphite on buff wove leaves, 3 3/4 x 6 1/4 in. Pennsylvania Academy of the Fine Arts*

Indeed, it did not. Balch married Eugenia Hargous MacFarlane in 1904 and after Eugenia died in 1921, he remarried three years later at the age of sixty-eight. Although Balch maintained a keen interest in art, in the 1890s he turned his attentions to his fascination with the natural world.[307] An avid mountaineer who had climbed some of Europe's most challenging peaks, Balch maintained a lifelong interest in mountain climbing and Antarctic exploration. He served as president of the Philadelphia Geographic Society, was a founder of the American Alpine Society, and authored more than forty articles and eight books, including *Antarctic* in 1902 and *Mount McKinley* and *Mountain Climbers' Proofs* in 1914. His reputation as an Antarctic historian was rewarded when Balch Glacier on the East Coast of Graham Land in Antarctica was named in his honor.

After Cecilia resolved her relationship with Edwin Balch, she turned her full attention to her career and soon decided that one season in Julian's atelier had not been adequate. She had arrived too late to complete a canvas for the Salon, and she had been too much of a novice to make the connections and alliances that would serve her to good advantage when she returned home. Because her family was expecting her to go back to Philadelphia in January,

24 Drawing

a spot of drapery falling in a straight direction.

Drapery may take the direction of the movement exaggerated.

Folds connect draperies.

Ornamental folds of drapery above send

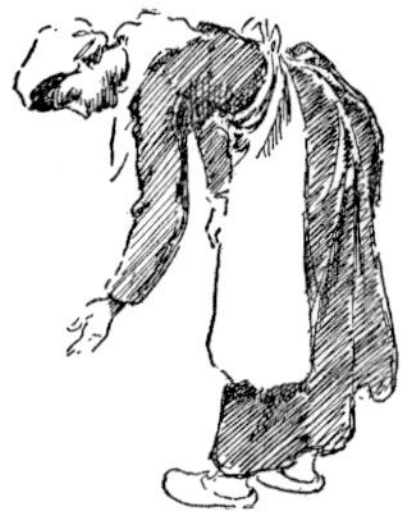

FIG. 28.

an arm or leg down while folds below send it up.

Have variety in bunching the folds when draping a figure. Drapery may be used to intensify movement in any desired direction.

76 Composition

Figure 24.—A showy character requires a large amount of oblique concentration of masses in a portrait.

Figure 25.—A cold nature will have very little oblique feeling in the figure.

Figure 26.—When a figure is bending over, the accessory masses should take the

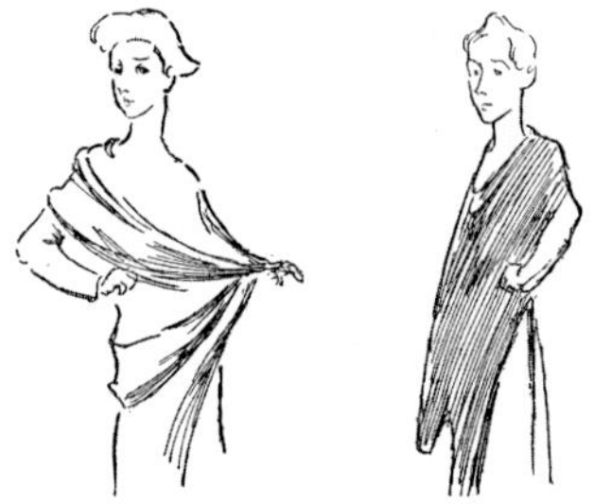

FIG. 24. FIG. 25.

reverse direction, which will emphasize the leaning movement.

Figure 27.—A stiff position can be made easy by keeping the dark spots oblique to one another; by keeping the darks vertical

48-49. LEFT TO RIGHT: *Charles A. Lasar.* ***"Movement"*** *and* ***"Composition,"*** *from* Practical Hints for Art Students *by Charles A. Lasar (Duffield & Co., 1910)*

and because the extra season in Paris would require their financial support, she had to convince them that her decision was a wise one. To this end, she enlisted the help of Lasar and Harrison, who both supported her decision. "They all praise me and say I must stay over one more winter to clinch it," she wrote to her uncle.[308] When he didn't respond, she waited a few weeks and again implored him to let her stay, first citing the emotional burden she would have to bear if she resided in the same geographic area as Mr. Balch, and then progressing to the real reason she was not prepared to return home.

> I am writing anxiously now to hear what you think about my staying over here a few months longer—you will easily understand that now I wish to stay as never before—It would be very painful for me to go home now—and for him too. I am besides very anxious to paint something for next year's Salon. I have nothing here now that I could leave that is as good as what I can do—and with the help that I have now, on account of Mr. Lasar and Mr. Harrison's interest as well as Mr. Julian's it is a chance I might never have again.[309]

Of course, Uncle Will acquiesced. He could not bear to deny Cecilia anything; indeed, years later in a last letter written in a shaky hand, he confessed that he had not realized the depth of his feelings for her until 1888, when she left to study in Paris. Aunt Eliza, who loved Cecilia no less, worried that although her Leilie would eventually return, she would be a different person. "You must not expand so enormously that this old home and these old hearts cannot hold you when you come home!" she wrote.[310]

With her immediate future decided, Beaux made the most of her last month in Brittany. She worked on three major paintings in Concarneau; the portraits of Harrison and Mrs. Conant and a life-sized study of two local women in their *coiffes*, a canvas she called her "two heads picture." The two heads presented the most challenging problem, as she attempted to reconstruct the pose from sketches, notes, her own memory of impressions glimpsed outdoors, and Lasar's theories on color and composition. Lasar told her that she had "bit off more than she could chew." For some reason this criticism affected Cecilia profoundly although it was offered idly and without malice.[311] "It is so hard for a woman to work with a system and science and calm good sense and infuse in it all the spirit and feeling—dignity and unity that place it on a high level—and it is such a mistake to think that the ideal of French art is anything less than this," she wrote in discouragement.[312]

While Cecilia was trying valiantly—within what she suspected were her limitations as a woman—to capture the ideal of French art, French painters were not waiting for foreign artists to grasp their theories but were pushing the boundaries of painting beyond the academic pictures popular in the Salon or the agreeable landscapes of the Impressionists. While Cecilia Beaux was carefully fashioning her career, stitch by stitch and note by careful note, a revolution was taking place ten miles down the road in the village of Pont Aven. Under the tutelage of Paul Gauguin (1848–1903), the young painters Emile Bernard (1868–1941) and Paul Serusier (1864–1927) were abandoning the principles of Impressionism and developing the colorful, decorative style that combined observation with imagination and came to be called Synthetism.

Cecilia, who knew nothing about the artistic insurrection in Pont Aven, happily ended the idyllic summer with a whirl of social events. Mr. Balch notwithstanding, Cecilia spent so much time with a furloughed British soldier named Radcliffe that when news of their friendship reached Etta in Philadelphia, Cecilia felt compelled to defend herself in a long explanatory letter. "It is the utmost absurdity to call it an 'affair,'" she wrote. "There was not a vestige of lovemaking about it beyond the fact that for the two weeks we knew him he was with me whenever he decently and sensibly could be. We liked each other immensely and when it came time for good-bye at Rennes—it was really a tough job to do it."[313] Beaux also spent as much time as possible with Alexander Harrison, although their relationship was entirely professional. As Etta later noted, "She found things out from Alexander Harrison (only about the sea, I may add!)."[314] Before the colony of American artists at Concarneau went their separate ways, Beaux, who had not lost her knack for writing clever verse, composed the following poem for her platonic friend.

Alexander Harrison

Oh who can bear comparison?
Was painter ever seen,
Who for ocean blue or green
Or glimmering opal sheen
With pinky throbs between,
Most mooningly marine,
Who can then bear comparison
With Alexander Harrison?

At the end of October, Cecilia and May left Concarneau for a trip to Italy financed by Uncle Will. The two cousins journeyed first to Venice, where they spent six days, enjoyed spectacular weather, ate gelato in Piazza San Marco, went for a gondola ride, and visited the glass studios at Murano. From Venice they journeyed to Florence, where Beaux was less enamored with the scenery but fell in love with the artwork. She admired portraits by the Renaissance painters Hans Holbein the Younger (1497–1543), Albrecht Dürer (1497–1528), and Lorenzo di Credi (1458–1537), whose distinction, she wrote, lay in the fact that they "had never seen pictures, only people, and when they sat down to paint a man they made him hair for hair."[315] The painting Beaux admired most was a portrait by Titian (1485–1576) at the Palazzo Pitti, which she felt was painted completely honestly without concessions to style or fashionable artifice. She called it

Young Florentine Gentleman, Unknown, but from her description, it was most probably the painting known today as *The Young Englishman* (ca. 1540–45). "It shows a young man disdainful of being painted, a mentally lonely mind, born at the wrong date and conscious of the anachronism, Perhaps an Englishman," Beaux recalled.[316]

Cecilia came down with the flu in Florence and spent three days in bed. When she recovered, the sojourn was almost over. The two cousins packed their bags and headed back to Paris. On their way they stopped in Avignon to pay homage to Papa Beaux's hometown. The Beaux relatives were dispersed, her father's siblings deceased. Uncle Edmund had died in 1875 and Aunt Marguerite Rousset in 1884. Cecilia apparently did not attempt to see her cousins Louise and Eugene Beaux or Paul Rousset, who were still living in the area, because years later Etta went to Avignon motivated by a desire to see if her daughter Ernesta's slim, dark beauty was a heritage from the Beaux side of the family. Etta was disappointed to discover that her French cousins were all plump and blonde.

Beaux did not linger in Avignon. She longed to get back to work, to rent a studio, and to establish the kind of community in Paris that she had enjoyed in Concarneau. "I must have a studio this winter and I don't want to go off to some remote part of Paris far from all my friends, especially Lasar and Harrison," she informed Uncle Will.[317] Paris was beckoning. In later years Beaux remembered that she headed toward the French capital "like a needle to the Pole."[318] Once the cousins arrived in the city, they wasted no time but went directly to 30 rue Vaugirard in the Latin Quarter and rented a room in the hotel where Florence Estes lived and where Beaux and May had first been introduced to Charles Lasar and Alexander Harrison.

"I would like to boast openly that I have lived in an attic in Paris, a tiny chamber in the mansard, with a dormer opening its *croissée* eastward and sunward," Beaux wrote many years later.[319] The little apartment was picturesque; a fulfillment of what Beaux had dreamed Paris would be. From her attic window she could see the Senate and the quarters of a Cavalry regiment, the Cuirassiers de l'Opéra. Sometimes Cecilia was awakened in the middle of the night by the sound of the soldiers returning from duty. Leaving her warm bed, she would rush to the window and fling it open to gaze at the spectacle of armored men on great war horses. As they rode in close ranks up the street, the horses' hooves beat out their majestic resonance through the somnolent neighborhood.

There was no restaurant in the hotel, and every morning the cousins descended five long flights of waxed steps in search of breakfast. Beaux, fit and healthy, negotiated them easily, sprinting up and down many times a day. At thirty-three she understood that she was getting a somewhat late start as a professional artist, yet she felt wonderful. "I suppose I must realize that life flows later with me though I feel so young and buoyant, that is as young as I ever did feel," she wrote to her uncle.[320]

Once established at rue de Vaugirard, Cecilia rented a small studio at 34 Notre Dame des Champs and informed Etta that she was thinking of purchasing an Aesthetic dress to wear with a buckle purchased in Venice and a string of turquoise beads.[321] Despite her new lodgings in the heart of the Parisian art community, the dress was as far into a Bohemian lifestyle as Cecilia Beaux was prepared to journey. From January through March she had one goal in mind—to paint a portrait for the spring Salon. To that end, she persuaded the beautiful Louise Kinsella, the sister of Kate Kinsella, an Irish artist Beaux had met in Concarneau, to pose for her. Louise was a stunning young woman, as fair as a baby. Her pale blonde hair cascaded down her back. And when she smiled, she revealed perfect white teeth and a single dimple. Louise set her own style, eschewing the bustles fashionable at the time and showing up at social occasions in clothes fashioned of soft material. Her only adornment other than her natural beauty was a shawl, which she draped over graceful shoulders.

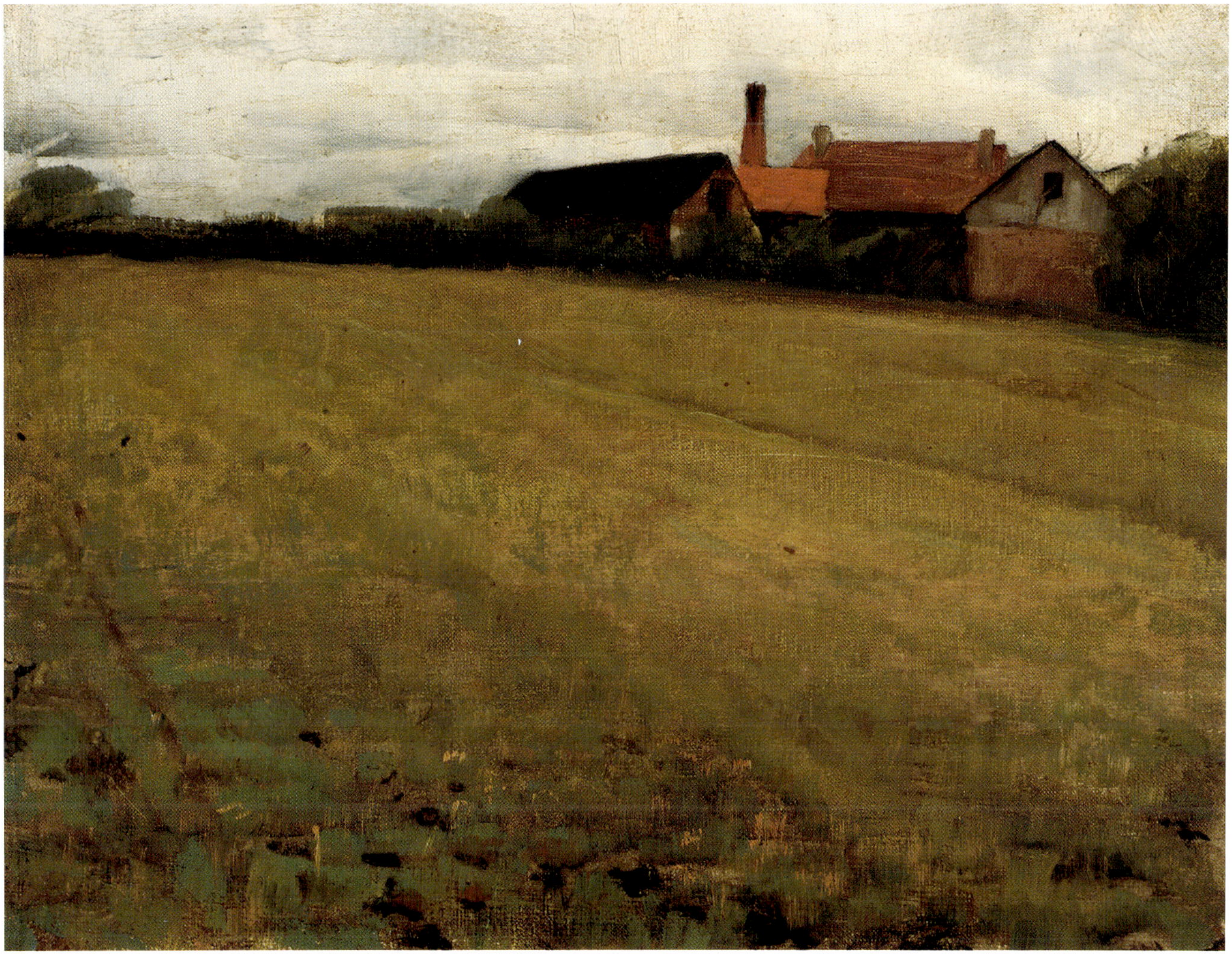

50. ***Landscape with Farm Building.*** *1888. Concarneau, France. Oil on canvas, 11 1/16 x 14 3/16 in. Pennsylvania Academy of the Fine Arts*

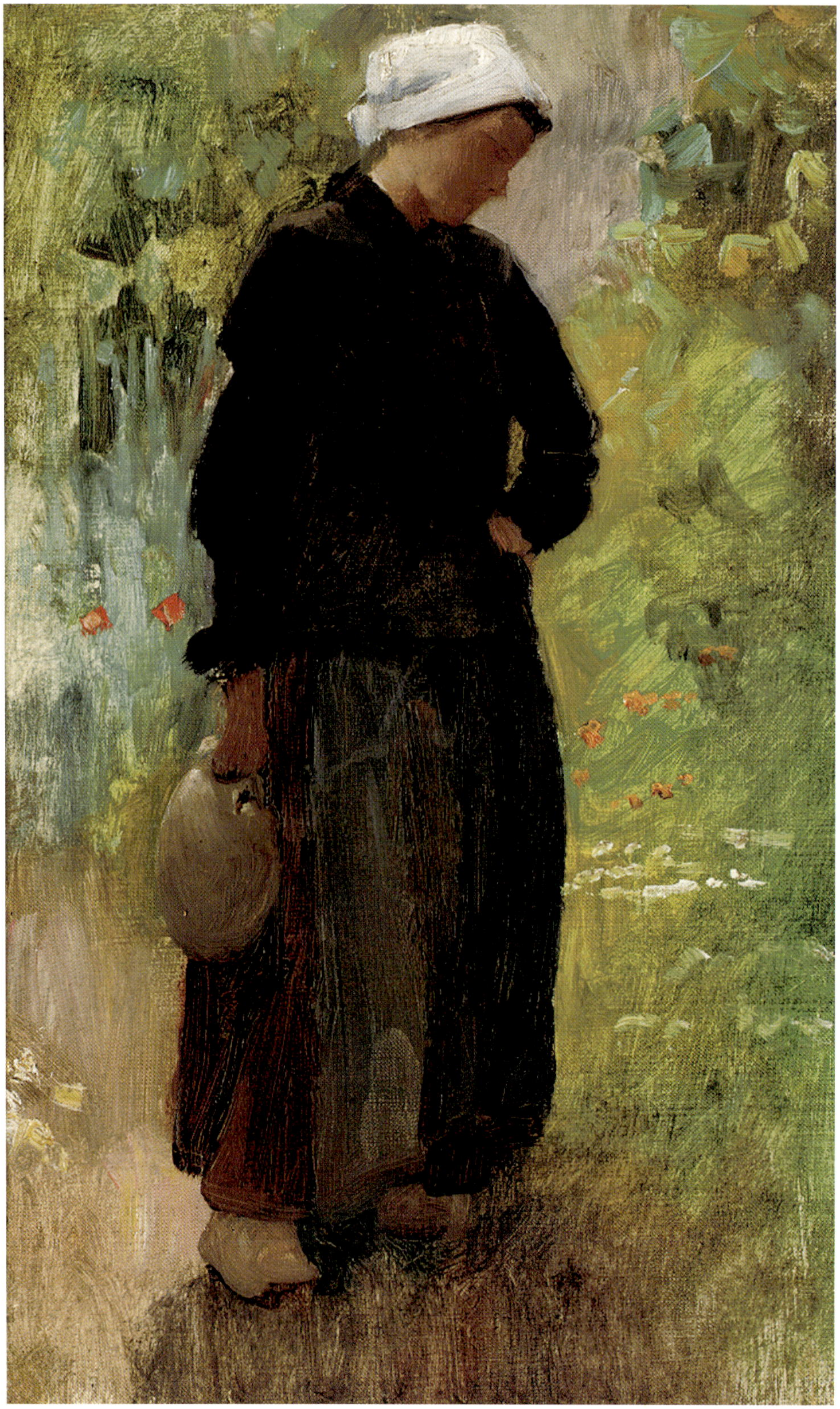

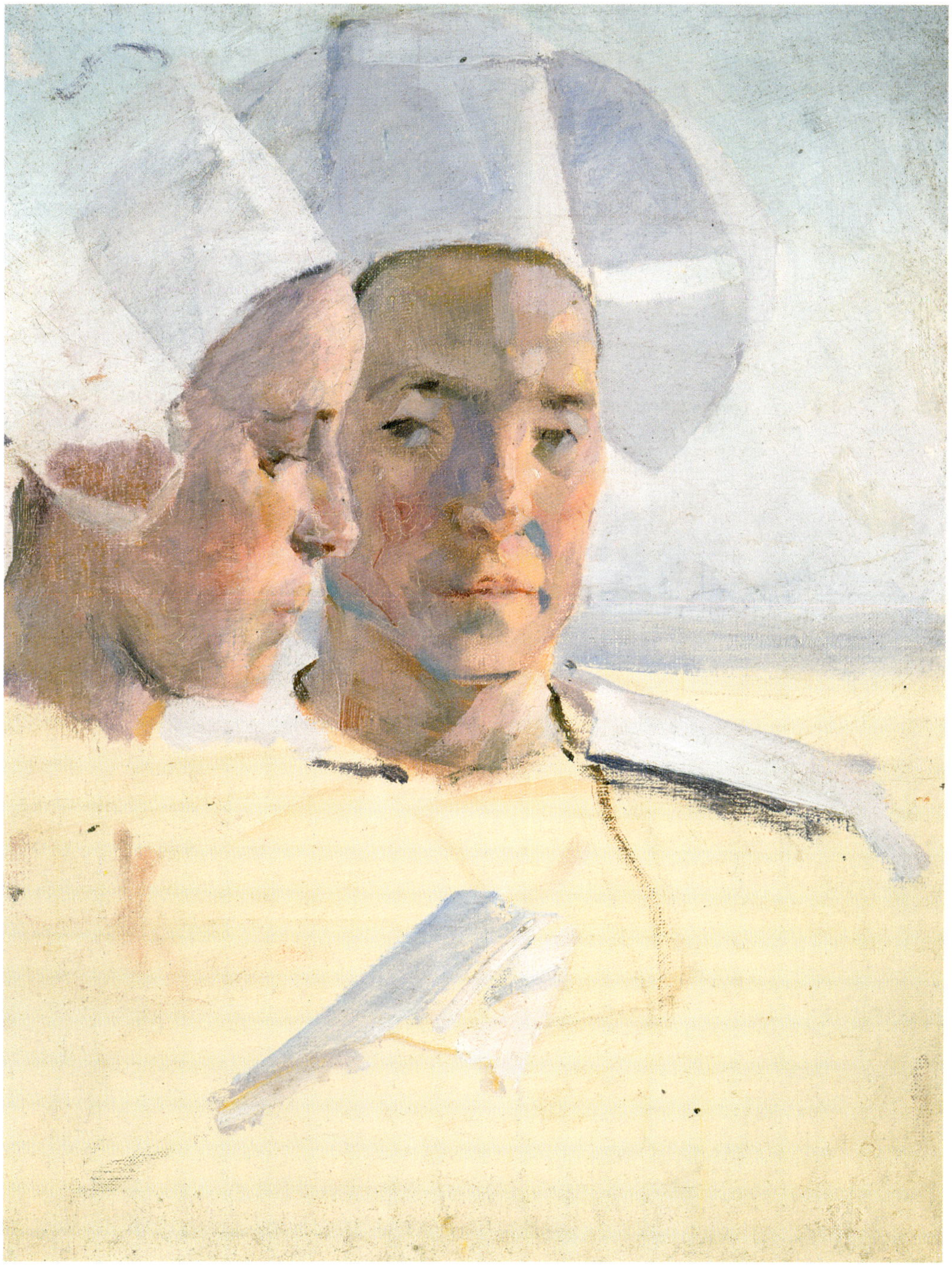

51. OPPOSITE: ***A Country Woman, Concarneau, France.*** *1888. Oil on canvas, 14 1/16 x 8 5/8 in., 1888. Pennsylvania Academy of the Fine Arts*

52. ABOVE: ***Study of Two Breton Women, Concarneau, France.*** *1888. Oil on canvas, 13 11/16 x 10 5/8 in., 1888. Pennsylvania Academy of the Fine Arts*

Beaux hoped that her portrait of Louise would progress quickly, so that by the first of February, she could enroll at the Académie Julian. However, the painting proved more difficult than expected, and although she understood the political advantage of being associated with Julian's school, Beaux felt that she should concentrate her attention on the Salon entry. "I found that it was impossible to work at the portrait and go to a *cours* [art school] at the same time as the sittings were irregular and occupied the middle of the day rather than the morning," Beaux explained in a letter to Etta. "Besides, I was too worried and tormented by it—and could not have undertaken *cours* work at the same time."[322]

Although she was unable to attend the Académie Juilian, Beaux found a school that offered evening sessions. After painting all day in her studio, she climbed many dark stairs to the vast gas-lit interior of the Académie Colorossi where many similarly ambitious women were working to improve their prospects. At Colorossi's, Beaux received criticism from the painters Gustave Courtois (1853–1923) and Pascal-Adolphe-Jean Dagnan-Bouveret (1852–1929). Colorossi's was a business enterprise modeled on the Académie Julian. The classes were less expensive, the atmosphere rough, the teachers considerably younger, but the atelier just as crowded. Perhaps the teachers were not well compensated because when Courtois came to criticize, Cecilia reported that he breezed through the studio in fifteen minutes saying only a word or two to each student.

Although Beaux worked conscientiously at Colorossi's and hung on every word of criticism offered by the busy and somewhat imperious teachers, she never forgot the purpose of her extended stay in Paris—her portrait of Louise Kinsella and the March deadline for Salon submissions. As she worked to complete the painting, her most valued advice came from the artists who generously agreed to visit her studio, which was conveniently located in a district frequented by painters. Carolus Duran, Jean-Léon Gérôme, and Jean-Paul Laurens were among the many notables who maintained ateliers in the area. Although some of their accommodations bordered on the lavish, Cecilia's space consisted of a rather shabby single-story lean-to illuminated by two long windows and a skylight. She was able to purchase most of the necessary accoutrements from the departing tenant, who had used the space for the same purpose. There was the essential stove, an easel, a few chairs, a long table to function as a taboret, and a couch. Cecilia purchased some rugs and a wall hanging to keep out the cold.

Beaux's absence from the Académie Julian did not deter her from asking the proprietor to stop by to see her painting. Within two days Julian arrived, squeezed his considerable bulk into the draughty room, and stood in front of her portrait with his arms folded. "I was alone and a good deal scared as what I had done to the background was sunken in and the whole thing looked weak and horrid," Beaux recalled. When Julian finally spoke, he was overcome with emotion. "I fear for you, I fear for you," he warned. "Then he went on to tell me that I was a real artist," Beaux reported. "But that he feared that in my enthusiasm for the ideal I would allow myself to fall into convention—that I must have more method more system. That I should compose areas in my picture, my portrait, as my taste and imagination dictated, search until I found exactly what I wanted and then copy it with the conscientiousness 'd'un religion'! He almost wept when he said this," she recalled.[323] Beaux thought the incident amusing, but in fact, Julian's remarks were prophetic, although not in the way he feared. Cecilia Beaux did not become a conventional, academic painter. Her work was honest, skillful, and free from artifice. However, she would later be branded with the disparaging term conventional, by twentieth-century critics who looked down on the method and system Rodolphe Julian advocated.

Cecilia's adherence to academic principles was the norm for most American artists of her generation. Children born before the Civil War grew up with respect for craftsmanship and tradition. There were rules that were not to be broken and conventions that were to be respected. The problem with Beaux's work developed when she took years off her age, thus associating herself with a younger generation of artists, who grew up in a profoundly different atmosphere. The American artists who would abandon academic principles and create a new aesthetic based on gritty realism and self-expression were already in Paris. That winter twenty-three-year-old Robert Henri, the man who was to lead this artistic insurrection, enrolled at the Académie Julian along with four of his friends. The group lived together in an attic, subsisting on rice and horsemeat. Their indiscretions caused them no concern. They drank too much, spent their evenings at the Folies Bergère and the Moulin Rouge, and soon paid little attention to the masters at the Académie Julian. Henri thought Bouguereau's canvases "tame and unlifelike."[324]

It is unlikely that Beaux met Henri, although they were both former Academy students. Henri was ten years younger, a fact that would not have bothered her if the young man had looked or behaved like a gentleman. Henri was scarred by acne, and in Beaux's opinion, his sloping forehead would have indicated a lack of intelligence. As to his indulgences, Beaux had no patience for such foolishness. She later wrote, "A girl from the beginning of her life as an artist should know that her physical energy must be conserved like precious oil, like water in the desert, like ammunition in a besieged camp, like food and fuel in a dash to the pole. . . . Art has no dealings with the dregs of life. The foam on the brimming cup is the only acceptable offering.[325]

Beaux did not deal with the dregs but only with artists she respected. Her naïveté protected her from understanding the complexities of the personal relationships among her colleagues in Paris. During her second winter she called on American painter Elizabeth Gardiner (1837–1922), who worked in a nearby studio on rue Notre Dame des Champs. "People say such horrid things about her and Bouguereau which are entirely untrue as anyone could tell who saw her,"[326] Beaux informed her family. "He has been anxious to marry her for a long time but his Maman won't let him and as he is a little fat old man this is funny to the American mind."[327] Bouguereau's maman, who objected to the match, died in 1896, and after a courtship of approximately nineteen years the pair married. Gardiner was fifty-nine and Bouguereau seventy-one.

Beaux considered the older generation of American painters to be suitably refined and was thrilled when both Harrison and Lasar, whose personal lives were kept private, visited her studio. "Mr. Lasar came the other day while Louise was posing and approved of it—leaned back in his chair and said 'that's nice, that's nice,' which was a great deal from him," Cecilia proudly informed her family.[328] Harrison told her that she was "getting" the model, and thus encouraged, Beaux persevered in the cold and damp until March 12, when Louise posed for the last time and the painting was finished. "The frame has come for the picture, and it looks quite well—not fresh nor free but it is noble and dignified," Cecilia wrote to her Aunt Eliza.[329] Cecilia framed the painting, stowed her supplies, swept the studio, and invited her friends in to see the result of so much concentrated effort. For each visitor there was a bunch of violets, "to give a sweet impression," Beaux wrote.

Many of Beaux's American colleagues were fortunate and finished their Salon paintings on time. Anna Klumpke sent a portrait of her mother, Florence Estes submitted an engraving, and Lucy Conant sent a work she called *Etude*. Charles Lasar submitted three paintings. Clifford Grayson finished his entry. Elizabeth Gardiner completed two paintings, as did Alexander Harrison. But others met with disappointment. "I suppose if all the heart aches and groaning in Paris had been audible for the last few weeks there would have been a lamentation louder than the rolling of cab wheels in the streets—but they are groanings which can not be uttered nor by any means comforted," Beaux explained.[330]

When her painting was completed, Beaux returned to the Académie Julian, although during her second year in Paris, she was savvy enough to attend class at

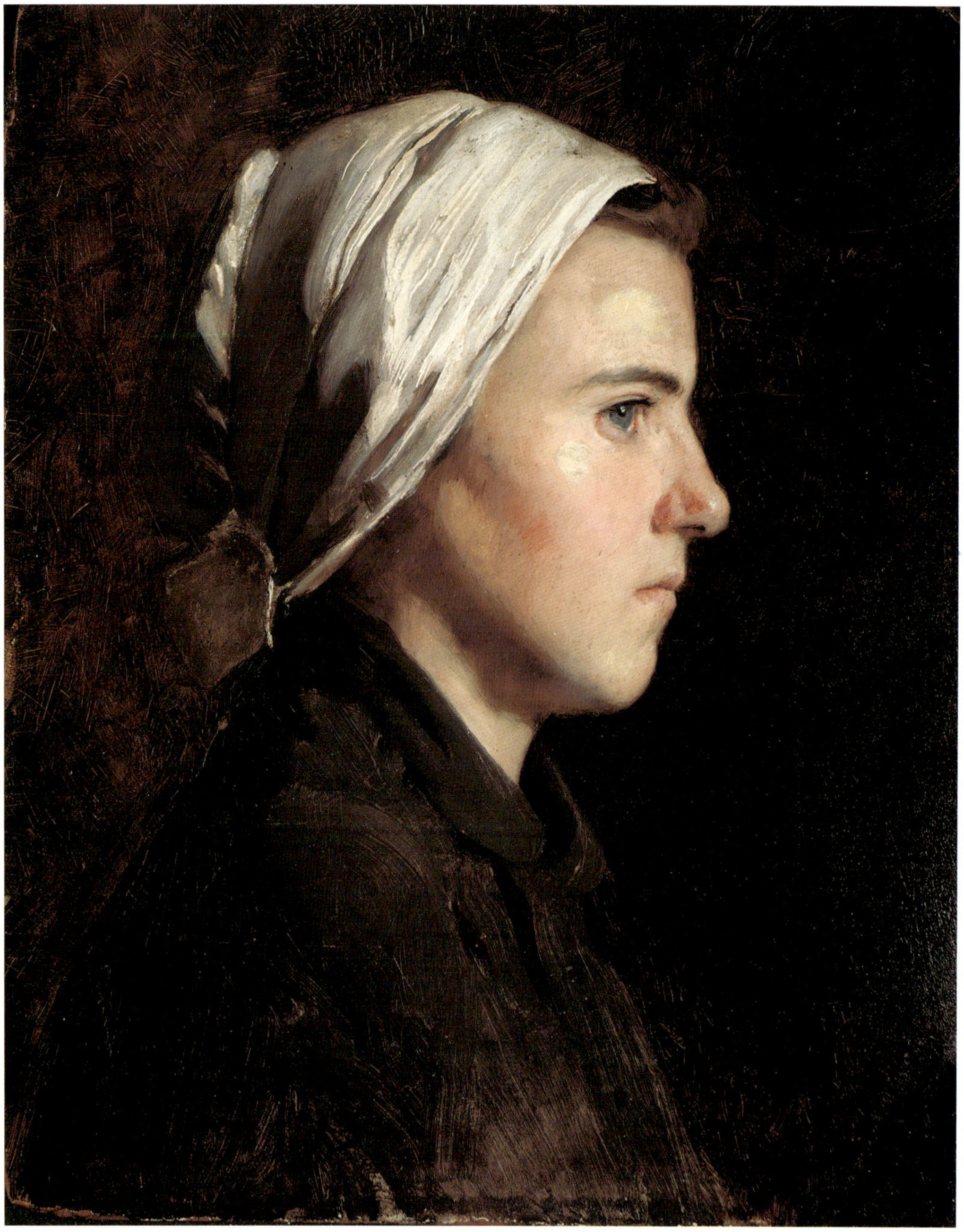

53. ABOVE: ***Head of a Woman.*** *1888. Oil on canvas, 16 x 12 7/8 in. Pennsylvania Academy of the Fine Arts*

54. OPPOSITE: ***Lady George Darwin.*** *1889. Pastel on paper, 19 x 13 1/2 in. Collection of Mr. and Mrs. John L. Huber*

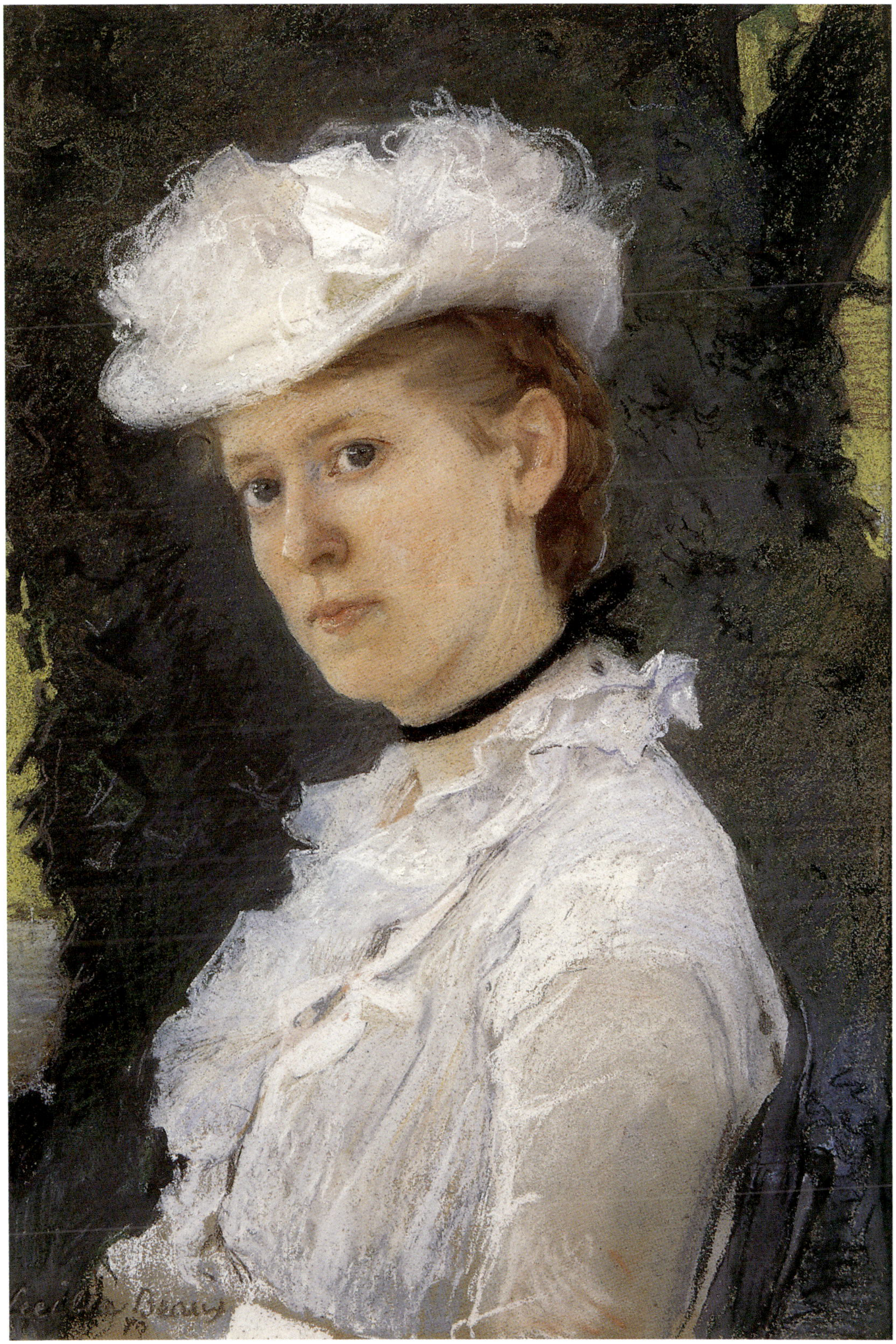

Atelier Passage des Panoramas where the most accomplished female students worked. Her return to Julian's was motivated by the opportunity to study with the painter Benjamin Constant (1845–1902), who was then offering criticism, as well as the desire to use the advantage the association would give her at the Salon. Concurrently with her enrollment, she provided Julian's assistant, Mademoiselle Amelie, with her entry number so that Julian could "boost" her painting at the Salon. Nevertheless, Beaux worried that after all she had learned and all she had sacrificed, her portrait of Louise Kinsella was not as accomplished as *Les Derniers Jours d'Enfance*, and that her association with Mr. Julian might not be sufficient cause for its inclusion in the exhibition.

By the end of the month the women at Julian's began to receive news about their submissions, and the atelier was filled with excitement. Beaux's French colleagues were effusive and emotional, laughing and hugging one another when they heard that their work had been accepted or crying and hugging one another when they received green rejection notices. The display of emotion disgusted Cecilia, who made a virtue of reserve and believed that the moral superiority of the Americans was evident in their more dignified deportment. "The excitement at Julian's has been intense among the French girls. They are such idiots—Crying for fear they will not get in and howling with joy through their tears when they find they are—and chattering incessantly," she wrote to her family with undisguised disgust.[331]

Cecilia heard nothing about her painting. Eventually, she took matters into her own hands and went to the Palais de l'Industrie to obtain the verdict. "It was with the courage of despair that I went alone as I was sure I had been refused—and I thought I would rather be about and have the long walk home to digest the calamity in," Beaux confided to her family.[332] It was a beautiful sunny day. With a pounding heart, Beaux took the omnibus up the Champs Elysées to the Palais.

> I had no idea how to get in or what to do but I went to the first small door and the official sent me to the office at the other end of the huge building. I saw a sign at the foot of some stairs "Administration de l'Exposition des Beaux Arts. . . . So I went up and there were doors but no signs—and I actually pushed one of them open. . . . I waited a minute in some trepidation when a man appeared who didn't seem surprised to see me—and took me along an entry and showed me into another room where about six men were writing and left me there.[333]

Mercifully, Cecilia did not have to wait long. One of the clerks asked her name, ran his finger down the columns of a register and uttered the long awaited word, *Admise*. Completely composed, Cecilia thanked him, walked out of the office, and immediately bumped into two friends, both hopeful female artists who had arrived on the same errand. Cecilia waited while her colleagues inquired about their own work, and when it was clear that all three women were successful, they fell into each other's arms, and Cecilia, forgetting propriety in the excitement of the moment, joined the celebration.

Cecilia occupied herself during the month of April by attending class. However, her enthusiasm for the female ateliers was fading. In the mornings she went to the Académie Julian. Although Benjamin Constant was complimentary about her drawings, she suspected that with ninety women working in the crowded studio, anything competent would catch his eye. In the afternoons she attended Lasar's atelier, even though she was growing increasingly impatient with his scientific system for painting. "I'm afraid that if I was with Lasar long I'd be reduced to a cipher," she told Uncle Will.[334] At the end of the month Beaux focused her attention on the Salon exhibition, on a costume ball that she would attend with the American painter William Amsden, and on Vernissage, when she would discover where her painting would hang and how it would compare to the others in the exhibition.

The ball was a success. Cecilia wrote to Etta that she had a wonderful time; "My coronet was stunning, gold with pearls in the points—and Amsden over whom we raved—was perfectly magnificent. He is a lovely fellow and was awfully proud of us."[335] Although Amsden was her official escort and an accomplished dancer, there was no dearth of other willing partners. "Some of them danced awfully," she complained to Etta. "And one of them walked the beads off my lovely slippers."[336] The ball was Beaux's first official social occasion after a long winter of work, and she enjoyed herself thoroughly, although she evidently harbored no romantic attachment to Mr. Amsden. "There will never be anyone as well suited to me as that much despised individual in Philadelphia—and that my soul knoweth right well," she wrote to Etta, referring to her rejected suitor, Edwin Balch.[337]

On Varnishing Day, Cecilia discovered that her painting was exhibited to advantage. Although it did not hang at eye level—"on the line" as it was called—the portrait was well placed in the middle of a wall with a number of smaller paintings grouped around it. "It is quite as well hung as it deserves, and looks a little better than I thought it would," Cecilia reported to Uncle Will.[338] After the Salon exhibition ended, Beaux gave the portrait to her beautiful model, Louise Kinsella. Whether Louise left the painting in Paris or took it to Ireland is unknown. There were no reproductions made, and if the painting still exists, its whereabouts are unknown. "After I left Paris, I did not hear from my lovely model for years, and when I did, it was to learn that she had passed from her own shadow to a deeper one, or perhaps to Light," Beaux wrote many years later. "I could not have imagined her growing old or changing. She was a poem and the best of these are never very long."[339]

Beaux accomplished her mission in Paris. She studied, painted in Brittany, toured Italy, and completed a portrait worthy of the Salon. In the end, it was all somewhat anticlimactic. "I suppose when I get home I shall look upon my sojourn here as one 'long dream of delirious joy' though of course it isn't that at all but a very quiet hum-drum round of days in which I don't seem to get half enough done," Beaux wrote to her family during her second season in Paris.[340] Beaux's relatives, who were waiting patiently on Spruce Street for her return to the fold, expected her to arrive in Philadelphia in early June, but once again she disappointed them by delaying her departure. This time the excuse was a chance to visit England. A friend from Philadelphia, Maud Du Puy, had married one of Charles Darwin's sons and was living in Cambridge, England, where her husband George Howard Darwin was a professor of astronomy and experimental philosophy at Cambridge University.[341]

May stayed behind in Paris, and Beaux made the torturous trip across the Channel alone. "The Channel crossing on a bad night I thought I knew how to dread," Beaux recalled. "But it was hideous far beyond my feeble imagination."[342] Once in England, the shipboard experience behind her, Beaux enjoyed her brief vacation with the Darwins. "Oh May, May if you could see me now I can well imagine your little shrieks of ecstasy, not at me, but my place—Think of my tea gown—that's the general tone and style of my room."[343] Cecilia loved Cambridge and thought Maud the very essence of quiet dignity, though she didn't care much for George Darwin, who reminded her of Dr. Bacon in both looks and "dyspeptic keenness." On Sundays the Darwins left their charming house on the banks of the Cam to attend church at Kings Chapel. During the week there were luncheons, teas, and garden parties with the city's elite. The Darwins introduced Beaux to many notable people, including George's mother, Emma Darwin, and John Couch Adams, the astronomer who discovered the planet Neptune. Beaux, who had just descended from her attic abode in Paris, was simultaneously charmed by the well-mannered society and dismayed by their provincialism. "I soon found that a polite silence followed any mention of French art, and the Lecturer on the Fine Arts had never heard of Bastien Lepage, or any other contemporary artist just across the Channel," Beaux later recalled.[344] However, when she completed a sketch of Maud Darwin's youngest child, Billy, her host and hostess were impressed and commissioned her to paint several portraits, an opportunity she was unable to refuse. So once again, Beaux informed her relatives that her homecoming would be postponed. She would return to Paris only long enough to settle her affairs and then spend the rest of the summer in Cambridge.

Because the two cousins had decided to give up their room at 30 rue Vaugirard, when Beaux returned to Paris she joined May in the studio on the rue Notre Dame des Champs. The summer had become unbearably hot, and the skylight added to the stifling atmosphere in the dusty room filled with the clutter of all their accumulated belongings—"squalor and wretchedness, into which no gleam of fun entered," Beaux recalled. Although there may have been nothing to amuse Beaux in the tiny studio, in the summer of 1889 Paris was alive with the excitement of the Exposition Universelle, a fair celebrating the centennial of the French Revolution. The centerpiece of the exposition was the Eiffel Tower, but there were more than eighty other structures housing a variety of exhibitions, including an impressive art gallery.

Cecilia had submitted her portrait of Mrs. Conant to the American Fine Art section, and one morning before she left for Cambridge she went to the fairgrounds to see her painting. Thirty-three-year-old John Singer Sargent was the star in a very strong showing by the Americans; six of his paintings were included in the exhibition. He was awarded a grand prize and decorated with France's highest honor for civilians, the Chevalier of the Légion d'Honneur. Although Beaux came to revere Sargent's work, she wrote no glowing letters praising his accomplishments. She saw her own painting, reported to her relatives that she was not ashamed of it, and as quickly as possible packed her belongings and, with May, headed to the Darwins' home in Cambridge. Her sojourn in Paris was over.

Once settled in Cambridge, the two cousins rented a room, and Cecilia set up a studio in a cottage on the Darwin property. There she completed portraits of Maud and George Darwin; Mrs. Horace Darwin, George's sister-in-law; and Ida Goodhart, one of the Darwins' neighbors. Beaux painted likenesses of George Darwin and Mrs. Horace Darwin in oil but used pastels for the portraits of Maud Darwin and Ida Goodhart. Because her training in Paris had been primarily in drawing, she felt comfortable with the medium, although she later remembered having a difficult time with the contrasting values of Mrs. Goodhart's pale white skin and her resplendent dark hair. All four portraits were successful, and as Cecilia charged only $75 each for them—an amount the Goodharts deemed "paltry"—her clients were thrilled. "They think me a wonder," she wrote to Grandma Leavitt.[345] The Darwins urged Beaux to stay in Cambridge. Several of their friends were eager to commission portraits, but although she was tempted, Cecilia and her patient cousin May were both ready to go home.

56. OPPOSITE: ***Cecil Kent Drinker.*** *1891. Oil on canvas, 64 x 34 1/2 in. Philadelphia Museum of Art*

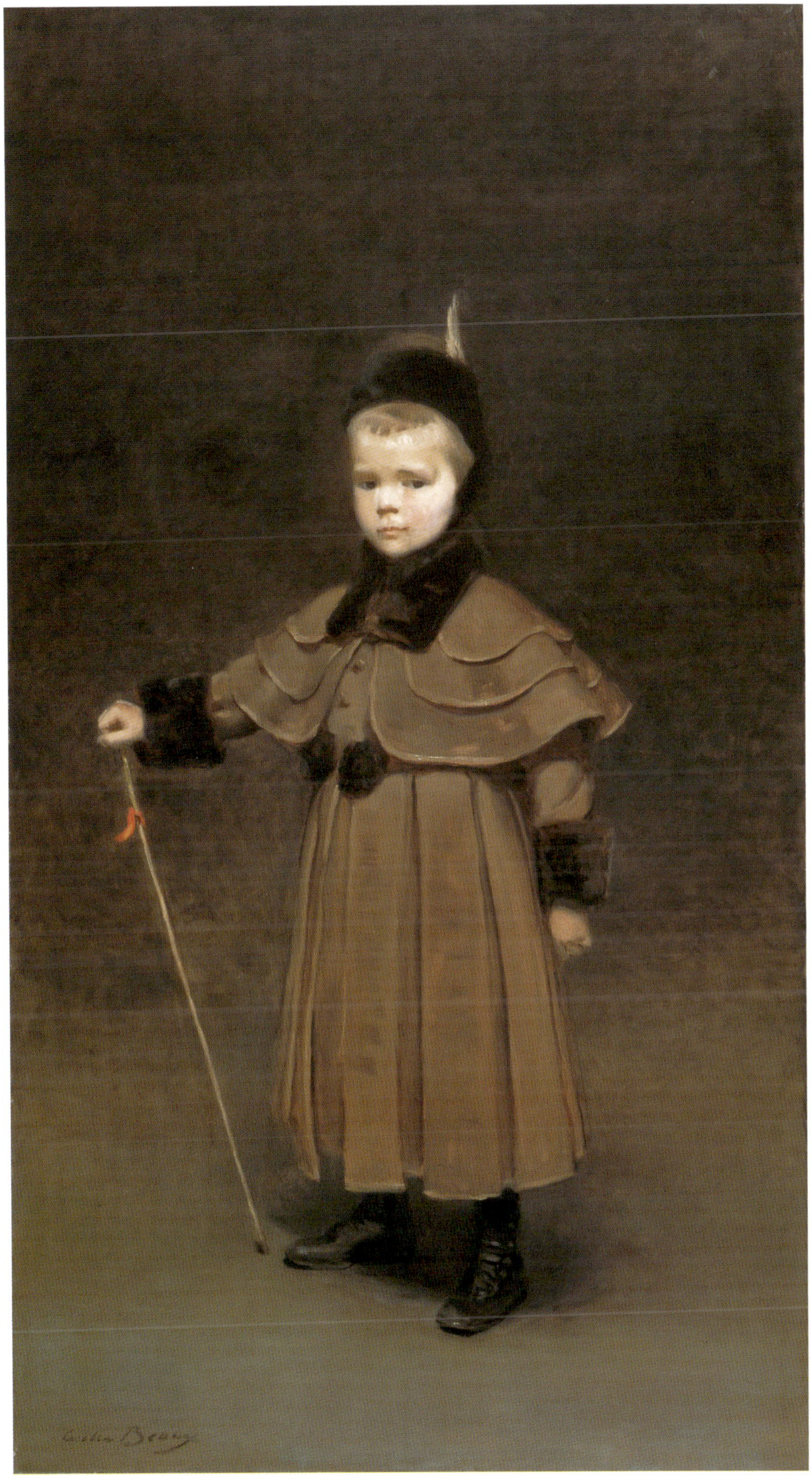

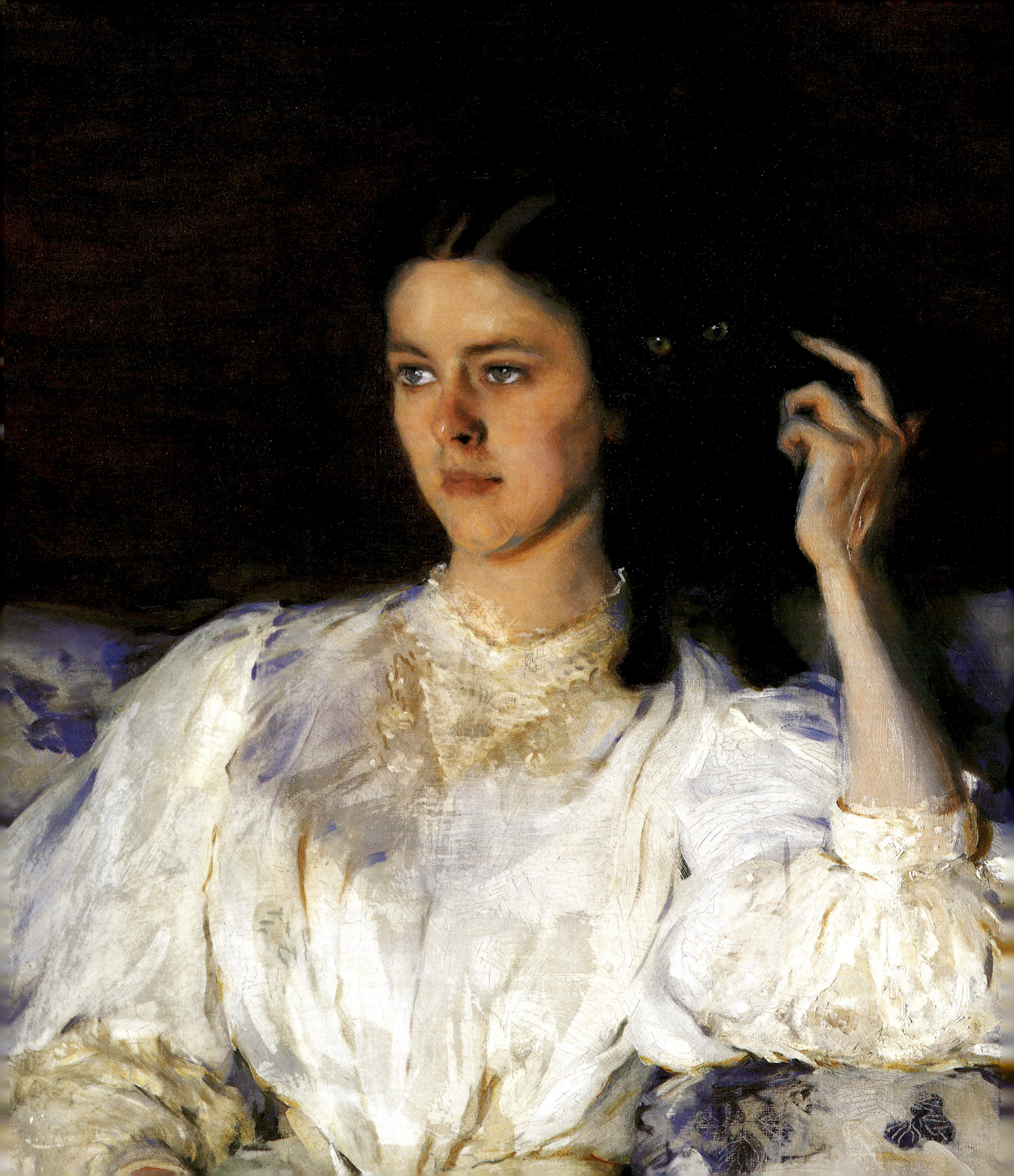

The Spring Salon

"Great works and great people meet nothing strong enough to oppose their destiny."
—Cecilia Beaux, *1930*

"To battle was Cecilia's life. Attainment without struggle seemed to her of little worth," Beaux's friend Thornton Oakley wrote.[346] And indeed, when Beaux returned to Philadelphia in 1889, it was with the idea of working tirelessly so that she could justify the expense of her European education by establishing herself as a respected painter. Toward that end she was prepared to make the necessary sacrifices, and her solicitous family was prepared to help. By the time Cecilia and May boarded the ship *Anchovia* in late August for the trip home, Uncle Will had already rented a suitable studio.

The crossing, while not as excruciating as her first experience with the North Atlantic, was still rough, and even in summer their small vessel left England enveloped in a cold fog that wrapped the masts like a shroud. However, on Cecilia's return voyage, the hardships were mitigated when she met a New Haven patent attorney named George Dudley Seymour. Beaux found Seymour fascinating. He shared her passion for achievement, and in subsequent years, in addition to his law practice, he became an active and influential historian. In 1914 his interest in the American patriot Nathan Hale culminated in his purchase of the Hale family home, which would have fallen into ruin without his intervention. Beaux's friendship with this intelligent young man never faltered. The two maintained a lively correspondence for the remainder of their lives. In George Seymour, who was traveling with a devoted male companion, Beaux found a man who was not interested in her either as a temporary adjunct to his romantic ambitions or as a prospective wife.

Beaux enjoyed male companionship. Yet once she had made the decision to devote her life to her profession and not to marry, she chose her male friends carefully, making sure that she could enjoy their companionship without the relationship taxing her time or emotional energy. Routinely, Beaux's male friends were either gay or so young that even with the eight years she subtracted from her age any possible romantic relationship would be out of the question. Beaux's niece, Catherine Drinker Bowen, remembered that when her Aunt Cecilia visited, a male admirer invariably accompanied her. "My aunt had possessed these willing followers ever since I could remember—ten or twenty years her junior as the case might be," Bowen wrote. "Most of them were noticeably good-looking; my aunt did not like to be with ill-favored people."[347]

Beaux's homecoming was joyous. She found her family much as she had left them, although Etta's three young sons had grown. The most obvious change was

OPPOSITE: *Detail;* ***Sita and Sarita****, or* ***Young Woman with Cat****. 1893–94. Oil on canvas, 37 1/4 x 25 in. Musee d'Orsay, Paris*

in the eldest, Harry, who by the age of nine was already decisive and ambitious. He had learned to play the piano well enough to give rise to the hope that the family tradition of musical excellence would carry over to the next generation. "After a separation of nearly nineteen months, the great emotion and happiness of return was in finding them all there," Beaux wrote. "The little ones were larger, and—this was best of all—the older unaltered, to my perception."[348] Grandma Leavitt was ninety-one-years old when Cecilia returned to Philadelphia and in miraculously good health. "Her health, except for the occasional small maladies, was perfect," Beaux remembered.[349] Etta recalled that when Grandma Leavitt was in her nineties, "she could see as well as anybody. She walked by the mirror one day and waved at it and said, 'I don't know that old woman.'"[350] Although Grandma Leavitt retained both her health and her humor, her energy had flagged. By 1889 Emily Biddle was running the household, and Grandma had retired to less strenuous occupations: offering advice when it was asked for, reading aloud to the family after supper, and knitting in time to the music that Uncle Will played on the piano.

It was reassuring for Beaux to discover that her family was so comfortably unaltered, especially since she felt that she had changed so much during her absence. Before she had gone to France, Beaux was a contributing member of the household who did her share of the chores, prepared meals, went shopping for groceries, and helped with the housekeeping. After her return she wanted to continue to live the life she had fashioned for herself in Paris—a life free of all but the most basic domestic responsibilities, a life devoted to her painting. Her relatives complied and asked nothing of her. Every morning Beaux left the house early to make the long trip to her studio at 1710 Chestnut Street. To facilitate her departure, Aunt Emily made her niece's bed, straightened her room, and followed her to the front door with a basket containing a bottle of milk and a buttered roll. In the evenings when she returned home after a full day of painting, Cecilia was free to do as she pleased. She often spent the late afternoons napping on the couch in the parlor. "Nothing was required of me," Cecilia recalled. "In all the years that followed my return from abroad, to the, alas, final breaking up of our circle, I was never once asked to do an errand in town, some bit of shopping, or a call, that would have put the slightest pressure upon me. So well did they understand."[351] Just how much Beaux's relatives understood is open to speculation. Certainly they admired her success in Paris and realized that she might establish an enduring reputation as a painter. But perhaps they worried about her, too. As Grandma Leavitt sat knitting and listening to her son-in-law conjuring the passion of Chopin out of the old piano, she may have wondered who would take care of Cecilia in her old age.

Cecilia harbored no such concerns. Freed from all domestic responsibility by her amazingly generous family, her professional life thrived. Every morning she accepted Emily's basket and left the house for the long walk to the trolley stop, where she would catch the car for the forty-minute ride to the city. Her studio on Chestnut Street was on the top of a rather tall building and consisted of two small connecting rooms. A skylight and two windows that faced the street provided good light. The furnishings were sparse: several casts, an old carved chest, a tapestry on the wall, some drapery fabric, and the necessary supplies for painting—easel, chair, and taboret. A reporter from the *New York Journal* seemed relieved to note that there were "No useless knick knacks, no 'odds and ends.'"[352]

Beaux arrived at her studio each morning promptly at 9 A.M. and expected the same promptness from her sitters.

> An hour was none too much for clearing the decks for action, preparing my palette, considering the canvas in progress, and my intentions concerning it, so that at ten I was more than ready for the subject who was expected to be prompt also, and who finding me always waiting, easily got the habit.[353]

Beaux was a taskmaster with her models, demanding the same degree of concentration from them that she required from herself. "The next five years were busy ones for me, and also for those who came to 'sit,' and who found that the rapid sketch in which they expected to find a compact of life was a long and laborious operation, and very exacting for them," Beaux recalled. One of her models, an accommodating bank president, informed her that she was like a little dog that walked round and round before settling.[354] Her friend Henry McCarter wrote more bluntly, "Cecilia Beaux painted me once upon a time or rather made a beginning. I personally could not stand it! Cecilia springs sideways and then makes faces at a sitter. When she paints she cries out—'Oh, your nose!'"[355]

When Cecilia Beaux returned to Philadelphia, she initially tried to recapitulate her success in Cambridge by working with pastels. However, she soon abandoned the medium and switched to oils, completing a number of successful portraits in the years immediately following her return from Europe. By her own count, Beaux produced more than forty pictures in her Chestnut Street studio, both commissioned paintings and noncommissioned portraits of family and friends. But having never had any formal instruction in painting other than her brief sessions with William Sartain, she continued to be confounded by color, and although her paintings appear effortless—the colors and values clear and masterful—she never painted easily. Thornton Oakley remembered Cecilia shouting in anger and defiance, "You would, would you!" to a bit of blue pigment that refused to assume the proper value on her canvas.[356] When Oakley asked Beaux how many times she had to repaint a portrait, Beaux surprised him by answering that she often repainted a single area hundreds of times. She simply refused to accept anything short of excellence. "You see," Beaux once told a reporter from the *New York Times*, "ours was a family of perfectionists. If they sewed they sewed beautifully. If they read they read thoroughly."[357]

When Grandma Leavitt reached the age of ninety-three and her health began to fail, her family of

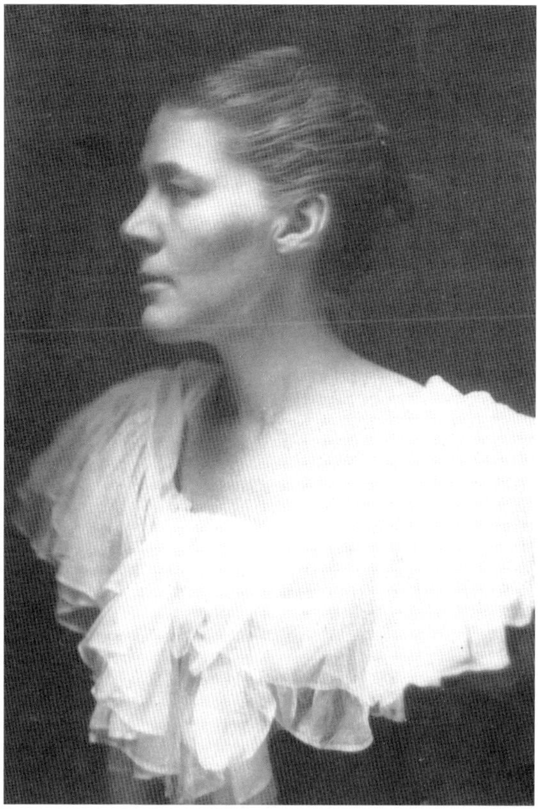

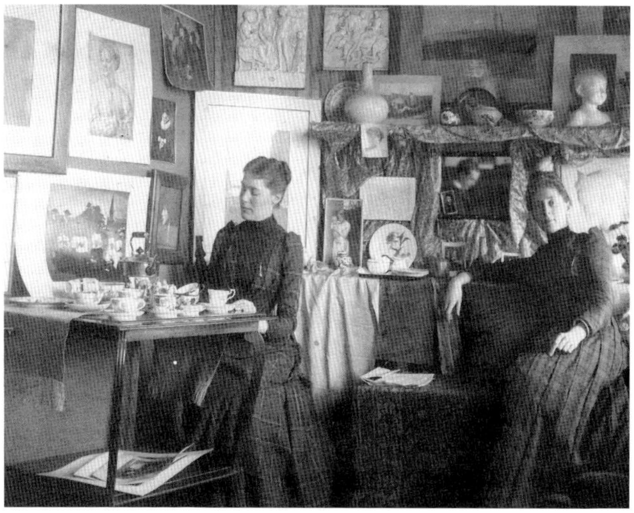

57. TOP: ***Cecilia Beaux in ruffled collar,*** *n.d. Pennsylvania Academy of the Fine Arts*

58. BOTTOM: ***Cecilia Beaux and Emma Leavitt after a tea party in Beaux's studio,*** *1889–90.*

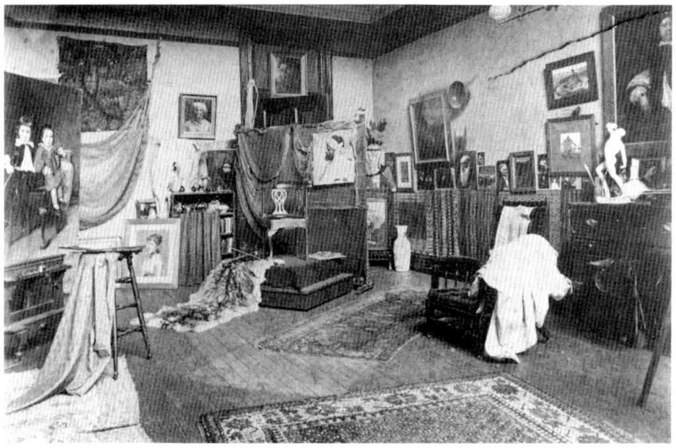

59. Interior of Cecilia Beaux's studio at 1710 Chestnut Street, 1889–90. Pennsylvania Academy of the Fine Arts

perfectionists rallied, hoping by sheer strength of will to keep her with them. They divided every day into shifts so that they could provide her with the best possible care. Cecilia spent the mornings in her studio, worked a full day, and by curtailing her customary social schedule, found time in the late afternoons to sit with her grandmother. At 8 P.M., Cecilia went to bed and slept until 2 A.M., when she would tiptoe downstairs in her nightdress to relieve her aunt. At 5 A.M. a nurse arrived, and Cecilia was able to go back to bed until 7 A.M., when she had to wake up and prepare for another day at her studio. "This programme [sic] never cost me either health or fatigue," Cecilia remembered with a certain amount of pride. "My work went on as usual and without strain."[358]

Grandma Leavitt's final illness lasted for eighteen months, during which time she was brave and stalwart, complaining to her granddaughter only once, telling her, "You are keeping me here when I ought to be gone."[359] On the night she died, Grandma Leavitt watched Cecilia as she cut out some material to make a smock. Rising from her chair and using the furniture to steady herself, Grandma Leavitt made her way to the sewing table to check on the quality and progress of her granddaughter's handiwork one last time. In this manner their relationship came full circle, ending where it began, with a sewing lesson.

During her grandmother's final illness and immediately following her death on May 9, 1892, Cecilia Beaux completed some of her most evocative canvases. Her loss seemed to awaken a sympathy for the human condition, which she invested in her portraits, so that they became emotionally charged as well as technically brilliant. Her virtuosity did not go unnoticed. In 1891 and again in 1892, she was awarded the Mary Smith Prize at the Pennsylvania Academy of the Fine Arts Annual Exhibition. In 1893 she was elected as a member of the Society of American Artists, won the Dodge Prize from the National Academy of Design, and received a gold medal from the Philadelphia Art Club for a large portrait of the Presbyterian minister Matthew Blackburne Grier. The Grier portrait was one of her strongest likenesses and an interesting amalgamation of the more sober work she completed before her sojourn in Paris and the lighter palette she developed as a result of her experimentation with color in Concarneau.

Many of the compelling portraits Beaux completed in the early 1890s were not commissioned but painted, as she described them, "*con amore*," with love. Most of them were of family members whom she was eager to immortalize on canvas. The fact that she was living at home and had very few expenses allowed her the luxury of selecting subjects who interested her. She painted her nephew Harry, the child who had inspired *Les Derniers Jours d'Enfance*, three times when she returned; once in 1889 in a watercolor with his mother and his brother Jamie, and again that same year seated at the piano. In 1891 she captured him on the edge of adolescence, reclining on a sofa. She painted her sister Etta, pregnant with her fourth child, in 1891 and also completed a full-length portrait of Etta's youngest, her four-year-old nephew, Cecil, dressed like a young prince in a long fur-trimmed coat and matching hat. The painting of Cecil was exhibited at the Philadelphia Art Club's Third Annual Exhibition and also at the 67th annual exhibition of the National Academy of Design in New York, where it received glowing critical reviews. "The picture of the exhibition is No. 319, a portrait of a child, by Cecilia Beaux," a journalist wrote. "It recalls Manet's *Boy with a Sword* . . . in its easy and certain apprehension of character and in the boldness and felicity of its execution."[360]

Beaux's portrait of Cecil did "apprehend" her nephew's character. In the painting the little boy looks determined and defiant, which he was. Beaux's youngest niece, Catherine Drinker Bowen, recalled a letter that her brother Jamie wrote to Cecilia Beaux about baby Cecil: "When we say Nonono to baby he says Ahaaaa very loud, the bad thing."[361] No one ever got away with saying "no" to Cecil Drinker, and as a young man his single-minded determination served him well. He was president of his senior class at Haverford College, graduated first in his class from medical school at the University of Pennsylvania, and by the age of thirty was the acting head of the physiology department at Harvard Medical School. However, the defiant side of his personality, evident to his perceptive aunt when he was only four years old, later stymied his family's efforts to curb his alcoholism, an addiction that eventually destroyed much that he had worked to achieve.

Beaux's ability to capture the personality of her models was remarkable and was the result of both careful observation and an innate sympathy for her subjects, whom she selected with care. She would not paint everyone. A person had to have attributes that interested her before she set brush to canvas, a fact that caused friction between Beaux and her youngest niece, Catherine, the only one of the Drinker children she never painted. "I hated her for this," Bowen wrote. "Nor did I love her more when I heard her tell a caller that when she first saw her niece Kitty in the cradle she knew that wasn't a forehead to paint, 'There's a forehead that will go to Bryn Mawr and write a book,'" Beaux explained. Although the remark infuriated Bowen, Cecilia Beaux's prediction came true: Catherine Drinker Bowen became a noted biographer and a prolific author.

Although Beaux never painted Catherine, her older sister, Ernesta, posed for Aunt Beaux nines times, beginning in 1894 when she was three years old. When Beaux saw Ernesta in the cradle, she apparently approved of her forehead and could see that the child would grow into an astonishingly beautiful woman.

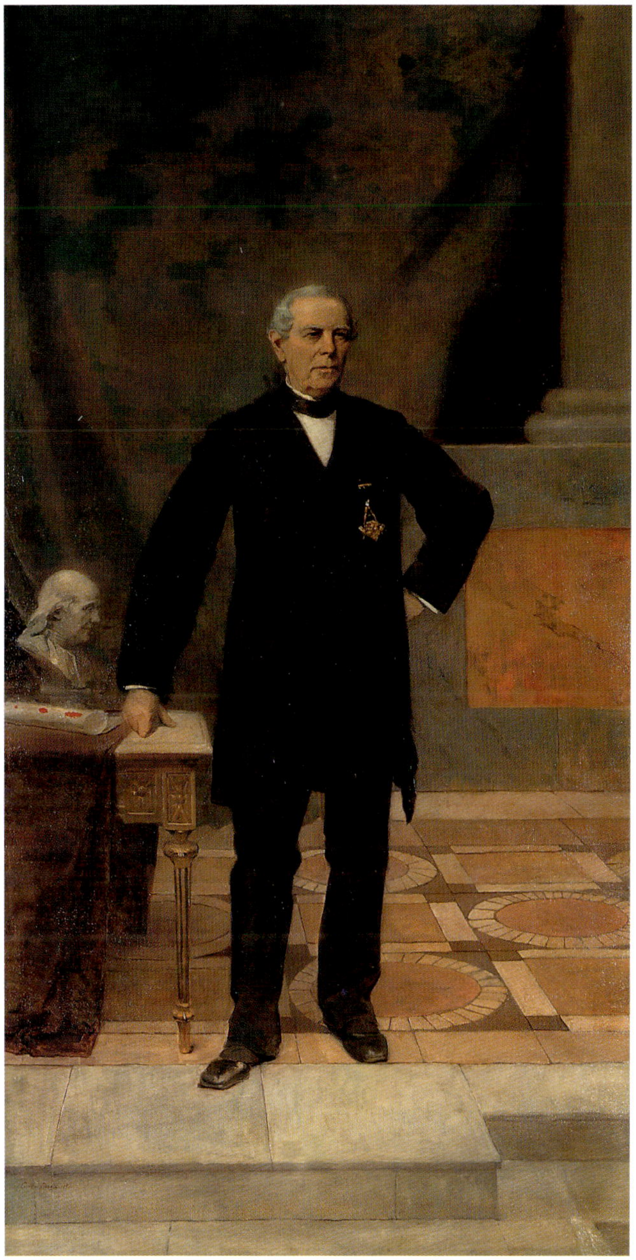

60. ***Peter Williamson.*** *1891. Oil on canvas, 113 x 59 in. Collections of the Grand Lodge of Pennsylvania on deposit with the Masonic Library and Museum of Pennsylvania*

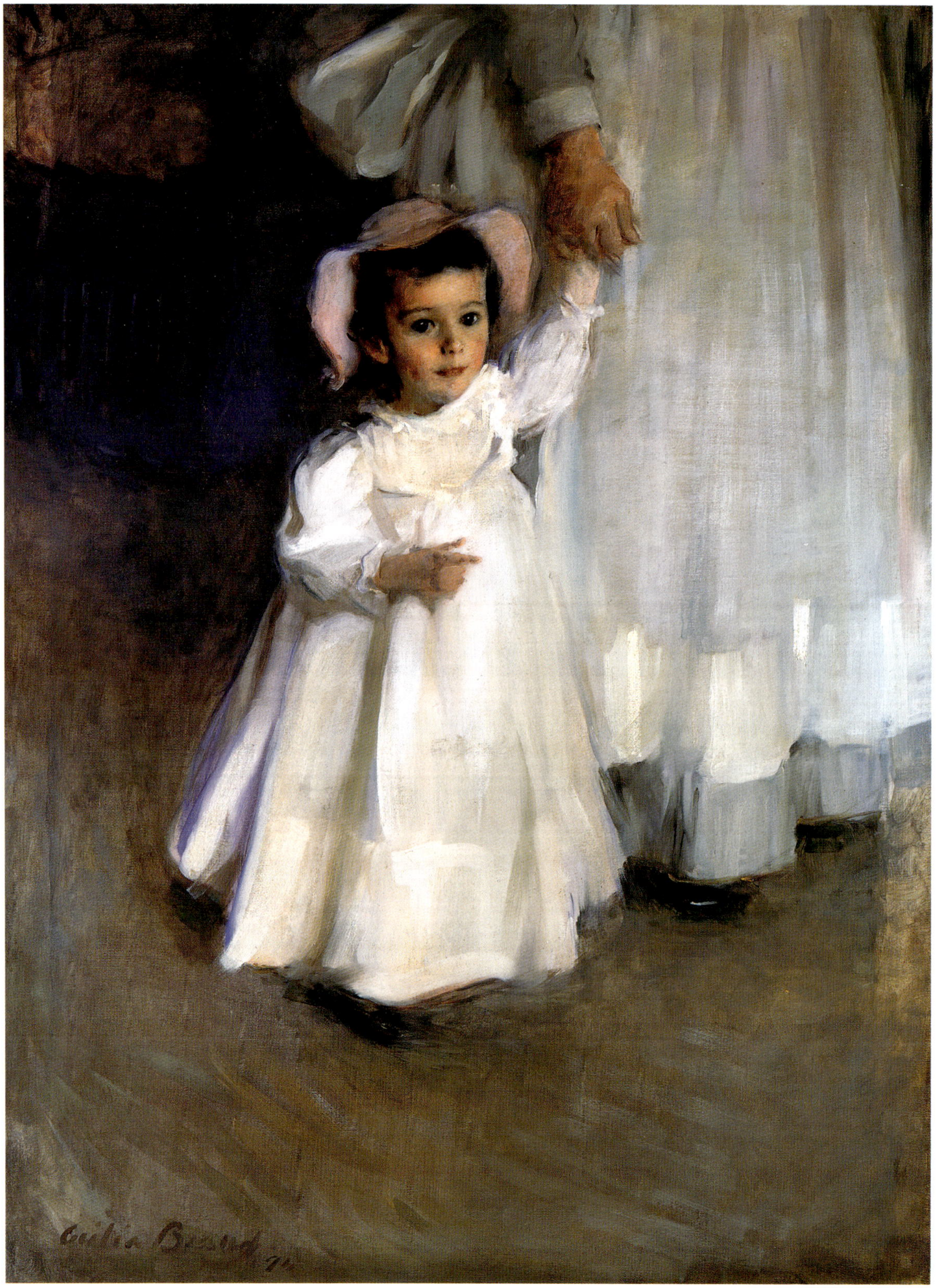

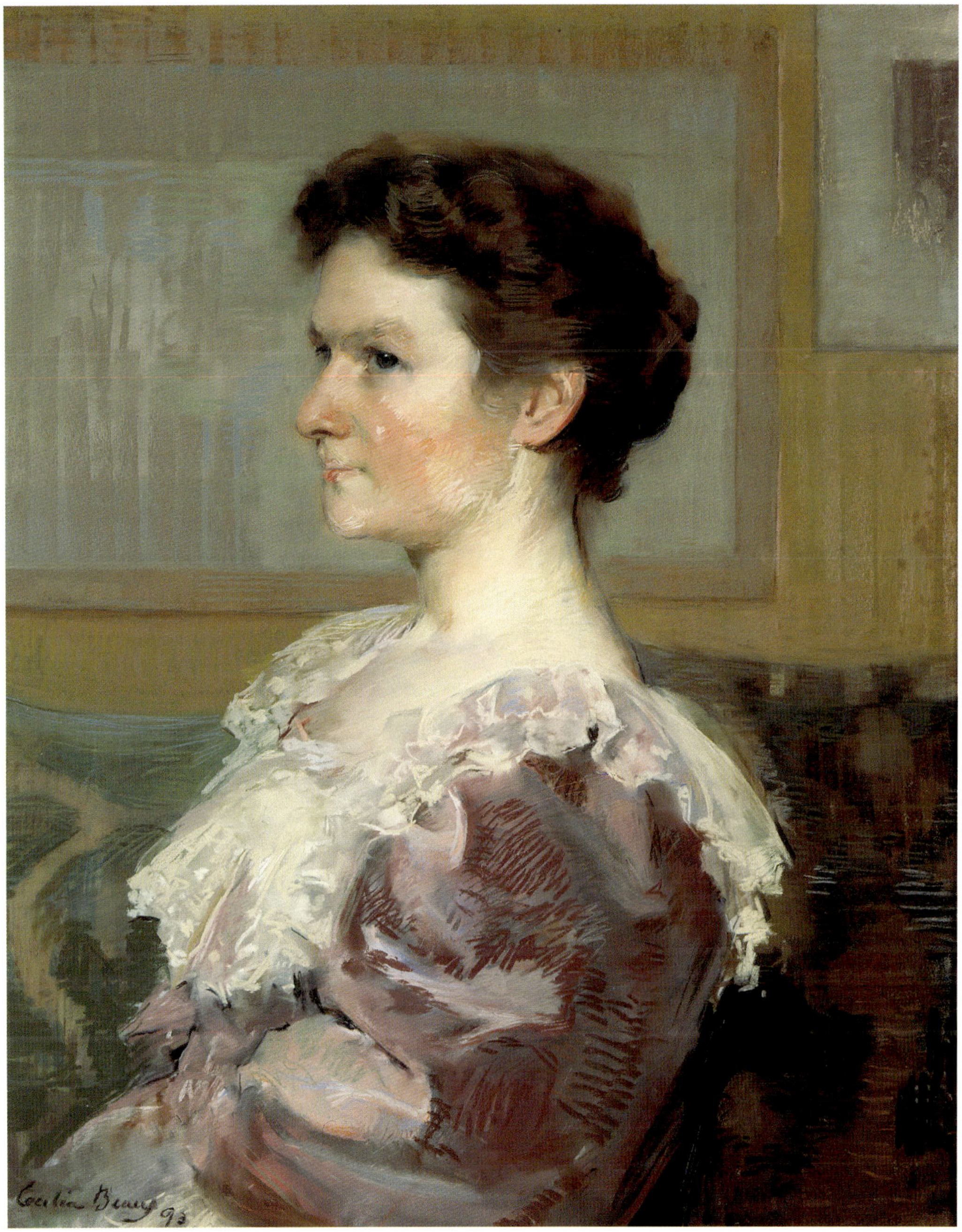

61. OPPOSITE: ***Ernesta,*** *or* ***Child with Nurse.*** *1894. Oil on canvas, 50 1/2 x 38 1/8 in. The Metropolitan Museum of Art*

62. ABOVE: ***Portrait of Helen Biddle Griscom.*** *1893. Pastel, 27 1/8 x 21 7/8 in. Pennsylvania Academy of the Fine Arts*

She was right. Catherine, who grew up harboring no resentment toward her stunning sister, wrote about the quality of Ernesta's beauty: "Actually it was the structure of her face that fascinated—the bones beneath, as Aunt Beaux had said, the line of brow and chin. Whichever way my sister turned her head on that long neck there was enchantment. I have seen men catch their breath looking at Ernesta."[362]

By the time Ernesta Drinker reached the age of twenty-two, she had turned down fifty marriage proposals. One suitor was said to have rushed into her room with a pistol and, putting the gun to his temple, threatened to commit suicide if Ernesta did not marry him. Fortunately the young man accepted her refusal valiantly and did not pull the trigger. Even after she found a suitable husband, Ernesta had legions of followers. In 1938, when she was forty-seven and living near Monte Carlo with her second husband, an admirer sent over a Bentley filled with roses. On another occasion an equally smitten man had seventy pairs of silk stockings delivered to her door. "Aunt Ernesta kept the stockings, spread the roses around the house and never would have anything to do with either suitor. . . . She left in her wake four outraged brothers and a pile of other male bodies which . . . looked like the casualties from the Light Brigade," her nephew Ezra Bowen recalled.[363] In a legendary feat at Bar Harbor, Maine, Ernesta won a bet by water-skiing in an evening gown without ever getting her dress wet. "I could never quite figure out how she stayed dry," Ezra wrote. "But according to legend, she started by sitting on the edge of the dock until the speedboat pulled her off and, at the end, she let go of the rope near the beach and just coasted up unto the sand."[364]

Ernesta Drinker's exquisite beauty was first revealed when Cecilia Beaux painted her as a charming toddler holding fast to her nurse's hand. In Beaux's painting, the nurse is almost entirely cropped out of the picture—only her hand and the edge of her dress are visible. It was an audacious composition reminiscent of some of the most innovative work of the French Impressionist Edgar Degas (1834–1917), whose paintings and pastels Beaux probably saw in Paris. Although her portrait of Ernesta received much attention and positive critical review, Beaux never again used such extreme cropping. Perhaps she understood that this particular child was destined to take center stage. When Ernesta Drinker entered a room, everyone else became part of the supporting cast.

Beaux's other family portraits painted "con amore" after her return from Paris were two likenesses of Leavitt relatives—a painting of her grandfather's cousin, Julia Leavitt Richards, and a portrait completed in 1894 of another cousin, twenty-nine-year-old Sarah A. Leavitt. Beaux painted Sarah with a small black kitten perched incongruously on her shoulder and titled the canvas *Sita and Sarita*. Like the portrait of Ernesta,

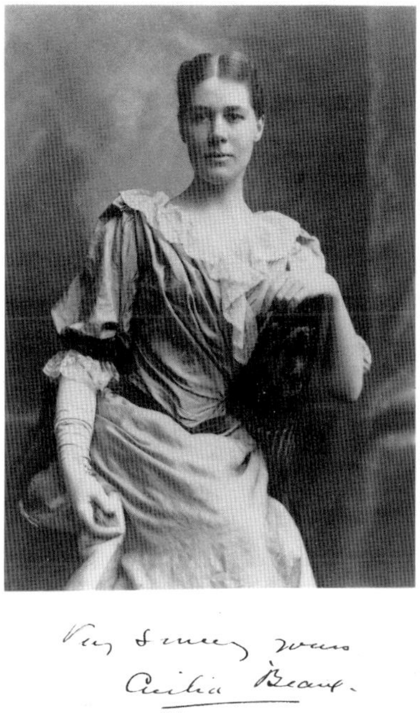

64. ***Cecilia Beaux***, *ca. 1895. Pennsylvania Academy of the Fine Arts*

63. OPPOSITE: ***The Reverend Matthew Blackburne Grier.*** *1892. Oil on canvas, mounted on wood, 49 5/8 x 39 3/8 in. Pennsylvania Academy of the Fine Arts*

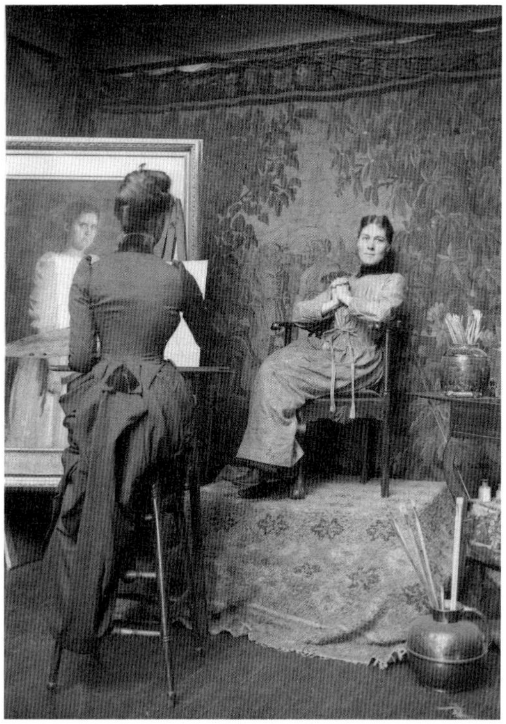

65. ***Cecilia Beaux posing for Emma Leavitt,*** *1889–90. Pennsylvania Academy of the Fine Arts*

this work was considered atypical and mysterious, not for any unconventional cropping or unusual visual effect, but for the subject matter; the forthright stare of Sarah Leavitt and what one commentator described as "the witch-like weirdness of the black kitten."[365] Critics and journalists inquired about the significance of the painting for years, and it was Etta who finally laid the matter to rest for her sister. "You ask about *Sita and Sarita,*" she wrote in response to a journalist's query. "Please make no mystery about it—it was only an idea to put the black kitten on her cousin's shoulder. Nothing deeper."[366]

For sixteen consecutive years, between 1879 and 1895, Beaux's paintings were honored with inclusion in the prestigious Pennsylvania Academy of the Fine Arts annual exhibitions. Critical notices of her work were impressive. "This item does not hesitate to pronounce Miss Beaux the best female portrait painter in America," a writer for one of the Philadelphia papers proclaimed.[367] In 1895, in recognition of her growing reputation, Cecilia Beaux was hired to teach at the Pennsylvania Academy of the Fine Arts at a salary of $1,200, succeeding the American Impressionist painter Robert Vonnoh (1858–1933), who had recently resigned. "Never before either in this country or abroad has a woman been chosen as a member of the faculty of a famous art school. It is a legitimate source of pride to Philadelphians that one of its most cherished institutions has made this innovation," announced one local newspaper.[368] Beaux, who had many years of teaching experience at the Miss Sanford's School and knew how to conduct a class, also brought to the Academy's students the knowledge she had acquired in France. She immediately became a popular and effective instructor. An anonymous note from a student attests to her abilities.

> I want to thank you for all the vigor and vitality you bring to your class at the Academy. Your criticisms are always such a lift over hard places; you go directly to the heart of the matter and clear away all the muddle. It must be wonderful to live with a mind like that—I often think yours is like an arrow, only you don't wound people with it, which is all the nicer. Perhaps we appear rather dull and uncomprehending or unresponsive sometimes. But oh we do appreciate fresh air and rejoice in a sense of humor.
>
> It is impossible to repay anything to the people who give the inestimable things but I like to thank them for existing. Some people are portraits—and others are just heads, and you are a very convincing portrait.[369]

Although the spring Salon was the focus of Beaux's ambitions when she was a student in Paris, after her return to Philadelphia, six years elapsed before she was again represented in the prestigious

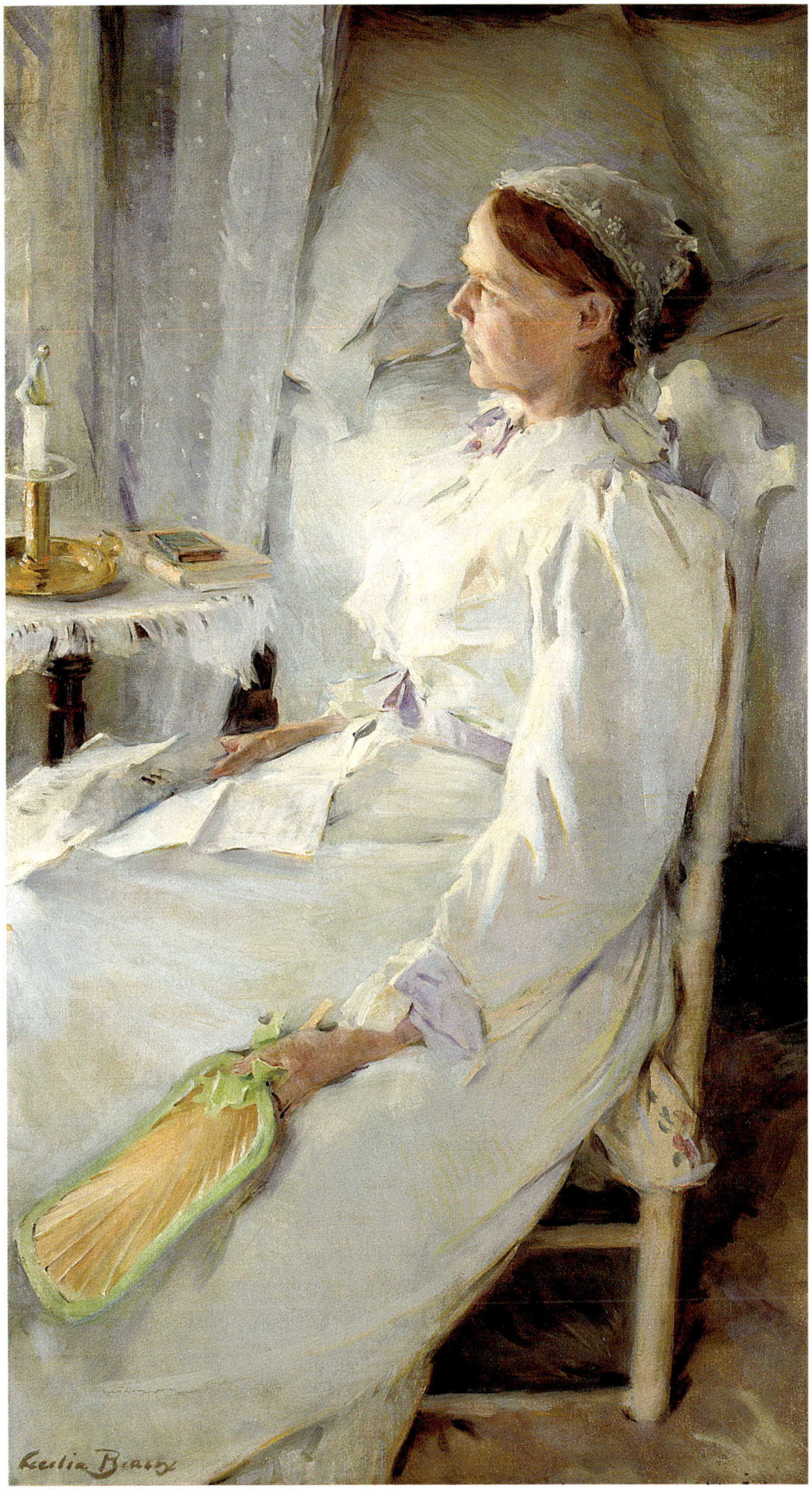

66. **New England Woman.** *1895. Oil on canvas, 43 x 24 1/4 in. Pennsylvania Academy of the Fine Arts*

67. RIGHT: **Mrs. Clement B. Newbold.** *1896. Oil on canvas, 78 1/2 x 48 in. Pennsylvania Academy of the Fine Arts*
68. OPPOSITE TOP: ***Henry Howard Houston, Jr.*** *1895. Oil on canvas, 33 3/4 x 25 3/8 in. Courtesy of the University of Pennsylvania Art Collection, Philadelphia*
69. OPPOSITE BOTTOM: ***Study for*** **The Dreamer.** *1894. Umber and chalk on gray-primed canvas, 32 x 24 in. Pennsylvania Academy of the Fine Arts*

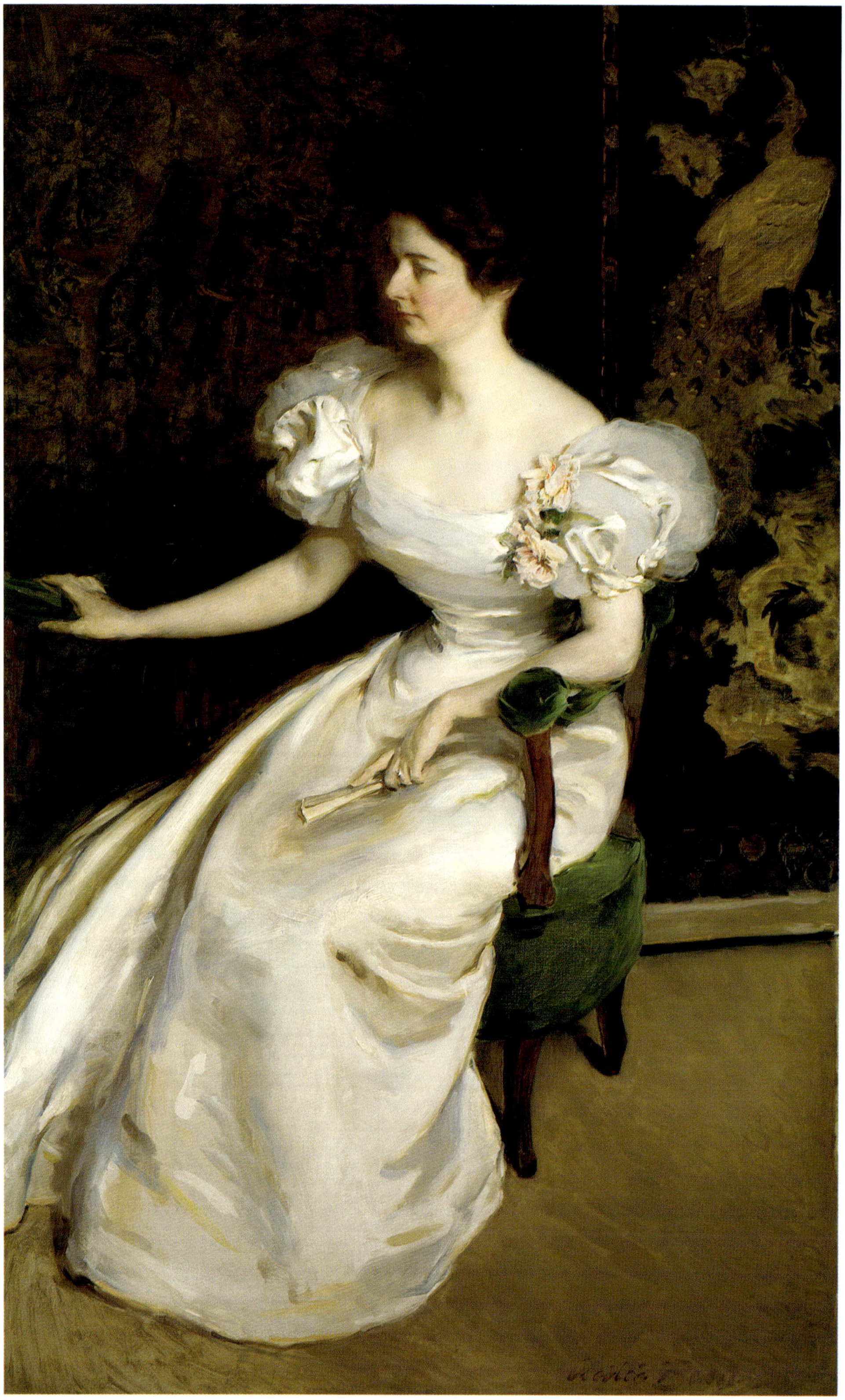

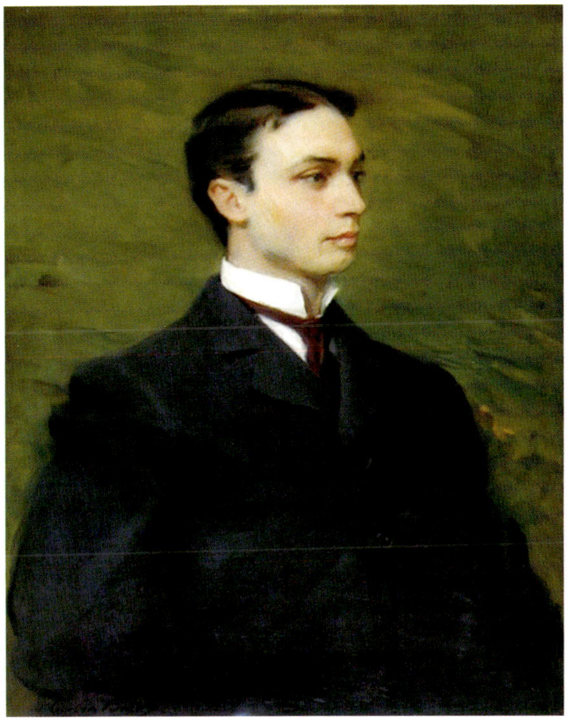

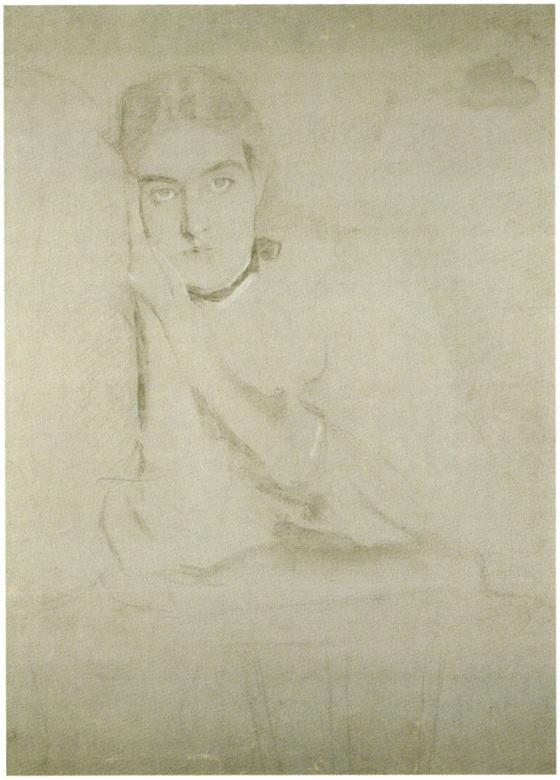

exhibition. Perhaps she worried that her initial triumph at the Salon had been a fluke, and that her second entry, the portrait of Louise Kinsella, was included in the show only because Rodolphe Julian had championed her cause. However, in 1896 John Lambert and Henry McCarter, two friends from Philadelphia who were studying art in Paris, persuaded her to send some of her paintings to the exhibition. Beaux chose six of her best canvases: the portraits of Dr. Grier, Ernesta, Julia Leavitt Richards, a portrait of Miss Caroline Kilby Smith titled *The Dreamer*, *Sita and Sarita*, and a small portrait of four-year-old Cynthia Sherwood, painted for the child's mother, the artist Rosina Emmet Sherwood (1854–1948). "Her picture of Cynthia will be a lifelong joy to me," Sherwood wrote in her diary in 1894. "It is not quite so pretty as Cynthia (this is not only a mother's opinion—everybody thinks so) but it has all her character & her intelligence & consistency & is a most delightful painting."[370]

Rosina Sherwood, who was an accomplished artist and might have become as famous as Beaux had marriage and family not interrupted her career, was not alone in her assessment of the portrait. Critics admired its technical facility and the bold way that Beaux left the arms unfinished, as if the child were either in motion or about to flee. The judges at the Salon of 1896 agreed. They admitted the painting to the exhibition along with Beaux's five other entries. All six of her paintings were hung "on the line" in a group—an unprecedented honor.

When word of this triumph came to Beaux by cable, she immediately made plans to return to France. This time, though, she stopped in England first to visit Maud Darwin, who accompanied her to Paris. Beaux did not arrive in time to go to the opening reception for the artists, so Henry McCarter wrote to tell her about the exhibition. "They've hung your pictures splendidly—in a group—with nothing above or below," he reported. "The vernissage is Friday next—today was exclusively for artists. Your panel holds its own definitely and makes a splendid showing, I wish you might see it. The portrait of Mr. X [Dr. Grier], which I cared

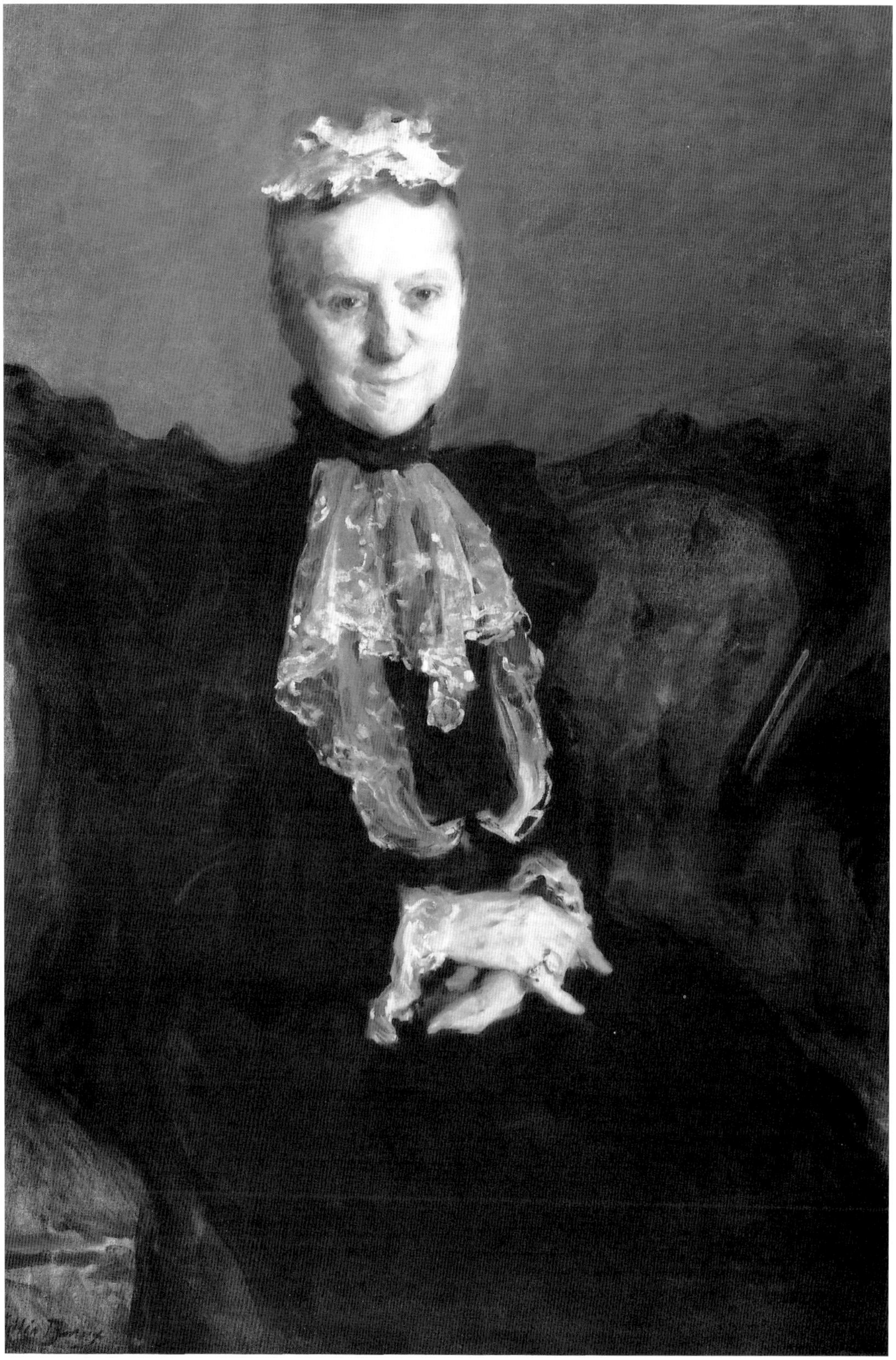

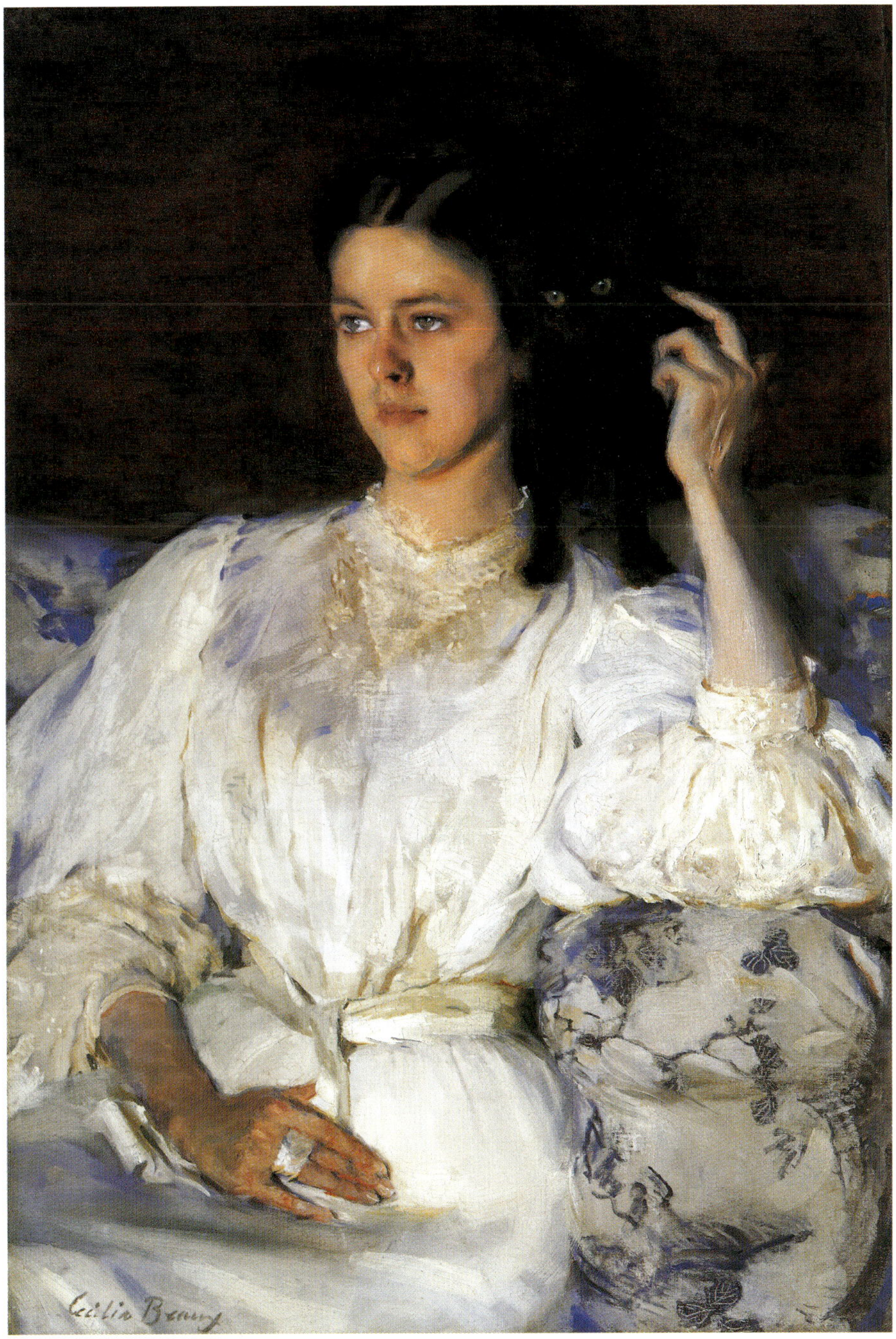

70. OPPOSITE: ***Mrs. Alexander Biddle.*** *1897. Oil on canvas, 40 1/4 x 30 3/16 in. Philadelphia Museum of Art*

71. ABOVE: ***Sita and Sarita,*** *or* ***Young Woman with Cat.*** *1893–94. Oil on canvas, 37 1/4 x 25 in. Musee d'Orsay, Paris*

least for—here counts tremendously. The black cat [*Sita and Sarita*] is best of all."[371]

By 1896 the Paris Salon had two venues, both officially sanctioned by the French government—the impressive galleries in the Palais de l'Industrie on the Champs Elysées, where Beaux's previous entries had been displayed, and the new exhibition hall in the Palais des Beaux-Arts on the Champ-de-Mars,[372] where Beaux sent her six works in 1896. According to Lois Marie Fink, who wrote a comprehensive history of American participation in the nineteenth-century French Salons, the Champ-de-Mars Salon was considered to be the more progressive of the two exhibitions. It attracted entries from a younger and more innovative group of artists and included more paintings by foreigners.[373]

In an age when fine art still supplied the most compelling visual images available, the late nineteenth-century Salons attracted huge crowds. Although by 1896 some artists were experimenting with genres that the public found puzzling, the preponderance of work still reflected French academic tradition, and most of the paintings had considerable popular appeal. Historical paintings were ubiquitous as were pictures with religious and moral themes. Classical imagery was also well represented, as it afforded viewers in an age of propriety the opportunity to admire unclad nymphs and goddesses.

In addition, the Salons were practically obligatory as social events, even for those who were beginning to be weary of the annual extravaganza. "All Parisians are standing shivering on the brink of a deluge of pictures which is rising steadily over the City of Light," the newspaper correspondent Nettie Hooper wrote on May 13, 1896. "One knows one must go to see these multitudinous works of art. First it is one's duty and secondly, not to be present on Varnishing Day at the two Salons is to be a degenerate citizen. Prolonged stations before the pictures however, brings on various disagreeable results. One contracts what Parisians call the 'Salon headache,' which is a combination of violent pain in the back of the head and an undeveloped but sanguinary wish that all artists who exhibit had died in their infancy."[374]

Hooper, who evidently did not suffer from "Salon headache," reported that on Varnishing Day an interested crowd surrounded Cecilia Beaux's group of paintings. Reviewers were interested, too. The influential French critic M. Henri Rochefort whose comments were translated and printed in the *The New Herald*, declared, "I am compelled to admit, not without some chagrin, that not one of our female artists . . . is strong enough to compete with the lady who has given us this year the portrait of Dr. Grier. Composition, flesh, texture, sound drawing—everything is there without affectation, and without seeking for effect."[375]

The *Harper's Bazaar* correspondent Katherine De Forest happened to be in the galleries when the awards committee, headed by Puvis de Chavannes (1824–1898), went through the Salon, and she reported on their deliberations. The painter Carolus Duran was dressed stylishly in a gray suit and hat, wore white kid gloves, and held an unlit cigarette between his second and third fingers while he cast his votes using black or white beans from bags carried by uniformed Salon employees. Among the distinguished group De Forest recognized the artists Gustave Courtois (1853–1923) and Jean Beraud (1849–1935), also elegantly attired for the occasion. Puvis de Chavannes marshaled this assembly through the exhibition by ringing a bell when it was time to cast their votes. When the jury stood in front of Miss Beaux's paintings, they must have seemed impressed because De Forest predicted that some honor would be awarded. Beaux was named an *associée* of the Société Nationale des Beaux-Arts, a title that brought with it the privilege of having one painting assured to hang each year at the Champ-de-Mars.

Beaux, who had never expected such honors, arrived in Paris to much acclaim. "At the Champ de Mars. With all Cecilia's group accepted. Enormous number of people and many celebrities," Henry McCarter wrote. "I was looking through a wide doorway—numbers of people were looking at someone approaching. It was Cecilia Beaux and John Lambert walking together. Tall, young, large—fresh as daisies—sweet and clean as new milk. They were absolutely alone and entirely unlike all the types and items around them. John was twenty-eight, Cecilia less, I hope. A little of that day has always remained with my Cecilia."[376] Cecilia Beaux was actually thirty-nine years old when McCarter spotted her in at the Salon galleries, and she had just realized an almost impossible goal. Within seven years the supplicant, who went trembling to the Palais de l'Industrie to learn the fate of her portrait of Louise Kinsella, had returned to the capital of the art world in triumph. And although she had reason to believe that this idyll would last, and that the best times were ahead of her, there was always that note of warning in Cecilia's nature. Something told her that even this great honor would not be enough.

Before she left France, Beaux went to Giverny to visit an American classmate from the Académie Julian and Académie Colorossi, Lilla Cabot Perry (1848–1933). Perry and her husband, Thomas, were close friends of Claude Monet (1840–1926), and for nine summers the Perrys rented a house at Giverny. When Lilla took Beaux to meet Monet, they found him in overalls and a large hat, standing in the middle of his sun-dappled garden amid a blaze of poppies and delphiniums. Genial Monet led the two women into his studio, where he showed them his latest landscapes—ethereal paintings of the river Seine. Lilla noticed that Monet had abandoned pointillism for this series and questioned him about this change of style. "*La Nature n'a pas de pointes*," Monet responded agreeably.[377] Beaux was delighted with this reply and in her autobiography recalled that while many other artists had just discovered pointillism and were rushing to embrace the new technique, Monet, the innovator, ever searching, had moved in a new direction. "Monet was never satisfied," Beaux wrote with profound understanding. Ever the perfectionist, she was never satisfied either.[378]

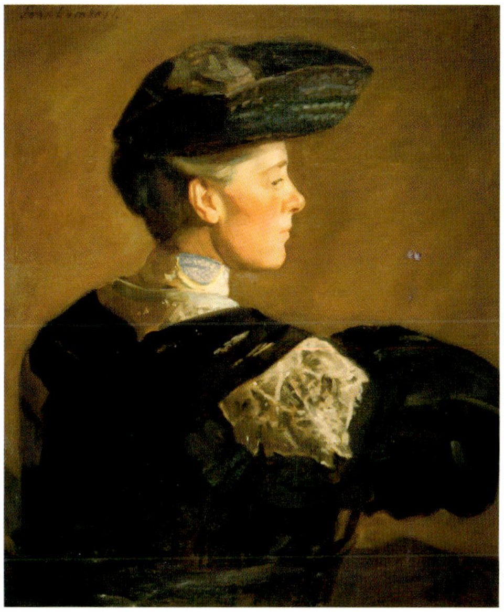

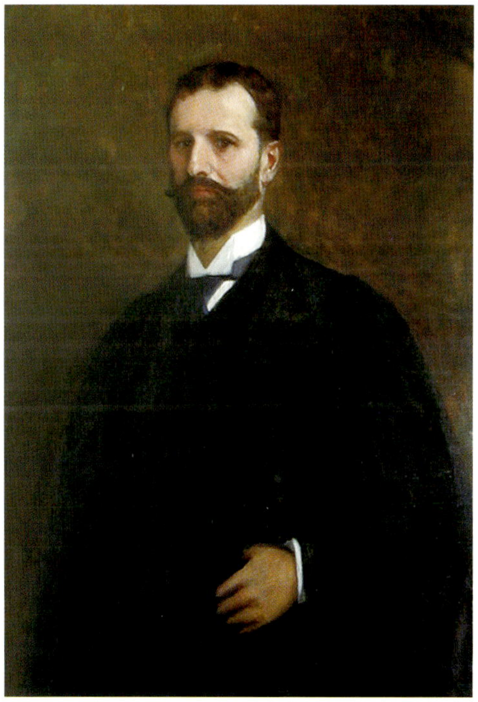

72. TOP: *John Lambert.* ***Cecilia Beaux.*** *ca. 1905. Oil on canvas, 29 15/16 x 24 3/4 in. Pennsylvania Academy of the Fine Arts*

73. BOTTOM: ***Algernon Sydney Biddle.*** *1891. Oil on canvas, 39 7/16 x 29 1/2 in. Courtesy of the University of Pennsylvania Art Collection, Philadelphia*

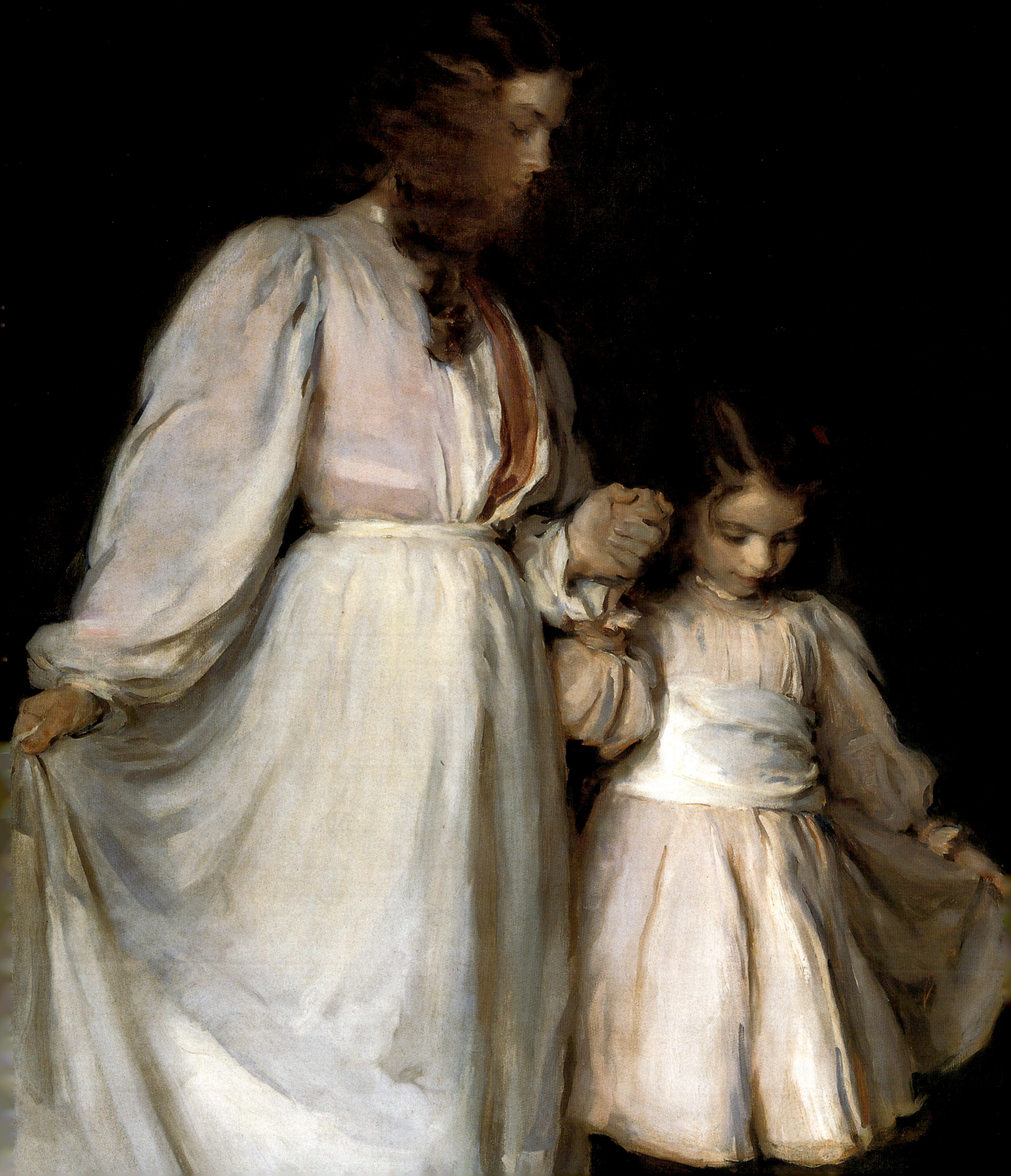

The Gilder Age

This is the place where we our love did hide:
That poor, fierce, fruitless mortal love of ours.
T'was here we crushed Life's perfumed crimson flowers
And drank the last sweet draught of Love Denied.

—Cecilia Beaux, *from her poem "Years After"*

Sometime after Cecilia Beaux's return from Paris in 1889, Cousin Kate Janvier introduced her to the poet and editor Richard Watson Gilder and his wife, the painter Helena DeKay Gilder. Richard Watson Gilder was the editor-in-chief of *The Century*, America's most popular late nineteenth-century literary magazine. Because of *The Century*'s wide circulation, Gilder's editorial decisions influenced the country's cultural life so profoundly that his biographer, Herbert F. Smith, concluded that the years between 1880 and 1890 should be renamed "The Gilder Age." In support of American literature, Gilder championed copyright laws that prevented American magazines from printing pirated works by English authors, thus creating a thriving market for American writers.

According to Smith, Gilder's greatest triumph as an editor was the magazine's February 1885 issue that included *The Rise of Silas Lapham* by William Dean Howells, a portion of *Huckleberry Finn* by Mark Twain, and Henry James's, *The Bostonians*. "That one issue," Smith asserted, "represents probably the greatest twenty-five cents worth of original American literature in the history of American periodicals."[379] Although Gilder's most significant influence on American taste was expressed through his promotion of domestic writers, he also supported the careers of American artists by featuring them in *The Century's American Artists Series*.

Gilder's wife, Helena DeKay Gilder (1846–1916), who studied at Cooper Union and The National Academy of Design, was also an advocate for American painters, especially artists who abandoned Victorian themes in favor of expressive, painterly work. With her encouragement, *The Century* promoted American realist Winslow Homer (1836–1910), American Impressionists William Merritt Chase and Julian Alden Weir (1852–1919), the sculptor Augustus Saint-Gaudens (1848–1907), visionary painter Albert Pinkham Ryder (1847–1917), and a host of others whose careers might have languished without the Gilders' help. Cecilia Beaux, also a beneficiary of their largess, was first featured in *The Century's American Artists Series* in the September 1894 issue. Thomas Janvier supplied the biographical information; an engraving of Beaux's painting *Reverie* (now titled *The Dreamer*) accompanied the text.

The Gilders' position as arbiters of American tastes was enhanced by the soirées held every Friday night at their home at 13 East Eighth Street. The list of celebrities who graced these legendary parties was impressive and included Jan Paderewski, Mark Twain, Bret Harte,

OPPOSITE: *Detail;* ***Dorothea and Francesca.*** *1898. Oil on canvas, 80 1/8 x 46 in. The Art Institute of Chicago*

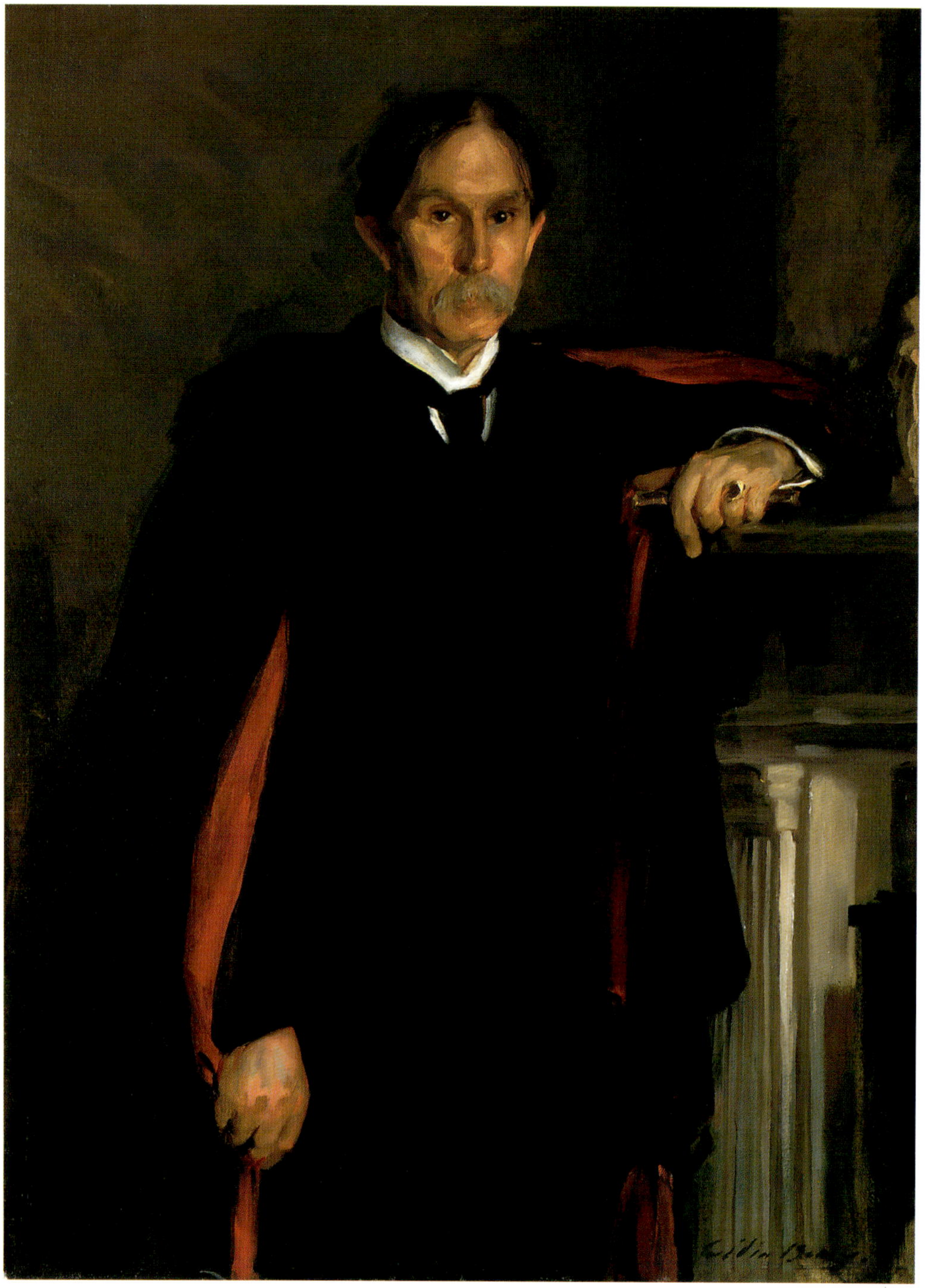

74. ABOVE: ***Richard Watson Gilder.*** *1902–3. Oil on canvas, 45 7/8 x 34 1/2 in. National Portrait Gallery, Smithsonian Institution, Washington, D.C.*

75. OPPOSITE: ***Miss Gilder [Francesca Gilder].*** *n.d. Oil on canvas, 26 1/2 x 18 1/4 in. National Academy of Design, New York*

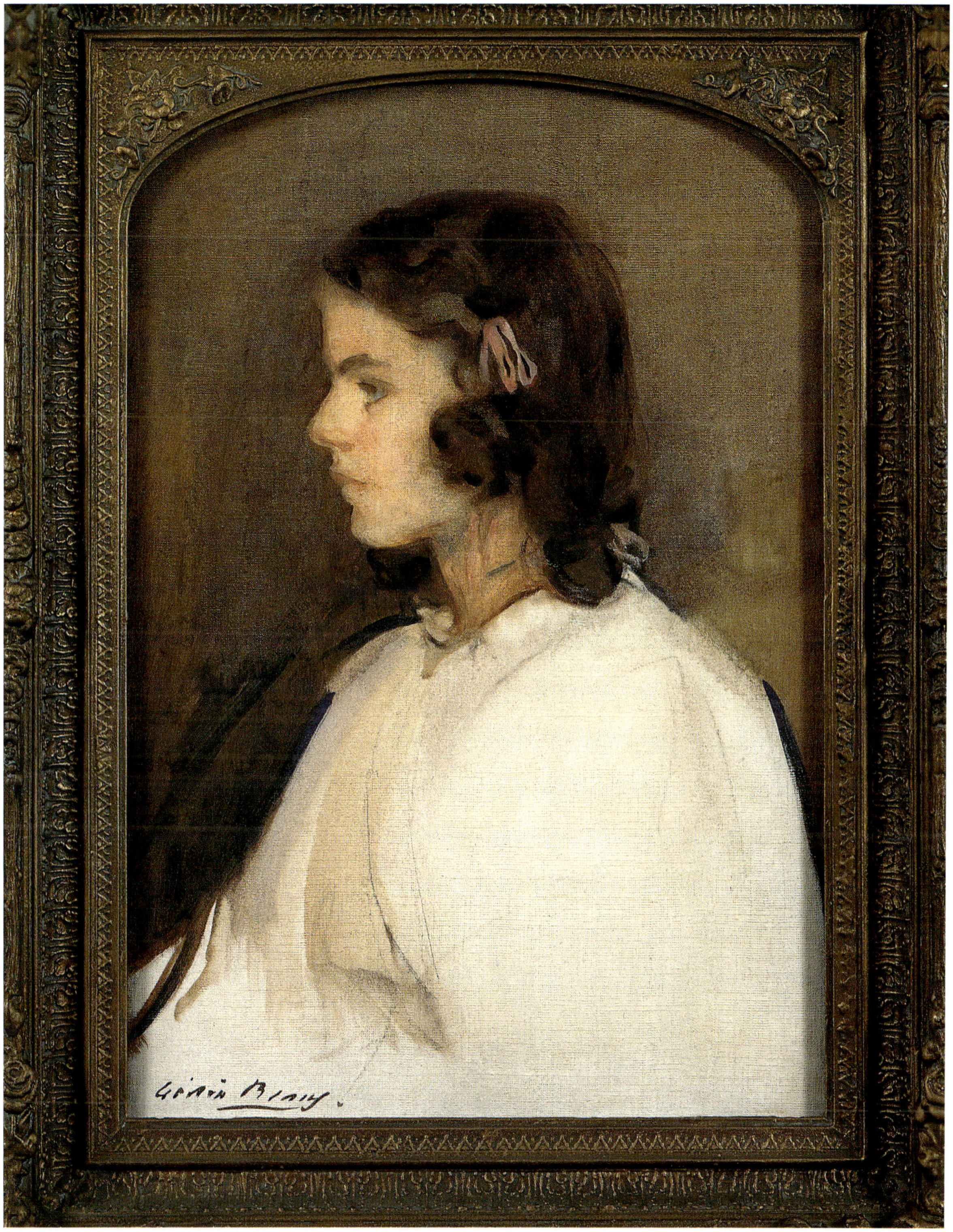

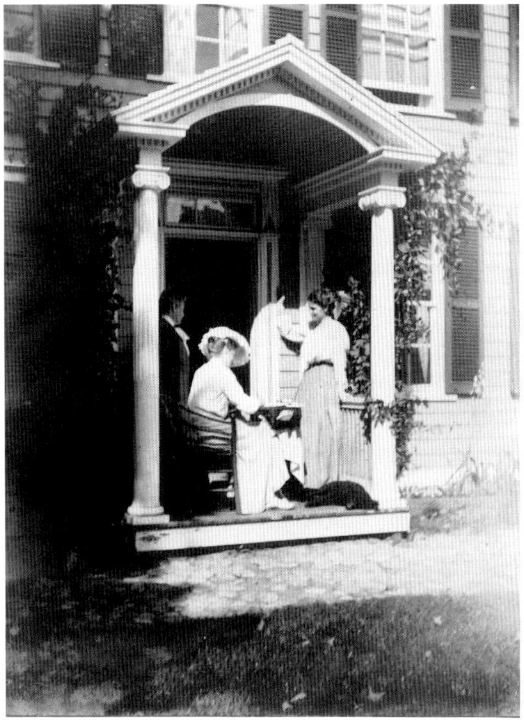

76. ***Cecilia Beaux** (seated) **Helena DeKay Gilder and Dorothea Gilder at Four Brooks Farm, Tyringham, Massachusetts,*** ca. 1900–5. *Pennsylvania Academy of the Fine Arts*

Grover Cleveland, Theodore Roosevelt, and Walt Whitman, who remembered, "At a time when most everybody in their set threw me down, they were notably and unhesitatingly hospitable."[380]

Richard and Helena Gilder also opened their home to Cecilia Beaux, providing her with social and professional connections she could never have achieved on her own. In the 1890s, when she was still living quietly in her third-floor room on Spruce Street, she would travel to New York and, in what must have seemed a stunning transformation, enter a world of sophistication and social standing that she found tremendously exciting. Beaux wrote that at the Gilders' she could take part in a life that "vividly joined and disseminated every form of intellectual and artistic activity. . . . Richard and Helena Gilder were complete and firmly defined individuals," she recalled. "In what their marriage meant to the world around them, they were phenomenal."[381]

In her autobiography Beaux wrote that although she made important contacts through her association with the Gilders, she was not always included in the parties. "I belonged to an intermediate generation, but was classed with the children, that is Rodman and Dorothea, my part being to assist with them and I often did not meet the personalities who gathered around Mrs. Gilder's tea-table, finding out who they were later."[382] Why Beaux, who was only nine years younger than Helena Gilder, who was an internationally acclaimed artist older than many of the Gilders' celebrity guests, who was old enough to be Rodman or Dorothea's mother, was classed with the Gilder children is bewildering. Perhaps, like many of her other close friends, the Gilders had no idea that Beaux was in her forties.

In the fall of 1898 the Gilders invited Beaux to accompany them to their family farm, Four Brooks, located on the side of a picturesque valley in the Berkshire town of Tyringham, Massachusetts. At the time, Rodman Gilder was twenty-one and Dorothea sixteen, and presumably, neither one required her assistance, so Cecilia took the opportunity to paint, selecting for her models Dorothea and her younger sister, Francesca. The Gilders renovated the old tobacco barn on the property for Cecilia's use as a studio, adding more windows to let in the light. When the improvements were complete, Cecilia set to work building a model stand so that the girls would not have to pose on the hard, dirt floor. Inspired by an impromptu dance invented by the two sisters, Beaux began an ambitious double portrait—a full-length oil of both girls.[383]

The painting progressed slowly, but the Gilder sisters were patient and posed for several months. When it rained in September, water poured into the barn, and although the girls were dry on their model stand, Beaux's easel was set up on the wet floor. Determined to finish, she donned rubber boots, stood in a puddle of water, and worked on through the fall. In October the weather turned bitterly cold, and the girls posed in their coats. When Beaux finally finished "on a dark autumnal night," the picture was packed by candlelight in the freezing barn and shipped to London, where it was exhibited in the 1899 International Exposition and received much critical praise. Beaux was pleased with the canvas, too; a reporter from the *Philadelphia Star* wrote that Beaux considered the painting to be "one of her best achievements."[384] And indeed, the portrait is remarkable. Beaux, who was perceptive and knew the character of both girls well, painted the Gilder sisters with elegance and deep sympathy. Little Francesca charmed her, and something in sixteen-year-old Dorothea Gilder awakened her heart.

The friendship between Cecilia Beaux and Dorothea Gilder grew over a period of years. Beaux's first surviving letter to Dorothea Gilder was mailed from Spruce Street in 1897. "Dearest Child," Beaux wrote, "This is only to tell you how dear and sweet your letter was—Ernesta does her best to love me enough for all of you—but don't stop." Dorothea, evidently pleased by the attention of her parents' illustrious friend, did not stop. And Beaux did nothing to discourage the girl's adulation.

By 1898 Cecilia Beaux was profoundly lonely, and although she was still a beautiful woman, she must have felt her youth slipping away. A reporter describing her appearance at the time seemed thankful to find that she was in "no sense mannish," and although he noted that she was "strikingly handsome," with a "face young and finely chiseled," he also mentioned that her hair was turning gray.[385] The signs of age were not only cosmetic. Beaux suffered from what she called "a kind of neuritis" in her right hand that belied her youthful appearance and made painting painful and writing sometimes impossible, as she could not grip a pen. Aspirin was not marketed until the following year and may not have helped in any case, as her problem persisted even after the drug was widely available. Beaux's only remedy for the pain aside from curtailing her hours at the easel, which she was not prepared to do, was to plunge her hand alternately into hot and cold water.[386]

Beaux's physical discomfort must have given her pause to reflect on the decisions that seemed so clear when she was young and imagined that her youth and beauty would last. Contrary to what she believed during her student days in Paris, Beaux discovered that her passion for her work would not be enough to sustain her. She longed for physical intimacy and for the kind of love that her faithful relatives could not supply. In 1899 she began to separate herself from her family in Philadelphia and started spending considerable time in New York. Aunt Emily and Uncle Will were in their sixties, and Aunt Eliza was seventy-three. They lived a quiet life centered on their church and the Drinker children, but Beaux was not ready to retire emotionally and wished for something more. She leased a studio at 64 Washington Square, close to the Gilders' home on Eighth Street, and spent a good deal of time with Dorothea.

Eighteen-ninety-nine was another year of professional triumph. On November 3 Beaux was awarded the Medal of the First Class and a $1,500 cash award from the Carnegie Institute in Pittsburgh for her double portrait of Mrs. Clement A. Griscom and her daughter Frances Canby, which she called *Mother and Daughter*. It was on the occasion of this award that William Merritt Chase, in a public speech, stated his admiration for Beaux's work: "Miss Beaux is not only the greatest woman painter, but the best that has ever lived. Miss Beaux has done away entirely with sex [gender] in art."[387] However, this accomplishment did nothing to remedy the loneliness in Beaux's heart. When she was handed the Carnegie Medal, she was thrilled to receive the handsome prize: "It was so glorious in saffron velvet and chamois, so great and splendid that I stooped to kiss it and it was cold—such is fame."

Cold as it was, Beaux's fame continued, and more medals were added to her growing cache. The following year she won another gold medal at the

Pennsylvania Academy of the Fine Arts for *Mother and Daughter* and was the only woman asked to serve on a jury to select American paintings to exhibit at the Paris Exposition. Her jury assignment was important; the Exposition was a unique opportunity for American painters to prove their worth by competing favorably for the prestigious international prizes to be awarded in Paris.

That summer, accompanied by Richard and Helena Gilder, Beaux set out for France to see the Exposition and to find out how the American work she had helped to select had fared with the judges in Paris. She stopped first at the Darwins' home in Cambridge, where she read in the *St. James Gazette* that not only had American painters been awarded more prizes than any other country except France but that she had received yet another gold medal. Beaux longed to share this good news with Dorothea, but because her hand hurt so badly, she had to dictate her letter to George Darwin. "You are so funny that all this will not surprise you," she wrote to Dorothea concerning the award, "but it did me for I honestly did not expect it."[388]

While Beaux was with the Gilders in Cambridge, they introduced her to their friends and generously included her in every outing and social occasion. "I go round as an appendage of your parents," she told Dorothea. "They try to pronounce my name with great clearness in introducing me; but it almost never has any effect; and perhaps it is good for me to understand the blank expression on the faces of many who would say: 'Why lay such stress upon the name of one who is just another woman.'"[389] Beaux's most profound fear was that somehow, in spite of all her struggles and personal sacrifices, she would be regarded as "just another woman." That fear led her to persevere in spite of any obstacles and to forgo time-consuming emotional attachments that might require her full attention. Initially, her friendship with Dorothea Gilder presented no such threat.

However, in 1901, when Dorothea was seventeen and Beaux forty-four, the content of their correspondence began to change. If the letters she sent to Dorothea were not in Beaux's hand, it would be difficult to believe that she wrote them. Beaux penned long letters throughout her life to family, close friends, and hopeful suitors, but these are unique. Many seem childish—the paroxysms of first love—and hardly what would be expected of a renowned professional with a droll wit and a gift for writing amusing anecdotes. But evidently she could not help herself. Beaux, the perfectionist who believed that she could best express her faith in God through perfect conduct, was inexplicably and inappropriately in love with the daughter of her kind benefactors. "At last, dear D. I get to you. . . . And must tell you first that I want terribly to be hugged. . . . This letter sounds too foolish to be handed about any more than our dear silly times together, and I want to be as foolish as I choose when I write to you," Beaux confessed.[390] By 1902 Beaux was sending gifts and poems to Dorothea.

She addressed her letters to "Dodo Dear, Dearest Do" and "My Beloved," and signed, "Your Own Cecilia" and "Your Bo-Ardor." She described her isolation and vulnerability, revelations that seem inappropriate for a forty-five-year-old woman to share with a teenager.[391] "I am dull and want petting terribly," Beaux wrote to Dorothea in March.[392] In April Dorothea, young and enamored in a way that at the time would have been considered quaint and entirely respectable had Beaux been her contemporary, responded in kind.

> I come from you and I would hold for a few minutes longer the deep joy of having kissed you. Now this one time holds its identity and is in itself a perfect whole. Soon it will slide half unconsciously into the company of other times adding indescribably to their dearness. The infinite desire, and the never ending growth of love seems to me to be the greatest proof we have of the possibility of eternity.[393]

If Beaux had not been serious about their relationship, the receipt of this letter would have been the

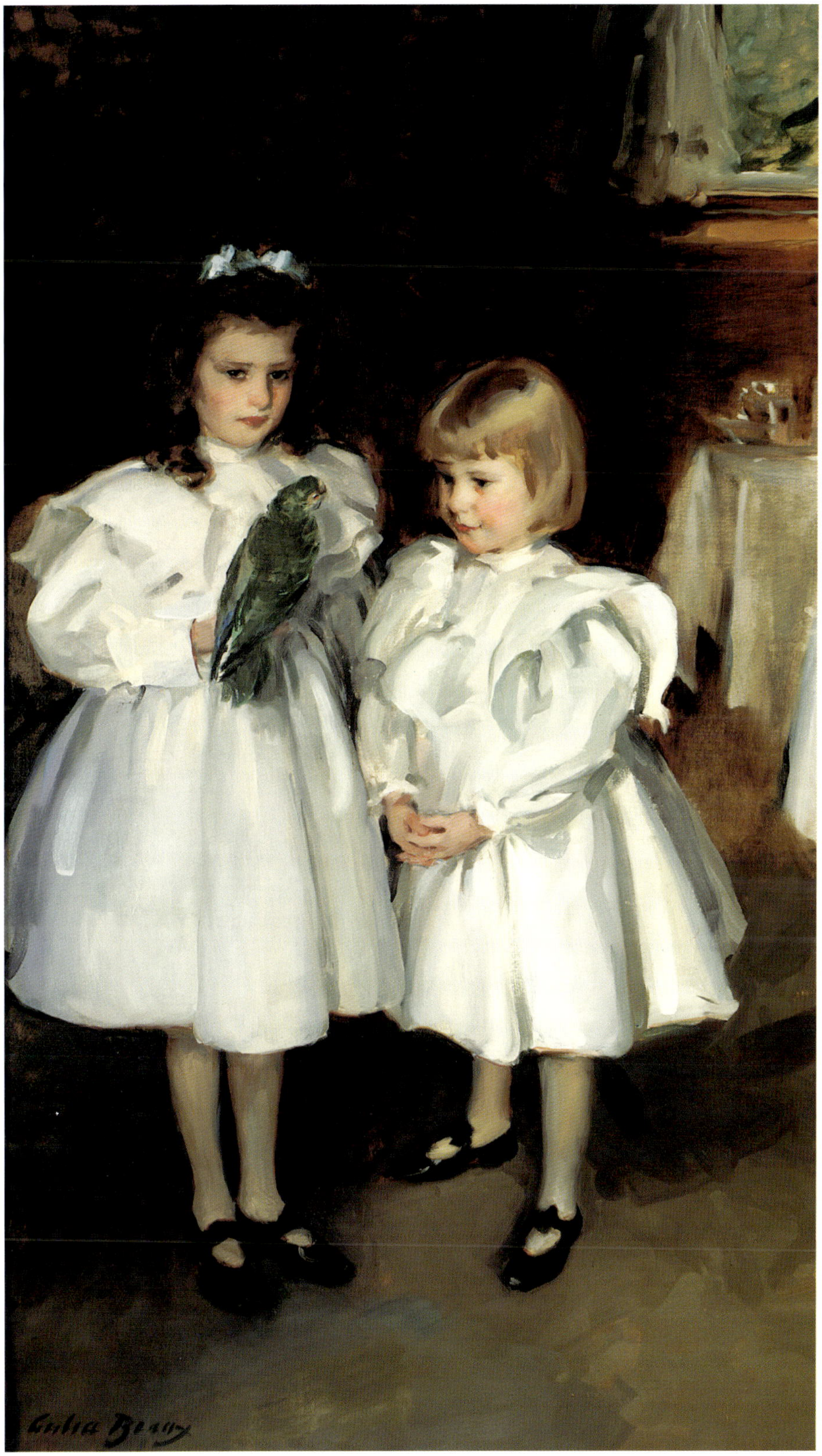

77. ***Gertrude and Elizabeth Henry.*** *1898–99. Oil on canvas, 64 x 37 1/4 in. Pennsylvania Academy of the Fine Arts*

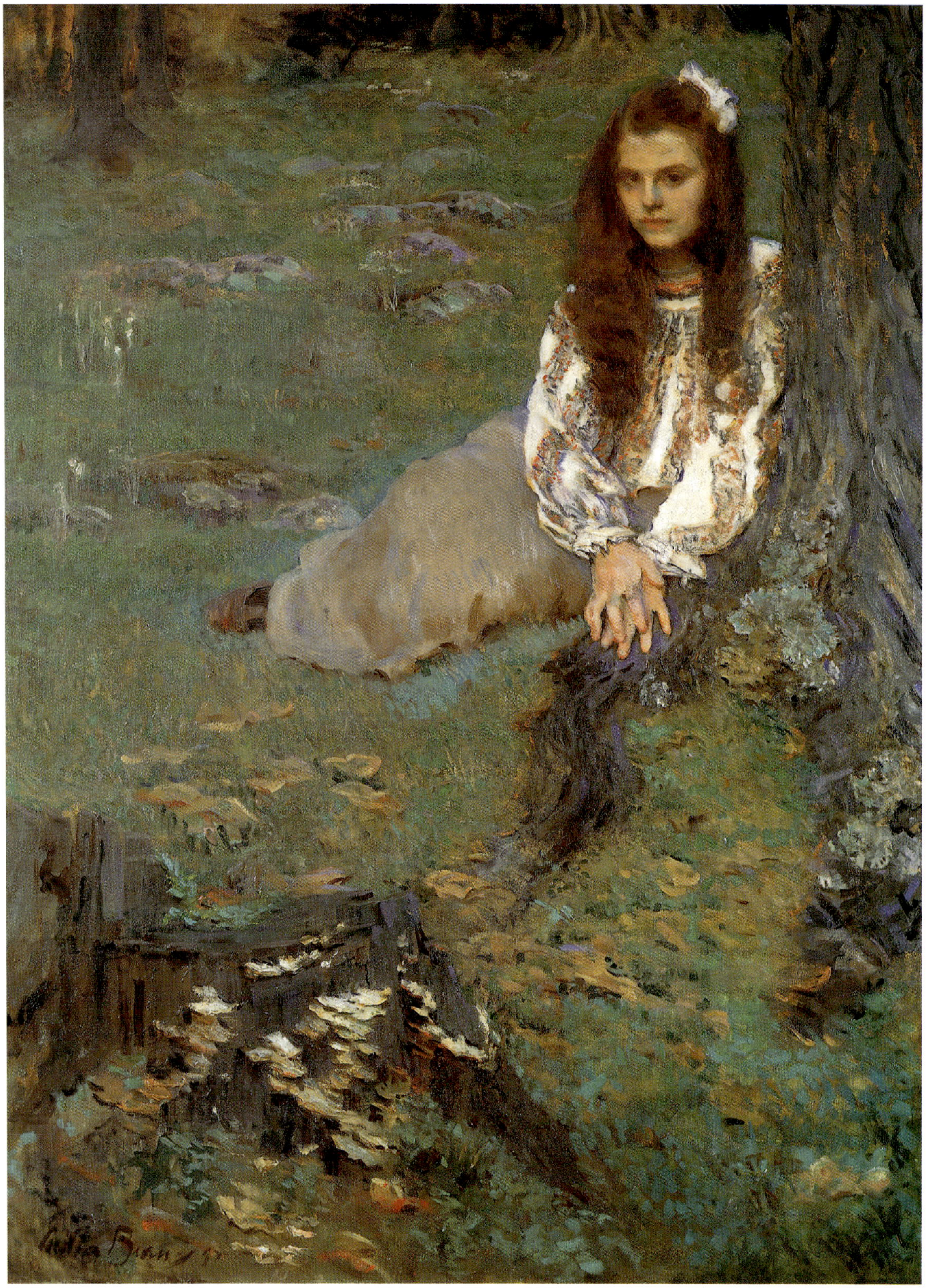

opportunity to establish the parameters of a more conventional friendship. Dorothea was a schoolgirl with a breathless crush on a celebrity. Beaux was a lonely woman, who should have been more prudent about allowing her middle-age malaise to intrude on the life of a vivacious young woman. Apparently, Beaux had no such qualms. In June she received another passionate letter from Dorothea, which she did not discourage. "When I am with you I can sometimes think of nothing else. Just as a man without air strives desperately to get it and can do nothing else," Dorothea wrote in June.[394] "Oh I am glad you love me D. glad—almost the only glad I have. And glad I can love you back," Cecilia responded. She hoped to have more time with Dorothea, to meet her at Four Brooks. "I am longing for the farm. . . . I want to go over several times a day. . . . Just you and I in the buggy. . . . To steal away in the morning and come home after supper. Not stay all night. . . we could not be comfortable and would get up feeling weary and dissipated."[395]

That fall Beaux was busy working on a portrait in Boston and sent many anxious letters to Dorothea in an attempt to arrange a meeting. When their plans did not work out, Beaux was disconsolate. "Oh dearest, dearest D. Believe that I am doing the best I can—Life is a queer puzzle and try as I can except in my work thus far—I am bound to be on the losing side. I am aching to see you so we can spend a day or two."[396] Two weeks later Beaux had to admit that because of the demands of her work, she would not be able to meet Dorothea. "Darling—Darling," she wrote. "You must not come down for this little time. . . . It is hard for me to plead a cause against myself—but oh, love me—love me still—dearest D." By October 14 they had evidently been able to arrange a rendezvous because Beaux wrote, "Darling –D. if I could only have had your arms around me a little longer—if I only could."[397]

Beaux understood that Richard and Helena Gilder would not approve of her familiarity with their daughter. She owed much to them and knew it. When they were all in Cambridge together she had written to Dorothea, "When your mother has said 'we' in her letters, it included me; for they took me to all the nice things they did, and the great heap of indebtedness grows apace."[398] That fall, in an attempt to conceal their intimacy, she began sending two kinds of letters to Dorothea—witty accounts of her commissions and travels that were appropriate for Dorothea to share with the family and more personal notes. To one cheerfully impersonal letter sent in October, she attached an addendum.

> Darling D. My letter today is not necessarily private unless you wish it to be. I think it is better for you not to have to hide them all. No—my letters must never feel like a hand of pity. For that is not true—It is clinging love—I can not do without you. Of the things that I want, you seem to be the only one that I may have—and I give thanks.[399]

It is hardly surprising that Beaux did not want the Gilders to discover the nature of her relationship with Dorothea. They had showed her kindness and promoted her career by publishing her paintings, illustrations, and even her poems. But, although Richard Gilder may have been troubled by their deception, passionate relationships between women were not unknown to him. Gilder's father had been a Methodist minister and the proprietor of a girls' school in Flushing, Queens, cheerfully nicknamed "The Flushing Female Academy" by local residents. Gilder was educated at his father's school, where he was the only male student, and presumably (as Beaux discovered at the Lyman School), romance between the girls was not uncommon. Even if Gilder had been oblivious to gossip at school, he published *The Bostonians*, Henry James's tale of love between an older and younger woman, a story that mirrored the relationship between Cecilia and Dorothea. He also

78. OPPOSITE: ***Dorothea in the Woods.*** *1897. Oil on canvas, 53 1/4 x 40 in. Whitney Museum of American Art*

79. RIGHT: ***Mother and Daughter.*** *1898. Oil on canvas, 83 x 44 in. Pennsylvania Academy of the Fine Arts*
80. OPPOSITE: ***Bertha Hallowell Vaughan.*** *1901. Oil on canvas, 58 x 38 in. Courtesy of the Harvard University Portrait Collection*

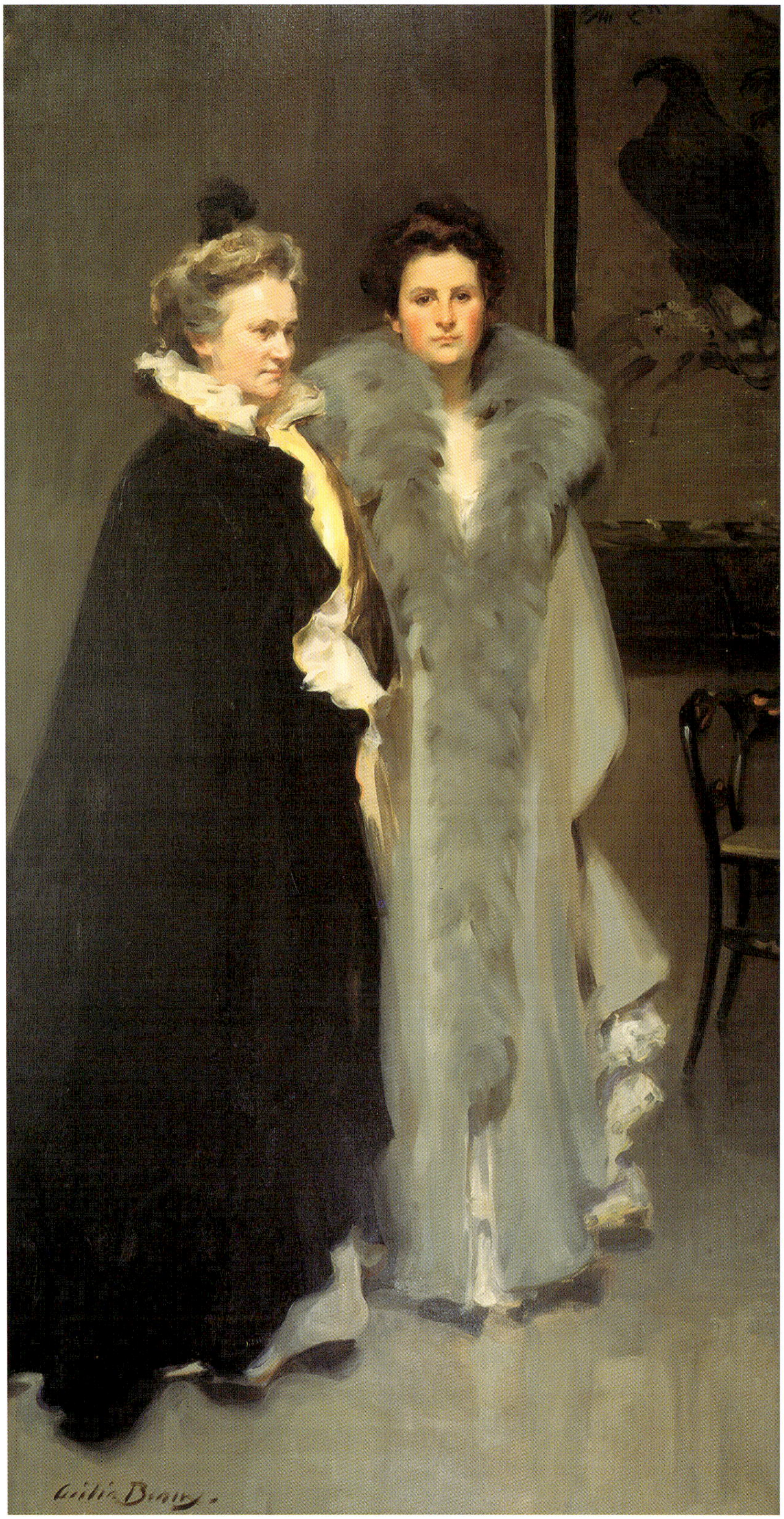

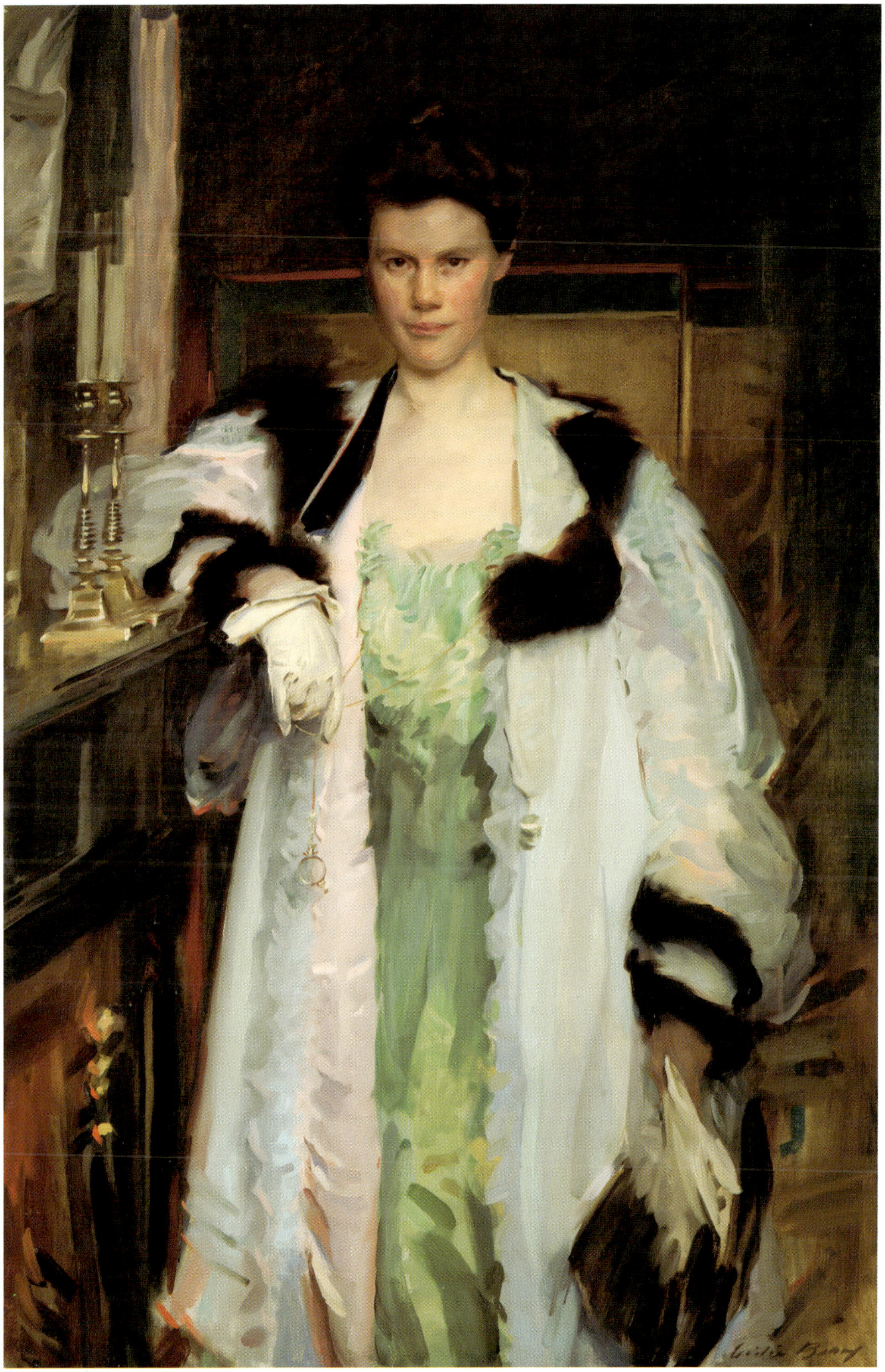

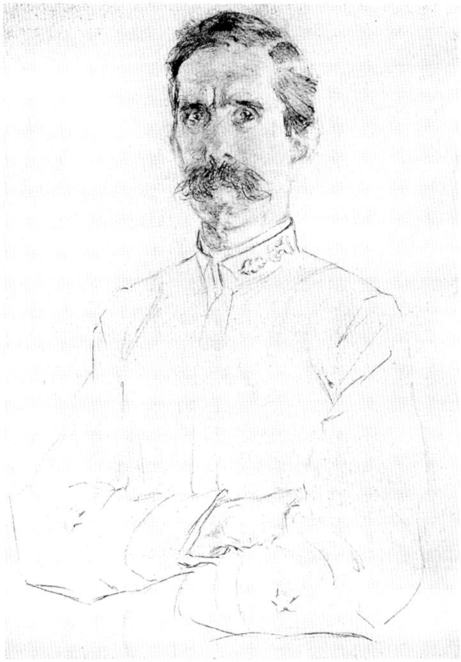

81. ***Richard Wainwright.*** *1898. Graphite on paper, 22 x 15 in. Cape Ann Historical Association, Gloucester, Massachusetts*

may have been aware that his wife, Helena DeKay Gilder, by every account a devoted and loving spouse, exchanged intimate and occasionally passionate letters with her childhood friend, the illustrator and writer Mary Hallock Foote, for most of their adult lives. The correspondence between the two women became the basis of Wallace Stegner's Pulitzer Prize–winning novel, *The Angle of Repose*, published in 1971.

Judging from their letters, the emotional and physical intimacy between Cecilia Beaux and Dorothea Gilder endured until 1906. During the time they were romantically involved, Dorothea grew from a schoolgirl into a beautiful young woman with a host of male admirers and Beaux was remarkably productive, completing portraits in her studios in Philadelphia, New York, Boston, and Gloucester, Massachusetts. Some of her most impressive commissions came through her association with the Gilders. A social occasion at Four Brooks resulted in a large oil of Mrs. Alexander Sedgwick and her daughter Christina. The Gilder connection with Theodore Roosevelt brought an invitation to go to the White House in 1902 and paint a portrait of First Lady Edith Roosevelt. The commission necessitated several visits to Washington, D.C., where Beaux painted Edith and her daughter Ethel in a double portrait. Beaux described her vision for the painting in a letter to Dorothea.

> The drama is . . . Mrs. R . . . cordially engaged with a visitor. . . . Modest-fearless little daughter impelled by mingled curiosity and affection, enters and plumps herself down beside Mama, who takes her little hand into her own lap to insure quiet and communicate maternal sympathy. Little daughter however, not interested in visitor, looks eagerly across her mother's bows at SOMETHING ELSE . . . for which I am an humble understudy. A pale blue velvet bow pins the eye to the middle of the canvas, and around it these various animations vibrate, and are finally lost in the ruby depths of the private-dining room wall-paper.[400]

While she was working on her portrait of Mrs. Roosevelt and Ethel, Beaux had a unique opportunity to become acquainted with the First Family. She dined with the Roosevelts in their private quarters and attended gala receptions and diplomatic functions. The experience was dazzling. "I love my president," she wrote enthusiastically to her relatives in Philadelphia. "I have made a sketch of him. He sat for two hours, talking most of the time, reciting Kipling, and reading scraps of Browning."[401] One evening she was invited to a State Dinner where Ignace Paderewski provided the entertainment and played one of her favorite pieces, Chopin's *Heroic* Polonaise. On this occasion Beaux did not hear the familiar warning in the cascading notes; she was too thrilled by the performance. "Paderewski out-did himself," she informed her aunts and uncle.[402]

> By the time he got to the Polonaise . . . the one with the tragic octaves—well—I think it may have been better than hearing Chopin himself. All of

Paderewski's gigantic power was back of it. I don't believe he has ever gone higher, farther, or deeper. I nearly broke under it—which means that I experienced all I could endure of joy—and was aware that I had tasted the best of its kind that creation can offer.[403]

In March 1903 Beaux borrowed the painting of Mrs. Roosevelt from the President and exhibited it along with twenty-eight of her other portraits in a solo show at the Durand-Ruel Gallery in New York. Reviews were generally positive, although critics were beginning to tire of Grand Manner portraits commissioned by wealthy patrons.[404] The reporter for the *Mail and Express* wrote that walking into the exhibition was like entering a well-ordered drawing room. "Children and grown folk are presented with an understanding of their own social attitudes toward life by an artist who in this respect is one of themselves."[405] Although Beaux's skill was unquestionable and much admired, there were comments about a certain superficial quality to the work, which reflected a growing attitude that no matter how masterful the painting, the subject matter did not provide enough substance to interest twentieth-century viewers. "Apart from their rare ability they have little to hold us," a writer for the *New York Evening Sun* commented.[406]

These barbs from the critics, the first indication that the aesthetic of the society portrait was in danger of falling from its lofty place in the hierarchy of genres, apparently did not concern Cecilia Beaux. Although she was often unsure of herself in social and personal situations, by 1903 Beaux harbored no doubts about the validity of painting portraits. Her professional confidence was bolstered by the acclaim her work had received in Paris. She treasured a review by the noted French critic Paul Bion, certain that his insights validated her work. Bion considered Beaux to be an ambassador of Americanism; at a time when the United States was still regarded as an intellectual backwater—the best of its citizenry rough-edged, brash pioneers. Bion maintained that Beaux's portraits were a revelation that

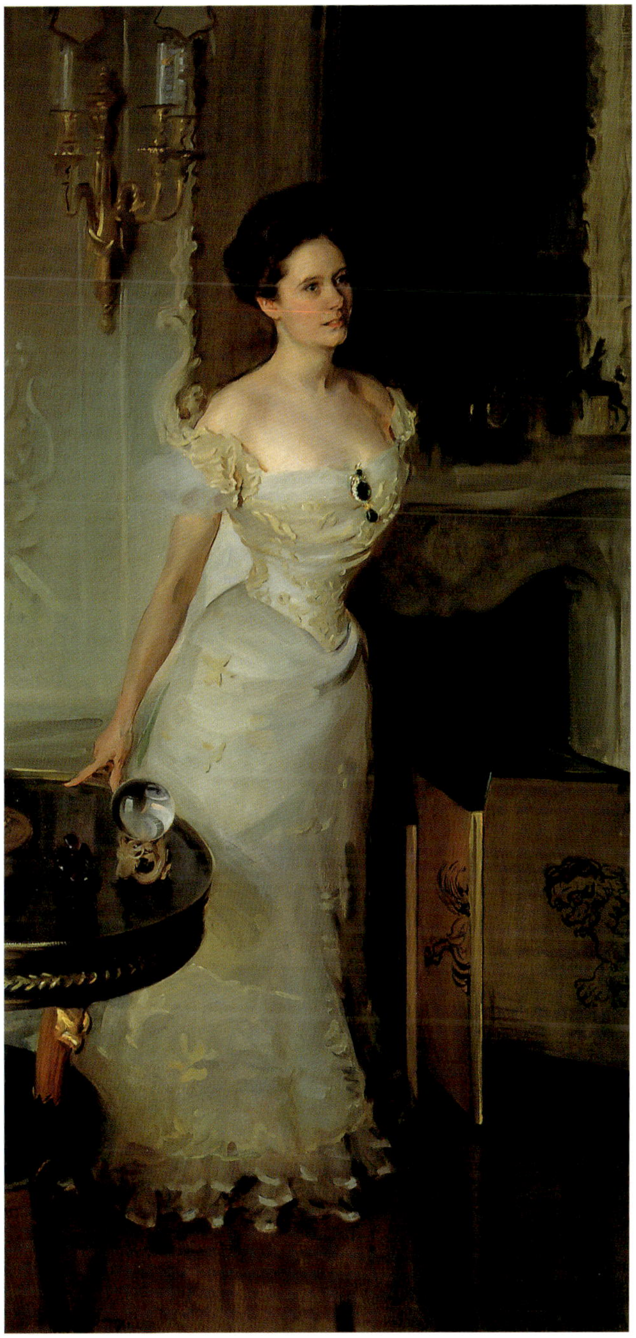

82. **Mrs. Larz Anderson.** *1901. Oil on canvas, 82 x 40 in. The Society of the Cincinnati*

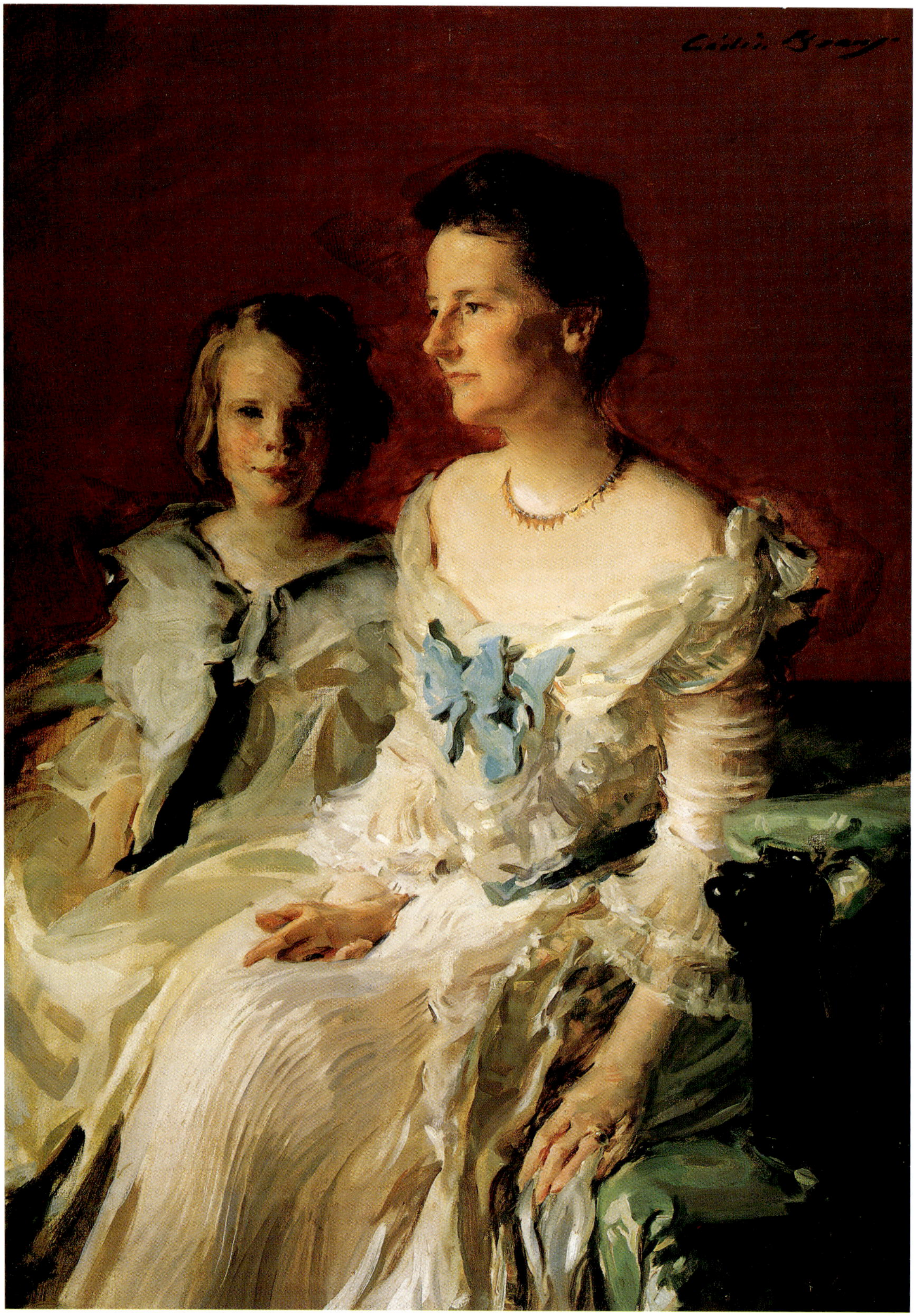
Cecilia Beaux

provided Europeans with a favorable view of the United States. "Here is the news she brings us," Bion wrote. "That not all American girls have enough confidence to run in front of the world and laugh in its face. . . . That there are also in Connecticut respectable grandmothers. . . . Here also is good Doctor Grier . . . a distinguished man, doubtlessly a scholar."[407] Although Beaux was proud of her dual heritage, she was an unapologetically patriotic American, and the idea that her work disseminated a positive image of the United States was immensely gratifying. Nevertheless, Beaux should have been more vigilant about the changes in American artistic tastes, and she might have been, had personal concerns not occupied so much of her time. Sustaining her discreet relationship with Dorothea Gilder required planning and emotional energy. In addition, Beaux was worried about both her sister Etta and her two aging aunts.

In 1903 Etta and Henry Drinker seemed to be living an idyllic life. They were settled comfortably with their six children, ranging in age from six to twenty-three, in a large gray house on the campus of Haverford College. Henry Drinker, employed as the counsel for the Lehigh Valley Railroad, found to his delight that he was able to support his family generously. Etta, who had grown up in an austere household where self-sufficiency was both a virtue and a necessity, was freed from most domestic tasks by a group of household servants. The Drinker family employed a cook, waitress, laundress, upstairs maid, coachman, gardener, children's nurse, stableman, and governess. Summers were spent in Beach Haven, New Jersey, where the family gathered at Curlew Cottage, a rambling beach house so beloved that taciturn Henry Drinker was moved to immortalize it in verse.

> I love my home, my home beside the sea.
> Where with pleasures meet, and in accord,
> The days drift on with those I love,
> Where joy attends my coming,
> And my going is but parting for a day.[408]

Obviously Henry Drinker was happy, and Etta, it would seem, had every reason to share his contentment. However, after the birth of her youngest child in 1897, she suffered from what was diagnosed as a serious nervous breakdown.[409] Ernesta recalled that when the crisis passed, her mother persevered but never fully recovered. "She became a very bad sleeper and remained highly nervous from that time on. We were all taught that she must not be put under any strain."[410]

Etta's illness developed at about the same time that Beaux was falling in love with Dorothea Gilder, and despite the intensity of her feelings for her young friend, Beaux was deeply concerned about her sister. She visited the Drinker family often and tried to add something positive to the lives of her nieces and nephews. "Every so often she would come to Haverford for a night," Ernesta recalled.

> To me these were gala occasions when I would go to her room at the head of the stairs, see her Paris clothes and delight in all she said or did. . . . Furthermore she introduced us to people in the world of artists and musicians, to the literary group led by Richard Watson Gilder. She gave us a glimpse of sophistication in manners, which we lacked. It would be impossible to overestimate the value to us of our contact with so positive and so inspiring an individual.[411]

Because it was understood that Beaux was busy with her professional career and should not be disturbed, the family on Spruce Street expected that Etta would take care of them in their old age, and indeed she did, with courage and fortitude. However, when Emily and Eliza both became ill in November 1903, Cecilia returned to Philadelphia to relieve Etta of the stress of nursing her ailing relatives. "I have decided to stay a day longer, just because I can't bear to leave them here. They cough so," Beaux wrote to Dorothea

83. ***Mrs. Theodore Roosevelt and Daughter Ethel.*** *1902. Oil on canvas, 44 1/2 x 31 1/2 in. Courtesy of Sarah Chapman*

on November 18. Aunt Emily did not recover. She died on December 19, 1903, at the age of sixty-five. Uncle Will and Aunt Eliza were both heartbroken. Their grief, added to Beaux's own, made visits to "the two lonely ones at 4305" almost unbearable.

Cecilia Beaux's relationship with Dorothea Gilder sustained her through this difficult time and during the following two years, when the house at 4305 Spruce Street was finally sold, and Aunt Eliza and Uncle Will moved to Haverford to be close to Etta and her family. Professionally, Beaux continued to thrive, but emotionally she was vulnerable. "Pleasant things are happening off and on," she wrote to Dorothea. "But I am lonely —lonely for that dear warm spot and your loving arms. Sometimes I feel as if I could not bear it—but what ridiculous talk that is. But in those precious hours there this last time, I am eternally grateful to remember that there was no, or almost no hurting moment. It was all gentleness—and much, much more—You were dearer dearer than ever—."[412]

Because of her family responsibilities and her teaching commitment at the Pennsylvania Academy of the Fine Arts, Beaux continued to make the trip to Philadelphia once a week during the school year. However, after the sale of the house on Spruce Street, she felt that the city was no longer her home, and it was several years before she was able to stand in front of her grandmother's house and confront her memories. On Christmas Eve, 1911, she finally made her pilgrimage. "We went for a walk down SPRUCE St. and looked at sacred 4305," she wrote in her diary.[413]

> A mystery poignant enough hangs around it. When I think of all I felt and lived there. . . . It is not BADLY changed . . . and my windows in the third story are so much the same. . . . Oh so many cool cloudy Sundays have I come home from church and gone up there to look out and wonder in that quiet room in the order and sweetness I always brought to it on Sunday morning—the recollection of my own reserved intensity was clear and wrapped in fire. The tulip trees over the way were the same. How often they fed my beauty sense before I knew I had one—.[414]

Cecilia's search for a permanent home led her away from the city of her birth, north to Gloucester, Massachusetts, America's oldest fishing port, located on rugged and picturesque Cape Ann. Beaux first visited Gloucester in the summer of 1887 and stayed with Aunt Eliza at the Fairview Inn at the entrance of Eastern Point. By the time Beaux met the Gilders in the late 1890s, summer vacations at the Fairview were something of a family tradition for Beaux and her Leavitt relatives. In 1903 Beaux decided that it would be prudent to spend her summers working in Gloucester, where her concentration would not be interrupted by professional obligations in New York or her commitments in Philadelphia. "Why not, I thought, have the summer for my working time, and take my rest in a short winter period," Beaux wrote in her autobiography. "I had never looked on painting as toil, but I had sometimes felt that the city contained too much of everything."[415]

That summer Beaux's friend A. Piatt Andrew, Jr., convinced her to abandon the Fairview Inn and rent a cottage, which she called "California Cottage." There, Beaux was welcomed by a group of single adults who had the means to enjoy an extended summer holiday and share a love of the rocky coastline, clear air, and the long, picturesque views of the harbor. During that summer in Gloucester, Beaux began to establish the same kind of camaraderie with a circle of fascinating people that she had enjoyed in Concarneau.[416]

The catalyst for the group was Beaux's new friend, dazzling thirty-one-year-old A. Piatt Andrew, an assistant professor of economics at Harvard University and a rising star in his profession. Blessed with inherited wealth, a lively intelligence, strikingly good looks, and an irresistible charm, he attracted a coterie of willing followers to parties at "Red Roof," his stunning home on Eastern Point. Andrew's friend Henry Davis Sleeper, heir to a manufacturing empire and an aspiring interior designer, also became part of

Beaux's social circle, as well as Kakuzo Okakura, the head of the Japanese Department at the Boston Museum of Fine Arts and author of *The Book of Tea*, a popular treatise on the significance of the tea ceremony in Japanese culture.

Beaux was not the only woman in the group. Andrew's magnetic charm drew female admirers, too, mostly older women either unmarried or widowed, and included Joanna Stewart Davidge, the principal of Miss Davidge's Classes, a private finishing school for girls in New York; Isabella Stewart Gardner, grande dame of Boston society, noted art collector, and close friend of John Singer Sargent; and the engaging and eccentric Caroline Sidney Sinkler, whom A. Piatt Andrew called the "Enchantress of Philadelphia." Sinkler, whose personality seemed to invite descriptive monikers, was more commonly known as the "Lavender Lady." In 1896, when her fiancé, the Philadelphia architect John Stewardson fell through the ice while skating on the Schuylkill River and drowned, she went into what she described as a state of "festive mourning" and dressed in shades of lavender for the rest of her life.[417]

Beaux also made friends with several young people. Twenty-three-year-old Dallas D. L. McGrew was a Harvard graduate working on the staff at the *Boston Journal*. Thornton Oakley (1881–1953), who was the same age as McGrew, was introduced to Beaux in 1898 when he was a teenager staying with his mother at the Fairview Inn.[418] When she met Oakley, he had just been admitted to architectural school at the University of Pennsylvania. Following his graduation, Oakley went on to study with Beaux's former classmate at Van der Wielen's, the illustrator Howard Pyle. At Pyle's school in Chadds Ford, Pennsylvania, Oakley joined an exceptional group of aspiring illustrators that included one young man who would stay in the area and start a dynasty of American artists, Newell Convers Wyeth (1882–1945).

By 1904, when Beaux was leasing California Cottage and enjoying the company of her new friends, Oakley had already established himself as a professional illustrator working for a variety of publications,

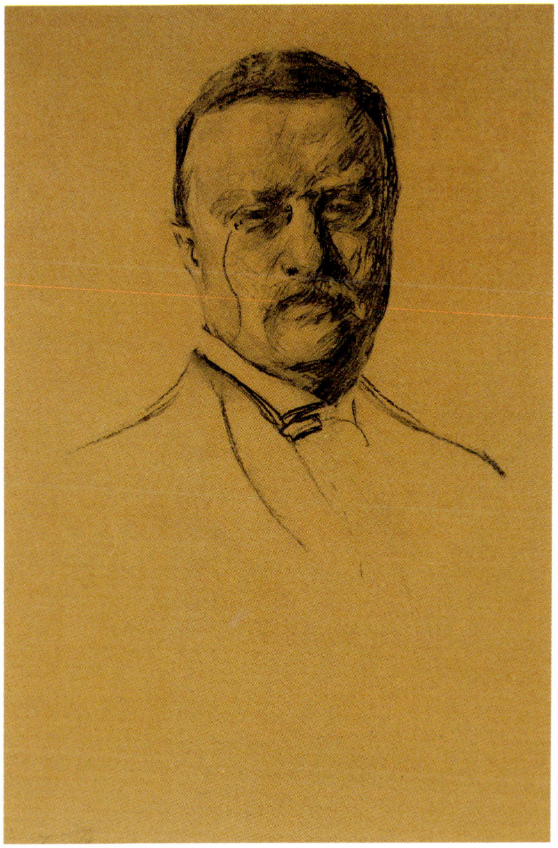

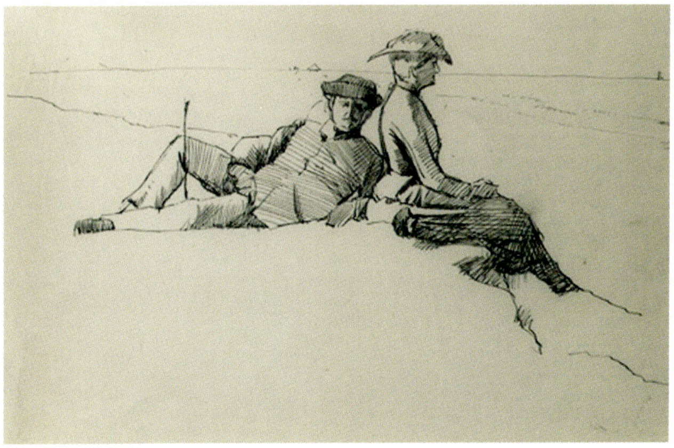

84. TOP: ***Portrait of Theodore Roosevelt.*** *1902. Charcoal on paper, 17 7/8 x 13 7/8 in.. Pennsylvania Academy of the Fine Arts*

85. BOTTOM: ***William Foster Biddle, Emily Leavitt Biddle at the Seashore.*** *ca. 1883. Ink on paper, 6 1/2 x 9 in. Private Collection. Courtesy of Alfred J. Walker Fine Art, Boston*

including the prestigious and widely circulated periodicals *Collier's*, *Leslie's Monthly*, and *Harper's*.[419] Beaux's friendship with Oakley grew that summer when they spent the first of what was to be many evenings together. Her relationship with the young illustrator belied the difference in their ages. Oakley was energetic—filled with excitement about his career and the world of art that his friend represented. Cecilia, whose enthusiasm for her profession had not wavered, was fit at the age of forty-nine, and despite her painful hand, able to match his energy. "Along the Grape-Vine Cove we wandered, or scrambled at low tide over seaweed . . . where surf thunders, where in pools then lurked fantastically colored crabs, starfish, plume-like creatures of the deep," Oakley recalled.[420]

Although her closest alliance among the remarkable people she met in Gloucester developed with Oakley, who shared her interest in art, the friendships Beaux established on Eastern Point endured and built her confidence. When Beaux was at ease, she was witty and entertaining. "Cecilia had a rich humor," wrote Henry McCarter, recalling an evening spent with Beaux and her friend, Anne Blake, who was visiting from Boston.

> One night in the bright moonlight we three sat on the end of a floating landing looking at the movement and living things down in the sea. Two minutes is all one can bear to look at too much beauty. When we had enough C. B. began to sing raucous Irish she had learned from her Uncle Will Biddle's cook "Stick a Fedder in Her Hat." Anne Blake meant to wear awful hats—this year was her worst of hats with a fedder in it. C. B. only remembered

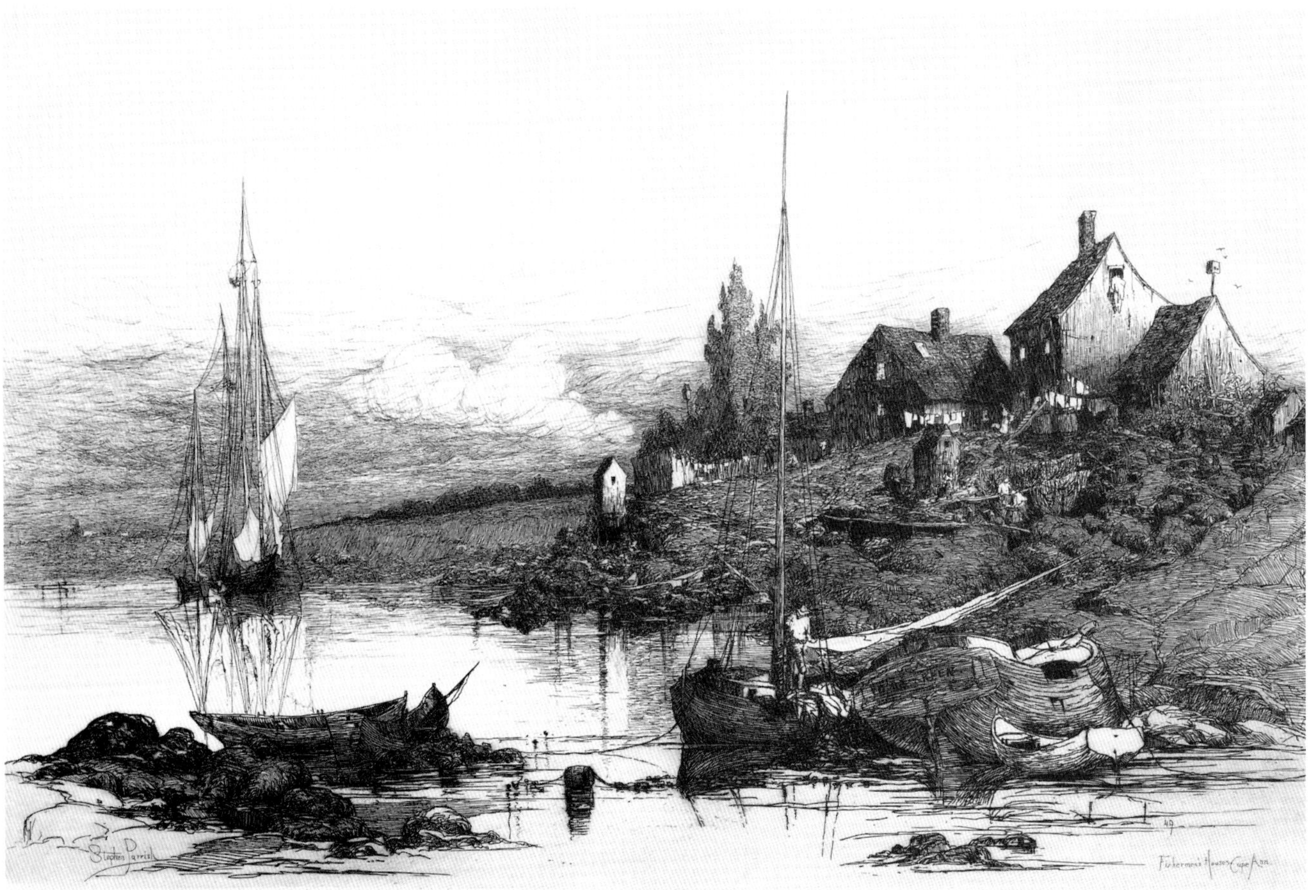

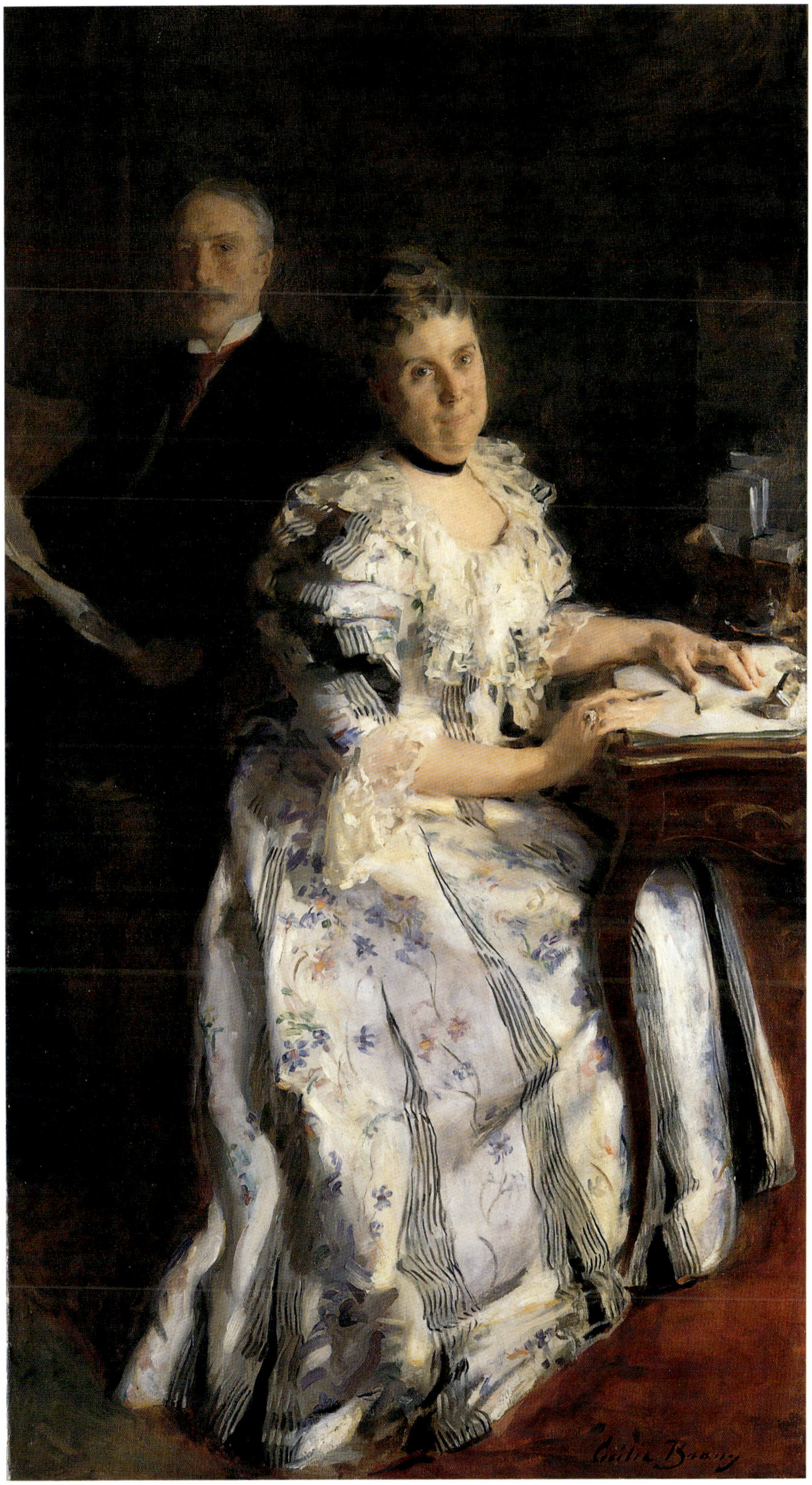

86. OPPOSITE: *Stephen Parrish.* ***Fishermen's Houses—Cape Ann.*** *1881. Etching, 11 x 18 11/16 in. Cape Ann Historical Association, Gloucester, Massachusetts*

87. LEFT: ***Mr. and Mrs. Anson Phelps Stokes.*** *1898. Oil on canvas, 72 1/16 x 39 7/8 in. The Metropolitan Museum of Art*

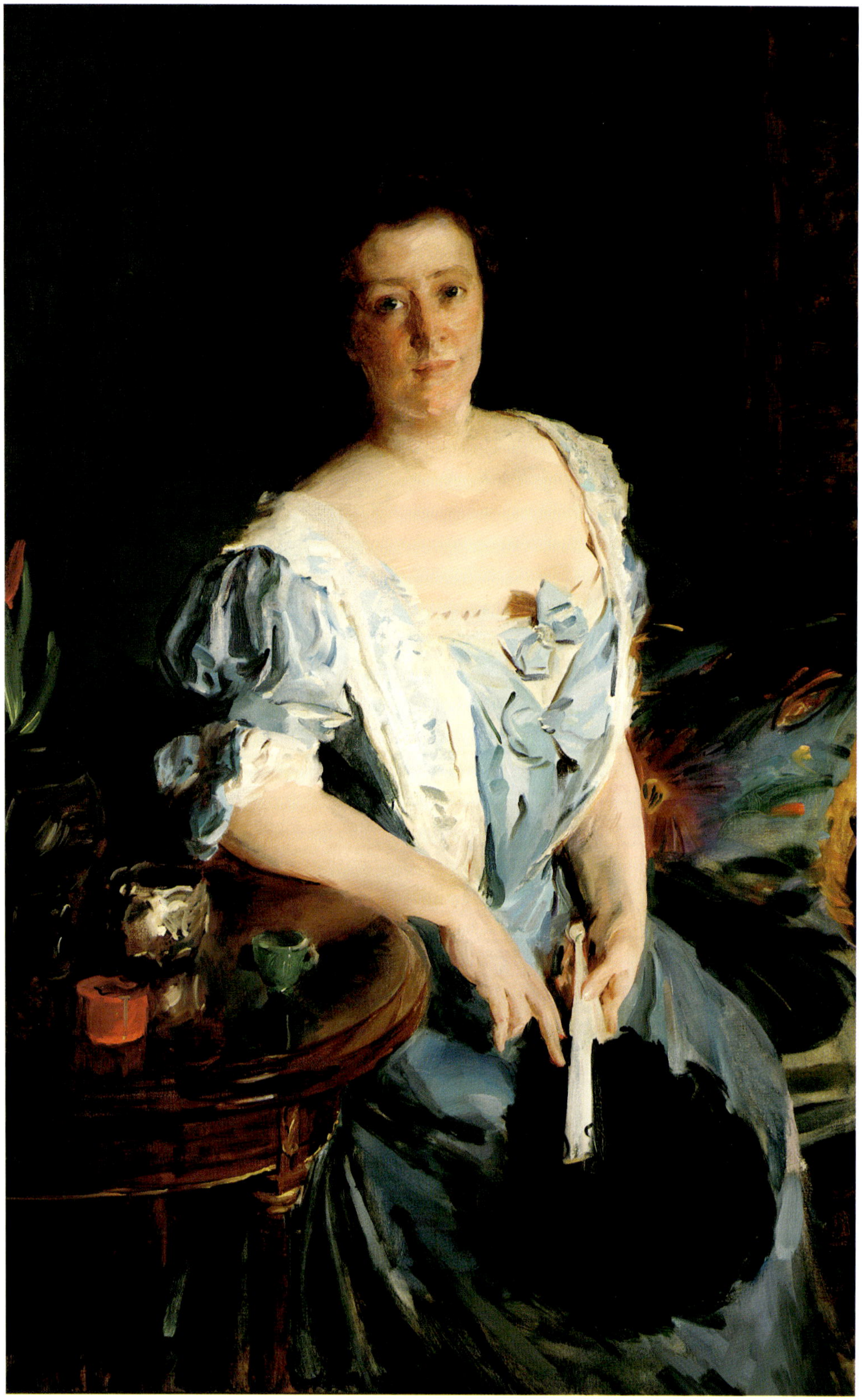

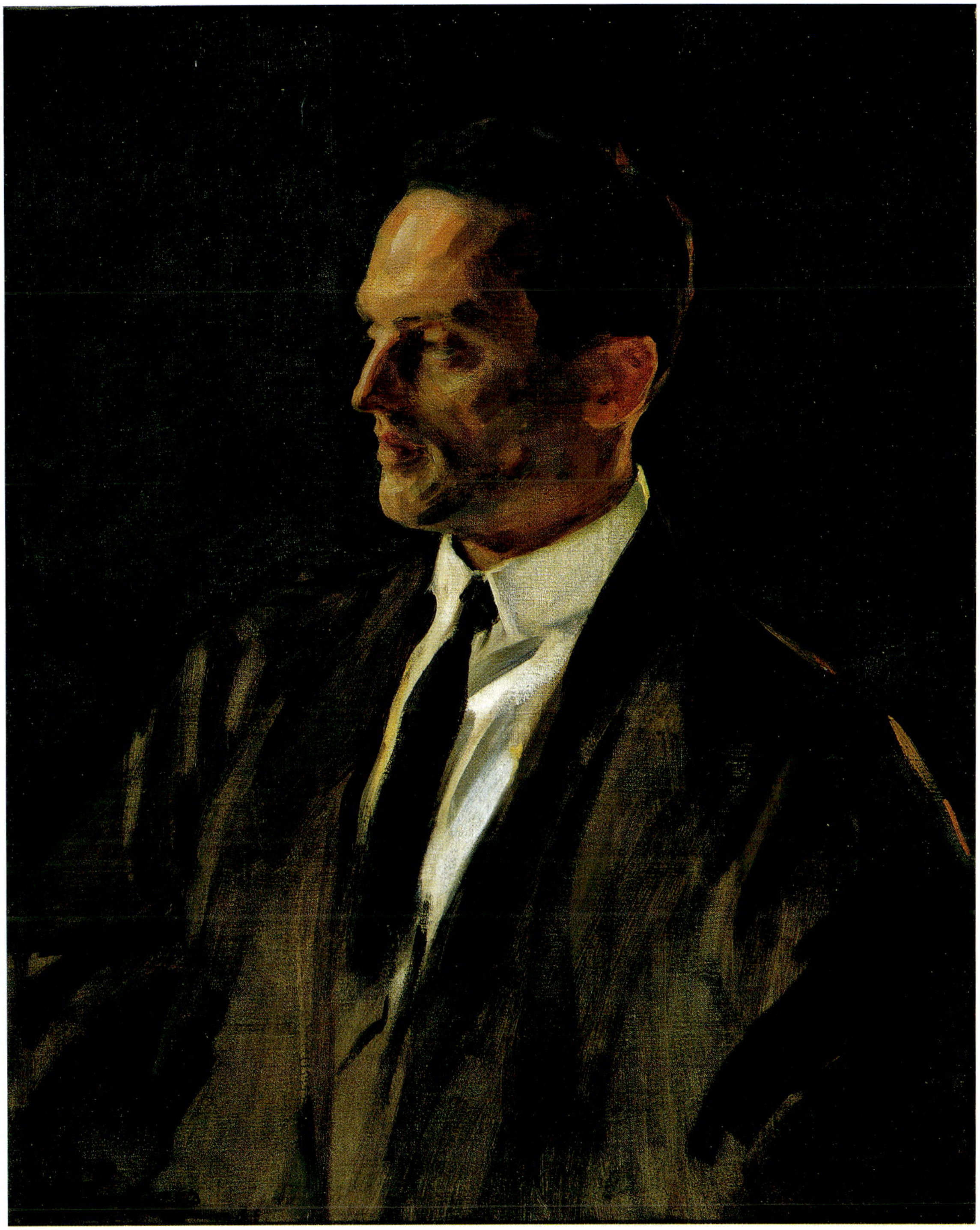

88. OPPOSITE: ***Mrs. John Frederick Lewis.*** *1906. Oil on canvas, 46 1/2 x 29 15/16 in. Pennsylvania Academy of the Fine Arts*

89. ABOVE: ***Piatt Andrew.*** *1903. Oil on canvas, 33 x 27 in. Cape Ann Historical Association, Gloucester, Massachusetts*

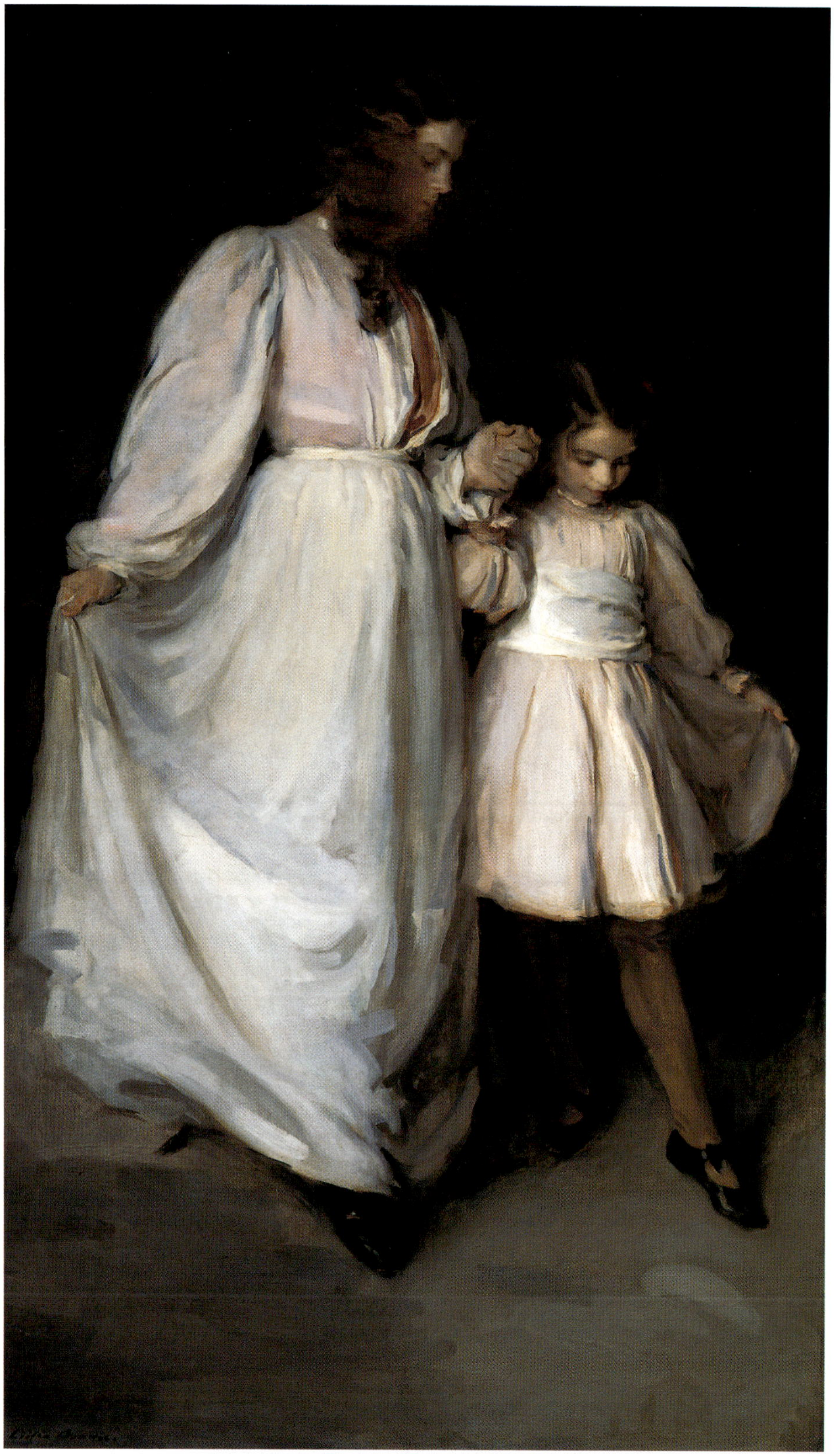

90. **Dorothea and Francesca.** *1898. Oil on canvas, 80 1/8 x 46 in. The Art Institute of Chicago*

two verses—when she had sung the two verses—
Anne Blake took up the song and sang the last two verses. Cecilia really had a grand life.[421]

Although the new friendships assuaged her loneliness and provided the companionship Beaux needed, working in Gloucester presented a challenge. Finding clients willing to travel from New York or Boston to pose proved difficult. So once again, Beaux turned to the Gilders for help, this time to Dorothea who at twenty-three was leading an active social life and had established contacts of her own. "KIP PERKINS . . . I would LOVE to do him. Do try to catch him," she begged Dorothea. "Do not scare him with the number of times he MIGHT have to pose. Nor with the price. Do write him at once . . . as cannily as you can . . . you see I have no order in prospect this summer . . . and just want a nice thing like this to do."[422] Dorothea must have been persuasive; John "Kip" Perkins posed for the painting, which Beaux called *Portrait of a Young Man.* The commission, coupled with the easy companionship of her new friends, convinced Beaux that she should build a permanent home in Gloucester. "She was full of plans, for her portraits to be sure, but in her mind her house-to-come was uppermost," Oakley wrote. "Texture, size, minute details of every room of every cranny, the management of light effects in the separate building of the studio were already vividly conceived."[423]

Beaux purchased a heavily wooded property near the homes of A. Piatt Andrew and Joanna Steward Davidge, between the Eastern Point lighthouse and the town of Gloucester. The land commanded a spectacular view of the harbor. There she envisioned a home and studio designed for "work—and friendship—the two main diversions of its owner's interest."[424] The house, built in a style that Beaux called "tropical colonial," was enchanting. Nestled among native blueberry, bay, sassafras, wild cherry, and maple, and adorned by forty ancient tupelo trees, the place spun a romantic magic that Beaux claimed made it "an unsafe place for lovers on the verge of yielding."[425] On August 7, 1906, a few weeks before the death of Aunt Eliza, the last of the three indomitable Leavitt women who had raised her,

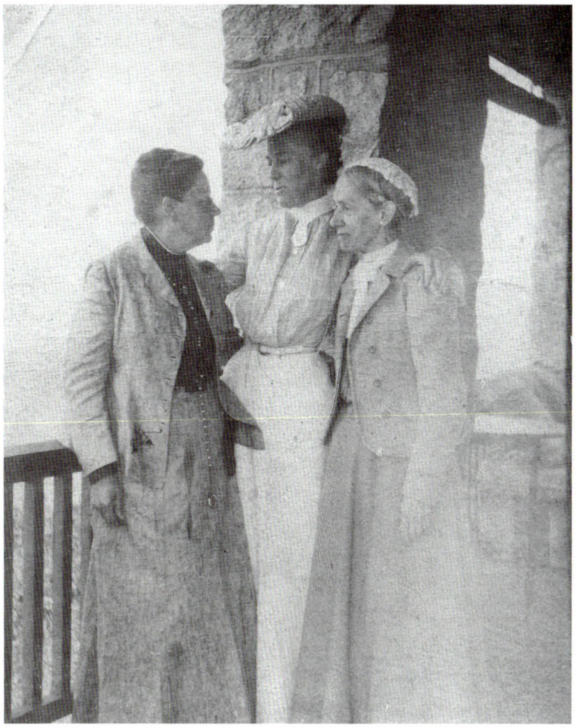

91. ***Emily Leavitt Biddle, Cecilia Beaux, and Eliza Leavitt,*** *ca.* 1903. *Pennsylvania Academy of the Fine Arts*

Cecilia lit her first fire on the hearth of the new home she called "Green Alley." There, away from the obligations and entanglements of the past, Beaux found what she described as "not rest . . . but a new life."[426] And indeed it was after moving to Green Alley that Beaux was finally able to withdraw from her dependence on Dorothea Gilder. Entries in Beaux's diaries indicate that the end of the romance was painful. For although she maintained a loving relationship with the Gilder family —which seemed to grow closer when she did not have anything to hide—as well as a true friendship with Dorothea, years passed before Beaux was able to reconcile herself to her loss. One night in August 1912, Dorothea telephoned, then dropped in at Green Alley. The two women talked until 2 A.M. "No sleep and very bad feelings," Beaux wrote in her diary. "It is not well to be made of glass if one is a locomotive."[427]

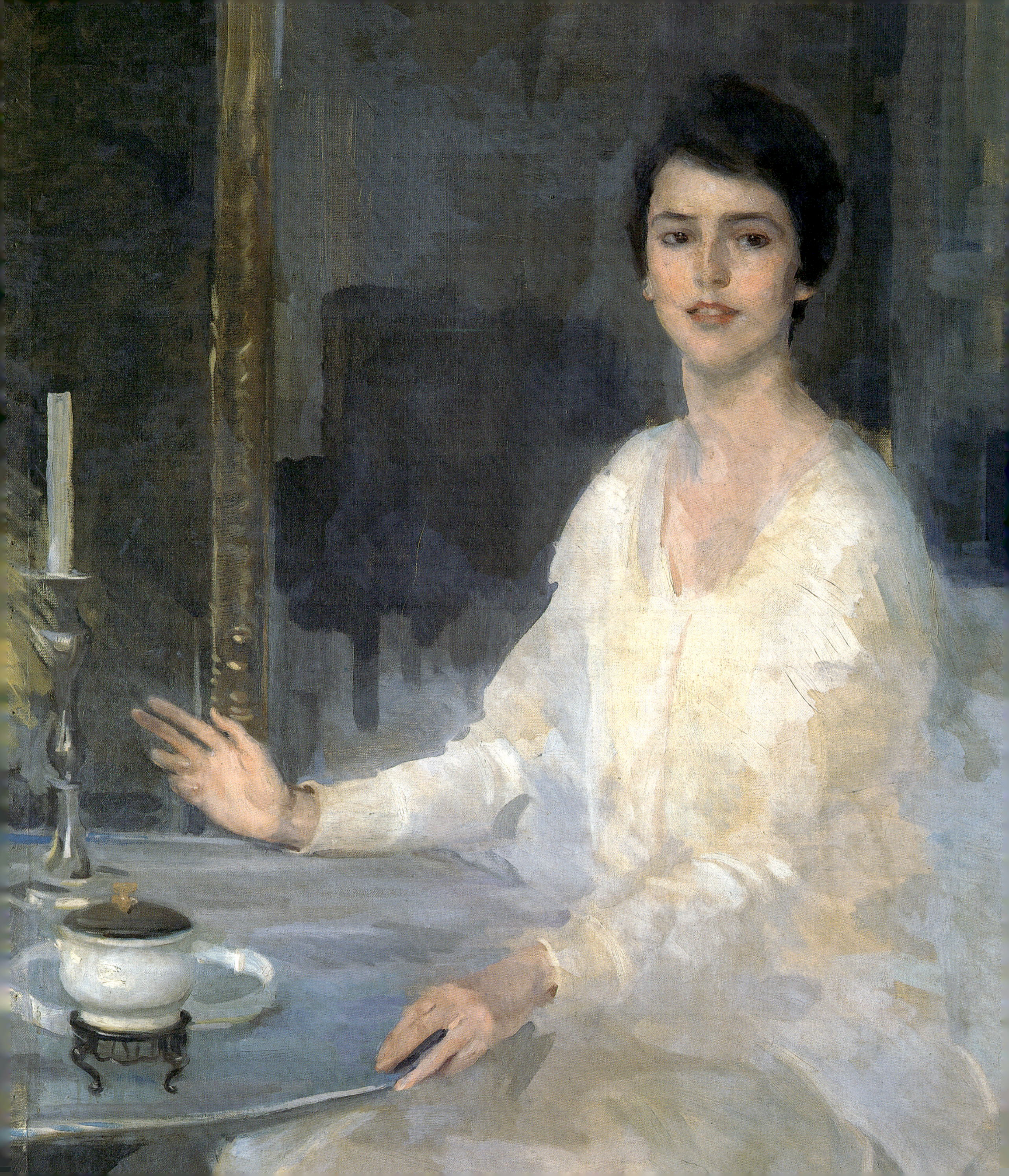

Dabsville at Eastern Point

"The sweet companionable presence; the austere
Demeanor, hiding a rich heart; the glance,
Intense and penetrant, that says a soul is here."

—Richard Watson Gilder *(1844–1909) on the portraits of Cecilia Beaux (1908)*

In 1905, Caroline Sidney Sinkler (the Lavender Lady) bought the house next to Andrew's Red Roof, and lightheartedly christened it Wrong Roof. On August 13, 1907, the interior designer Henry Davis Sleeper purchased the property next door to Sinkler and built a home of his own. Although he continued to add to the house for the rest of his life, the basic structure was completed the following spring. So by 1908, Beaux's friends in Gloucester were also her adjacent neighbors, all living in privileged comfort in uniquely beautiful homes that they modestly called cottages and assigned names, as if each house were more of a friend than a dwelling. Beaux's Green Alley was at the north end of the road. Next door, heading south was Joanna Davidge's Pier Lane, followed by Red Roof, Wrong Roof, and Sleeper's fantastic and ever-expanding mansion, which he named Beauport.[428] The five residents called their little community Dabsville, a title devised by the female residents using their initials—D for Davidge, B for Beaux, and S for Sinkler.

The enclave was secluded. A visitor traveling the winding road that led to Eastern Point would pass fish-drying tents and a bathing beach before noticing that the track narrowed. By 1910 a sign had to be posted: "Dangerous Passing. Automobiles not allowed." But horse and carriage might continue. A little way down the road a small picketed gate marked the beginning of a dirt path that led into a tangle of old tupelo trees, cat briar, wild grape, and Virginia creeper. Birds lived in the greenery and took flight when someone passed by—cat-bird, thrush, warbler, and whitethroat. At the end of the path, invisible from the road, was the first house on the point, Green Alley. Beaux's clients arrived in the morning, opened the gate, and walked through the wild tunnel of native plants that inspired the name of the property. Beaux's maid, Anna Murphy, met them at the front door and escorted them through a courtyard that led to the studio. The studio was decorated sparingly—bare walls, a large fireplace with a huge bearskin rug on the hearth, a piano, and the essential painting equipment. Beaux worked there every morning except Sunday. "I paint four hours and then I am through for the day. I am tired out. I could no more paint another stroke until I had time to recuperate than I could if I never painted at all," she told a reporter from the *Boston Herald*.[429] Although her hours at the easel were short, Beaux worked in what she called a "white heat." It was understood that when she was painting, she was not to be disturbed. Callers were told to return in the afternoon. When her niece Ernesta fell on the stairs and broke her arm, the girl did not alert

OPPOSITE: *Detail;* ***Ernesta.*** *1914. Oil on canvas, 71 3/4 x 43 3/8 in. The Metropolitan Museum of Art*

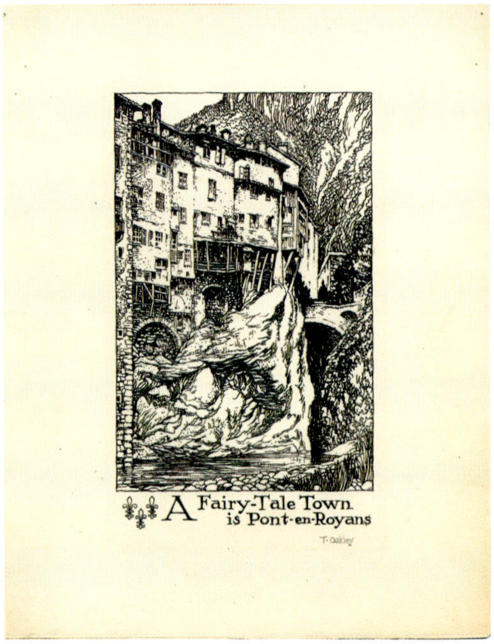

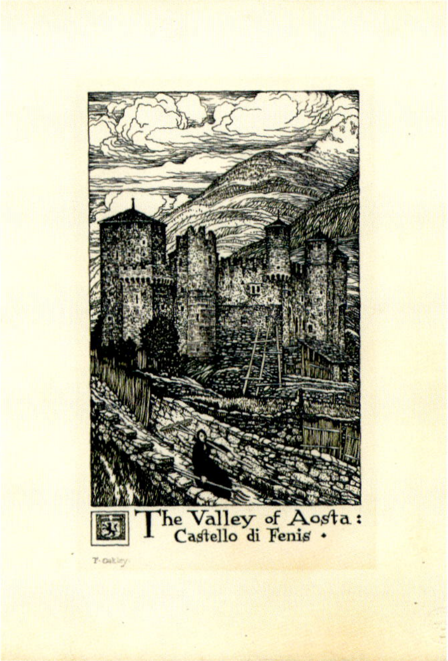

92–94. LEFT TO RIGHT: *Thornton Oakley.* ***A Fairy-Tale Town Is Pont-en-Royans, The Valley of Aosta: Castello di Fenis,*** *and* ***The Erstwhile Abbey of Sixt.*** *1927. Pen and ink on board, 10 x 6 in. each. The Eisenstat Collection of American Illustration*

her aunt but called a doctor and was at the hospital when Beaux walked up the hill to the main house at noon. "Ernesta was well trained," her sister Kitty recalled. "Nobody interrupted those working hours . . . nor did Ernesta resent the incident. Caring for the sick and heedless was not Cecilia's business. That lay elsewhere. We all knew and respected it."[430]

Beaux's dedication to her work yielded the desired result, and during her first two summers at Green Alley she completed seven major portraits, including a likeness of the Revolutionary War naval hero John Paul Jones commissioned by the U.S. Naval Academy, a portrait of Miss Adelaide Nutting, superintendent of Nurses at Johns Hopkins Hospital, and a portrait of Frances Elizabeth Bennett, presented in her memory to the University of Pennsylvania where Miss Bennett had been a member of the Board of Managers for the Post-Graduate Department for Women.

Each day at noon, when she put down her brushes, Beaux left her ambitions in the studio and lived the life of a wealthy socialite. Dressed in a long skirt and simple blouse, she put on her silk jacket and straw hat, took a deep breath of sea air, and went out to the flowerbeds. Having never before had a plot of land of her own, she found joy in the simple care of her phlox, roses, and hollyhocks. In New York, her diary indicates that she felt isolated. In Gloucester, she never did. She had frequent houseguests. For a time, May Whitlock lived with her and managed the house when Beaux was in New York. The Gilder family visited often, as did her nieces and nephews. Ernesta Drinker, recalling Green Alley, later wrote: "In the summer I was her child for weeks at a time, staying with her in Gloucester, minus nurse or governess. When I became of reasonable age, I was known as that terrible brat who ran over the sea cliffs like a goat and scared the life out of all of them."[431] Ernesta was not entirely unsupervised. Her aunt's two hardworking servants, Anna Murphy, whom Beaux had acquired from her sister's household, and houseman Natale Gavagnin, a former Venetian gondolier brought to the United States by the

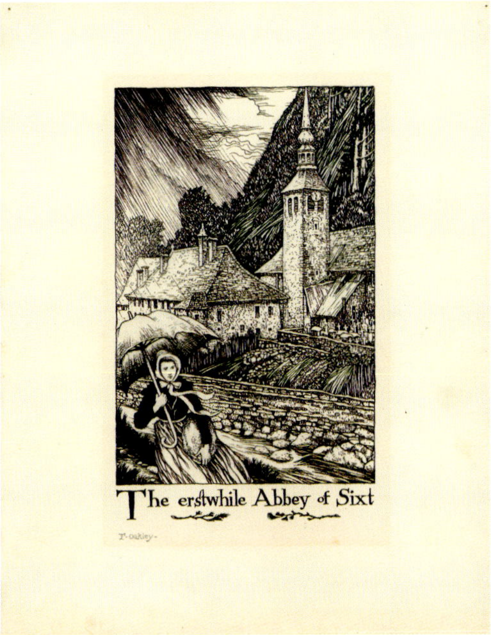

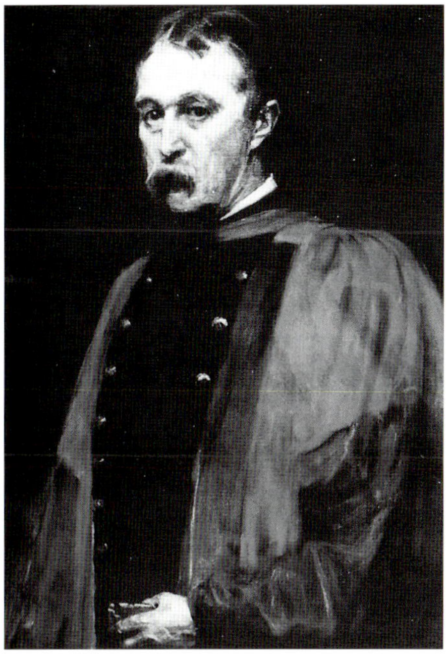

95. Detail; ***Dr. John Shaw Billings.*** *1895. Oil on canvas, 77 x 52 in. United States National Library of Medicine*

Gilder family, were attentive and saw to it that the children were safe and the visitors comfortable.[432] They also took care of all the domestic chores, so that Beaux would not have to tax her energy. Their good services allowed Beaux the luxury of leisure time. In the afternoons she took a nap, a habit developed when she was a girl and never abandoned. Her profession, she believed, demanded physical strength. When asked repeatedly why so few women succeeded in art, Beaux always cited a lack of vigor. "Strength is the stumbling block," she said. "They [women] are sometimes unable to stand the hard work of it day in and day out. They become tired and cannot reenergize themselves."[433]

In the evenings Beaux reenergized herself by socializing with her neighbors. A. Piatt Andrew's Red Roof became the group's hub, where business leaders, architects, opera singers, writers, socialites, and Harvard students, attracted by Andrew's charm and magnetism, came to enjoy summer parties. The gatherings were sometimes formal—Beaux sat next to President Taft at a Gloucester party in 1909—but most often they were casual. People dropped in and stayed unless a thirteenth guest arrived.[434] That number was considered unlucky, and unwilling to tempt fate, the neighbors would immediately disperse. Of Andrew's many admirers, none was more ardent than his neighbor, Henry Davis Sleeper, who loved him with an almost pathetic devotion, which seemed to alternately flatter and burden Andrew. For Christmas in 1907 Andrew gave Sleeper a Napoleon medal. "I haven't loved a present so much since I was a child," Sleeper wrote in thanks. "Every single night it goes into the pocket of my pajamas."[435] The next year, not to be outdone, Sleeper gave Andrew two bear cubs for Christmas, and for a time the animals lived "odiferously" (Andrew noted in his diary) in cages at Red Roof.

In spite of her own feelings for Dorothea Gilder, initially Beaux did not seem to understand that the relationship between the two bachelors on Eastern Point was anything more than friendship. And when she arrived at Red Roof to find the house filled with young men and got a less than enthusiastic reception, it stung her pride. Later when she understood that her

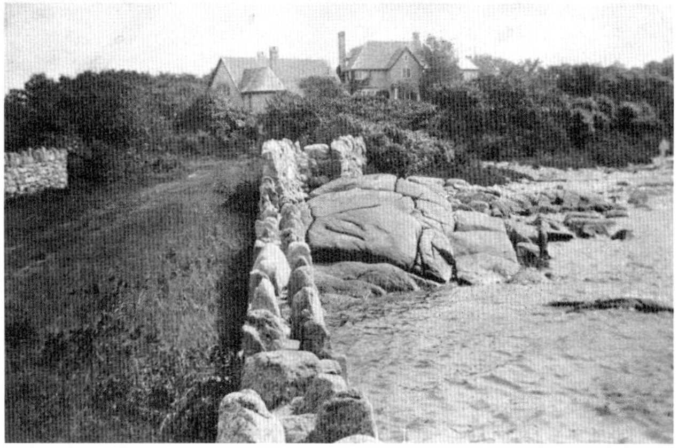

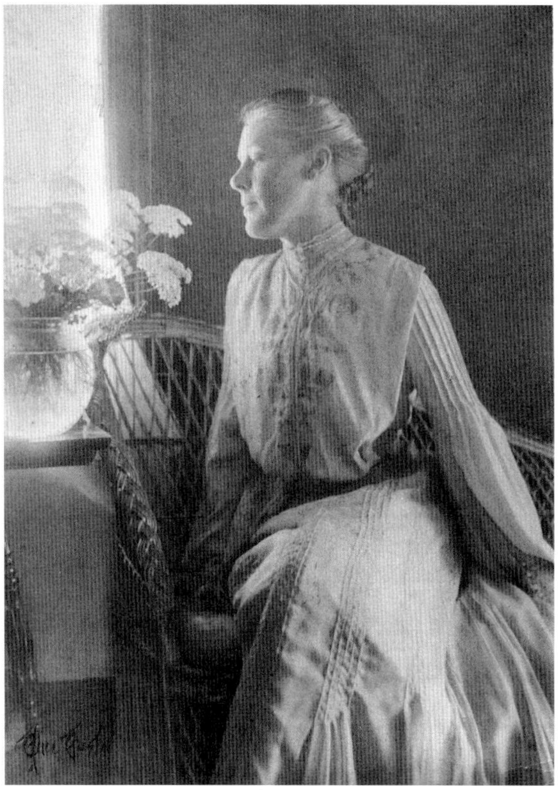

96. TOP: *View of Green Alley from the shoreline. n.d. Pennsylvania Academy of the Fine Arts*

97. BOTTOM: *Cecilia Beaux in wicker chair, 1898–1905. Pennsylvania Academy of the Fine Arts*

friends were homosexuals, she was not entirely sympathetic. When the two men called her in New York to invite her to a party, she was delighted. "Long talk. Very inspiring to hear THEM. . . . But I have to remember the one appalling FACT."[436]

The "fact" notwithstanding, Beaux adored Andrew and was proud to know him. But although the neighbors all shared a genuine affection, the two men often made fun of the three older women. When friends proposed to descend on Beauport, Henry Sleeper, who didn't feel up to the strain, wrote to Andrew that he was able to discourage the visit by stating that he had no automobile, no motorboat, no horses, and a poor cook—and that all his neighbors were middle-aged unmarried women. On another occasion Sleeper wrote gleefully to Andrew that stopping by Green Alley one evening he had discovered fifty-three-year-old Beaux on the roof of the studio admiring the view with some friends—May Whitlock, a man he didn't recognize, and a Mr. Storck. "In the evening we all called on Miss Beaux & found her sitting on the cloister roof—with a strange man & her stork [sic]. I told her I thought it impudent to let him perch so near her chimney."[437]

While Beaux enjoyed her new life in Gloucester, the currents of American art that defined the twentieth century were sweeping by her. Leading these revolutionary changes was Mr. Robert Henri, the young man who was in Paris during Beaux's second winter there, eating rice and horsemeat and eschewing the advice of his Parisian masters in favor of his own expressive style. In the intervening years, while Beaux was winning accolades in Europe and America, Henri was not idle. In April 1899 four of his paintings were accepted at the Paris Salon. The French government purchased one of Henri's canvases for the Luxembourg Gallery: a painterly but starkly realistic impression of a contemporary and somewhat dirty Parisian Street in winter, titled *La Neige*. The picture was typical of Henri's work and mirrored his theories on modern art—that all of life was suitable subject matter for painters—not just the beautiful, but also the commonplace.

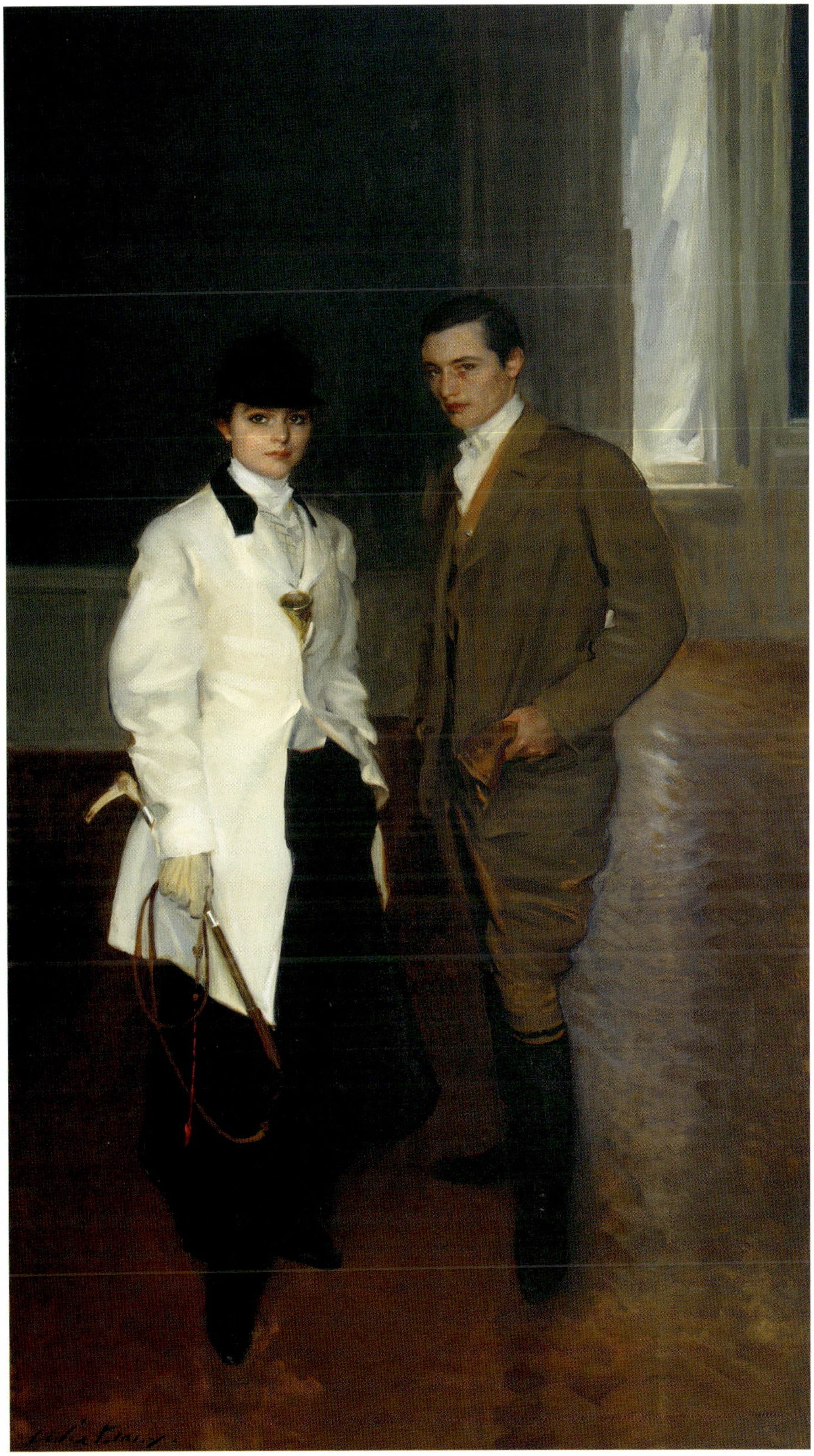

98. ***Charles Sumner Bird and His Sister Edith Bird Bass.*** *1907. Oil on canvas, $94^{5}/_{8}$ x $53^{1}/_{2}$ in. Museum of Fine Arts, Boston*

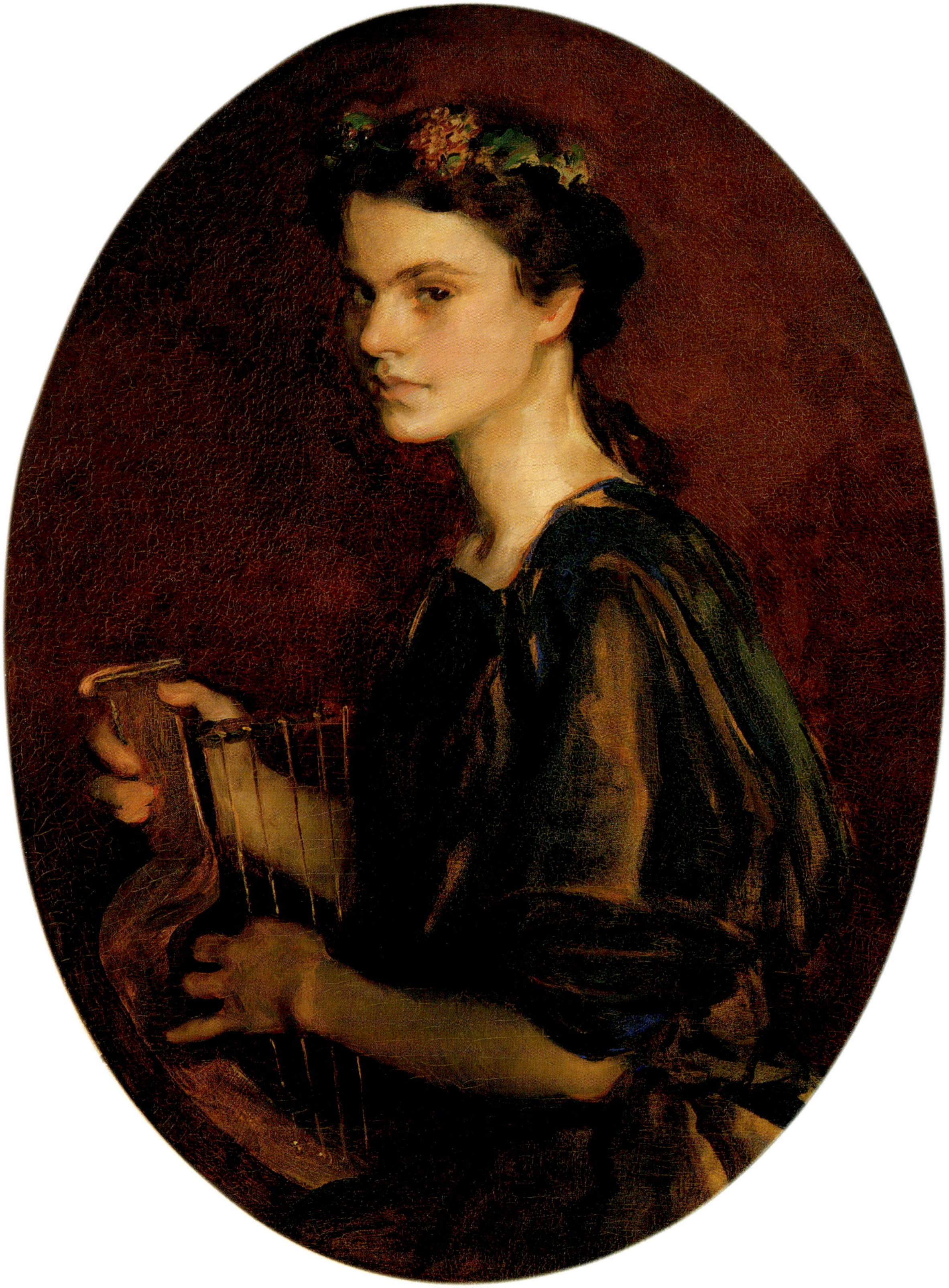

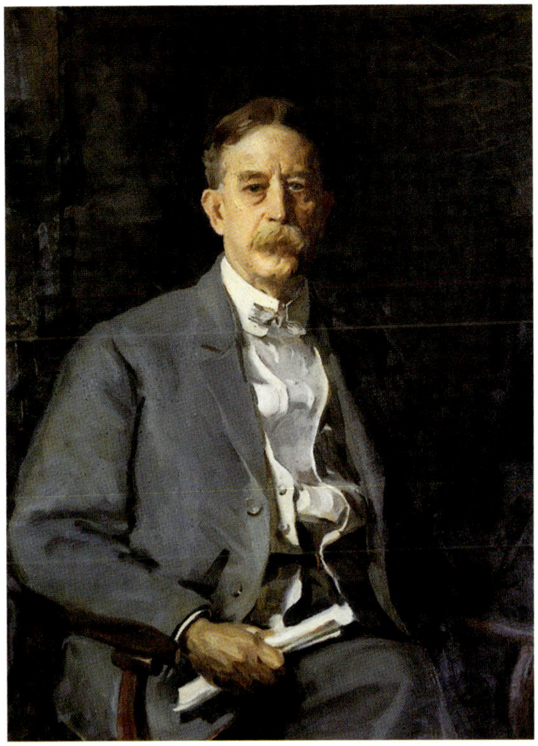

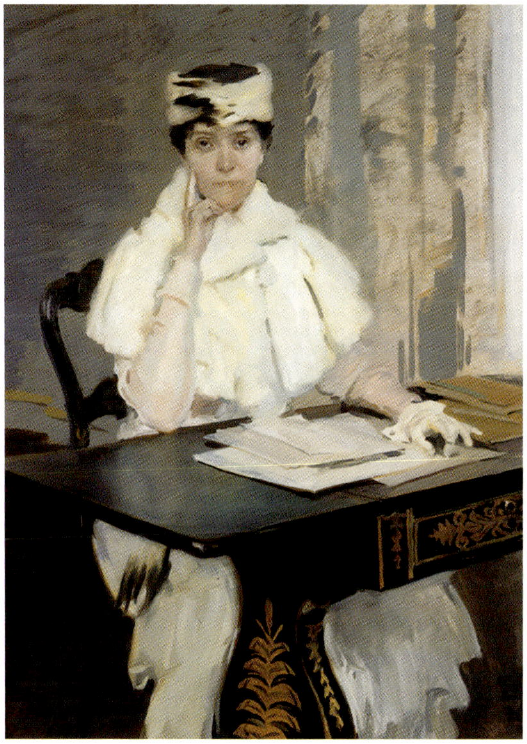

100. LEFT: ***Samuel Hamilton Brooks.*** *1911. Oil on canvas, 39 5/16 x 29 1/8 in. Memphis Brooks Museum of Art*

101. RIGHT: ***Bessie Vance Brooks.*** *1911. Oil on canvas, 47 1/4 x 34 1/4 in. Memphis Brooks Museum of Art*

By 1906, when Cecilia Beaux moved into Green Alley, Henri was successfully established in New York as a painter and an influential teacher at the New York School of Art. The institution was founded in 1896 by Beaux's advocate, William Merritt Chase, and veritably hijacked from him by the younger, more dynamic Henri. Chase, who had held sway over the New York art world since the late 1870s taught the academic principles he had embraced as a student at Munich's Royal Academy. He believed in careful study, proscribed methods, and "delicacy of detail." Henri believed in working quickly. "Work with great speed," he advised his eager students. "Have your energies alert, up and active. Do it all in one sitting if you can. In one minute if you can. There is no use delaying."[438]

Although American aesthetic tastes were changing with Henri at the vanguard, William Merritt Chase maintained his popularity as a painter through the first decade of the twentieth century. His canvases had enough dash to classify as contemporary, and his subject matter was noncontroversial—Impressionist landscapes, adept portraits, and the still life, a genre that Henri did not consider important for artists grappling with the complexities of urban society. "Stop studying water pitchers and bananas and paint everyday life," he admonished his class.[439] Henri urged his students to live among the common people of the city, and many did, moving to Greenwich Village among New York's working poor, beginning an exodus that resulted in a vibrant artistic and intellectual community. Many of the young men in Henri's thrall would adapt his principles and go on to make their mark in American art. Among them were Edward Hopper (1882–1967), Rockwell Kent

99. OPPOSITE: ***Girl with Lyre.*** *1905. Oil on canvas, 32 x 25 in. Berry Hill Gallery, New York*

(1882–1971), Guy Pène du Bois (1884–1958), and George Bellows (1882–1925).

Two such different men were bound to clash, and ultimately, Chase and Henri were on opposite sides of an artistic controversy that changed the direction of American painting. The dispute became public in 1907, when the thirty-man jury for the annual spring show at the National Academy of Design rejected many of the paintings submitted by Henri's students and associates. In protest, Henri withdrew two of his own paintings and vowed to stage an independent show that would promote the work of artists who shared his opinions concerning the viability of recording commonplace, contemporary life. The resulting exhibition, which featured the work of Henri, William J. Glackens (1870–1938), Everitt Shinn (1876–1953), John Sloan (1871–1951), Ernest Lawson (1873–1939), George Luks (1866–1933), Maurice Prendergast (1858–1924), and Arthur B. Davies (1862–1928), opened at the Macbeth Gallery on February 3, 1908, and caused a sensation. An estimated three hundred people an hour arrived on opening day, and the crowded conditions continued for the twelve-day run of the exhibition. Seven paintings were sold. The sculptor and doyenne of New York society, Gertrude Vanderbilt Whitney (1875–1942) purchased four.[440]

Although the event was a popular success, the press, which called the group of artists "The Eight," gave the show mixed reviews. James Huneker, the critic for the *New York Sun*, and Frederick James Gregg of the *Evening Sun* applauded the independent exhibition, as did Henri's student Guy Pène du Bois, who edited a column for the *New York American*. Lined up against "The Eight" or "The Ashcan School," as they came to be called, were Beaux's friend from Concarneau, Arthur Hoeber, who wrote for the *Globe*, and the exhibition's most rancorous detractor, Helena Gilder's brother, Charles DeKay, the art critic for the *New York Times*. "His patronym (DeKay) is a compliment," John Sloan commented, "for decay implies some original quality gone by."[441]

Although Cecilia Beaux took no public part in this controversy, it was to affect her profoundly. Her friends and associates, who twenty years earlier had been eager to unseat the Victorian aesthetic, were entrenched in their opposition to the new ideas that Henri and his compatriots represented. A review in *Town Topics* signed "The Gilder," and doubtlessly penned by a member of the Gilder family, was among the most vitriolic.

> Vulgarity smites one in the face at this exhibition and I defy you to find anyone in a healthy frame of mind who, for instance, wants to hang Luk's posterior of pigs, or Glackens' At *Mouquin's* or John Sloan's *Hairdresser's Window* in his living rooms or gallery, and not get disgusted two days later. . . . As for Prendergast, his work is unadulterated artistic slop, and Shinn's is only several degrees better. . . . Arthur B. Davies is on a slightly different plane, that place which leaves you in doubt between genius and insanity.[442]

Beaux's own opinion of the new aesthetic was that it was a momentary aberration destined to fail. After visiting an exhibition of works by the Expressionist painter Max Weber (1881–1961) at the Photo-Secessionists gallery, Beaux commented in her diary, "Pseudo-Egypto-Primitive-Hysterico-morbid-cellulal-vanitito-infans-masquerado-exuditions. Pretended to be solemn over it and heard some characteristic talk by devotees. . . . Shall go again in old clothes and stan [sic] on one leg."[443]

Although Beaux did not take these independent exhibitions seriously, she should have. Even the previously unassailable John Singer Sargent would be affected. "Many painters are to be found who question whether the object of his effort is of a sufficiently high order, while admitting his genius in the use of the medium," wrote one reviewer commenting on a group of Sargent portraits.[444] It is hardly surprising, given the

102. OPPOSITE: ***John Paul Jones.*** *1906. Oil on canvas, 41 15/16 x 31 15/16 in. United States Naval Academy*

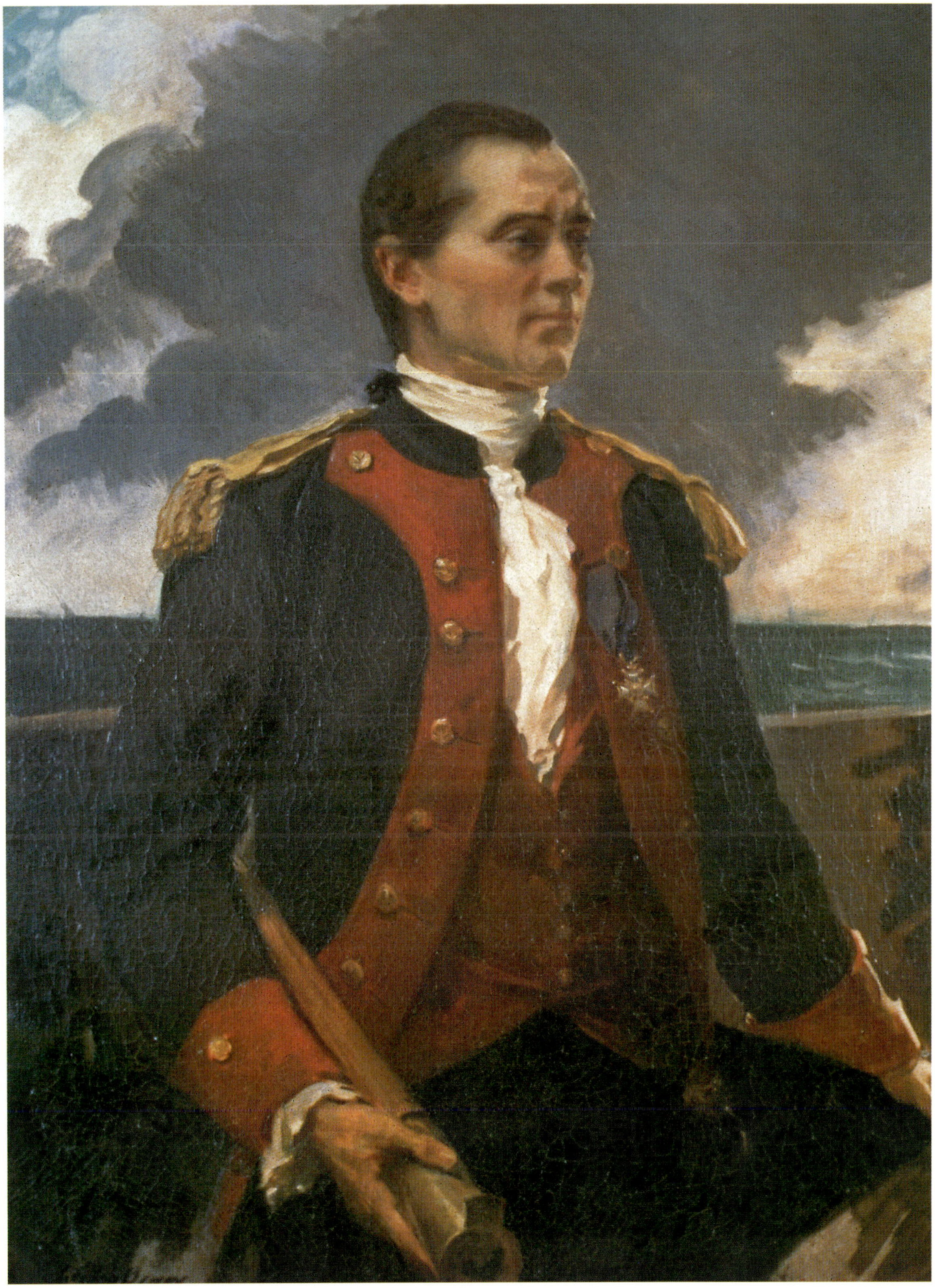

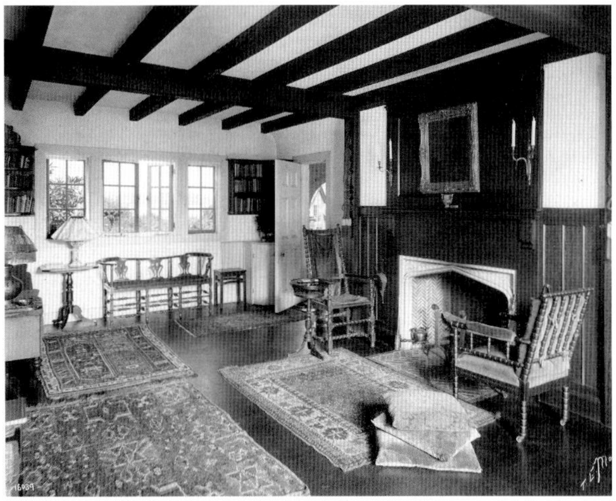

103. *T. E. Morr.* ***Cecilia Beaux's home, Green Alley,*** *interior view, 1910–20. Pennsylvania Academy of the Fine Arts*

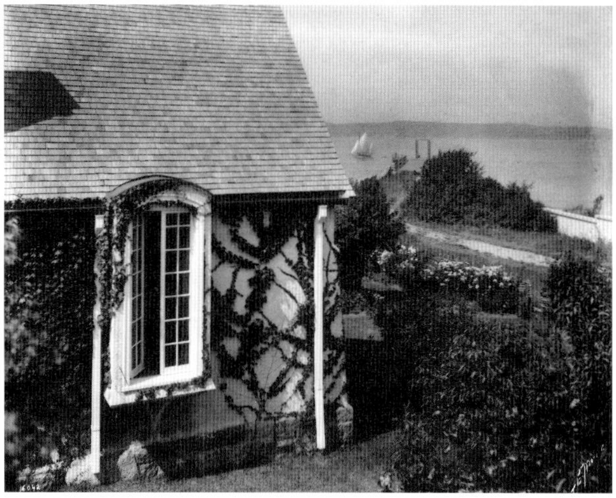

104. *T. E. Morr.* ***Cecilia Beaux's studio at Green Alley,*** *1910–20. Pennsylvania Academy of the Fine Arts*

similarities between the paintings of Sargent and Beaux, that when critics supporting the new innovations in painting later reconsidered her work, it suffered the same censure. Eager to have a woman included in the firmament of artistic excellence and reluctant to support Beaux in that position, they looked for a new champion of female achievement. Ironically, their choice for the successor to Chase's title of "the greatest woman painter of modern times," was not among the young students at the New York School of Art, but an irritable sixty-four-year-old expatriate living in Paris, Miss Mary Cassatt. Beaux and Cassatt had crossed paths on at least one occasion. In 1902 Cassatt wrote to her friend Louisine Havermeyer, "How did you like Miss Beaux? I hope you did not make my Beaux mistake and talk Art."[445]

Cassatt noticed Beaux's work and thought it superficial and academic, but Beaux ignored Cassatt. The older woman rarely visited the United States and didn't begin marketing her work in America until 1895, when the Durand-Ruel Galleries mounted an exhibition. Because the show was a modest critical and financial success, Cassatt exhibited again at Ruel's in 1898. Nevertheless, Beaux apparently took little notice. She never expected a threat to her primacy to come from someone older and had little respect for Impressionism. She loved a story about the American painter Frederic Remington (1861–1909), concerning his response to the Impressionists, and recorded it in her diary: "When Remington went to Paris and was shown some of the crumply impressionism he said, 'Why I have an old aunt in New Bedford who can KNIT better pictures than those.'"[446]

Had the critical excitement over the show by "The Eight" made her worry about a rival, any fears would have been mitigated by yet another honor. On Washington's birthday, a few weeks after the opening of Henri's show, Beaux, who had no formal academic training beyond her year at the Misses Lyman School, was awarded an honorary degree of doctor of laws by the University of Pennsylvania. Richard Watson Gilder introduced her with a poem composed for the occasion. The third stanza captures the spirit of his tribute:

> Lady, shrink not that you, today we name
> In the same breath with the age conquering fame
> Of them most glorious in a mighty line.
> Not for the living is it to assign

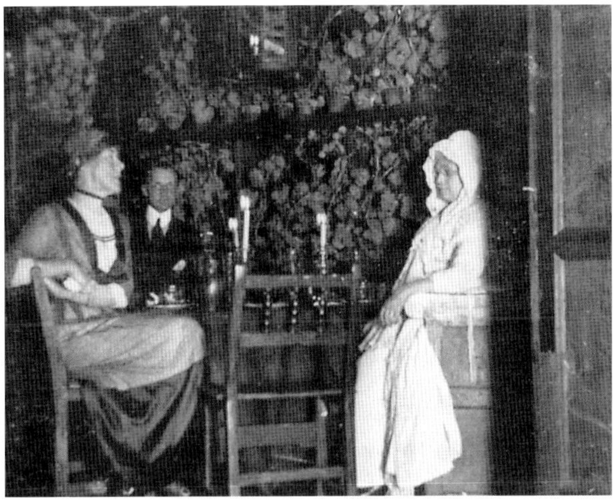

105. ***Cecilia Beaux, Henry Davis Sleeper, and unidentified woman, Gloucester, Massachusetts,*** *n.d. Cape Ann Historical Association, Gloucester*

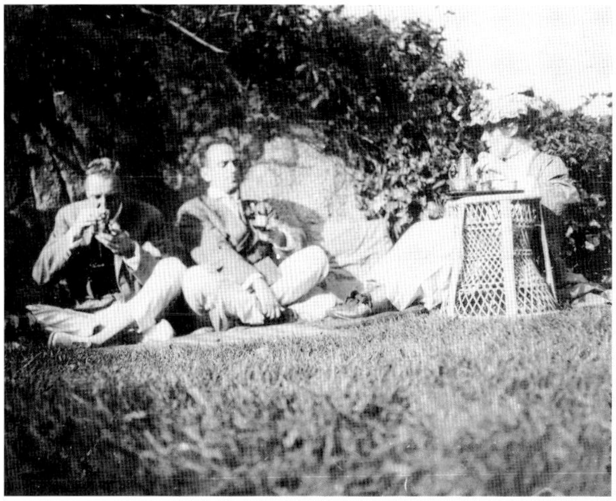

106. ***A. Piatt Andrew, Henry Davis Sleeper and Cecilia Beaux,*** *1907. Pennsylvania Academy of the Fine Arts*

Rank to the living in the long roll of art.
But blame us not if here we crown the intent
Not less than the sincere accomplishment.
We only know the art we see and love.
Is beautiful, intense, most subtle, rare,
And tho' with something of our new world air
Athrill—Yet it is masterful, above,
All else with the old mastery—not old
But fresh forever as the dawn's new gold.

It is unlikely that the sentiment of Gilder's poem seemed quaint or Victorian to Beaux. She sat on the front of the stage at the University of Pennsylvania clad in cap and gown—the three velvet stripes on her sleeve designating entrance into the academic elite. When Gilder finished reading, the crowd rose and applauded. This latest honor fed Beaux's expectation that her portraits were favored to endure—to remain fresh forever. In February of 1908 Mary Cassatt was comfortably ensconced in France, and Cecilia Beaux was on top of the world. Her respected position as an artist seemed secure, and among her friends in Gloucester she had found a soul mate, a true and loyal companion and perhaps more.

By February 1908 Cecilia Beaux and Thornton Oakley had been friends for ten years. Oakley idolized Beaux and felt honored to be on close terms with such an eminent painter, and Beaux, flattered by the attention of the handsome young man, adored him. In June Oakley came to Green Alley and stayed for several days. "T. O. and I went to Pine woods all day. Rather wonderful day," Beaux noted in her diary. Later Oakley wrote sentimentally about visits to Gloucester: "Evenings with Cecilia! They crowd my recollections—evenings in 'Green Alley,' our lingerings beside the fire, Natale, Anna, rendering silent service, harbor sounds falling softly on the ear, the cry of gulls, the eerie warning of the buoy on Reef of Norman's Woe."[447] If Green Alley was casting its spell on the two friends turning them into "lovers on the verge of yielding," there is no evidence that they did so. Oakley may have been delighted by Cecilia's interest in him, but he had his own plans, which he kept to himself. On February 3, 1909, when he wrote to Beaux announcing his engagement, she was taken completely by surprise. Evidently, during their long walks and evenings by the fire, they had talked of other things. "Letter from Thornton Oakley announcing his engagement . . . very bad news

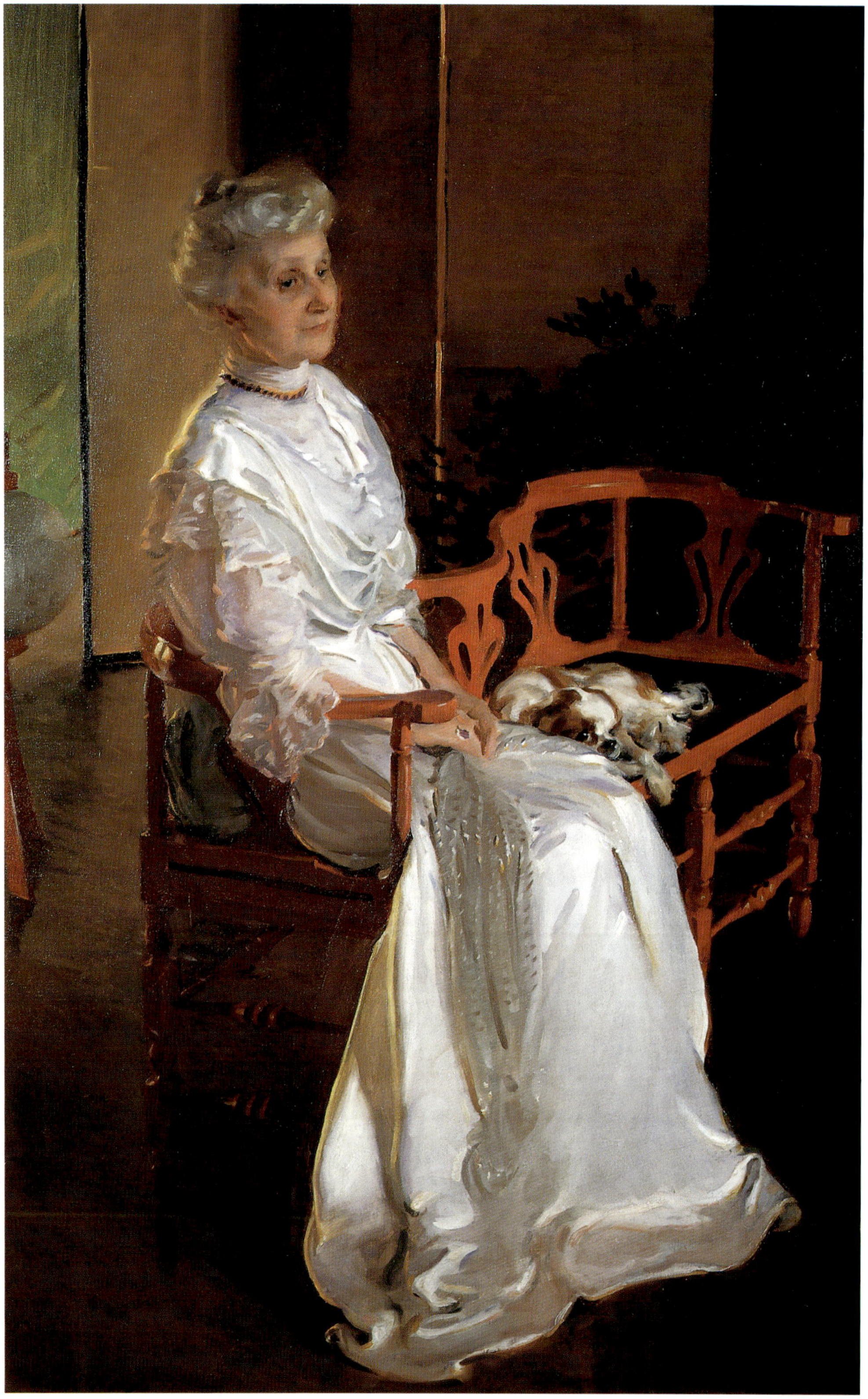

for me. . . . Bad period . . . must look out," Beaux wrote in her diary. To Thornton, responding immediately in a letter, she was gracious.

> I must tell you first that it is the best news I could have of you . . . and if any one had given me a chance to wish any thing for you, it would be this. . . . Though I never knew "AMY". . . . The one I knew was Alice. . . . They can not be the same? Having said this, truth compels me to say that your news was a sharp blow to my contentment with life in general on my own account. . . . There is no use talking, what I had of you is gone now and I shall never have any good of you again after this. . . . I can hear your happy giggle as you read these words. . . . But I shall miss you terribly. . . . Why you are the only near and familiar companion artist friend I had. The only one I would have. Your visit last summer had all the brightness of illusion . . . of unthinking days of reprieve. . . . I have hated to write you on this machine. . . . But my hand has been very bad. . . . But it has been a dear thought that you were there. . . .Tell me more of it if you can and will. . . . You have known her for years. . . . That much I know. Everything but my selfish self rejoices . . . but I am selfish.[448]

Beaux was fifty-two and Oakley twenty-six when he announced his engagement to Amy Ewing. At the time Beaux's neighbor Joanna Davidge was dating Dr. Randall MacIver, a man thirteen years her junior. So if Beaux had hoped for a romantic relationship with Oakley, the idea would not have seemed entirely out of the question. However, there is no reason to believe that Beaux expected anything more from Oakley than a true friendship. When her neighbor Joanna married Dr. MacIver a few years later, Beaux showed no envy. "A note came from Joanna announcing her ENGAGEMENT. . . . To Dr. MacIvor [sic] of course," Beaux noted in her diary. "I am enchanted with this. She says all is well forever now. . . . After all her long years of teaching how good this is."[449]

What was good for Joanna Davidge might never have satisfied Cecilia Beaux. She wrote many letters to Oakley over the years. They are witty and sometimes tender, but there is not one that shows anything close to the passion and longing expressed in her letters to Dorothea Gilder. Whether Beaux ever considered her preferences or thought of herself as a lesbian is not easy to discern. In the nineteenth century "romantic friendships" between women were accepted and considered harmless, as the general opinion was that women's sexual feeling were in abeyance until awakened by a man. Women like Cecilia Beaux and Dorothea Gilder, who had a physical bond as well as an emotional attachment, would have been loath to describe themselves as lesbians. The lesbian historian Lillian Faderman contends that proper women would not have been comfortable "defining themselves in terms they had been taught were indecent, even if they did have sexual relationships."[450] The strict observance

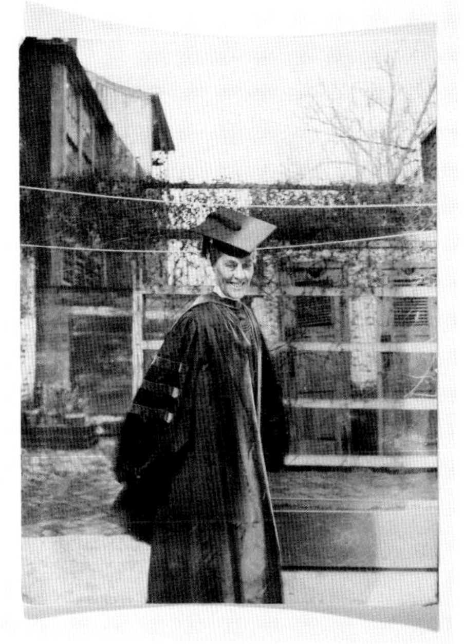

108. ***Cecilia Beaux in cap and gown***, *1908. Pennsylvania Academy of the Fine Arts*

107. OPPOSITE: ***Mrs. Richard Low Divine.*** *1907. Oil on canvas, 74¾ x 48 in. Columbus Museum of Art*

of conventional proprieties was important to Beaux, who once expressed shock when she saw a grown woman ride a horse astride.

Despite her infatuation with Dorothea Gilder, Beaux clearly enjoyed the attentions of men. She dressed carefully in flowing, feminine gowns and made an effort to be amusing enough to attract their interest. "[William Merritt] Chase from down the table came to tell me how 'charming I looked.' . . . Guess it was the bandeau," she noted in her diary when she was fifty-six years old.[451] Approaching the age of sixty, Beaux was still a handsome woman. "Having a nice talk when Jack came in. W. not much pleased I think," she wrote in her diary. "Very gay time . . . very teasy . . . and I don't know how to convince him of the truth. Hints don't seem to take. He thinks me young. Shall I tell him I watched Lincoln's funeral?"[452] Beaux's good looks and easy charm attracted the attention of numerous men for most of her adult life. She called this casual flirtation "EYES" and enjoyed it.[453] However, once she achieved a man's interest, she always backed away. Her excuse to friends and family, even to herself, was always the same, that something was not quite right and that she required perfection.

Thornton Oakley maintained his friendship with Cecilia Beaux following his marriage to Amy Ewing on March 28, 1910. When he returned from a thirteen-month honeymoon and came to see her, Beaux described the visit in her diary.

> It was glorious. First we talked and then had tea and walked over to the park which was quite deserted and very sweet. Then we went down to a little restaurant and sat long to talk. . . . Out again for a walk . . . and up to the apartment. I put on the Indian robe he bought me and lay on the floor while he read me his "Impressions on China . . . " he calls "In the Land of The Red Dragon.". . . A delightful time. . . . If only I could have a succession of such hours during the leisure times I would ask for nothing better.[454]

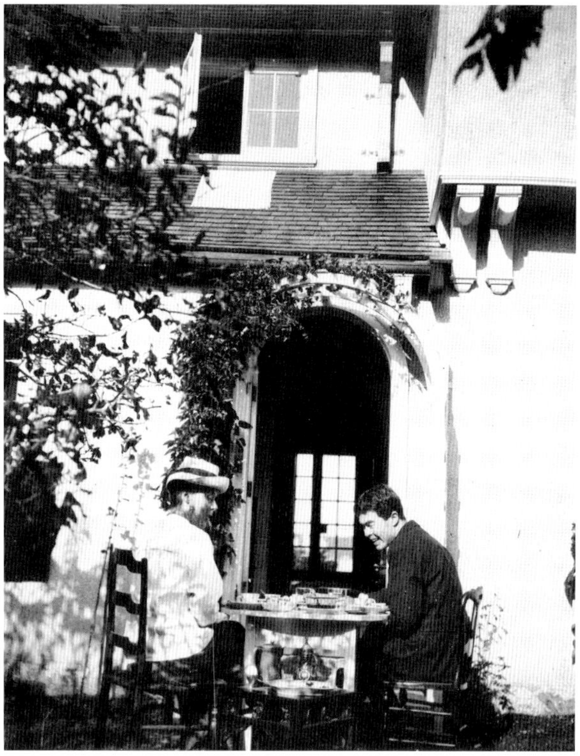

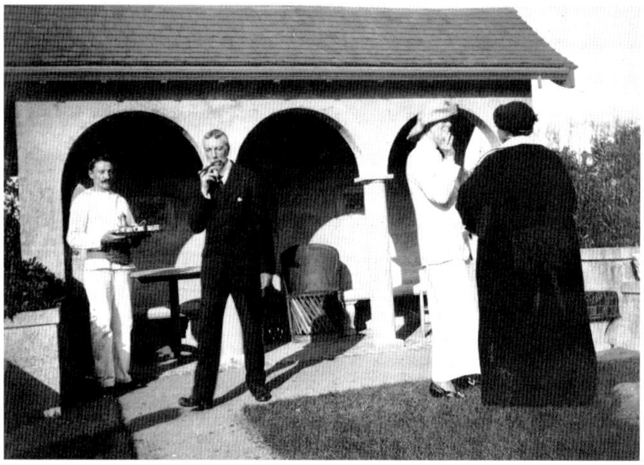

109. TOP: ***Cecilia Beaux and Thornton Oakley at Green Alley,*** *1907. Pennsylvania Academy of the Fine Arts*

110. BOTTOM: ***Beaux with friends and her houseman at Green Alley,*** *1912. From left to right, Natale Gavagnin, Arthur Hadley, Cecilia Beaux, and Isabella Stewart Gardner. Pennsylvania Academy of the Fine Arts*

111. OPPOSITE: ***Mrs. Stedman Buttrick and Son John.*** *1909. Oil on canvas, 33 1/2 x 25 1/2 in. Courtesy Mr. John D. Bryson*

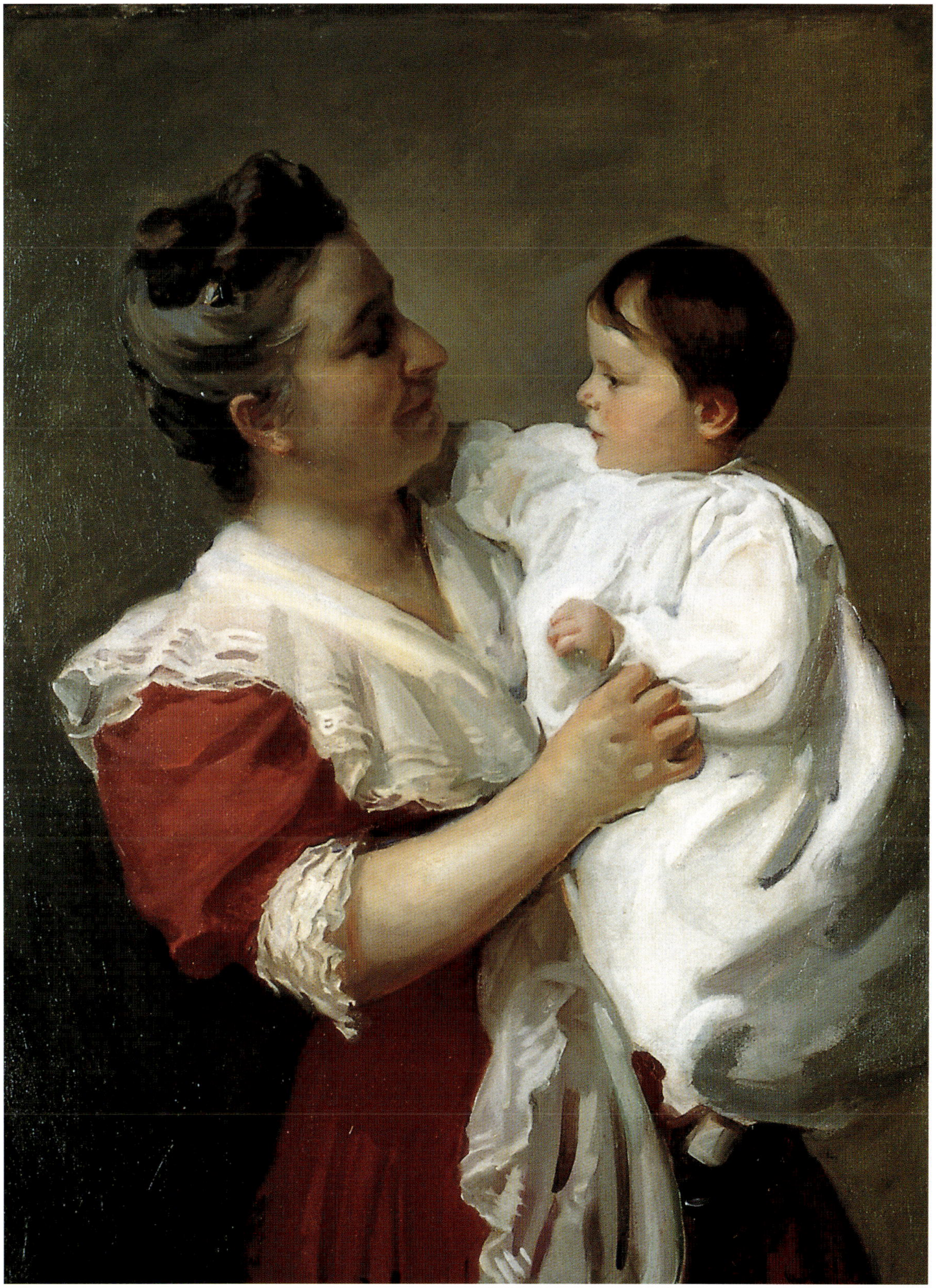

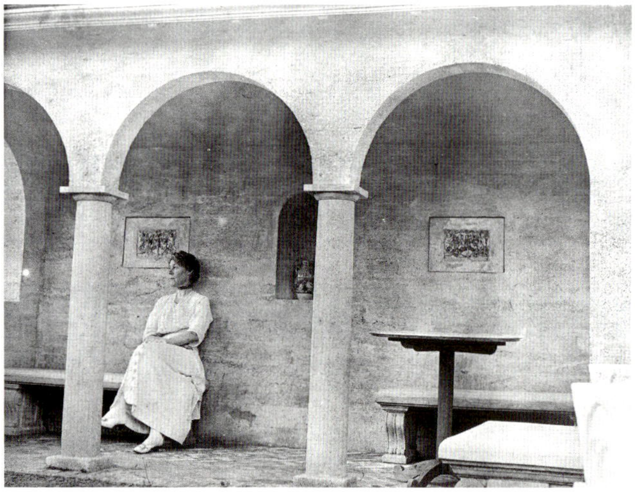

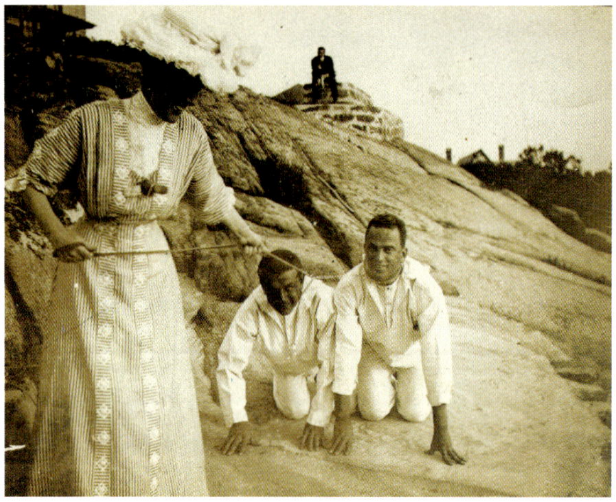

112. TOP: ***Cecilia Beaux seated in the loggia at Green Alley,*** *mid-1920s. Pennsylvania Academy of the Fine Arts*
113. BOTTOM: ***Cecilia Beaux with A. Piatt Andrew*** *(left)* ***and Jack Mabbett*** *(William James Jr., in background). 1908. Pennsylvania Academy of the Fine Arts*

In a letter to Dorothea, she explained, "Adores his wife but don't propose to lose hold of C. B."[455] Beaux was right on both accounts. Thornton and Amy enjoyed a loving and enduring marriage, but both were attentive to their friend Cecilia. Thornton, who understood that Beaux never mentioned her age or celebrated her birthday, remembered her every year with a valentine. "When you think of your Valentine / Say she is grateful / And Remembering / And always wanting more hearts / More Messages, more tokens / And more comforting," Beaux wrote to Thornton in 1925 after receiving his annual greeting.[456]

Although many of Beaux's relationships with men were baffling, there was no question that she adored her uncle, whose steadfast love sustained her. A few months after Oakley's marriage, when Beaux received word that Uncle Will was gravely ill, she closed her studio in Gloucester and rushed to his side. Writing to Dorothea, who had lost her father the previous autumn, Beaux confided, "Oh D. be thankful that you did not have to watch your beloved fading—slowly fading—and have—as we have now—no hope."[457] When Biddle died on August 9, 1910, Beaux was devastated. Nevertheless, she knew how to deal with tragedy. Following the example set by her grandmother and her aunts, she got to work. In the five years following her uncle's death, Beaux produced close to 25 percent of her total lifetime output. In order to accomplish so much, she often had two clients pose in a single day, abandoning her long-held habit of working only in the morning.

Beaux's increase in productivity did nothing to diminish the quality of her portraits, which capture both the personality of the sitter and the charm of the era. Her yield was unprecedented, and so were her honors, which continued unabated. A solo show in 1910 at the Macbeth Gallery received a glowing review in the *Evening Globe* from her friend critic Arthur Hoeber. In 1911 she was chosen to be on the jury for the Carnegie Institute's annual international exhibition, the only woman ever awarded that honor. In 1912, fortified with a glass of sherry to calm her nerves, Beaux received another honorary degree, a Master of Arts from Yale University. That same year she exhibited thirty-five paintings in a major show at the Corcoran Art Gallery in Washington, D.C.

In spite of these accolades, there was nothing Beaux could do to alter the course of American art, which was (as far as she was concerned) heading for a disaster as inevitable as the *Titanic*. On February 15, 1913, largely due to the efforts of one of "The Eight," painter Arthur B. Davies, the first International Exposition of Modern

Art in the United States opened at New York's 69th Regiment Armory. The controversial exhibition, popularly known as The Armory Show, presented more than 1,200 works of art, including paintings by Georges Braque (1882–1963), Pablo Picasso (1881–1973), Marcel Duchamp (1887–1968), Henri Matisse (1869–1954), Paul Gauguin (1848– 1903), and Vincent Van Gogh (1853–1890) to an astonished American public and attracted more than 70,000 viewers. Arthur Hoeber declared that the "public rubbed its eyes and laughed out loud." Writing for the *Century*, critic Royal Cortissoz declared the Post-Impressionists "not only incompetent, but grotesque."[458]

The critical furor over the exhibition proved irrelevant. New Yorkers had been enlightened. The course of American painting was changed—irrevocably influenced by the innovations of European art. In a lecture Cecilia Beaux delivered at Simmons College titled "The Public and Modern Art," she contended that it was ultimately the American public, not critics or artists, who would dictate national taste and establish a unique American style. A believer in the tenants of American democracy, she trusted the good sense of the people and was confident that they would not embrace the novelty of modernism and that her work would triumph. And indeed for a time, the facts seemed to support her faith in the conservative wisdom of the populace.

Women artists, even very accomplished ones, were expected to paint feminine subjects, and it was unusual for a female painter to be hired to portray important men. However, Beaux's stature and reputation as an artist transcended such stereotypes, and her skill as a painter coupled with her many awards and honors resulted in commissions that were unprecedented. Posing for a Cecilia Beaux portrait became a mark of prestige. Between 1910 and 1916, she painted the Philadelphia banker Clement Newbold; Sereno E. Payne, Chairman of the House Ways and Means Committee; a bank president and close friend of Abraham Lincoln, John W. Bunn; the philanthropist and manufacturer Henry Phipps; Dr. Andrew F. West, dean of the Graduate School at Princeton University; Dr. William Henry Howell, dean of the medical faculty at Johns Hopkins University; and Robert de Forest, President of The Metropolitan Museum of Art.

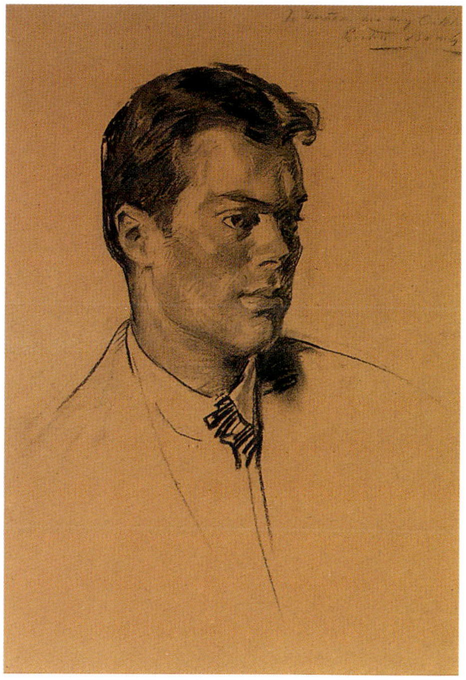

114. ***Thornton Oakley.*** *1911. Charcoal on board, 19 5/8 x 14 1/8 in. Courtesy Mrs. Lansdale Humphreys*

Beaux also painted women and children, and during this productive period, when she was busy with lucrative commissions, she still found time to complete portraits, "con amore," of her family and friends. Among her most successful paintings are likenesses of Dorothea Gilder and her niece Ernesta Drinker, both painted in 1914. Dorothea looks sophisticated in a portrait titled *After the Meeting*. Dressed for business in a fashionable striped dress, black hat adorned with a white egret feather, and a brown fur stole, she is portrayed in conversation—suspended by her friend's brush in the middle of some lively discourse. She looks nothing like the innocent girl Beaux painted dancing in the tobacco barn fifteen years earlier. In 1914 Dorothea Gilder was thirty-two years old and had enjoyed a brief stage career. Using the name Dorothea Coleman, she played a flower girl in *Kismet*, had a small part in

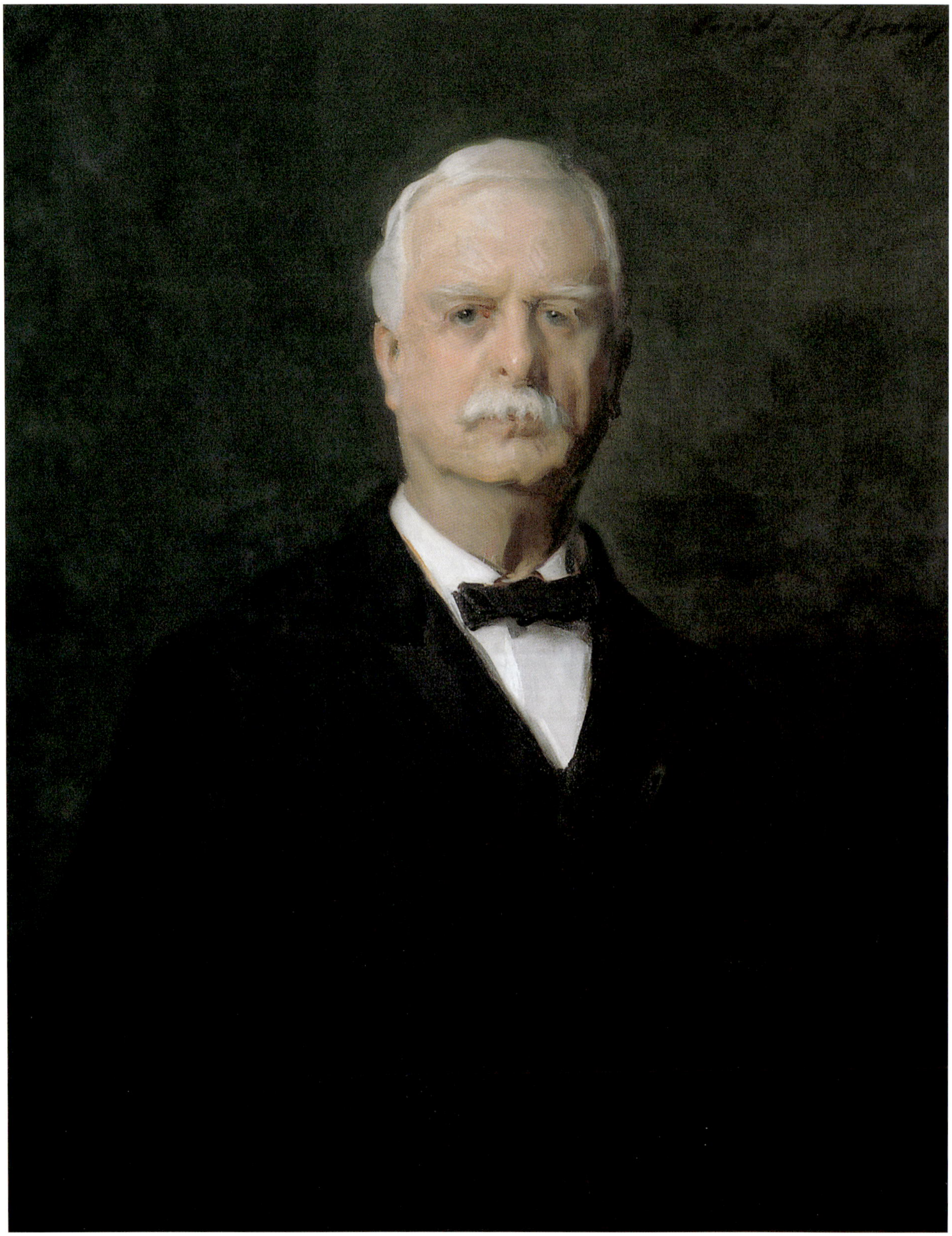

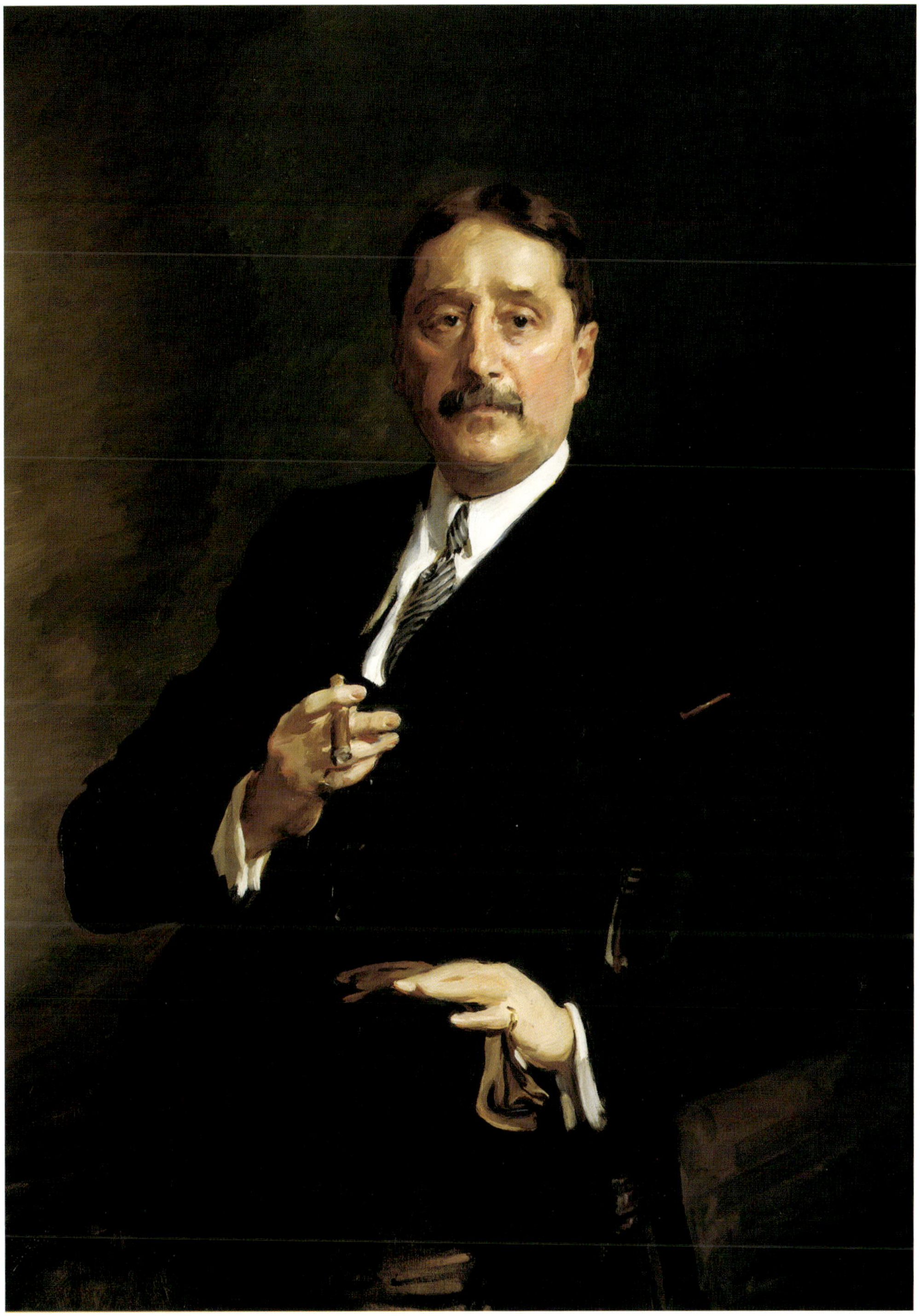

115. OPPOSITE: ***Sereno Elisha Payne.*** *1912. Oil on canvas, 41 1/2 x 31 1/2 in. Architect of the Capitol*

116. ABOVE: ***Clement B. Newbold.*** *1912. Oil on canvas, 47 3/8 x 35 in. Pennsylvania Academy of the Fine Arts*

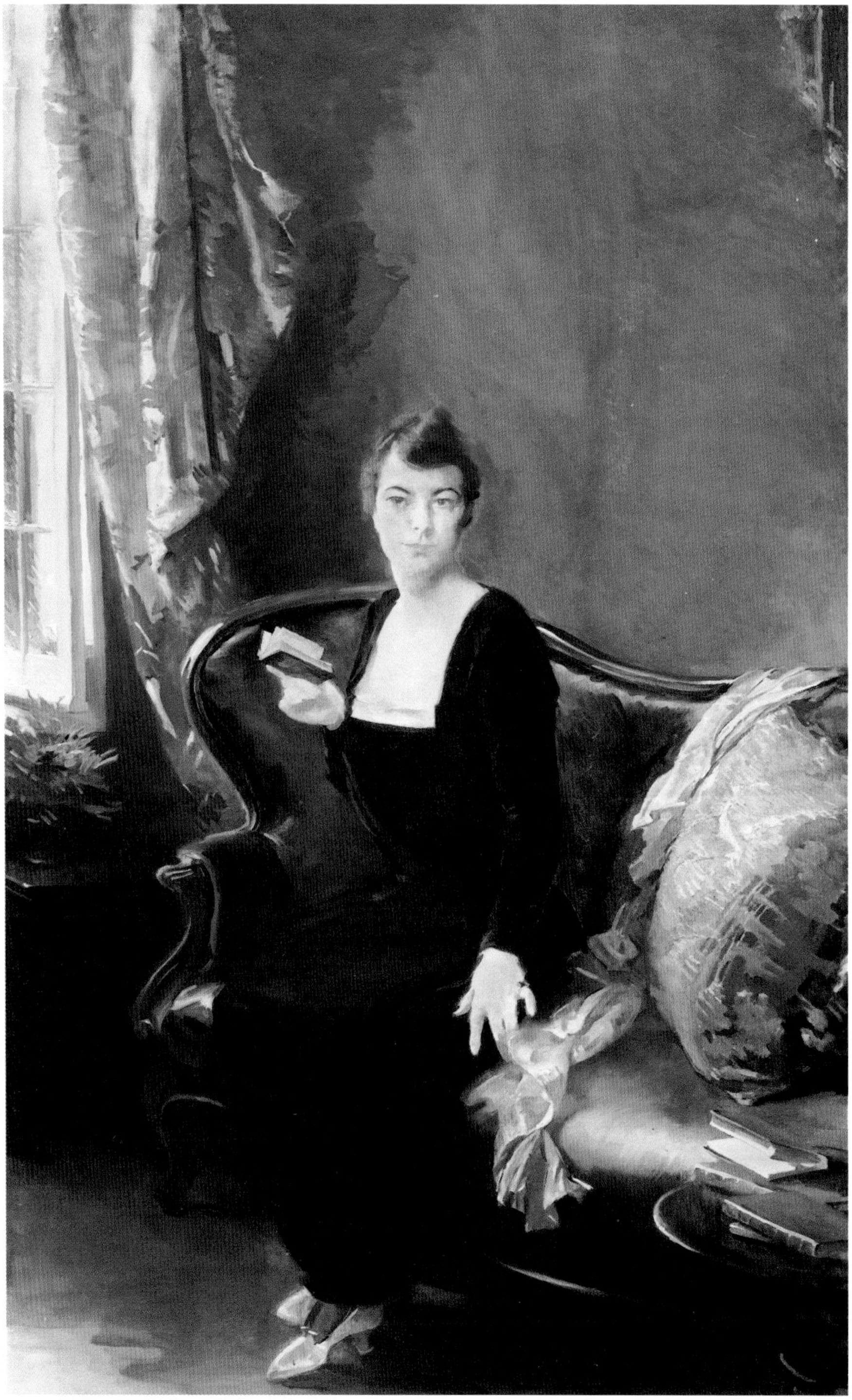

117. ABOVE: ***A Lady in Black.*** *ca. 1916. Oil on canvas, 78 3/8 x 47 1/2 in.*
Museum of Fine Arts, Boston

118. OPPOSITE: ***Ernesta.*** *1914. Oil on canvas, 71 3/4 x 43 3/8 in.*
The Metropolitan Museum of Art

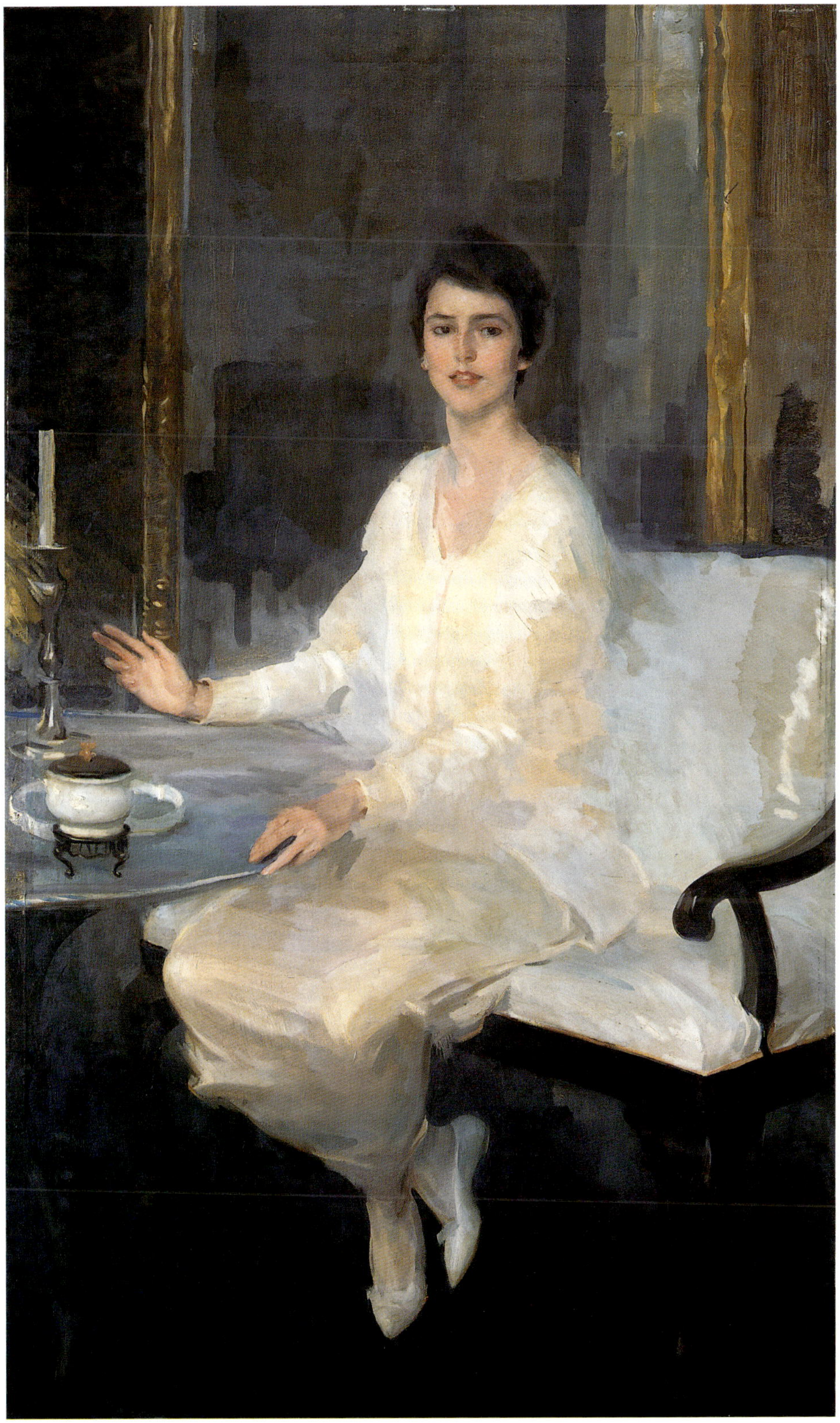

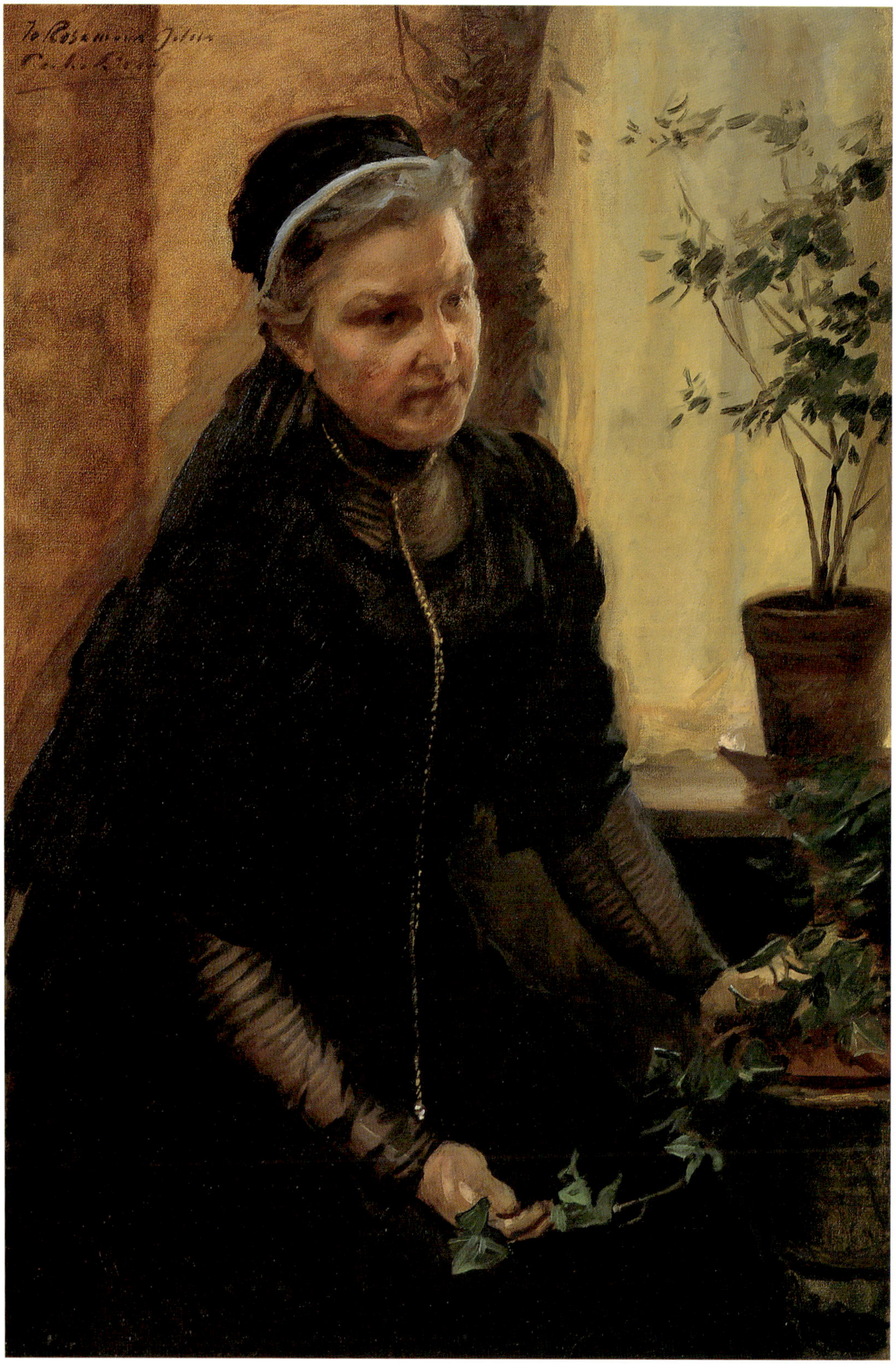

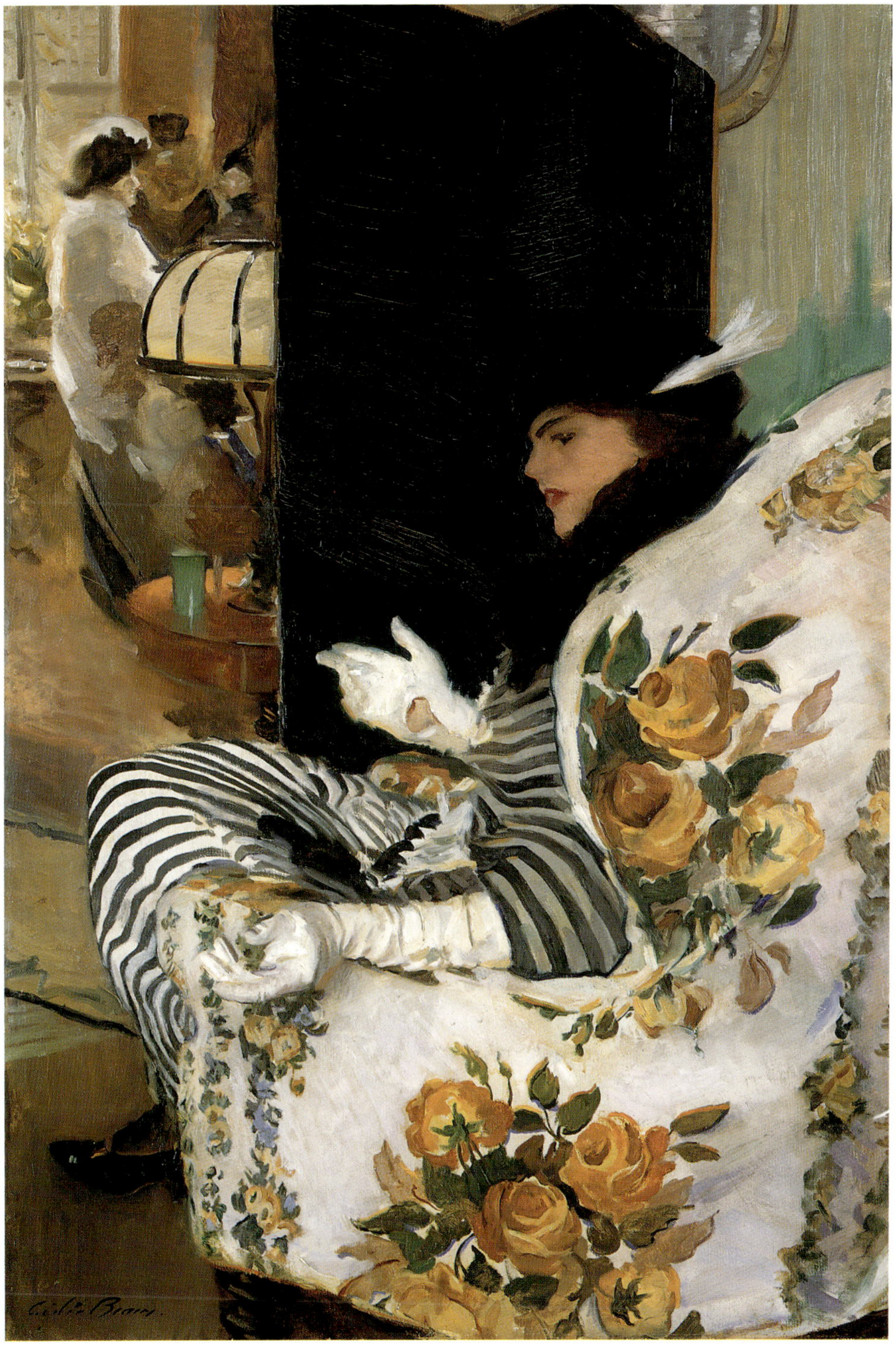

119. OPPOSITE: ***Helena DeKay Gilder.*** *1911. Oil on canvas, 31 x 21 in. Collection of the family*

120. ABOVE: ***After the Meeting.*** *1914. Oil on canvas, 40 15/16 x 28 1/8 in. Toledo Museum of Art*

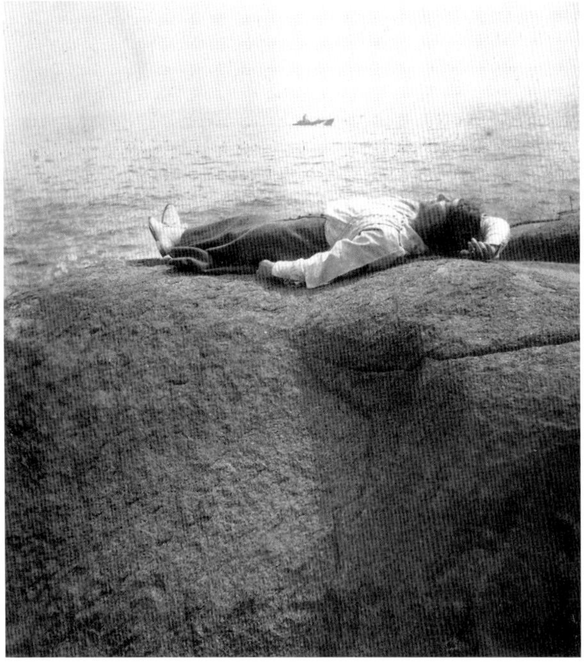

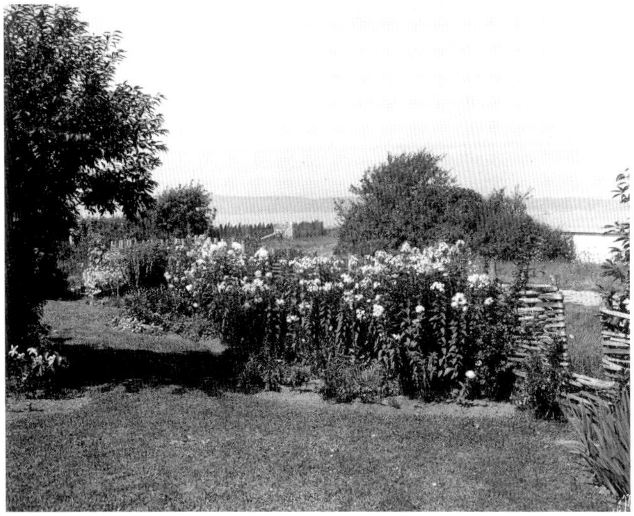

121. TOP: ***Cecilia Beaux lying prone on the rocks at Gloucester, Massachusetts,*** *ca. 1910–20. Pennsylvania Academy of the Fine Arts*
122. BOTTOM: *T. E. Morr.* ***View of the harbor from Cecilia Beaux's studio,*** *1910–20. Pennsylvania Academy of the Fine Arts*
123. OPPOSITE: ***Helena Dorothea McGrew.*** *ca. 1920. Oil on canvas, 24 1/2 x 18 1/4 in. Courtesy of Skinner, Inc., Auctioneers of Fine Art and Antiques, Boston and Bolton, Massachusetts*

Edward Sheldon's play *Egypt*, and later worked with the Shakespearean actress Julia Marlow and actor E. H. Sothern.

In contrast, twenty-two-year-old Ernesta looks demure in her portrait and stunningly beautiful. Dressed in white, she regards the viewer directly. In 1915 The Metropolitan Museum of Art purchased the painting of Ernesta. At the time, Beaux was thrilled by the acclamation and sold the painting to the museum for $3,000, her customary fee for a portrait. Later she was sorry that she had sold the painting. She disapproved of the way it was handled and displayed—"not becomingly," she told her nephew Harry.[459] Beaux also disagreed with what she perceived as the museum's policy of buying small canvases by struggling modern painters. She believed that purchasing decisions at a major museum should be based on the merit of the work and not on the financial needs of the artist.

In the midst of this demanding professional schedule, Beaux still made time to socialize with friends in New York and in Gloucester. After the death of her uncle, she formed a closer bond with Helena DeKay Gilder, who was in mourning for her husband. Beaux painted her portrait and spent almost every evening at the Gilders' home, although she avoided Dorothea. At some point after 1911, Beaux had introduced Dorothea to her young friend from Gloucester, Mr. Dallas McGrew, who by then was working for the International Banking Corporation in New York. In 1916 Dorothea and Dallas announced their engagement. It was another defeat for Cecilia, but by the age of sixty-one she had grown accustomed to losses. Dorothea Gilder married Dallas McGrew on May 19, 1916, at the Gilders' home in New York. Only the immediate family attended the wedding, as Helena Gilder was gravely ill and would die before the month was out. Beaux sent a gift with a note, "Here is your wedding gift with a halo if you can see it of surrounding love."[460] By 1917 the McGrews were living in China, where Dallas was working. Ten months later the couple had a baby girl and named her Helena.

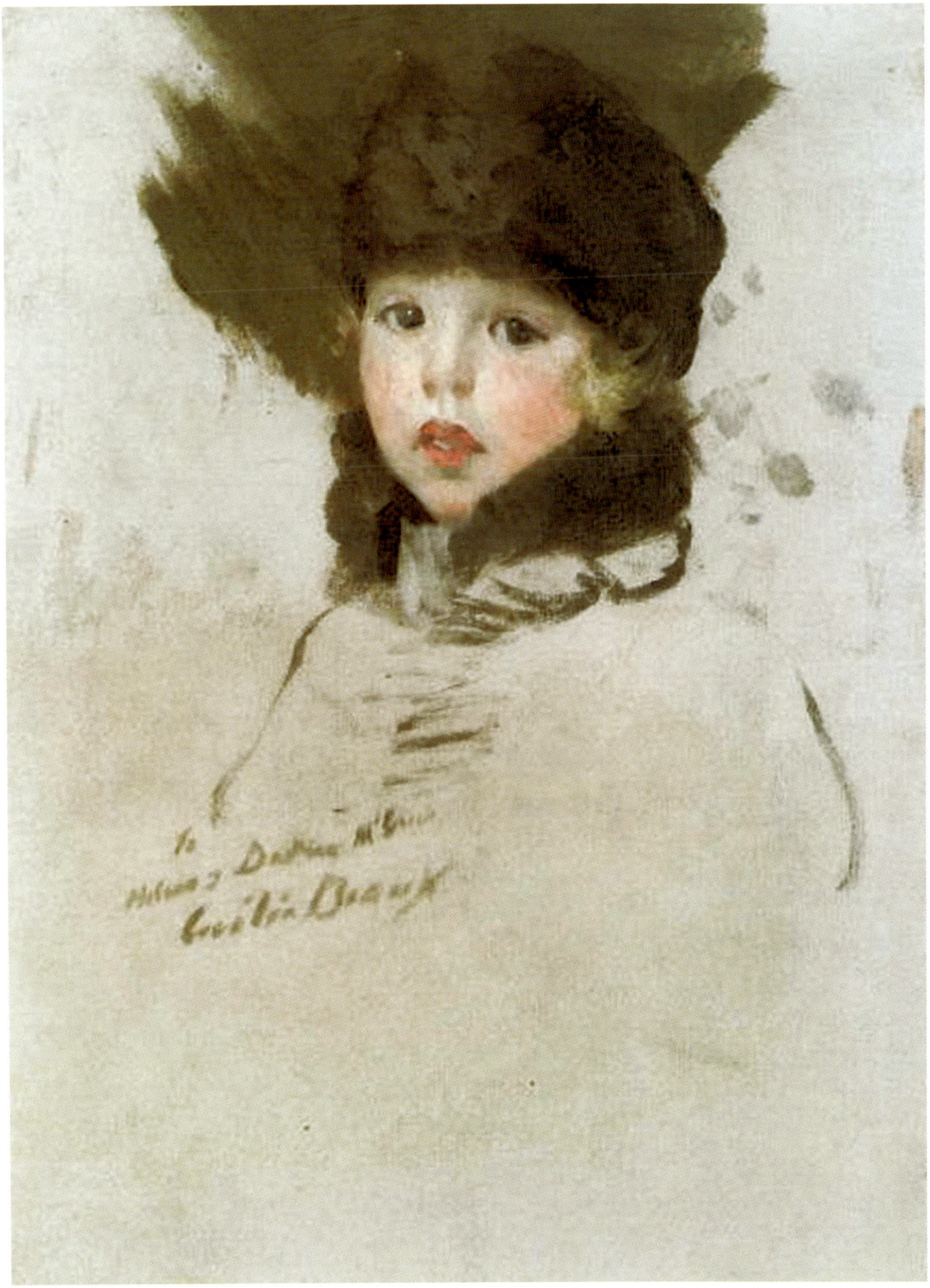

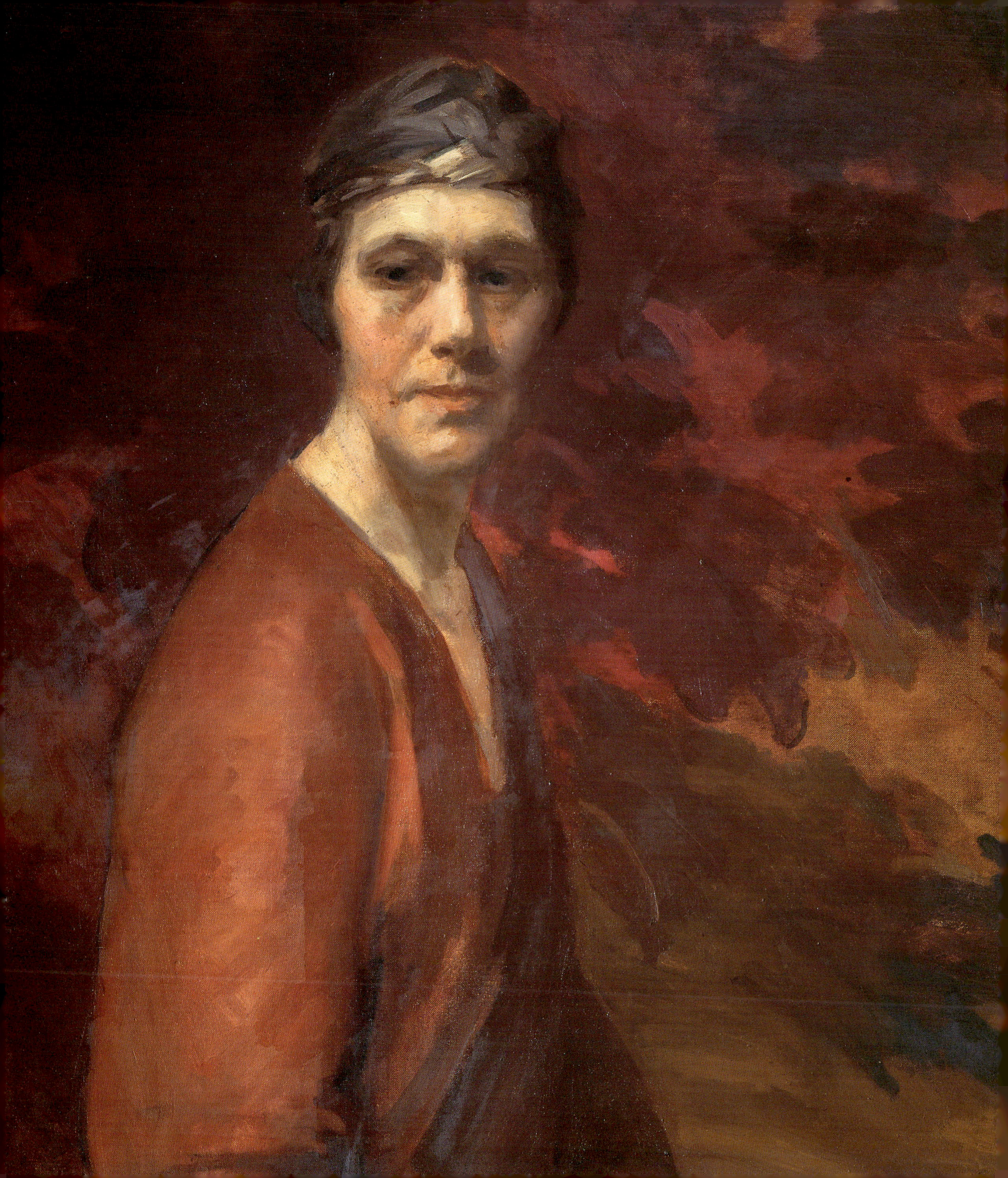

Green Alley Autumn

"Art exacts everything, no matter what the power of the effort—or the result of it may be."

—Cecilia Beaux, *April 9, 1911*

Following Helena Gilder's death and Dorothea's marriage, Beaux's strongest ties to New York dissolved. It would have been understandable if, given her age, position, and circumstances, she had drifted into stylish retirement among her wealthy friends in Gloucester. But it was not in her nature to stop working. In a revealing interview in the *American Magazine* published when Beaux was approaching seventy, she told the writer, Allison Gray, "I can say this: When I attempt anything, I have a *passionate determination* to overcome every obstacle. Work is a struggle to conquer something. And I do my own work with a refusal to accept defeat that might almost be called pitiful."[461] Gray noted that as Beaux uttered this extraordinary sentiment, she clenched her fists as if gripping something intangible.

Had Allison Gray known Beaux well, she might have understood that the artist's entire life had been about gripping the intangible—which for Beaux was an artistic ideal that could not be achieved without a continual struggle for perfection. "A perfect technique in anything," Beaux maintained, "means that there has been no break in continuity between the conception and the act of performance."[462] As Beaux aged, her determination to achieve did not falter. For as the people she loved grew up, grew old, or died, increasingly it was her work that defined her. She had little time for anything else. Her complete focus on her painting caused resentment in her youngest niece, Catherine Drinker Bowen, who felt that Beaux ignored her. When her siblings were young, Bowen recalled, Aunt Bo was attentive. Although Beaux's health was good and she wrote in her diary that she always felt like the youngest person at every party, she was aware that her productive years were finite. So it became progressively more important that her paintings weather the onslaught of modernism and emerge victorious. This was the legacy she had worked toward for more than forty years.

Beaux understood that to assure herself a place in the canon of American art she would have to do something extraordinary. Her chance to achieve that goal came with the opening of hostilities in Europe that led to the beginning of World War I. In 1914 Beaux's neighbor in Gloucester, A. Piatt Andrew, became one of the first Americans to take an active part in the conflict. Armed with energy, intelligence, and personal charm, Andrew went to France and convinced government officials that American volunteers could aid French troops by providing ambulance service to soldiers at the front. Once permission was granted, Andrew steamed home to the United States and easily persuaded the eager Henry Davis Sleeper to take charge of fundraising.

OPPOSITE: *Detail;* ***Self-Portrait.*** *1925. Oil on canvas, 43 x 28 in. Uffizi Gallery, Florence, Italy*

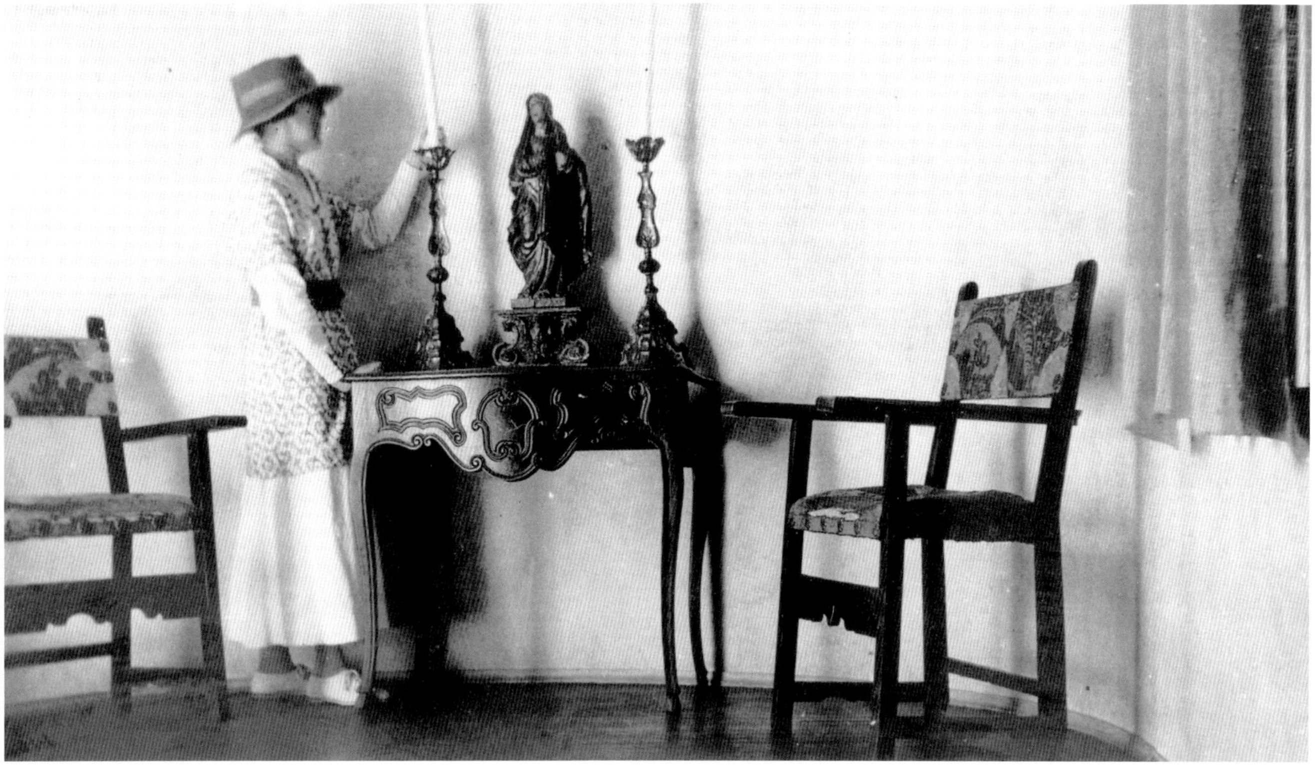

124. *Cecilia Beaux in the vestibule of her studio at Green Alley.* *1917. Pennsylvania Academy of the Fine Arts*

The two men did the impossible. By 1917 Andrew operated 1,220 donated ambulances and supervised 2,500 volunteers. His organization later became known as the American Field Service. "It is worthy of remembrance that the little group of American volunteers . . . numbering at no one time much more than two thousand, formed, for the first three years of the Great War, the most considerable organized representation which the United States had on the battle front," Andrew later wrote.[463] The American Field Service ambulance corps served at the battle of Verdun, in the Balkans, and in every engagement of the French army in the year 1917, from April until October. Accolades for the organization came from all quarters. The French Ambassador to the United States sent a telegram, which summarized the general response to the bravery and selflessness of Andrew's volunteers. "Lives saved by thousands, suffering attenuated, amputations avoided, families spared their fathers for after the war; these form only a part of the French debt toward the American Field Service."[464]

Inspired by the accomplishments of her neighbors, Beaux longed to contribute something toward the war effort. She donated money to help Andrew and Sleeper but hoped to do something significant on her own. In 1917, when she had a solo show at the Knoedler Gallery, she donated two small landscapes to be auctioned. All proceeds were designated for a relief fund for the families of artists enlisted as soldiers in the French army. However, this effort seemed small and did little to satisfy her patriotism, her love for France, or her more personal quest for artistic immortality. In 1918 she conceived of a plan that would accomplish her goal. Toward that end she composed a letter to her friend Robert de Forest President of The Metropolitan Museum of Art:

It seems to me that it would be highly fitting and appropriate, that portraits from life of some of the distinguished leaders among our Allies should be executed during Victory year, by an American artist, to be ultimately the property of the Nation or some National or public Institution.

I want to offer my services to go to France to paint two or more of such portraits, if sittings can be given for them. I desire no remuneration of any kind, and of course will see to all expenses in the matter if my offer should be accepted.

I realize that it is asking much of the great men in question, to propose that they should give time for the sittings; of course not now but perhaps next summer, when the immediate stress of the world situation may be relieved. Naturally I am thinking of the most distinguished—
Mr. Clemenceau, Marshal Foch, General Joffre.

I am not unknown in France, as I have been medaillee, and am Sociétaire des Beaux Arts. I exhibited at the exposition of 1900, and have frequently exhibited at the Champ de Mars, and I have always been given distinguished positions and notices.

I am writing to you, dear Mr. de Forest, in the first instance, because I feel that it will be necessary for me to be fully vouched for in this enterprise, and to what higher authority can I go?

I must present my appeal finally to those best able to offer my request with success, provided they are willing to do so, and beg you to advise me if you think well of it, and to whom I should turn.

You know my standing as an artist, and I hope you will consider that I am as able as any other American painter to undertake such a work.

Beaux's proposal intrigued de Forest and became the impetus for the formation of the National Art Committee—an eleven-member board headed by the Commissioner Plenipotentiary of the United States, the Honorable Henry White. The board created to put Beaux's plan into action expanded on her original idea. Eight artists were commissioned to paint twenty-three portraits of the heroes of the Great War. Cities around the country were to raise money to sponsor the artists, and the resulting canvases would become the property of the National Portrait Gallery in Washington, D.C. Beaux, who was funded by the city of San Francisco, was allocated three portraits. However, only one of the personalities she origially proposed to paint was assignd to her—Georges Clemenceau. Edmund Tarbell (1862–1938), an adept painter and Director of the Corcoran School of Art in Washington, D.C., was assigned Marshal Foch, Commander of the Allied Forces. The Danish-born artist John C. Johansen (1876–1964) was commissioned to paint the Commander-in-Chief of the French Army, Joseph Joffre. If Beaux was disappointed that her original plan had been commandeered and Foch and Joffre consigned to other artists, she never mentioned it. In fact, in her autobiography she wrote that she was chosen for the work by the committee and made no mention that the project had been her idea.

Any disappointment she might have felt about having to share the honors of the enterprise was probably mitigated when she was assigned two other distinguisehd subjects: Cardinal Désiré Joseph Mercier of Belgium and Admiral Sir David Beatty, Commander of the British Fleet. Conscious of the great opportunity before her, Beaux booked passage to Paris. Thornton Oakley went to see her off and watched her wave gaily from the railing of the ship. "So as she waved that day I love to think of her," he later recalled. "Radiant, clad in crimsons, wealth of greens, scarf blowing, headdress touched with gleams of gold—departing on the culminating adventure of her career."[465]

By May 1919, when the Peace Conference was still in session, Beaux was in Paris preparing to begin her

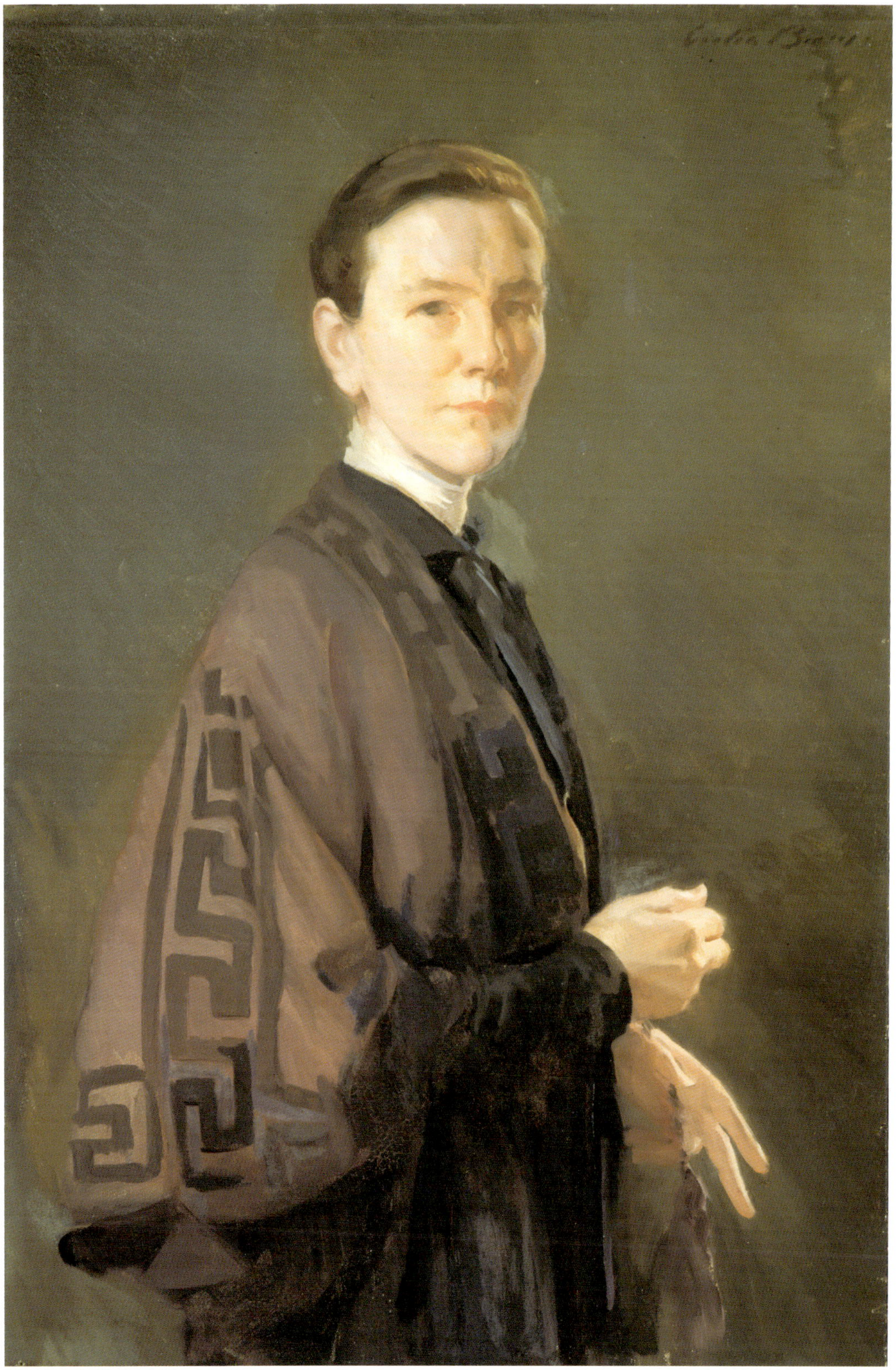

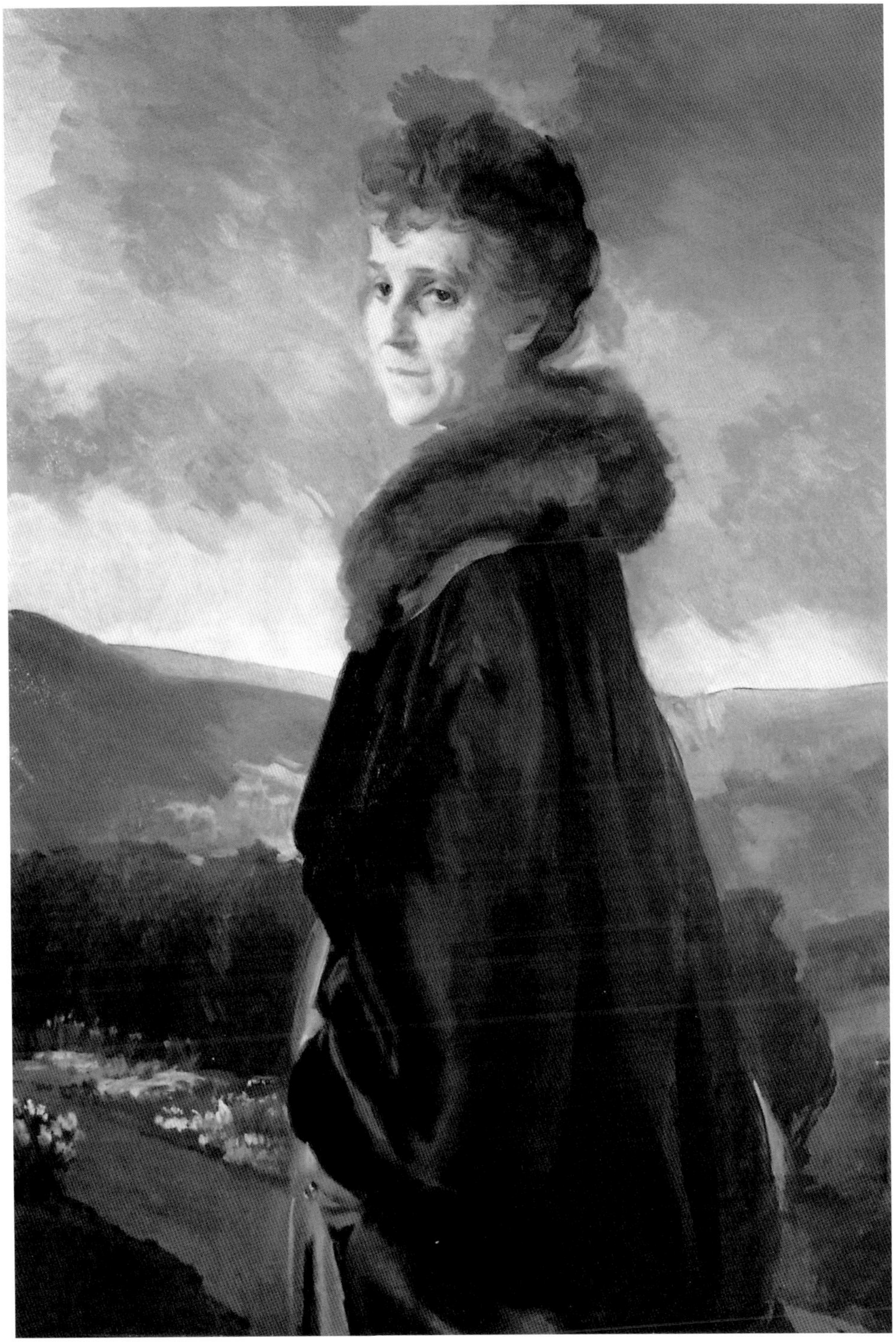

125. OPPOSITE: ***Marion Reilly.*** *1918. Oil on canvas, 39¼ x 26¼ in. Bryn Mawr College Collection*

126. ABOVE: ***Mrs. Andrew Carnegie.*** *1917–18. Oil on canvas, 52 x 36½ in. Carnegie Museum of Art*

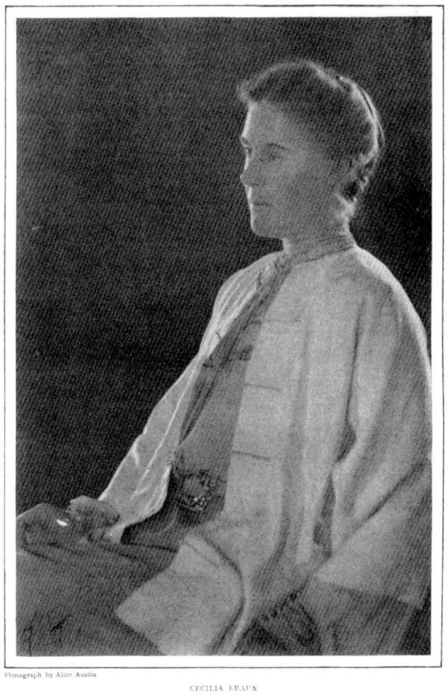

127. *Alice Austin.* ***Cecilia Beaux.*** *ca. 1910–20. Pennsylvania Academy of the Fine Arts*

portrait of Clemenceau and looking for lodging and a suitable studio. Spring in Paris was as glorious as she remembered. "I am glad to revel in the beauty. Every leaf and flower is as perfectly done as ever," she reported to Etta. "Nothing will stop them from the right way of doing everything."[466] But although the war had spared Parisian gardens, the French people were not unscathed. In the well-manicured parks Beaux noticed young widows tending their small children. Maimed soldiers proudly wearing newly minted medals regarded the wealth of spring with haunted eyes that bore testament to their suffering. One morning Henry Davis Sleeper, who was in France with the American Field Service, picked up Beaux and her traveling companion, the artist Lucy Taggart (1880–1960), in one of the ambulances and set out to show them the devastation at Rheims, Noyons, Soissons, and Chemin des Dames. The battlefields were bright with a spectacular display of poppies, daisies, and bluets, each in separate masses that seemed to form the tricolor of the French flag. Stooped laborers moved amid the flowers collecting huge mounds of rusting barbed wire and shell casings and stacking them by the roadsides. "Soft summer sunshine, songs of invisible birds, hope, comradeship were ours," Beaux wrote. "Why, so near death and ruin, were we so blessed?"[467]

Beaux did feel blessed. She expected that the heroes who had triumphed over Germany in "The War to End All Wars" would achieve mythic status and was overjoyed that she was to meet three of them, capture their personalities, immortalize traits that only she could perceive, and present the results to a grateful American public. Beaux may have recalled Gilbert Stuart's (1755–1828) portraits of Washington, or Benjamin West's dramatic *Death of General Wolfe*. But her dream was not to be fulfilled. Her subjects never achieved anything close to the revered standing of Washington, and the flawed portraits, which she was unable to paint with her customary skill, did not compare with West's masterful canvas.

Nothing went as planned. Beaux was afraid to have anyone approach Clemenceau, who had come into sharp disagreement with President Woodrow Wilson over the terms of the Treaty of Versailles. Given the circumstances, Beaux feared that he would not consent to pose for an American artist. Since the National Art Committee had set no deadline for her work, she decided to wait for a more opportune time. While she waited, she would go to Belgium and begin the portrait of Cardinal Mercier, who had agreed to pose. However, before she left Paris, she was determined to catch a glimpse of the Prime Minister. On June 30, the Monday following the signing of the Treaty of Versailles, the American Embassy procured a seat for Beaux in the diplomatic gallery of the Senate where Clemenceau was to present the Treaty to the senators. "It was a great occasion," she wrote to Etta. "He came in among shouts & roars, mounted a tribune directly opposite where I was and read his address quietly as if he feared his own emotions."[468] The senate chamber was illuminated only by natural light, which shone on Clemenceau from above like a sanction from God. Beaux decided that if she ever had the opportunity to paint the man they called

"Le Tigre," she would duplicate the dramatic scene before her from memory. For someone who was used to having sitters pose for three hours at a time and confessed that she gave them orders and "pulled them about," constructing a major portrait without the benefit of a model would be a monumental task. Nevertheless, heady with the great honor entrusted to her, she believed that it was possible.

Filled with optimism, Beaux set out for Belgium with Lucy Taggart. On July 2, 1919, the pair arrived in Brussels in a driving thunderstorm, wet and bedraggled. From Brussels they took a train to Malines, and on July 6 Beaux was escorted to the Archevêché where Cardinal Mercier received her. He was a tall, thin man and looked weary, as if the responsibilities he had shouldered during the war had left a weight on him that could not be easily removed. Beaux described him as a shepherd well acquainted with the sorrows of his flock. Throughout the German occupation of neutral Belgium, through a series of letters read in churches, Mercier openly criticized the injustices perpetrated on the people by the German army. His opposition to the invading forces coupled with his courage in expressing his resistance provided hope during dark times. For his bravery and defiance, Mercier was revered in Belgium and respected in the United States.

Beaux expected to see the strength of Mercier's character in his manner and bearing, but she was unprepared for the depths of her feelings when the Cardinal appeared before her. She was completely besotted. If Papa Beaux and his Huguenot forebears looked down from their place of eternal reward and saw their daughter so taken with a Cardinal, they would certainly have been dismayed. "I have no doubt he knew more of me in those five minutes than I have ever known myself. . . . He had the grandeur, the universality, and the unconsciousness of Nature; the highest peak, the deepest river, and the way of the butterfly in the air,"[469] Beaux wrote, recording the occasion in her autobiography. To Etta she confided, "I almost wept when I told him how he was beloved in America, and he saw at once as he sees everything, that I was modest and sincere and would not take a mean advantage."[470]

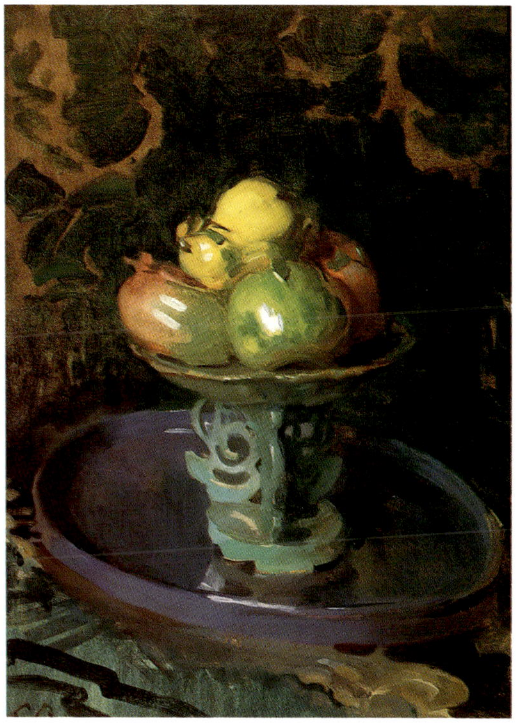

128. ***Still Life with Fruit.*** *1918. Oil on canvas, 24 1/4 x 18 in. Westmoreland Museum of American Art*

The Cardinal generously offered a spacious, bare hall, the Salle des Evêques (Bishop's room) for Beaux's use as a studio. He explained, "*Madame, vous êtes chez vous.*"[471] The room had eight large windows overlooking the garden. High in the ceiling an enormous hole left by a German shell served as a reminder of the Cardinal's courage. Beaux rented an easel from a photographer, donned rubber-soled shoes and a crownless, brimmed hat, and tried to begin. It was impossible. The light in the room was not consistent. At certain hours, large patches of sunlight would appear on her canvas making it difficult to see what she was doing. His Eminence posed infrequently and for short periods, as Beaux was reluctant to tax his strength. When he did arrive in the Salle, Beaux, intimidated by his presence, never worked on the actual canvas, preferring to make notes and quick sketches while the two chatted. During one session, Beaux mentioned that she began her career drawing fossils. "And you still are!" Mercier replied.[472]

Beaux had conceived of a portrait that showed Mercier's moral force. Here was the man who had "carried Belgium in his arms," for five years. Yet as the Cardinal posed, she realized that when the war ended, he had taken off his armor. He looked frail and exhausted. "I have never fought anything as I have this whole experience," Beaux wrote to Etta.[473] Beaux struggled with the portrait until the end of August, when the Cardinal was leaving for a trip to the United States. "The hands were chaos, the background a mess, and there was very little really good painting on the whole canvas," Beaux admitted in her autobiography. But if she had been inclined to lose heart, the Cardinal, who appraised her work before he left, boosted her morale. Of all the portraits by all the painters, he told her, "*Vous êtes la seule qui a fait l'Ame*,"—you alone have painted the soul.[474] Heartened, Beaux was confident that given good light in a Paris studio, she could complete the painting.

Beaux finished the canvas in Paris. Although it was not among her finest, it represented her best effort. "The true artist never perfectly materializes his vision," she wrote. "How can he be but humble?"[475] Discouraged but undefeated, Beaux made plans to go to London in November 1919 to begin her portrait of the British Admiral Sir David Beatty. She trusted that Beatty, who was married to an American, would be cooperative and agree to pose. Beaux met the Admiral at his attractive home in Regents Park and was not intimidated. He was a soldier, not a saint, and although he was universally respected, questions had been raised about the impetuous nature of his attack on the German High Fleet at the Battle of Jutland, where he gained his reputation as a bold commander at the cost of many British lives. Beatty, who received Beaux as a courtesy to the American Ambassador, had no idea who she was or why she had come. Nevertheless, once she explained her purpose, he agreed to pose the next day, remarking with a smile, "It's just as well to get disagreeable things over, eh?"[476] As it turned out, the process was not disagreeable at all.

Beatty was a handsome man in his forties, cordial yet businesslike. At 11 A.M. the following day, he arrived at Beaux's airy studio at 3A Claireville Grove.

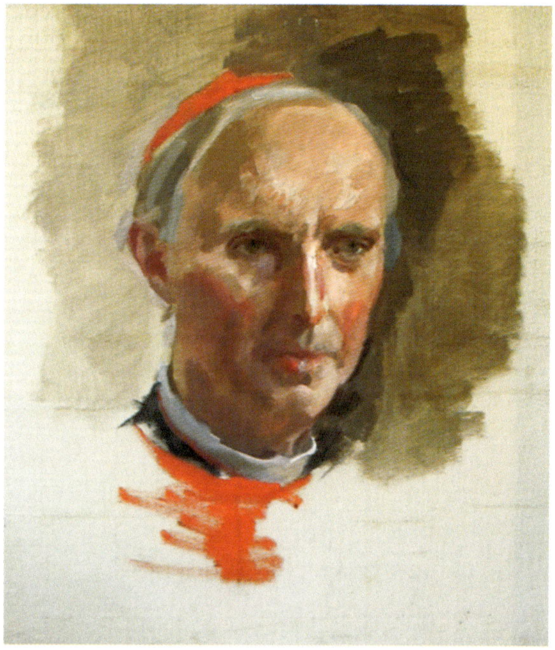

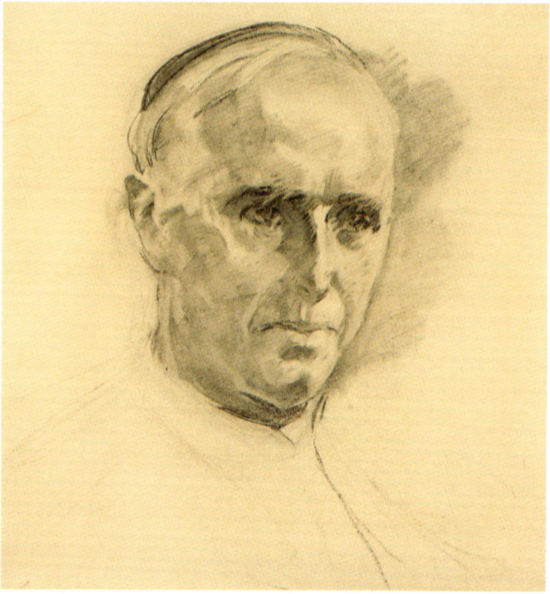

129. TOP: ***Study for Cardinal Joseph Mercier.*** *1919. Oil on canvas, 25 x 21 in. Courtesy of Alfred J. Walker Fine Art*

130. BOTTOM: ***Sketch for Cardinal Mercier.*** *1919. Charcoal on paper, 24 1/4 x 19 1/2 in. Pennsylvania Academy of the Fine Arts*

131. OPPOSITE: ***Cardinal Mercier.*** *1919. Oil on canvas, 78 x 51 3/4 in. Smithsonian American Art Museum, Washington, D.C.*

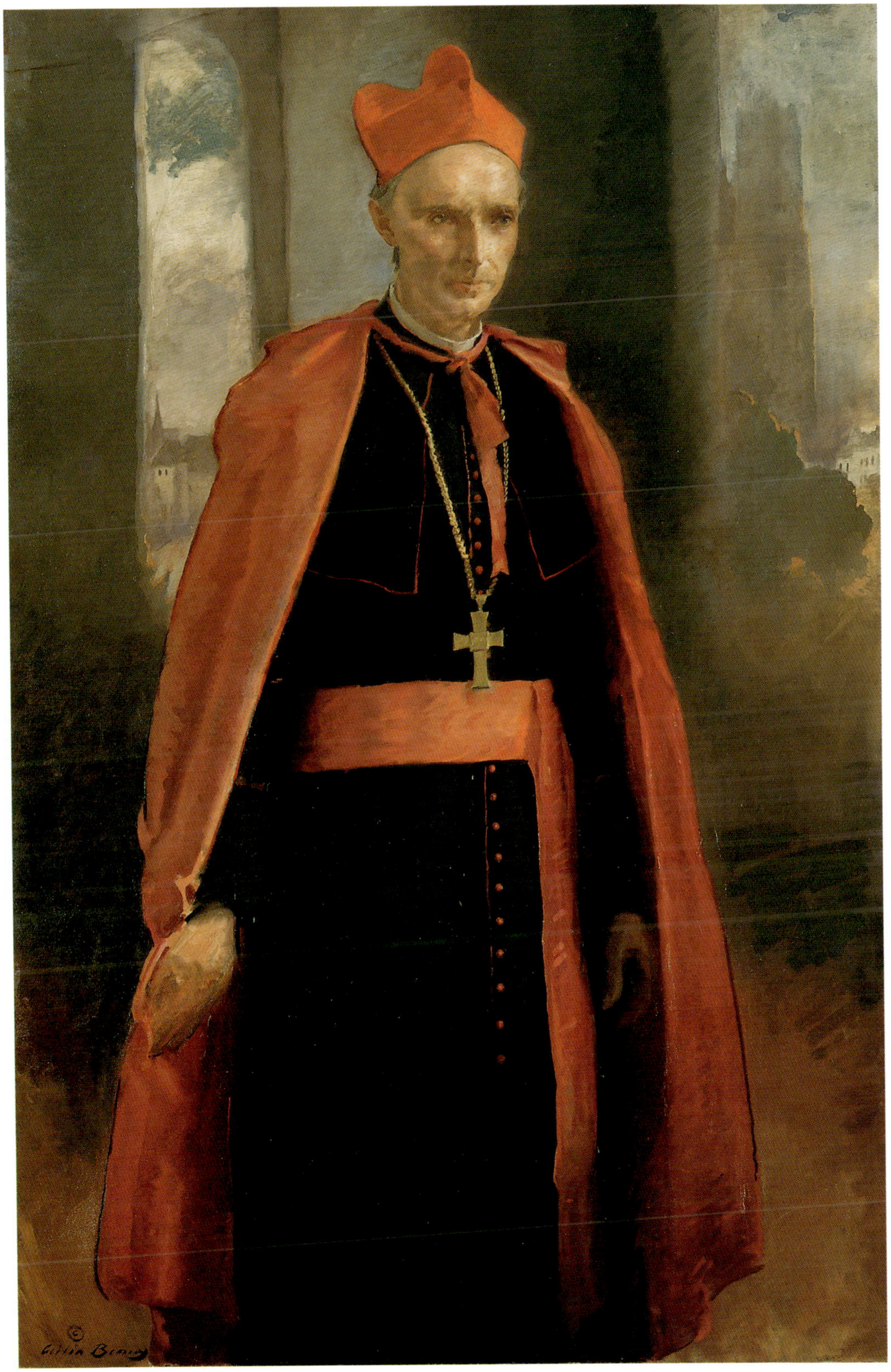

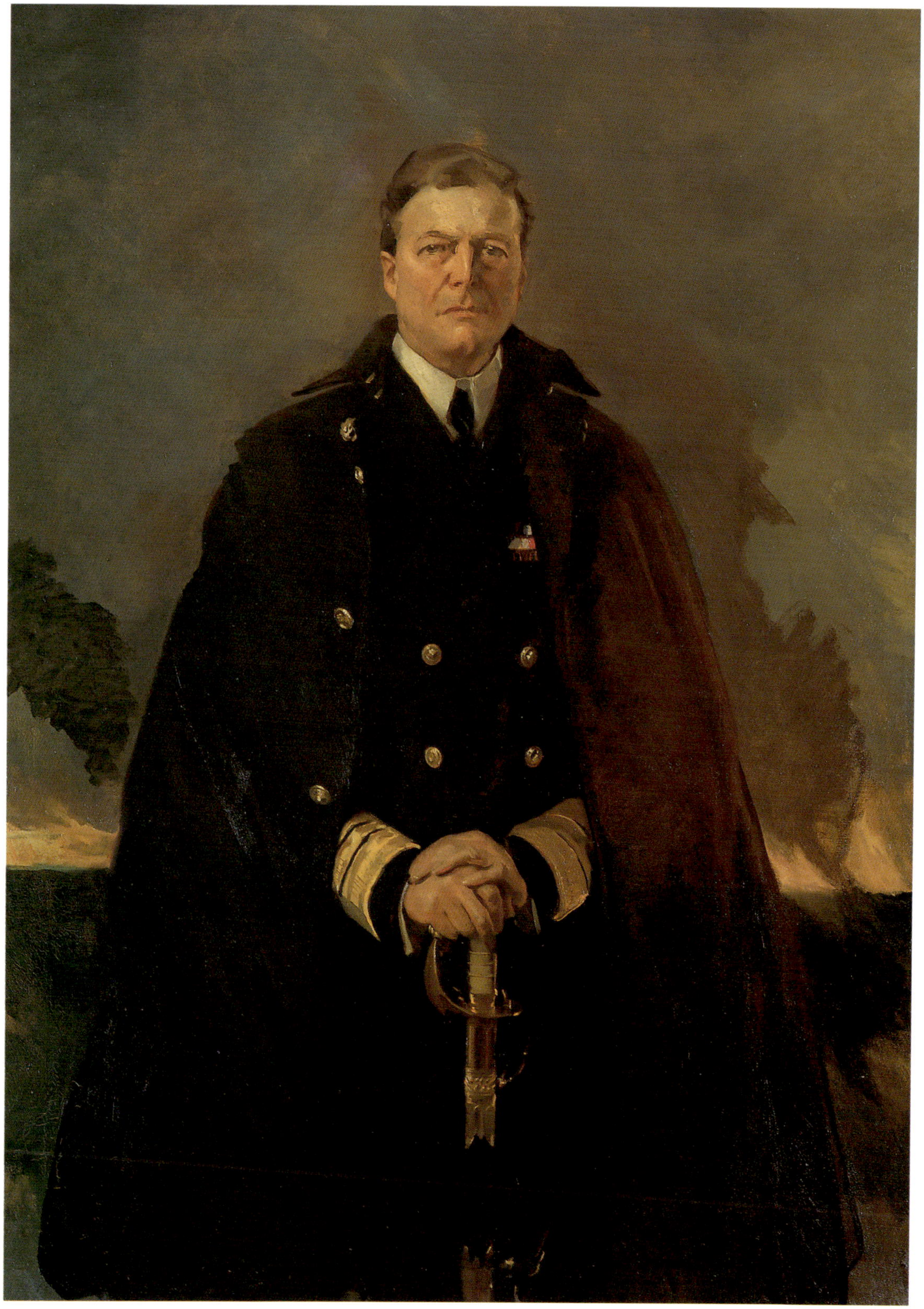

During the short session she took notes and made some decisions about the composition of the portrait, which she felt should be traditional, as Beatty seemed to be a traditional man. The Admiral promised to come back for another sitting, but because Beaux was not sure whether he would consent to a third visit, she hired a model and laid out the entire picture, leaving a space for Beatty's head which she would render in charcoal and transfer to the canvas. "The drawing turned out to be, for its purpose, the most comprehensive as well as the most direct drawing I ever made," Beaux later recalled, "just less than life-sized and easily transferable."[477]

The portrait progressed quickly. Beatty was cooperative and posed seven times, although he once asked, "What is America going to do for me?" "What would you like to have her do, Lord Beatty?" Beaux replied. "Ratify the Treaty," he said.[478] Beaux finished the canvas in two months. Although she would have liked to spend more time on the painting and later thought it adequate yet uninspired, she had done a professional job. The portrait was strong and expert.

When Beaux returned to Paris in January 1920, Georges Clemenceau was in Egypt. Beaux waited in vain for word of his homecoming, and finally in April, when she heard that he was back in France, she went to the American Embassy determined to find a way to contact the Prime Minister and arrange an appointment. This time she was successful; a meeting was scheduled for the following day. "It has happened! Take time to leap to the ceiling. It is worth a vigorous whoop," she wrote to her sixty-seven-year-old-sister, whose feet had been firmly planted on the ground for many years.[479] Beaux, who still felt vigorous enough to cheer her good fortune, celebrated along with Rosamond Gilder, Helena's youngest daughter, who was in Paris at the time and agreed to accompany Beaux to her appointment.

132. OPPOSITE: ***Admiral Sir David Beatty**, or **Lord Beatty**. 1920. Oil on canvas, 62 1/2 x 45 5/8 in. Smithsonian American Art Museum, Washington, D.C.*

When Clemenceau entered his study, Beaux was stunned to discover that he was a little old man, whose physiognomy and bearing caused her to discard long-cherished beliefs concerning the way character showed in the bones. In the placing of the head and the prominent brow, "one could trace primitive man to an endlessly remote root," Beaux admitted.[480] Later a reporter asked her about Clemenceau and his primordial head. "You did Clemenceau's portrait. He is a man of powerful mind. Yet his head looks like that of a caveman with his retreating forehead and—" Beaux protested immediately. "Oh, no! That's where you are mistaken, you get the impression of a retreating forehead because of the great overhanging brow, but that in itself is a mark of intelligence. Notice his strong cheekbones, too. . . . You almost always find them in persons of powerful mentality."[481]

During her first interview with Clemenceau, the caveman sat in the embrace of a polished, curved desk and eyed Beaux with hostility. "Well, to begin with, we hate each other," he said. "No, Monsieur," Beaux replied. "That's only half true."[482] Charmed, the Prime Minister threw up his hands and laughed. "The assault was over and the breach opened," Beaux recalled.[483] By the time Beaux conducted this first dialogue with Clemenceau, she had already laid out her canvas using photographs and drawings as reference, staying true to her original idea—to replicate the image of him reading the Treaty of Versailles before the Senate.

When she arrived for her second appointment, Beaux brought a pad to jot down her impressions. Suddenly realizing that she was going to take notes, Clemenceau took her by both arms, gave her what she described as a good-natured shake, and said, "Well, I would like to kill you but our laws do not permit it."[484] Awed by the honor of having a private conversation with the French Prime Minister but not intimidated by his gruff manner, Beaux made her notes; clear eyes, dark depths with yellow lights, grizzled gray eyebrows and moustache. But although Clemenceau generously permitted Beaux to make numerous visits to his office on rue Franklin, the portrait did not go well. The lighting in the Prime Minister's office came from a large window opposite his desk and not from above, so Beaux had to invent the modeling. Only Sargent, Beaux maintained, could have successfully completed the portrait given the circumstances.

When Clemenceau was called away from the city, Beaux decided to return to the United States where she hoped that with greater distance between herself and the force of the Prime Minister's personality, she could improve the painting. Beaux worked on the canvas in her studio in New York, but could do little to rectify the flaws. After almost two years of concentrated effort, she was forced to admit her disappointment in all three paintings. "This is an apology," Beaux wrote in an introduction to a section of her autobiography describing the war portraits. "Whatever is lacking in the result—which of course fell far behind my hopes—I may lay the story of my adventure, a small wreath among the heaped tributes that lie along the pathway of the great."[484]

In 1921 the National Art Committee organized a touring exhibition of the entire collection of war portraits and published a catalogue containing biographies of all eight artists, six men and two women. Of the eight, Beaux was the oldest and the only one who refused to list her age. Although Beaux was not satisfied with her work, her paintings looked competent in the company of the other portraits, and neither the critics nor the public were disposed to find fault with an exhibition that paid tribute to the heroes of the Great War.

After her return home, Beaux continued to paint, although her production dropped considerably. She did a poster for the American Legion, an organization that her neighbor, A. Piatt Andrew, helped found and painted several commissioned portraits. She continued to exhibit her work and receive honors. In 1921 she was awarded a gold medal from the Art Institute of Chicago. In 1922 the League of Women Voters listed her name among the twelve greatest living American women.

At the age of sixty-eight Beaux made a final visit to Paris recapitulating the first by traveling once again with her cousin, May Whitlock. Soon after their arrival, both women were bedridden, Beaux with a virus and May with bronchitis. The cousins stayed in a hotel in Versailles while they recuperated. Beaux made plans to salvage the rest of the trip, but illness had exhausted her and her hand hurt. "It is hard to know what to do," she wrote to Thornton Oakley. "I have decided positively not to pioneer with my cousin in tow. I am not equal to it. . . . Oh how I long to follow, not to lead."[486] The two women recuperated and stayed on until the summer of 1924, planning to return on July 5. Then disaster. "Oh Thornton—Thornton," Beaux wrote to her friend. "Instead of sailing on the 5th I fell on my side and broke my hip. . . . You know what this means to your light footed C. B."[487]

Beaux spent three months at the English Clinic in Paris immobilized on her back. She sent for her maid, Anna Murphy, who arrived at the end of July. Ernesta rushed to her aid in the interim. When Beaux finally returned home in the fall, she was permanently disabled. "Never again was she to take a step save to hobble on mechanical support," Oakley recalled.[488] Beaux was in despair, but fate was to offer her another opportunity. Sorting through the mail that had piled up in Gloucester during her long absence, she tackled the contents of a box labeled "To be disposed on return do not forward." After discarding all the other letters, Beaux opened one from the Italian Embassy in Washington, D.C., that looked vaguely promising. Inside was a note from the Italian Ambassador and a letter from the Uffizi Gallery in Florence, requesting a self-portrait for their collection. The letter explained, as if an explanation was needed, that should Beaux accept this honor she would join a respected group of artists represented in the gallery that included Peter Paul Rubens (1577–1640), William Holman Hunt (1827–1910), Sir Joshua Reynolds (1723–1792), George Romney (1734–1802), and Eugène Delacroix (1798–1863). "My astonishment and satisfaction were witness to my deep appreciation of such an honor," Beaux recalled. "Although I had not tried to paint since my accident, I at once began dragging myself about."[489]

The portrait Beaux painted for the Uffizi Gallery in 1925 is astonishing. Although she was able to maintain all sorts of lies and evasions concerning her personal history in interviews and later in her autobiography, Beaux's brush was honest. She captured her own

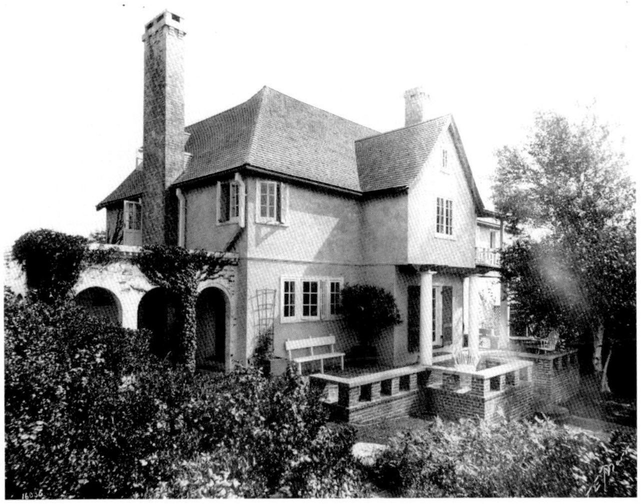

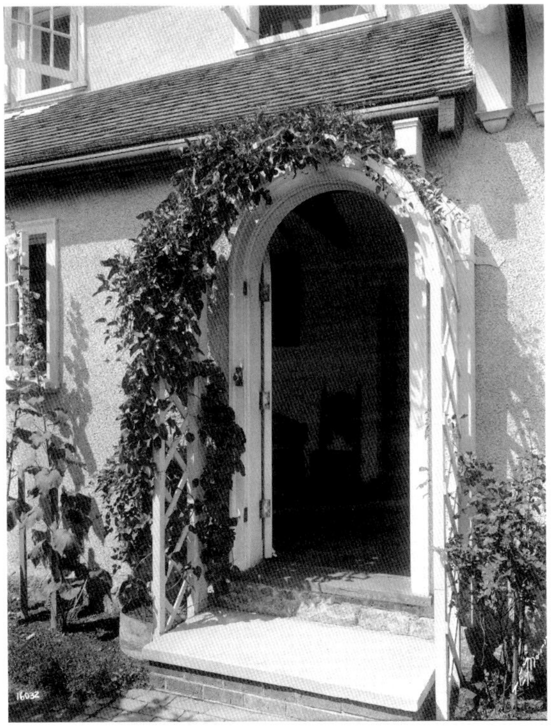

133. TOP: *T. E. Morr.* ***Green Alley, house and terrace,*** *1910–20. Pennsylvania Academy of the Fine Arts*

134. BOTTOM: *T. E. Morr.* ***"The Door Is Always Open at Green Alley,"*** *labeled by Beaux, 1910–20. Pennsylvania Academy of the Fine Arts*

personality as deftly and impartially as she had rendered her clients during her long career. Beaux appears tired in the painting, and although still handsome, the weight of her seventy years shows. Her right hand is posed awkwardly and looks arthritic and painful. Beaux disliked the portrait. Perhaps when it was completed, she wished that she had tempered the realism. The portrait, she wrote, "will always be a source of regret to me."[490] In an article published in the *Washington Star*, the critic Leila Mechlin wrote at length about the painting, which was on display at the Corcoran Gallery of Art. "It is essentially a spiritual interpretation, though probably this was not the painter's intention. But she is the one who has always insisted that she painted what she saw."[491]

In the years following her accident, Beaux worked very little. She wore a steel brace and used a crutch. Standing at her easel exhausted her. Her nephew Cecil Drinker, a physiology professor at Harvard University, later told his family that it was Aunt Beaux's own fault that she had to wear the brace—that in the 1930s, when new surgical techniques were available, she could have had a steel pin implanted and gone on to live a normal life. Beaux's friend Kit Wright might have disputed Cecil's claim: "One day when I was in Dr. Reisman's waiting room I saw to my amazement Miss Beaux, hobbling out. He had just told her it would be no use to have an operation—time was too short. I think he was very much moved by the occasion himself."[492]

In April 1926 Beaux received a Gold Medal from the American Academy of Arts and Letters. The award was the first the Academy had bestowed on a woman in twenty-one years, and as such, it carried the implication that Beaux's name would endure as the principal female artist of her era. But this latest award combined with all her other accomplishments would not suffice. Three months later, Mary Cassatt died in Paris. Within a year memorial exhibitions were organized at the Durand-Ruel Galleries, The New York Public Library, The Metropolitan Museum of Art, the Art Institute of Chicago, and the Philadelphia Museum of Art.[493] Response to Cassatt's work was exceptionally positive. French Impressionism had become fashionable in the

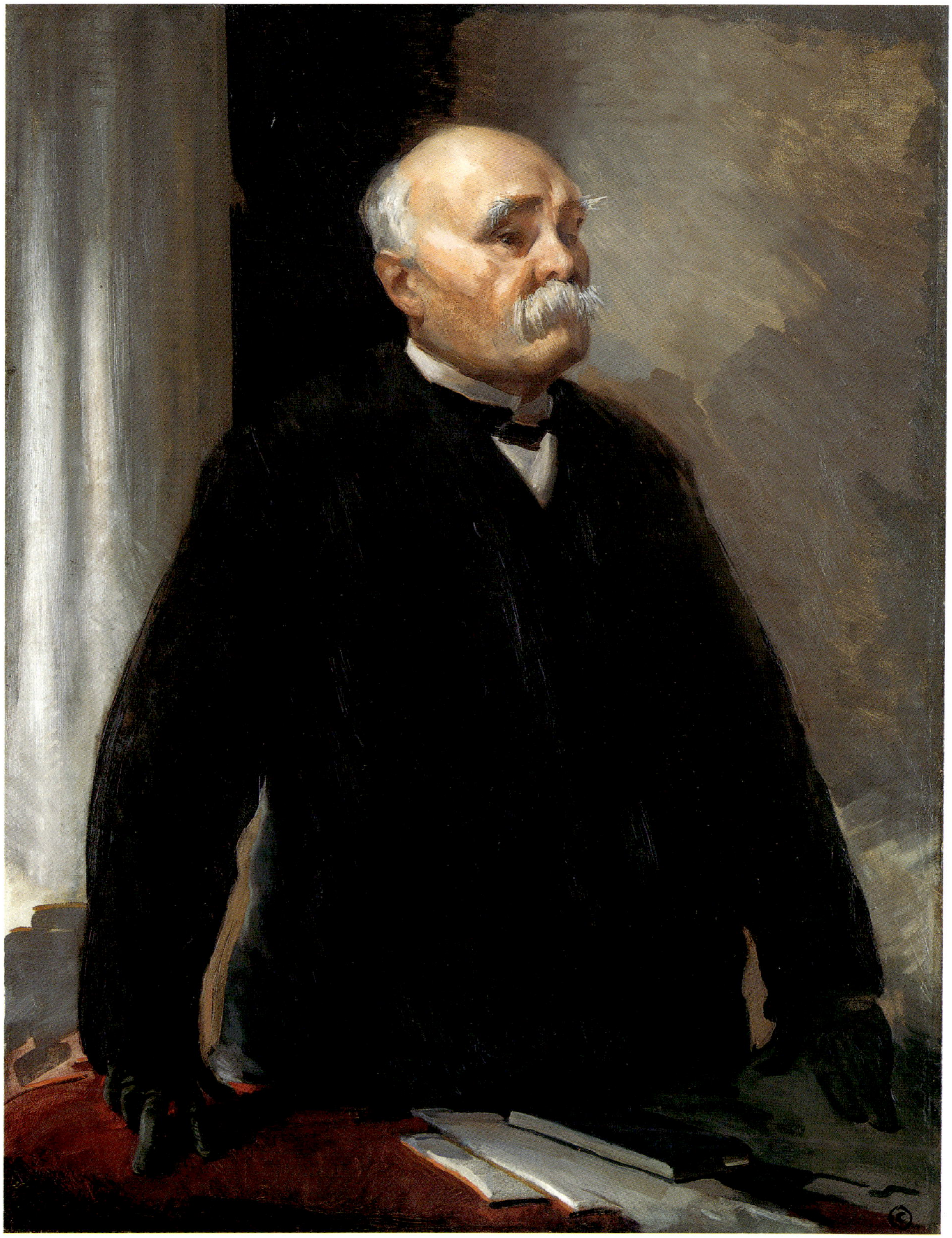

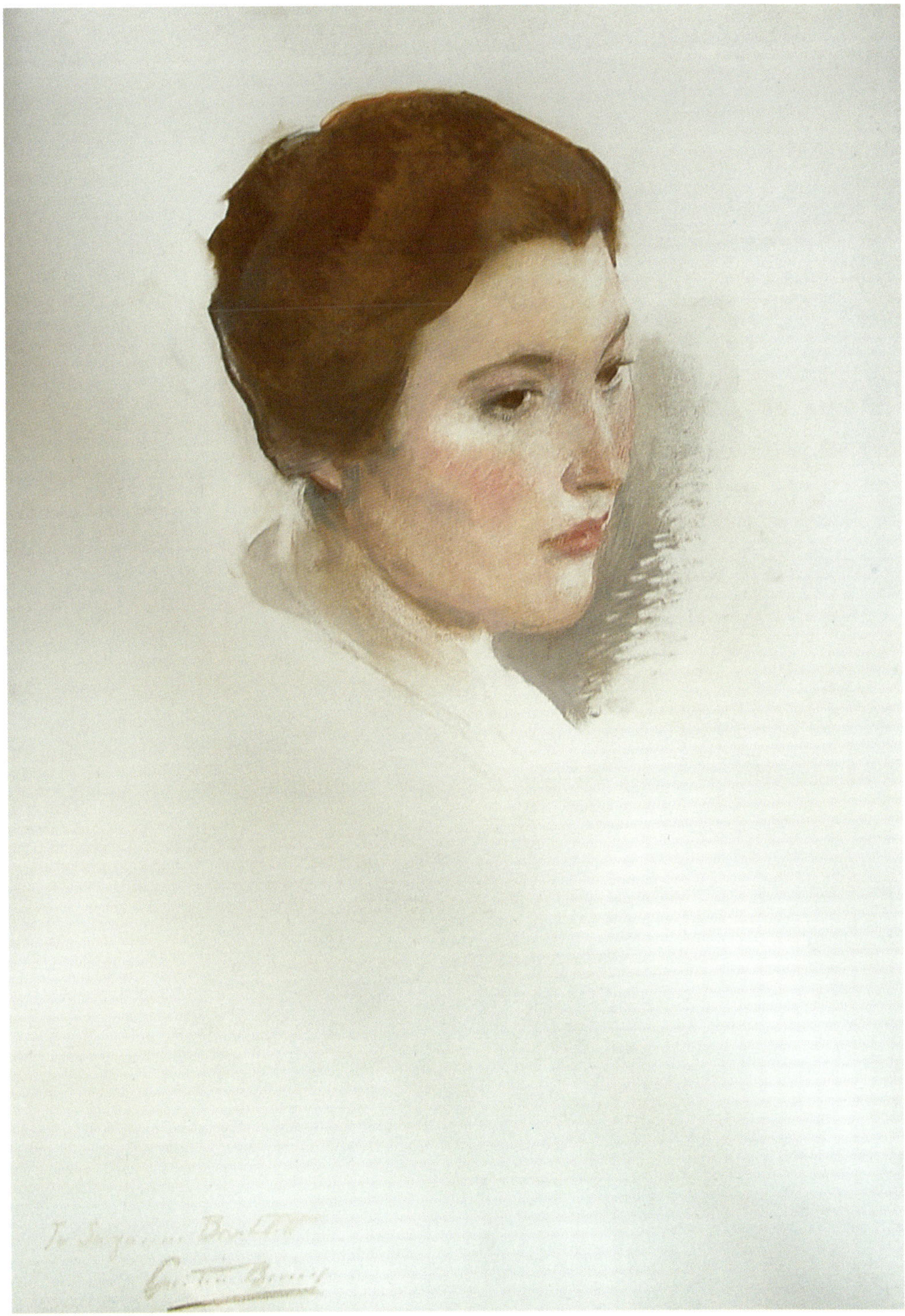

135. OPPOSITE: **Georges Clemenceau.** *1920. Oil on canvas, 46 7/8 x 36 3/4 in. Smithsonian American Art Museum, Washington, D.C.*

136. ABOVE: **Caroline Ogden-Jones Peter.** *1920. Oil on board, 21 1/16 x 14 3/8 in. Tudor Place Historic House and Garden*

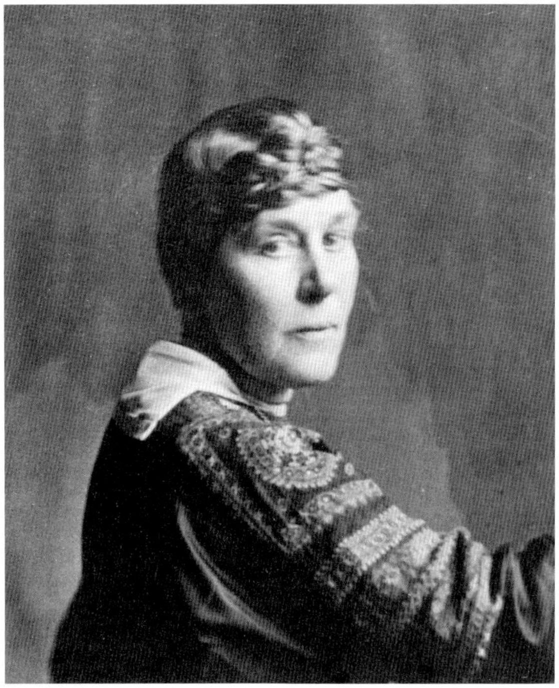

137. ***Cecilia Beaux,*** *1920s. Pennsylvania Academy of the Fine Arts*

United States. Degas and Monet were revered, and here was a woman who was their compatriot, a vital member of the Impressionists' inner circle, yet also one of their own—an American. Beaux must have noted the excitement over Cassatt's work with dismay. Unwilling to yield her position as the greatest female painter America had yet produced, Beaux decided to make one final attempt to explain herself and her art. In 1928 she began to work on an autobiography.

It took Beaux two years to complete *Background with Figures*. Thornton Oakley recalled that while she was busy writing, a new era dawned in American art, and "tradition was cast to the winds." Beaux was aware of the changes and although she abhorred them, she was comforted by her conviction that the new art was destined for destruction. Throughout the centuries, Beaux reasoned, it was order and craftsmanship that endured and prevailed. "It was clear to Cecilia Beaux," Oakley wrote "that this scoffing, by the new régime, at laws that govern order is the reason for the present suffering in the world. Hatreds, passions, carnage, are the results of the refusal of mankind to recognize the eternal precepts of the Master Artist, the Designer of all things."[494]

Beaux's autobiography was published by the Houghton Mifflin Company in 1930 when she was seventy-five years old. The book garnered favorable reviews, although their content must have caused Beaux some consternation. Writing for the *New York Telegram*, Margaret Lowengrund noted, "Though on the fringe of modernism, Miss Beaux was of the group that remained blissfully detached from its influence and spent her talent in that school of sophisticated portraiture which has discreetly passed."[495] Another reviewer wrote that Beaux's autobiography brought back the "charm of the old-fashioned life." The *Chicago Journal of Commerce* titled their review of her book, "A Victorian Canvas."[496] A writer for *The New Republic* gently explained, "I can not go the whole way with Miss Beaux in a number of her enthusiasms, not by a good deal; St. Gaudens' sculpture, the literary circle of Richard Watson Gilder's day, Sargent—these are some of them."[497]

Although Beaux's autobiography is rich in detail concerning both American art and the remarkable development of her career, there are many evasions and omissions. The lack of dates is irritating, although the reason is clear. Beaux did not want to reveal her age. In this, she was successful. A critic for *California Art and Architecture*, commenting on *Background with Figures*, wrote, " Dates . . . are conspicuously absent, but one infers that in the early seventies this little girl in Philadelphia was very, very young."[498] There are other puzzling gaps in Beaux's autobiography. Thornton Oakley, her dearest friend, is never mentioned. There is also very little written about Dorothea Gilder, who died from complications of diabetes and tuberculosis in 1920 at the age of thirty-eight. Beaux refers to her only in passing, while describing the process of painting *Dorothea and Francesca*, "One of us, Dorothea, has passed from her own remembering—but not ours—Dorothea, dear companion and playmate."[499]

138. OPPOSITE: ***Self-Portrait.*** *1925. Oil on canvas, 43 x 28 in. Uffizi Gallery, Florence, Italy*

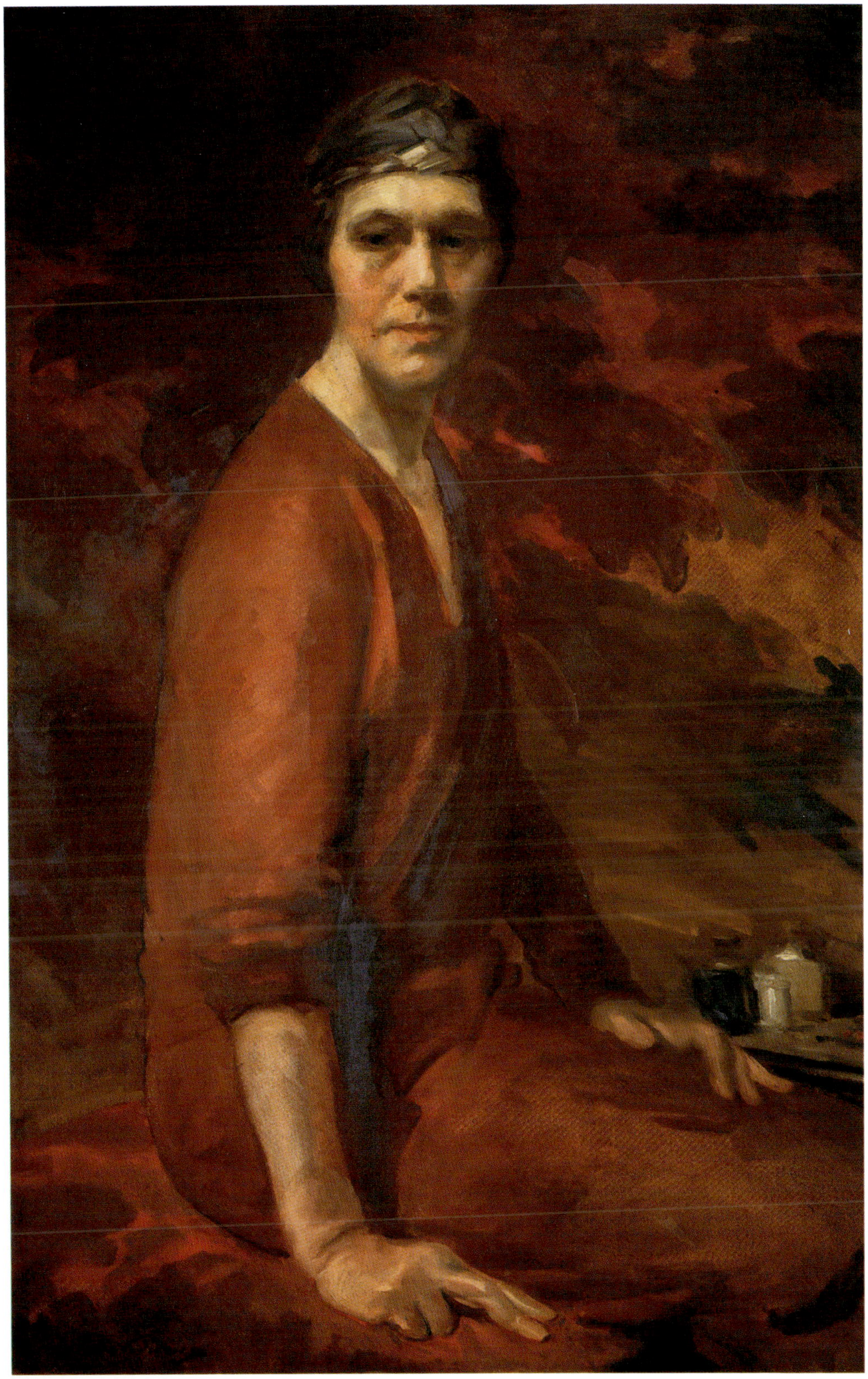

Beaux might have expected that the publication of her autobiography would be her last creative endeavor. Her injury exhausted her. She may have heard in her heart the ominous bass chords of Chopin's *Heroic* Polonaise and in her pain, been sure that the soaring melody would not return. But there was to be one last triumph. In 1935 The American Academy of Arts and Letters put together a retrospective exhibition of sixty-two of Beaux's paintings. Oakley recalled watching his friend in delight at the opening, eighty years old and still impressive. The occasion was to be Beaux's last public appearance.

> A vivid picture I cherish of my friend at the opening reception, sumptuous as ever in attire, responding to homage, surrounded, extolled, the cause, the living center, of the ranks of glowing portraits which looked down from those gallery walls, looked down upon the throngs that rendered praise, looked down and spoke as clearly as with words of the years of devotion to their creation, of the free flow of the artist's genius, of the joy that was hers in recording for posterity the beauty she perceived in man, the beauty visual, spiritual, intangible, indefinable save by her brush.[500]

The following autumn, Beaux made a final visit to the Drinkers' house in Merion, Pennsylvania. Through the years the two sisters had remained close, and Beaux's visit was an annual event. Etta's youngest daughter, Catherine Drinker Bowen, dreaded these occasions. She had never been fond of her aunt, and in her old age Beaux had not mellowed. "Aunt Beaux," Bowen recalled, "Possessed a self-absorption which at the same time attracted and repelled, bringing to mind Nietzsche's remark about 'the artist's egotism, which shines like brass and will not be denied.'"[501]

Etta, who was intimidated by Beaux's fame and self-assurance, made such elaborate arrangements for her sister's arrival that each year the family worried she might not survive. Henry Drinker retired to his study. The maid cleaned and rearranged furniture. The cook baked and Etta fretted. "If my mother had expected President Roosevelt himself she could not have made more fuss," Bowen recalled.[502] Beaux arrived at teatime with her maid Anna Murphy in an old bright blue Packard touring car that Bowen recalled was driven by one of Beaux's admirers. Although the two sisters wrote each other long letters proclaiming their mutual affection, when they were together there were invariably quarrels and disagreements that Bowen recalled exploded like strings of small firecrackers. However, on Beaux's final visit there were no quarrels. Shortly after her arrival, Beaux was stricken with pneumonia.

Beaux lay in the Drinkers' guest room all through October and into November, as the leaves fell and the cold winds scattered them across the front lawn and into the street where they crackled on the pavement. While the family watched and waited, Etta began to talk about the old house at 4305 Spruce Street, as if her memories could hold death at bay: Grandma Leavitt, Aunt Eliza, Aunt Emily, Uncle Will, the two motherless sisters and the generous relatives who took them in, recognized their individual strengths, and armed them both with the fortitude to pursue their separate destinies.

Beaux did not die that autumn. She recovered and outlived both Henry and Etta Drinker. After a long convalescence she rose from her bed, called for the Packard, and went back to New York. Before Beaux left, Catherine Drinker Bowen heard voices in the living room and looked in to see her mother and aunt, sitting on the old sofa that Henry Sandwith Drinker had sent back from China in the 1840s. The two sisters, giggling like schoolgirls, were reciting the Shorter Catechism.

> What is the chief end of man?
> Man's end is to glorify God, and to enjoy him forever.

After recovering from her illness, Cecilia Beaux returned to her established routine spending winters in the city and summers at Green Alley. Although she regained much of her strength, her eyes were failing. When she was in New York, Gilder Palmer, Francesca's teenaged son, often visited Beaux's apartment, sometimes taking her walking in Gramercy Park but more often replicating Grandma Leavitt's thoughtfulness so many years before by reading to her aloud. Palmer remembers Beaux as a marvelous woman, filled with vivacity and energy. Her preference in literature was for Shakespeare. *Richard II* was a particular favorite, although as she aged Beaux preferred the comedies. "I've heard enough of tragedy," she once told her young companion.[503]

Every spring Thornton Oakley left his family in Philadelphia and went to New York to collect Beaux for the drive north. The two friends then set off driving past bright fields of blossoms from the city to Eastern Point. Every fall he returned faithfully to Gloucester, and after packing up the car Oakley and Beaux would motor back to New York admiring forests ablaze with golden maples. Beaux, who loved this annual ritual would throw back her head and sing, and Oakley, no longer young, would push his shock of white hair off his forehead, and smiling broadly, negotiate the miles. The last year of her life, Beaux was almost completely blind and too weak to travel. She wrote to Thornton in a shaky hand:

> Oh Thornton my friend. This is my message to you. I cannot write I am in prison. But I have Anna. Come when you can. Morning hour is best . . . call up first. I long to see you. Pity and Love,
> Your Cecilia

Eliza-Cecilia Beaux died on September 17, 1942, at Green Alley. Two hundred people attended her memorial service at the Calvary Protestant Episcopal Church in New York. The sculptor Paul Manship gave the eulogy and read a formal tribute written by the *New York Herald Tribune* art critic Royal Cortissoz. Henry McCarter wrote a personal eulogy, which he mailed to a friend: "You know Fanny, It was not Cecilia's honors and medals—it is as you know that Cecilia had the thrill in living. It was in her painting as well, but not so much as it was in Cecilia. You know my friends do not die. I find them in everything years afterward."[504]

Cecilia Beaux spent a lifetime trying to atone for her mother's death, her father's grief, and her grandmother's sacrifice in the only way she could—by accomplishing something significant. Although she did not know for

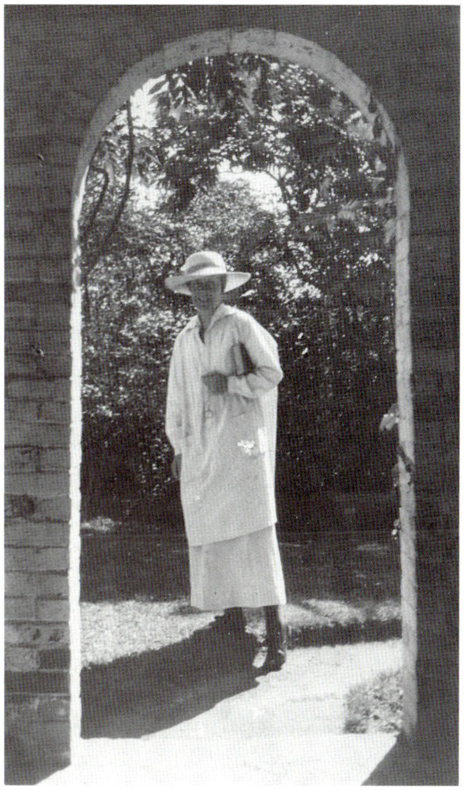

139. ***"Morning at Green Alley,"*** *included in Beaux's autobiography, 1930. Pennsylvania Academy of the Fine Arts*

certain that her portraits would endure, she suspected they would. She poured her own life and vitality into each one, and as a result her subjects are alive on the canvas, their time and their unique humanity captured and held. Etta with little Harry on her lap—their hands clasped, Henry Sturgis Drinker in his white summer suit, Cecil looking defiant, Ernesta holding her nurse's hand and later beautiful in a white dress, Dorothea Gilder dancing. Beaux's inheritance from her mother was the knowledge that life is fleeting. Armed with this certainty she observed and recorded the world she knew with the uncompromising honesty that is the hallmark of any artist worth remembering. She once wrote to Thornton Oakley, "I never cease to be conscious of what is happening—and when the parting is over and the loss begins I shall be glad that at least I have missed nothing."[505]

List of Works

Frontis

1. Cecilia Beaux. *Self-Portrait*. Oil on canvas, 25 x 20 in., 1894. National Academy of Design, New York (67-P)

The Beaux Sisters

2. Cecilia Beaux's grandmother, Cecilia Kent Leavitt, ca. 1850. Pennsylvania Academy of the Fine Arts, Philadelphia. Gift of Cecilia Saltonstall through Tara Leigh Tappert

3. Jean Adolphe Beaux and Cecilia Leavitt Beaux, ca. 1850

4. Eliza Leavitt, n.d. Photographer: J. E. McClees. Pennsylvania Academy of the Fine Arts, Philadelphia. Gift of Cecilia Saltonstall through Tara Leigh Tappert

5. Cecilia Beaux. *Dressing Dolls*. Oil on canvas, 35 x 28 in., 1928. From a Private Collection. Photograph courtesy of Spanierman Gallery Ltd.

   At the end of her career when Beaux was seventy-three years old and in declining health, she went back to her studio, set out her supplies, and painted this canvas recalling her childhood enthusiasm for dolls. Although physically weak by 1928 and not willing to cope with clients and deadlines, Beaux was artistically strong. This painting is one of her best; the brush strokes are fluid and masterful, creating solid form with an effortless skill, the extraordinary result of years of dedication to her craft.

6. Cecilia Beaux. *Madonna*. Oil on paper, 16 3/8 x 10 3/4 in., ca. 1900. Private Collection, Courtesy of Alfred J. Walker Fine Art, Boston

West Philadelphia

7. Emily Leavitt Biddle, n.d. Photographer: Peter A. Juley and Son. Pennsylvania Academy of the Fine Arts, Philadelphia. Gift of Cecilia Saltonstall through Tara Leigh Tappert

8. William Foster Biddle (1834–1910), ca. 1890. Pennsylvania Academy of the Fine Arts, Philadelphia. Gift of Cecilia Saltonstall through Tara Leigh Tappert

9. "Old Pennsylvania Academy of the Fine Arts," from *History of Philadelphia: 1609–1884* by J. Thomas Scharf and Thompson Westcott (L. H. Everts & Co., 1884).

   The Pennsylvania Academy of the Fine Arts, the oldest institution of its kind in the country, was housed in this building designed by the architect John Dorsey. When the Academy officially opened in 1806, citizens paid twenty-five cents to view the impressive collection of paintings and the casts of classical sculpture. The casts included some of the most famous pieces then in the Louvre, including the *Fighting Gladiator*, the *Apollo Belvedere*, and the *Laocoön*. Because the subjects were undraped, it was considered improper to view them in mixed company. Consequently, on Mondays the gallery was reserved exclusively for women.

10. J. D. Harding. "Lesson 114, A Cattle Shed," from *Lessons on Art* by J. D. Harding (W. Kent & Co., ca. 1850).

    Cecilia Beaux began copying the drawings of J. D. Harding at the age of thirteen.

11. J. D. Harding. "Lesson 115, Farm-Buildings at Penshurst," from *Lessons on Art* by J. D. Harding (W. Kent & Co., ca. 1850).

12. J. D. Harding. "Lesson 119, Buildings at Puzzano, Lago Maggiore," from *Lessons on Art* by J. D. Harding (W. Kent & Co., ca. 1850).

13. Cecilia Beaux. *Mrs. John Wheeler Leavitt* (born Cecilia Kent, 1798–1892). Oil on canvas, 45 1/2 x 34 in., 1885. Westmoreland Museum of American Art. In honor of Philip Drinker and Susan Aldrich Drinker as a gift from Mary Eliza Drinker Scudder and Thayer Scudder, 1996.10

A Fashionable Education

14. Cecilia Beaux at age twelve, ca. 1867. Photographer: O. H. Willard. Pennsylvania Academy of the Fine Arts, Philadelphia. Gift of Cecilia Saltonstall through Tara Leigh Tappert

15. Cecilia Beaux. *Thomas Allibone Janvier* (1849–1913). Charcoal on paper, 19 1/2 x 13 1/4 in., n.d. The Century Association, New York; gift of the relatives and friends of Thomas Allibone Janvier through Roland Gibson Hazzard, 1917

Cecilia Beaux met Thomas Janvier in 1871 when she was sixteen years old and beginning an apprenticeship with Catharine (Kate) Drinker. Twenty-two-year-old Janvier, whose parents were both writers, was working as a journalist and often visited Drinker's home and studio. "One young gentleman, as handsome as a troubadour, with a gay romantic head, came often," Beaux wrote describing her initial impression of the man who would marry Kate in 1878. Kate and Thomas eventually settled in New York, and when Beaux returned from her studies in France, the Janviers introduced her to a group of writers, artists, and journalists who would be instrumental in promoting her career.

16. Cecilia Beaux. *Left Temporal Bone*. Graphite on paper 7 x 5 in., 1873. Courtesy of Alfred J. Walker Fine Art, Boston

17. "Pennsylvania Academy of Fine Arts," from *History of Philadelphia: 1609–1884* by J. Thomas Scharf and Thompson Westcott (L. H. Everts & Co., 1884).

Following a disastrous fire in 1845, the old Academy building was rebuilt. However, by 1870 the institution had outgrown its quarters and a site in downtown Philadelphia was selected for an expanded facility. The new building designed by the architects Frank Furness and George W. Hewitt opened in 1876 when Cecilia Beaux was twenty-one years old.

18. Cecilia Beaux. *The Dreamer* (Caroline Kilby Smith). Oil on canvas, 32 1/4 x 24 1/2 in., 1894. Collection of the Butler Institute of American Art, Youngstown, Ohio

Cecilia Beaux exhibited *The Dreamer* at the National Academy of Design in 1894 and at the Carnegie Institute in 1896, where the painting was awarded a bronze medal. Beaux continued to submit *The Dreamer* to numerous exhibitions with great success. In spite of a growing cache of awards and favorable critical reviews, the painting did not sell for twenty-three years. In 1917 Beaux exhibited it for the last time at the Galleries of M. Knoedler in New York, where it was finally sold to a private collector for the considerable sum of $3,000. Before agreeing to part with the painting, Beaux wrote to her model and friend Caroline Smith offering her the first right of refusal. Smith sent a telegram, "REGRET DEEPLY CANNOT BUY BEAUTIFUL PORTRAIT CONGRATULATIONS ON YOUR SUCCESS." Beaux also came to regret Smith's inability to purchase the canvas. Some years later when Beaux heard that the owner of the painting had either died or sold the canvas, she attempted to locate her painting. When her efforts proved futile, she considered the work lost. It did not surface again until 1931, when the painting was offered to the Butler Institute of American Art.

The Academy

19. Edward Drinker Cope. 1876. Photograph from a private collection courtesy of Maxilla and Mandible, Ltd., New York

20. Cecilia Beaux. *Mother and Son* (Mrs. Beauveau Borie, 1845–1940, Adolphe Borie, 1877–1934). Oil on canvas, 57 1/4 x 40 in., 1896. Photograph courtesy of Christie's Images

Studio on Chestnut Street

21. Cecilia Beaux. *Shell Studies*. Graphite and wash on off-white wove paper (a. 2 5/16 x 2 9/16, b. 2 7/16 x 1 1/2, c. 2 13/16 x 5 11/16 in., ca. 1875. Pennsylvania Academy of the Fine Arts, Philadelphia. Gift of Henry Sandwith Drinker, 1942.29

22. Cecilia Beaux and cousin Emma Leavitt reading in their Chestnut Street studio. Pennsylvania Academy of the Fine Arts, Philadelphia. Gift of Cecilia Saltonstall through Tara Leigh Tappert

23. Cecilia Beaux's sister, Aimee Ernesta Beaux Drinker, n.d. Photographer: Broadbent & Phillips. Pennsylvania Academy of the Fine Arts, Philadelphia. Gift of Cecilia Saltonstall through Tara Leigh Tappert

24. William Sartain. *The Young Musician.* Oil on canvas, 18 x 14 13/16 in., ca. 1870. Pennsylvania Academy of the Fine Arts, Philadelphia. Gift of Mrs. James Mapes Dodge in accordance with the wishes of the artist, 1931.13.2

25. Cecilia Beaux. Circular plaque with bust-length portrait of a boy. Porcelain plaque, 11 1/4 in. in diameter, 1880. The Metropolitan Museum of Art, Purchase, Friends of the American Wing Fund, 2002. (2002.214) Photograph © 2004 The Metropolitan Museum of Art

26. Cecilia Beaux. *Sketchbook #2* [Landscape study inscribed "Roadside, August 4"]. Graphite, pen, and white highlight on buff wove leaves, 5 3/4 x 9 1/4 in., 1879–1891. Pennsylvania Academy of the Fine Arts, Philadelphia. Gift of Henry Sandwith Drinker, 1950.17.57 a-ff

27. Cecilia Beaux. *Self-Portrait.* Oil on canvas, 18 x 14 in., ca. 1880–85. National Portrait Gallery, Smithsonian Institution, Washington D.C. Photo courtesy of National Portrait Gallery, Washington D.C./Art Resource, NY

28. Robert Redfield, May Whitlock, and Cecilia Beaux. ca. 1885–86. Pennsylvania Academy of the Fine Arts, Philadelphia. Gift of Cecilia Saltonstall through Tara Leigh Tappert

29. Cecilia Beaux. *A Little Girl* (Fanny Travis Cochran, 1876–1977). Oil on canvas, 36 x 29 3/16 in., 1887. Pennsylvania Academy of the Fine Arts, Philadelphia. Gift of Fanny Travis Cochran, 1955.12

30. Cecilia Beaux. *Les Derniers Jours d'Enfance* (Aimee Ernesta Beaux Drinker, 1852–1939, Henry Sandwith Drinker, 1880–1965). Oil on canvas, 46 x 54 in., 1883–1885. Pennsylvania Academy of the Fine Arts, Philadelphia. Gift of Cecilia Saltonstall Drinker, 1989.21

31. Cecilia Beaux. *Portrait of Howard and Mildred Colton* (Howard, 1881–1970, Mildred, 1883–1977). Oil on canvas, 55 7/8 x 42 in., 1887. Pennsylvania Academy of the Fine Arts, Philadelphia. Partial gift of Captain and Mrs. J. Ferrell Colton and partial purchase from the Academy purchase fund, 1998.7

32. Cecilia Beaux, 1885–90. Pennsylvania Academy of the Fine Arts, Philadelphia. Gift of Cecilia Saltonstall through Tara Leigh Tappert

33. Cecilia Beaux. *Edmund James Drifton Coxe* (1881–1934). Watercolor on wove paper, 24 1/8 x 18 1/4 in., 1884. Pennsylvania Academy of the Fine Arts, Philadelphia. Gift of Maria M. Skinner, granddaughter of the sitter, 1992.6

34. Cecilia Beaux. *George C. Troutman* (1818–date unknown). Oil on canvas, 48 1/8 in. x 38 1/4 in., 1886. Berry Hill Gallery, New York

35. Cecilia Beaux. *Man with a Cat* (Henry Sturgis Drinker, 1850–1937). Oil on canvas, 48 x 34 5/8 in., 1898. Smithsonian American Art Museum, Washington, D.C.; bequest of Henry Ward Ranger through the National Academy of Design. Photography courtesy of Smithsonian American Art Museum, Washington, D.C./Art Resource, NY

Paris, 1888

36. Cecilia Beaux. *Seated Girl in a Long Black Dress.* Oil on cardboard, 19 5/8 x 12 1/4 in., ca. 1885. Pennsylvania Academy of the Fine Arts, Philadelphia. Gift of Henry Sandwith Drinker, 1950.17.5

37. Eliza Leavitt, carte de visite, ca. 1880. Photographer: Wenderoth, Taylor & Brown. Pennsylvania Academy of the Fine Arts, Philadelphia. Gift of Cecilia Saltonstall through Tara Leigh Tappert

38. Cecilia Beaux (seated) with her cousin May Whitlock. Pennsylvania Academy of the Fine Arts, Philadelphia. Gift of Cecilia Saltonstall through Tara Leigh Tappert

39. Artist unknown. *M. Julian, August 11, 11:30* am. Caricature from the album *Croquis de Mme Geraldi.* André Del Debbio Collection, Paris

40. Académie Julian at rue de Berri, Atelier with Students, 1889. André Del Debbio Collection, Paris

41. Anna Bilińska. *Woman with a Japanese Parasol.* 1888. Pastel, 37 x 29 1/8 in. André Del Debbio Collection, Paris

42. Académie Julian at Passage des Panoramas. André Del Debbio Collection, Paris

43. Alexander Harrison. *The Wave*. Oil on canvas, $39\frac{1}{4}$ x 118 in., ca. 1885. Pennsylvania Academy of the Fine Arts, Philadelphia. Joseph E. Temple Fund, 1891.5

44. Cecilia Beaux. *Little Lamerche*. Oil on canvas, 24 x 19 in., ca. 1900. Fine Arts Museums of San Francisco, Gift of Mr. and Mrs. John D. Rockefeller III, 1979.7.7

45. Cecilia Beaux. Sketch of Concarneau House. Brown ink on cream wove paper, $5\frac{1}{2}$ x $8\frac{1}{2}$ in., 1888. Pennsylvania Academy of the Fine Arts, Philadelphia. Gift of Henry Sandwith Drinker, 1950.17.47.1a

46. Leonard Woolsey Bacon and family, ca. 1886. Photograph courtesy of Jack B. Bacon

Back Row:
Seated: Mrs Leonard Woolsey Bacon (Susan Bacon)
Standing: Reverend Leonard Woolsey Bacon, MD, Reverend Benjamin Wisner Bacon

Middle Row:
Seated: Susan Almira Bacon, Mrs. Benjamin Wisner Bacon (Lila B. Aiken)
On her lap: Elizabeth Bacon (later Mrs. Prescott Greene)

Front Row:
Standing: Leonard Woolsey Bacon (Later MD), Theodore Davenport Bacon (Reverend) Mabel Bacon (later Mrs. Phillip Ripley)
Seated: Katherine Bacon (Later Mrs. Joseph Fyffe), Mrs. Nathaniel Terry Bacon (Helen Hazard), Nathaniel Terry Bacon

47. Cecilia Beaux. *Sketchbook #3 (Concarneau)* [Breton Man and Woman in Native Dress]. Graphite on buff wove leaves, $3\frac{3}{4}$ x $6\frac{1}{4}$ in., 1888. Pennsylvania Academy of the Fine Arts, Philadelphia. Gift of Henry Sandwith Drinker, 1950.17.58 a-j

48. Charles A. Lasar. "Movement," from *Practical Hints for Art Students* by Charles A. Lasar (Duffield & Co., 1910).

The American painter Charles Lasar was a popular art teacher in Paris in the late 1880s. Although Beaux was fond of Lasar and they were both part of a close-knit group of American artists working in Brittany in the summer of 1888, Beaux did not always approve of his teaching methods. "I should not like to be altogether under Mr. Lasar's influence," she explained in a letter to her uncle. "He tells you what to do and the scientific reason almost too much."

49. Charles A. Lasar. "Composition," from *Practical Hints for Art Students* by Charles A. Lasar (Duffield & Co., 1910).

50. Cecilia Beaux, *Landscape with Farm Buildings, Concarneau, France*. Oil on canvas, $11\frac{1}{16}$ x $14\frac{3}{16}$ in., 1888. Pennsylvania Academy of the Fine Arts. Gift of Henry Sandwith Drinker, 1950.17.31

51. Cecilia Beaux. *A Country Woman*, Concarneau, France. Oil on canvas, $14\frac{1}{16}$ x $8\frac{5}{8}$ in., 1888. Pennsylvania Academy of the Fine Arts, Philadelphia. Gift of Henry Sandwith Drinker, 1950.17.32

52. Cecilia Beaux. *Study of Two Breton Women*, Concarneau, France. Oil on canvas, $13\frac{11}{16}$ x $10\frac{5}{8}$ in., 1888. Pennsylvania Academy of the Fine Arts, Philadelphia. Gift of Henry Sandwith Drinker, 1950.17.7

53. Cecilia Beaux. *Head of a Woman*. Oil on canvas, 16 x $12\frac{7}{8}$ in., 1888. Pennsylvania Academy of the Fine Arts, Philadelphia. Gift of Henry Sandwith Drinker, 1950.17.4

54. Cecilia Beaux. *Lady George Darwin* (born Maud DuPuy, 1861–1947). Pastel on paper, 19 x $13\frac{1}{2}$ in., 1889. Collection of Mr. and Mrs. John L. Huber

When she completed her studies in Paris, Cecilia Beaux went to Cambridge, England, to stay with her friend Maud DuPuy Darwin. Maud's daughter Gwen later recalled the visit in a book she wrote about her family: "In summer tea was in the garden, under the great cooper-beech by the river. It was here that Miss Cecilia Beaux, a well-known American artist, painted my mother's portrait in pastel. . . . Miss Beaux was a great friend of my mother's, and was one of the ladies I used to chaperone. She was certainly one of the few visitors whom I really liked; I believe I was even then interested in her painting."

—Gwen Raverat, *Period Piece* (New York: W. W. Norton & Co. Inc., 1952), 37.

56. Cecilia Beaux. *Cecil Kent Drinker* (1887–1950). Oil on canvas, 64 x 34½ in., 1891. Philadelphia Museum of Art: The Joseph E. Temple Fund, 1891. Photograph by Graydon Wood, 1993

The Spring Salon

57. Cecilia Beaux in ruffled collar. Pennsylvania Academy of the Fine Arts, Philadelphia. Gift of Cecilia Saltonstall through Tara Leigh Tappert

58. Cecilia Beaux and Emma Leavitt after a tea party in their studio. 1889–90. Pennsylvania Academy of the Fine Arts, Philadelphia. Gift of Cecilia Saltonstall through Tara Leigh Tappert

59. Interior of Cecilia Beaux's studio at 1710 Chestnut Street, 1889–90. Pennsylvania Academy of the Fine Arts, Philadelphia. Gift of Cecilia Saltonstall through Tara Leigh Tappert

60. Cecilia Beaux. *Peter Williamson* (1795–1886). Oil on canvas, 113 x 59 in., 1891. Collections of the Grand Lodge of Pennsylvania on deposit with the Masonic Library and Museum of Pennsylvania

Peter Williamson was a Philadelphia pharmacist who acquired a fortune and retired comfortably in his mid-fifties. A dedicated philanthropist throughout his life, Williamson was one of the founders of the Philadelphia College of Pharmacy as well as an organizer of the Southern Dispensary and the Southwark Soup Society. In 1856–57 Williamson was elected Grand Master of Pennsylvania's Grand Lodge of Free and Accepted Masons.

61. Cecilia Beaux. *Ernesta*, or *Child with Nurse* (Ernesta Drinker, 1892–1981). Oil on canvas, 50½ x 38⅛ in., 1894. The Metropolitan Museum of Art, Maria DeWitt Jesup Fund, 1965. (65.49) Photograph © 1993 The Metropolitan Museum of Art

62. Cecilia Beaux. *Portrait of Helen Biddle Griscom* (1866–1950). Pastel, 27⅛ x 21⅞ in., 1893. Pennsylvania Academy of the Fine Arts, Philadelphia. John S. Phillips Fund, 1989.16

63. Cecilia Beaux. *The Reverend Matthew Blackburne Grier* (1820–1899). Oil on canvas, mounted on wood, 49⅝ x 39⅜ in., 1892. Pennsylvania Academy of the Fine Arts, Philadelphia. Gift of Anne Farr Bartol, 1961.10

64. Cecilia Beaux, ca. 1895. Pennsylvania Academy of the Fine Arts, Philadelphia. Gift of Cecilia Saltonstall through Tara Leigh Tappert

65. Cecilia Beaux posing for Emma Leavitt, 1889–90. Pennsylvania Academy of the Fine Arts, Philadelphia. Gift of Cecilia Saltonstall through Tara Leigh Tappert

66. Cecilia Beaux. *New England Woman* (Mrs. Jedediah H. Richards, née Julia Leavitt). Oil on canvas, 43 x 24¼ in., 1895. Pennsylvania Academy of the Fine Arts, Philadelphia. Joseph E. Temple Fund, 1896.1

67. Cecilia Beaux. *Mrs. Clement B. Newbold* (born Mary Dickenson Scott, 1870–1903). Oil on canvas, 78½ x 48 in., 1896. Pennsylvania Academy of the Fine Arts, Philadelphia. Gift of Clement B. Newbold, 1973.25.2

Mary Cassatt painted a portrait of family friend Mary Scott in 1865 and was insulted when she heard that her efforts were to be quickly replicated by Cecilia Beaux. She was further angered when she saw Beaux's finished composition—an almost exact copy of her own. She surmised, probably correctly, that Beaux was chosen to create a more flattering portrait. The following year Mary Newbold's mother, Anna, bypassed Cassatt and commissioned Beaux to paint her portrait. Cassatt never forgave the Scott family for this insult and re-claimed the paintings she had given them. Seventeen years later when Cassatt was famous and dealers and museums were clamoring for her work, a Scott relative tried to retrieve one of Cassatt's portraits. Cassatt adamantly refused to release it and wrote to a friend, "Well let her rejoice in Miss Beaux's portraits & leave me alone."

68. Cecilia Beaux. *Henry Howard Houston, Jr.* (1858–1879). Oil on canvas, 33 3/4 x 25 3/8 in., 1895. Courtesy of the University of Pennsylvania Art Collection, Philadelphia

In 1894 Pennsylvania Railroad executive Henry Howard Houston and his wife, Sallie, donated funds to build Houston Hall on the campus of the University of Pennsylvania. The building, which opened in 1896, was dedicated to the memory of their son, who died of typhoid fever one year after his graduation from the University. Houston Hall was the first student union in the country and housed a swimming pool, billiard room, gymnasium, bowling alley, and chapel. Beaux's portrait of Houston was painted from photographs.

69. Cecilia Beaux. Study for *The Dreamer* (Caroline Kilby Smith). Umber and chalk on gray-primed canvas, 32 3/4 x 24 in., 1894. Pennsylvania Academy of the Fine Arts, Philadelphia. Gift of Henry Sandwith Drinker, 1950.17.48

70. Cecilia Beaux. *Mrs. Alexander Biddle* (born Julia Williams Rush, 1832–1898). Oil on canvas, 40 1/4 x 30 3/16 in., 1897. Philadelphia Museum of Art: Gift of Horace Brock, 1978

71. Cecilia Beaux. *Sita and Sarita*, or *Young Woman with Cat* (Sarah Allibone Leavitt, 1865–1930). Oil on canvas, 37 1/4 x 25 in., 1893–94. R.F 1980–160. Musée d'Orsay, Paris. Photograph by Erich Lessing/Art Resource, NY

72. John Lambert. *Cecilia Beaux*. Oil on canvas, 29 15/16 x 24 3/4 in., ca. 1905. Pennsylvania Academy of the Fine Arts, Philadelphia. Gift of Henry Sandwith Drinker, 1950.17.53

John Lambert (1861–1907) was born in Philadelphia and studied at the Pennsylvania Academy of the Fine Arts. He sailed to Paris in 1888, the same year Cecilia Beaux made her journey, and like Beaux attended the Académie Julian. When he returned home he continued his career in art, exhibiting his work at the Pennsylvania Academy of the Fine Arts annually from 1892 until 1908 and at exhibitions at The Chicago Art Institute, the St. Botolph Club in Boston, and the Paris Salons of 1891 and 1896. When Lambert died at the age of forty-seven, he willed his Philadelphia studio to Cecilia Beaux.

73. Cecilia Beaux. *Algernon Sydney Biddle* (1847–1891). Oil on canvas, 39 7/16 x 29 1/2 in., 1891. Courtesy of the University of Pennsylvania Art Collection, Philadelphia

Algernon Sydney Biddle was a law professor at the University of Pennsylvania.

The Gilder Age

74. Cecilia Beaux. *Richard Watson Gilder* (1844–1909). Oil on canvas, 45 7/8 x 34 1/2 in., 1902–1903. Gift of Rodman and Mary Ellen Gilder, National Portrait Gallery, Smithsonian Institution, Washington, D.C. Photo courtesy of National Portrait Gallery, Washington D.C./Art Resource, NY

75. Cecilia Beaux. *Miss Gilder* (Francesca Gilder, 1888–1984). Oil on canvas, 26 1/2 x 18 1/4 in., n.d. National Academy of Design, New York (68-P)

76. Cecilia Beaux (seated) Helena DeKay Gilder, and Dorothea Gilder at Four Brooks Farm, Tyringham, Massachusetts, ca. 1900–1905. Pennsylvania Academy of the Fine Arts, Philadelphia. Gift of Cecilia Saltonstall through Tara Leigh Tappert

77. Cecilia Beaux. *Gertrude and Elizabeth Henry* (Gertrude Henry, 1891–1974, Elizabeth Henry, 1894–1973). Oil on canvas, 64 x 37 1/4 in., 1898–99. Pennsylvania Academy of the Fine Arts, Philadelphia. Funds provided by the descendants and relatives of Gertrude and Elizabeth Henry and by the Pennsylvania Academy, 1986.9

78. Cecilia Beaux. *Dorothea in the Woods* (Dorothea Gilder, 1882–1920). Oil on canvas, 53 1/4 x 40 in., 1897. Whitney Museum of American Art, New York; Gift of Mr. and Mrs. Raymond J. Horowitz 70.1587

79. Cecilia Beaux. *Mother and Daughter* (Mrs. Clement A. Griscom nee Frances Canby Biddle, 1840–1924 and Frances Canby Griscom, 1879–1974). Oil on canvas, 83 x 44 in., 1898. Pennsylvania Academy of the Fine Arts, Philadelphia. Gift of Frances C. Griscom, 1950.15

80. Cecilia Beaux. *Bertha Hallowell Vaughan* (1866–1948). Oil on canvas, 58 x 38 in., 1901. Courtesy of the Harvard University Portrait Collection, Gift of Samuel Vaughan and Mrs. Langdon P. Marvin to the Radcliffe Institute for Advanced Study, 1954. Direct digital capture by Katya Kallsen © President and Fellows of Harvard College

81. Cecilia Beaux. *Richard Wainwright* (1849–1926). Graphite on paper, 22 x 15 in., 1898. Cape Ann Historical Association, Gloucester, Massachusetts

This drawing by Cecilia Beaux was commissioned by her friend Richard Watson Gilder to accompany an article written by U.S. Naval Commander Richard Wainwright describing an engagement between an American gunboat and Spanish destroyers during the Spanish American War. The article appeared in the May 1899 issue of *The Century*. Beaux was commissioned to draw a number of portrait illustrations for the magazine. Gilder also published Beaux's poetry.

82. Cecilia Beaux. *Mrs. Larz Anderson* (born Isabel Weld Perkins, 1876–1948). Oil on canvas, 82 x 40 in., 1901. Reproduced by permission of The Society of the Cincinnati

In 1896, while touring the world as a young debutante, Isabel Anderson met her future husband, who was then serving as a diplomat at the United States Embassy in Rome. Although Larz Anderson was wealthy and well connected, his resources did not match Isabel's, who at the age of five had inherited $17 million dollars from her grandfather. Three years after their marriage, Beaux began this portrait at *Weld*, the couple's 64-acre estate in Brookline, Massachusetts.

83. Cecilia Beaux. *Mrs. Theodore Roosevelt and Daughter Ethel* (Edith Kermit Carow Roosevelt, 1861–1948, Ethel Roosevelt, 1891–1977). Oil on canvas, $44\frac{1}{2}$ x $31\frac{1}{2}$ in., 1902. Courtesy Sarah Chapman

84. Cecilia Beaux. *Portrait of Theodore Roosevelt* (1858–1919). Charcoal on paper ($17\frac{7}{8}$ x $13\frac{7}{8}$ in., 1902. Pennsylvania Academy of the Fine Arts, Philadelphia. Gift of Henry Sandwith Drinker, 1950.17.46

85. Cecilia Beaux. *William Foster Biddle, Emily Leavitt Biddle at the Seashore*. Ink on paper, $6\frac{1}{2}$ x 9 in., ca. 1883. Private Collection, Courtesy of Alfred J. Walker Fine Art

86. Stephen Parrish (1846–1938). *Fishermen's Houses—Cape Ann*. Etching, 11 x $18\frac{11}{16}$ in., 1881. Cape Ann Historical Association, Gloucester, Massachusetts

Although his reputation as an artist was eclipsed by the success of his son, the illustrator Maxfield Parrish, in the 1880s Stephen Parrish became one of the most successful etchers in the United States. His landscapes and marine views of the New England coast were particularly popular. Stephen Parrish was a frequent visitor to Gloucester and may have been responsible for introducing Cecilia Beaux to the area.

87. Cecilia Beaux. *Mr. and Mrs. Anson Phelps Stokes* (Anson Phelps Stokes, 1838–1913, Helen Louisa Phelps 1846–1930). Oil on canvas, $72\frac{1}{16}$ x $39\frac{7}{8}$, 1898. The Metropolitan Museum of Art, Gift of the Family of the Rev. and Mrs. Anson Phelps Stokes, 1965 (65.252). Photograph © 1995 The Metropolitan Museum of Art

Anson Phelps Stokes, a merchant, banker, and director and trustee of several companies built a summer "cottage" on 900 acres near the Gilders' summer home in Tyringham, Massachusetts. Beaux probably met the Stokes family through her association with the Gilders. One year before Beaux painted this canvas, John Singer Sargent finished a double portrait of the Stokeses' eldest son, Isaac Newton Stokes, and his wife, Edith.

88. Cecilia Beaux. *Mrs. John Frederick Lewis* (born Anne Henrietta Rush Baker, 1863–1937). Oil on canvas, $46\frac{1}{2}$ x $29\frac{15}{16}$ in., 1906. Pennsylvania Academy of the Fine Arts, Philadelphia. Gift of Alfred Baker Lewis, 1974.13

Anne H. Rush Baker married John Lewis in 1894. Her husband, a prominent attorney by vocation and an avid art collector of American portraits by avocation, served as President of the Pennsylvania Academy of the Fine Arts, Vice President of the Historical Society of Pennsylvania, and a director of the Genealogical Society of Pennsylvania.

89. Cecilia Beaux. *A. Piatt Andrew* (1873–1936). Oil on canvas, 33 x 27 in., 1903. Cape Ann Historical Association, Gloucester, Massachusetts

90. Cecilia Beaux. Dorothea and Francesca (Dorothea Gilder, 1882–1920, Francesca Gilder, 1888–1984). Oil on canvas, 80 1/8 x 46 in., 1898. A. A. Munger Collection, 1921.109. Reproduction, The Art Institute of Chicago

91. Emily Leavitt Biddle, Cecilia Beaux, and Eliza Leavitt, ca 1903. Pennsylvania Academy of the Fine Arts, Philadelphia. Gift of Cecilia Saltonstall through Tara Leigh Tappert

Dabsville at Eastern Point

92. Thornton Oakley. *A Fairy-Tale Town Is Pont-en-Royans*. Pen and ink on board, 10 x 6 in., 1927. The Eisenstat Collection of American Illustration

93. Thornton Oakley. *The Valley of Aosta: Castello di Fenis*. Pen and ink on board, 10 x 6 in., 1927. The Eisenstat Collection of American Illustration

94. Thornton Oakley. *The Erstwhile Abbey of Sixt*. Pen and ink on board, 10 x 6 in., 1927. The Eisenstat Collection of American Illustration

Thornton Oakley composed these drawings and more than ninety others for *The Cloud-Lands of France*, a travel log written by his wife, Amy. In a "Forward by the Artist," Oakley waxed poetic: "Reader, thou who longest to escape the routine of a humdrum life, thou who yearnest for a realm of fancy, a domain where thou mayst wander unconstrained, amidst a pageantry of light and color,—crags bearing on the brows glistening diadems of ice; vales o'erflowing with romance; towns of medieval lure, and folk arrayed as though of some long-vanished century,—reader, come, and forth together we shall fare into such a land that waits us."

95. Cecilia Beaux. Detail; *Dr. John Shaw Billings* (1838–1913). Oil on canvas, 77 x 52 in., 1895. United States National Library of Medicine

At the start of the Civil War twenty-three-year-old Dr. John Shaw Billings entered the U.S. Army Medical Department. For the next two years he distinguished himself as a field surgeon at the battles of Chancellorsville and Gettysburg as well as in the Wilderness Campaign and the Siege of Petersburg. In 1864 Dr. Billings accepted a less harrowing assignment as librarian for the Surgeon General's Office, a post he held for the next thirty years. In 1865, at the age of fifty-seven, Billings retired from the Army and came to Philadelphia with the intention of continuing his career as a professor of Hygiene at the University of Pennsylvania. His plans changed when he was offered a position as the director of the New York Public Library. During his short stay in Philadelphia, Beaux painted this portrait, commissioned by a group of physicians for presentation to the National Library of Medicine.

Beaux posed Dr. Billings wearing academic robes over his military uniform, a costume that reflected his various honors. However, Beaux made no other concessions to his celebrity. In the portrait Dr. Billings appears just as he probably looked—strong but tired, his jaw slack, his hands veined, and his face gazing at the viewer with weathered resignation.

96. View of Green Alley from the shoreline. Pennsylvania Academy of the Fine Arts, Philadelphia. Gift of Cecilia Saltonstall through Tara Leigh Tappert

97. Cecilia Beaux in wicker chair, 1898–1905. Pennsylvania Academy of the Fine Arts, Philadelphia. Gift of Cecilia Saltonstall through Tara Leigh Tappert

98. Cecilia Beaux. *Charles Sumner Bird and His Sister Edith Bird Bass*. Oil on canvas, 94 5/8 x 53 1/2 in., 1907. Museum of Fine Arts, Boston: Gift of Mrs. Charles Sumner Bird 1981.720

99. Cecilia Beaux. *Girl with a Lyre* (Dorothea Gilder, 1882–1920). Oil on canvas, 32 x 25 in., 1905. Berry Hill Gallery, New York

In 1973, while researching an article for *Antiques Magazine*, Fred Berry was invited to the Gilder's home on Gramercy Park. At the time it was occupied by the Gilders' two surviving daughters, Rosamond and Francesca, who were both in their eighties. "It was absolutely fascinating, a glimpse into a world of the previous turn-of-the-century when people like Henry James and Cecilia Beaux spent time with Richard Watson Gilder and his family," Berry recalls. "The apartment was pretty much as it had been almost a century earlier . . . and I suspect that the furniture and paintings and books at least were all unchanged." Among the paintings hanging on the walls was a Winslow Homer portrait of Helena Gilder (now in the Thyssen Bornemisza Museum in Madrid) and several portraits by Beaux including *Girl with a Lyre.*

100. Cecilia Beaux. *Samuel Hamilton Brooks* (1834–1912). Oil on canvas, $39\frac{5}{16}$ x $29\frac{1}{8}$ in., 1911. Memphis Brooks Museum of Art. Gift of Brooks S. Hamilton, 1916

101. Cecilia Beaux. *Bessie Vance Brooks* (1868–1943). Oil on canvas, $47\frac{1}{4}$ x $34\frac{1}{4}$ in., 1911. Memphis Brooks Museum of Art. Gift of Bessie Vance Brooks, 1916

102. Cecilia Beaux. *John Paul Jones* (1747–1792). Oil on canvas, $41\frac{15}{16}$ x $31\frac{15}{16}$ in., 1906. United States Naval Academy

103. Cecilia Beaux's home, Green Alley, interior view, 1910–20. Photographer: T. E. Morr. Pennsylvania Academy of the Fine Arts, Philadelphia. Gift of Cecilia Saltonstall through Tara Leigh Tappert

104. Cecilia Beaux's studio at Green Alley, 1910–20. Photographer: T. E. Morr. Pennsylvania Academy of the Fine Arts, Philadelphia. Gift of Cecilia Saltonstall through Tara Leigh Tappert

105. Cecilia Beaux, Henry Davis Sleeper, and unidentified woman, n.d. Cape Ann Historical Association, Gloucester, Massachusetts

106. A. Piatt Andrew, Henry Davis Sleeper, and Cecilia Beaux, 1907. Pennsylvania Academy of the Fine Arts, Philadelphia. Gift of Cecilia Saltonstall through Tara Leigh Tappert

107. Cecilia Beaux. *Mrs. Richard Low Divine* (born Susan Sophia Smith, 1843–1927). Oil on canvas, $74\frac{3}{4}$ x 48 in., 1907. Bequest of Gertrude Divine Webster, 1947.080. Columbus Museum of Art

108. Cecilia Beaux in cap and gown, 1908. Pennsylvania Academy of the Fine Arts, Philadelphia. Gift of Cecilia Saltonstall through Tara Leigh Tappert

109. Cecilia Beaux and Thornton Oakley at Green Alley, 1907. Pennsylvania Academy of the Fine Arts, Philadelphia. Gift of Cecilia Saltonstall through Tara Leigh Tappert

110. Beaux with friends and her houseman at Green Alley, 1912. From left to right: Natale Gavagnin, Arthur Hadley, Cecilia Beaux, and Isabella Stewart Gardner. Pennsylvania Academy of the Fine Arts, Philadelphia. Gift of Cecilia Saltonstall through Tara Leigh Tappert

Gardner, a friend and patron of John Singer Sargent, was a frequent visitor to Eastern Point and Green Alley. Beaux never asked Gardner to sit for a portrait and later explained to a reporter (somewhat enigmatically) that Gardner was too "violent" to be painted. "She was not handsome or pretty and yet she fascinated people," Beaux recalled. "Once she borrowed two lion cubs from the keeper in the zoo—charmed them out of him because she liked them."

111. Cecilia Beaux. *Mrs. Stedman Buttrick and Son John* (born Olive Bagley, 1868–1909, John Butterick, 1905–1954). Oil on canvas, $33\frac{1}{2}$ x $25\frac{1}{2}$ in., 1909. Mrs. John D. Bryson

This portrait is a commemorative canvas painted from photographs and commissioned after Mrs. Buttrick died giving birth to Mary, her fifth child.

112. Cecilia Beaux seated in the loggia at Green Alley, mid-1920s. Pennsylvania Academy of the Fine Arts, Philadelphia. Gift of Cecilia Saltonstall through Tara Leigh Tappert

113. Cecilia Beaux with A. Piatt Andrew (left) and Jack Mabbett (William James Jr., in background). Photograph, 1908. Pennsylvania Academy of the Fine Arts. Gift of Cecilia Saltomstall through Tara Leigh Tappert

114. Cecilia Beaux. *Thornton Oakley* (1881–1953). Charcoal on board, $19\frac{5}{8}$ x $14\frac{1}{8}$ in., 1911. Mrs. Lansdale Humphreys

115. Cecilia Beaux. *Sereno Elisha Payne* (1843–1914). Oil on canvas, 41 1/2 x 31 1/2 in., 1912. Architect of the Capitol

Sereno E. Payne was a Republican Representative from New York who served in Congress almost continuously from 1883 until his death in 1914. He was the Chairman of the Ways and Means Committee of the House of Representatives from 1899 to 1911, a record for longevity in the position at the time. Payne sat for his portrait in Beaux's studio at Green Alley in Gloucester.

116. Cecilia Beaux. *Clement B. Newbold* (1857–1926). Oil on canvas, 47 3/8 x 35 in., 1912. Pennsylvania Academy of the Fine Arts, Philadelphia. Gift of Clement B. Newbold, 1973.25.1

117. Cecilia Beaux. *A Lady in Black*. Oil on canvas, 78 3/8 x 47 1/2 in., ca. 1916. Museum of Fine Arts, Boston: Gift of Alfred I. Du Pont 21.1841

118. Cecilia Beaux. *Ernesta* (Ernesta Drinker, 1892–1981). Oil on canvas, 71 3/4 x 43 3/8 in., 1914. The Metropolitan Museum of Art, Arthur Hoppock Hearn Fund, 1915 (15.82). Photograph © 1995 The Metropolitan Museum of Art

119. Cecilia Beaux. *Helena DeKay Gilder* (1848–1916). Oil on canvas, 31 x 21 in., 1911. Collection of the family

120. Cecilia Beaux. *After the Meeting* (Dorothea Gilder, 1882–1920). Oil on canvas, 40 15/16 x 28 1/8 in., 1914. Toledo Art Museum, Gift of Florence Scott Libbey, 1915.163

121. Cecilia Beaux lying on the rocks at Gloucester, Massachusetts, ca. 1910–20. Pennsylvania Academy of the Fine Arts, Philadelphia. Gift of Cecilia Saltonstall through Tara Leigh Tappert

122. View of the harbor from Cecilia Beaux's studio, 1910–20. Photographer: T. E. Morr. Pennsylvania Academy of the Fine Arts, Philadelphia. Gift of Cecilia Saltonstall through Tara Leigh Tappert

The view of the harbor from Cecilia Beaux's house did not come easily but was revealed after much hard work. "Here we work still at cutting, cutting," Beaux wrote to her friend Thornton Oakley. "The trees are making walls of leaves and choking out air and sun."

123. Cecilia Beaux. *Helena Dorothea McGrew*. Oil on canvas, 24 1/2 x 18 1/4 in., ca 1920. Courtesy of Skinner, Inc., Auctioneers of Fine Art and Antiques, Boston and Bolton, Massachusetts

Green Alley Autumn

124. Cecilia Beaux in the vestibule of her studio at Green Alley, n.d. Pennsylvania Academy of the Fine Arts, Philadelphia. Gift of Cecilia Saltonstall through Tara Leigh Tappert

125. Cecilia Beaux. *Marion Reilly*. 1918. Oil on canvas, 39 1/4 x 26 1/4 in. Bryn Mawr College Collection.

126. Cecilia Beaux. *Mrs. Andrew Carnegie* (Louise Whitfield Carnegie, 1857–1946). Oil on canvas, 52 x 36 1/2 in., 1917–18. Carnegie Museum of Art, Pittsburgh: Carnegie Institute Purchase 12.8

Louise Whitfield Carnegie was the wife of the steel maker and philanthropist Andrew Carnegie. Known for his great wealth and amazing generosity (he gave away approximately $350 million dollars during his lifetime), Carnegie considered his wife "Lou" to be his greatest treasure. Reminiscing about their rewarding life together, Carnegie wondered, "Why, oh why, are we compelled to leave the heaven we have found on earth and go we know not where?"

127. Cecilia Beaux, ca. 1910–20. Photographer: Alice Austin. Pennsylvania Academy of the Fine Arts, Philadelphia. Gift of Cecilia Saltonstall through Tara Leigh Tappert

In an article for the *Pittsburgh Dispatch* published in April 1911, journalist Maud Carrell wrote the following description of Beaux: "No doubt feminine readers will be interested in the personality of Miss Beaux. She is tall and slender, has gray eyes that look directly at one and are sometimes as luminous as her canvases. She has that gift of witty speech and the laugh that comes readily. She suggests the woman of highest breeding, of poise, of grace, or reserve. One would say that Bohemia and Cecilia Beaux were strangers. It would be hard to imagine this elegant woman in velvet and rich furs claiming any license allowed to genius, adopting any bizarre habits of dress or familiar cameraderie [sic] that it sometimes affects."

128. Cecilia Beaux. *Still Life with Fruit*. Oil on canvas, $24\frac{1}{4}$ x 18 in., 1918. Westmoreland Museum of American Art. Gift of the Women's Committee, 1977.2

129. Cecilia Beaux. *Study for Cardinal Joseph Mercier* (1851–1926). Oil on canvas, 25 x 21 in., 1919. Courtesy of Alfred J. Walker Fine Art, Boston

130. Cecilia Beaux. *Sketch for Cardinal Mercier*. Charcoal on paper, $24\frac{1}{4}$ x $19\frac{1}{2}$ in., 1919. Pennsylvania Academy of the Fine Arts, Philadelphia. Gift of Henry Sandwith Drinker, 1950.17.38

131. Cecilia Beaux. *Cardinal Mercier* (1851–1926). Oil on canvas, 78 x $51\frac{3}{4}$ in., 1919. Smithsonian American Art Museum, Washington, D.C. Photography courtesy of Smithsonian American Art Museum, Washington, D.C./Art Resource, NY

"When I was painting Cardinal Mercier's portrait . . . he was sometimes very tired and worn out when he came to the studio; just a gray old man—his face colorless, his eyes so sunken that I could hardly see them," Beaux recalled. "But as I began to work, we would talk together; and in a little while, as he became interested, the color would creep into his cheeks, his eyes would dilate, and it seemed as if twenty-five years fell away from him in just a few moments."

132. Cecilia Beaux. Admiral Sir David Beatty, or Lord Beatty (1871–1936). Oil on canvas, $62\frac{1}{2}$ x $45\frac{5}{8}$ in., 1920. Smithsonian American Art Museum, Washington, D.C. Photography courtesy of Smithsonian American Art Museum, Washington, D.C./Art Resource, NY.

133. Green Alley, house and terrace, 1910–20. Photographer: T. E. Morr. Pennsylvania Academy of the Fine Arts, Philadelphia. Gift of Cecilia Saltonstall through Tara Leigh Tappert

134. Beaux labeled this photograph "The Door Is Always Open at Green Alley," 1910–20. Photographer: T. E. Morr. Pennsylvania Academy of the Fine Arts, Philadelphia. Gift of Cecilia Saltonstall through Tara Leigh Tappert

135. Cecilia Beaux. *Georges Clemenceau* (1841–1929). Oil on canvas, $46\frac{7}{8}$ x $36\frac{3}{4}$ in., 1920. Smithsonian American Art Museum, Washington, D.C. Photography courtesy of Smithsonian American Art Museum, Washington, D.C./Art Resource, NY.

136. Cecilia Beaux. *Caroline Ogden-Jones Peter* (1894–1965). Oil on board, $21\frac{1}{16}$ x $14\frac{3}{8}$ in., 1920. Tudor Place Historic House and Garden. Photograph by Emily Rusch

137. Cecilia Beaux, 1920s. Pennsylvania Academy of the Fine Arts, Philadelphia. Gift of Cecilia Saltonstall through Tara Leigh Tappert

138. Cecilia Beaux. *Self-Portrait*. Oil on canvas, 43 x 28 in., 1925. Uffizi Gallery, Florence, Italy. Photograph Scala/Art Resource, NY

Cecilia Beaux was recovering from a debilitating injury and considering retirement when she received a letter requesting a painting to hang with a collection of self-portraits in the Uffizi Gallery in Florence, Italy. Beaux was the first female American artist to be honored with inclusion in the august group that included Rubens, Rembrandt, and Delacroix. "My astonishment and satisfaction were witness to my deep appreciation of such an honor," Beaux later recalled. "Although I had not tried to paint since my accident, I at once began dragging myself about."

139. "Morning at Green Alley." Cecilia Beaux published this photograph in her autobiography in 1930. Pennsylvania Academy of the Fine Arts, Philadelphia. Gift of Cecilia Saltonstall through Tara Leigh Tappert

Notes

1 Beaux, Cecilia. *Background with Figures* (Boston and New York: Houghton Mifflin Company, 1930), 33.

2 Hunekar, James. *Chopin: The Man and His Music* (New York: Scribners, 1900), 188. In this early biography of Chopin, James Hunekar, who had studied to be a concert pianist, wrote about the difficulty of Chopin's "Heroic" Polonaise in A flat major, Op. 53: "That Chopin ever played it as intended is incredible; none but the heroes of the keyboard may grasp its dense chordal masses, its fiery projectiles of tone."

3 Powell, Alvin. "Defeating Infection: How Oliver Wendell Holmes Helped Conquer the 'Black Death of Childbed.'" *Harvard University Gazette* (Sept. 8, 1997). Online at www.news.harvard. edu/gazette/1997/09.18/ DefeatingInfect.html

4 Ibid.

5 Beaux, Cecilia. *Background with Figures*, 12.

6 Tappert, Tara Leigh. *Choices—The Life and Career of Cecilia Beaux: A Professional Biography* (diss,. George Washington University, 1990), 9.

7 Beaux, *Background with Figures*, 9.

8 Leavitt, William P., Leavitt *Pioneers: Western Migration and Colonization.* (PDBK Enterprises, ca. 1985–2003): http://users.lasvegas.net/~wmpl/Leavitt1.htm#content. The Mattapan Plantation was renamed Dorcester in 1630 by the General Court of the Massachusetts Bay Colony.

9 The Dey Street neighborhood occupied the approximate site of the World Trade Center.

10 Beaux, *Background with Figures*, 6.

11 Ibid.

12 Ibid., 7 and Grace Leavitt Peck to Cecilia Beaux. March 1914. Cecilia Beaux Papers, Archives of American Art.

13 Ibid.

14 Ibid., 25.

15 Ibid., 8.

16 Ibid., 9.

17 Archives départementales du Vaucluse (Palais des Papes, Avignon), Sous-série 5 E : civil status of Mialet.

18 Oakley, Thornton. *Cecilia Beaux* (Howard Biddle Printing Company, 1943), 13.

19 The translation of "A l'Asard Bautezar," was obtained from The Office of Tourism, Les Baux de Provence, in an E-mail message, December 23, 2002, and from the brochure, "A Sense of Place: Les Baux de Provence," Les Baux Tourist Office 13520 Les Baux-de-Provence.

20 Bowen, Catherine Drinker. *Family Portrait* (Little, Brown and Company, 1970), 138, 139.

21 Beaux, *Background with Figures*, 9.

22 Tappert, Tara Leigh. "Aimée Ernesta and Eliza Cecilia: Two Sisters, Two Choices." *The Pennsylvania Magazine of History and Biography.* vol cxxiv, no. 3 (July 2000), 251.

23 Although current research indicates that Cecilia Beaux was the third child of Cecilia Leavitt Beaux and Jean Adolphe Beaux, in a letter that Cecilia Beaux wrote to the editor of the *Saturday Review of Literature* published on March 7, 1891, she said: "I was their fourth child."

24 Ibid., 11.

25 Bowen, 136.

26 Beaux, *Background with Figures*, 9.

27 Scharf, Thomas J. and Westcott, Thompson. *History of Philadelphia 1609–1884* (L. H. Everts & Co., 1884), vol 1, 720.

28 Pennell, Joseph. *The Adventures of an Illustrator* (Little, Brown, and Company, 1925), 9.

29 Scharf, vol. 2, 1684.

30 Beaux, *Background with Figures*, 13.

31 When the Philadelphia horse-cars began regular operations in 1858, seats were reserved for the white population. Blacks wishing to ride stood on platforms attached to the fronts of the cars. In 1867 the State Legislature passed a bill allowing Negroes to sit in the cars. Cox, H. E. *Negro History Bulletin*, 1962, 26 (3), 119–123.

32 Hershberg, Theodore. *Philadelphia: Work, Space, Family, and Group Experience in the Nineteenth Century* (New York and Oxford: Oxford University Press, 1981), 141, 142.

33 Watson, John F. *Annals of Philadelphia and Pennsylvania in the Olden Times* (Philadelphia: J. M. Stoddart & Co., 1881), 613, 614.

34 Hershberg, 45.

35 Ibid., 65. In 1860 there were 709 textile firms in Philadelphia.

36 Letter from Aimée Ernesta Drinker to Mrs. Bedford, April 10, 1902. Cecilia Beaux Papers. Archives of American Art.

37 Bowen, 137, and Beaux, *Background with Figures*, 10. "The rock of Jacob / All his work is perfect / What he promises / His hand accomplishes / Alleluia, Alleluia."

38 Bowen, 136, 137.

39 Beaux, Jean Adolphe. Beaux to his employees. Cecilia Beaux Papers. Archives of American Art.

40 Bowen, 138.

41 Beaux, *Background with Figures*, 205.

42 Tappert, 15.

43 Ibid., 15.

44 Beaux, *Background with Figures*, 41.

45 Ibid., 25.

46 Ibid., 23.

47 Letter from Aimée Ernesta Drinker to Mrs. Bedford, April 10, 1902. Cecilia Beaux Papers. Archives of American Art.

48 Drinker, 144.

49 Beaux, *Background with Figures*, 29.

50 Tappert, Tara Leigh. "Aimée Ernesta and Eliza Cecilia: Two Sisters, Two Choices." *The Pennsylvania Magazine of History and Biography*, vol. cxxiv, no. 3 (July 2000), 254.

51 Beaux, *Background with Figures*, 14.

52 Cecilia Beaux to Jean Adolphe Beaux, December 9, 1863. Cecilia Beaux Papers. Archives of American Art.

53 Letter from Aimée Ernesta Drinker to Mrs. Bedford, April 10, 1902. Cecilia Beaux Papers. Archives of American Art.

54 Bowen, 204.

55 Emily Leavitt to Jean Adolphe Beaux, December 9, 1863. Cecilia Beaux Papers. Archives of American Art.

56 Ibid.

57 Penn State Sustainable Forest Teacher Resource Center and "American Institute of Mining Engineers Monthly Bulletin," No. 46, October 1910.

58 Beaux, 33.

59 Ibid., 203.

60 Ibid., 31.

61 Mendelssohn, Felix. *Elijah*, Op. 70, no. 28, 1846.

62 Beaux, *Background with Figures*, 33.

63 Trumbell, Rebecca. "Spruce Hill Historic District. Nomination for the Spruce Hill Historic District." submitted to the Philadelphia Historical Commission, 1985. Online at http://uchs.net/HistoricDistricts/S42.DOC

64 Watson, 811.

65 Watson, 814.

66 Milroy, Elizabeth. "Avenue of Dreams: Patriotism and the Spectator at Philadelphia's Great Central Sanitary Fair." *Pennsylvania's Civil War*, William Blair and William Peneak, eds. (University Park: The Pennsylvania State University Press, 2001), 33.

67 Ibid., 48.

68 Beaux, *Background with Figures*, 38.

69 Ibid.

70 Beaux, *Background with Figures*, 35.

71 Ibid.

72 Henderson, Helen W. *The Pennsylvania Academy of the Fine Arts* (L. C. Page and Company, 1911), 19. John Sartain. *The Reminiscences of a Very Old Man* (Appleton and Company, 1899), 167.

73 Scharf, 298, 301, 311, 322, 336, 341, 409.

74 Bowen, 140.

75 Ibid. William Foster Biddle expressed his views on opera in an article, "Opera Before the Court of Reason," *The Atlantic Monthly*, vol. 77, issue 464, 1896, 786–96.

76 Beaux, *Background with Figures*, 36.

77 Ibid., 39.

78 Ibid.

79 Ibid., 14.

80 Letter from Aimée Ernesta Drinker to Mrs. Bedford, April 10, 1902. Cecilia Beaux Papers. Archives of American Art.

81 Beaux, 39.

82 Ibid., 57.

83 Harding, J. D. "Preface to the First Edition." *Lessons on Art* (London: W. Kent & Co., 1866).

84 Beaux, *Background with Figures*, 43.

85 Ibid., 44.

86 Ibid.

87 Beaux, Cecilia. Untitled, undated manuscript. Cecilia Beaux Papers. Archives of American Art.

88 Bowen, 144.

89 Beaux, untitled, undated manuscript. Cecilia Beaux Papers. Archives of American Art.

90 Beaux, *Background with Figures*, 25.

91 Ibid., 24.

92 Bowen, 147.

93 Agnes Irwin gained a national reputation as an educator and in 1894 became the first Dean of Radcliffe College. Years later, in 1906, Cecilia Beaux was commissioned to paint Ms. Irwin's portrait.

94 Beaux, *Background with Figures*, 53.

95 Ibid.

96 Ibid., 53.

97 Ibid., 49.

98 Beaux, *Background with Figures*, 51.

99 Bowen, 144.

100 Beaux, *Background with Figures*, 50.

101 Beaux, *Background with Figures*, 56.

102 Bowen, 150.

103 Bowen, 153.

104 Biddle, Henry D. *The Drinker Family in America* (Philadelphia: privately printed, 1893), 27.

105 "Mrs. Janvier's Varied Life." *New York Times*, Sunday, Oct 1, 1922, section 8, p.xx.

106 Ibid.

107 Bowen, 157.

108 This account is related in more detail in Catherine Drinker Bowen's chronicle of her family, *Family Portrait*, 252–60.

109 Drinker, Henry S. *History of the Drinker Family* (Philadelphia: privately printed, 1961), 60.

110 Tappert, 41.

111 Huber, Christine Jones. *The Pennsylvania Academy and Its Women, 1850 to 1920* (Philadelphia: Pennsylvania Academy of the Fine Arts, 1973).

112 Beaux, *Background with Figures*, 59.

113 Letheve, Jaques. *The Daily Life of French Artists.* (New York: Praeger Publishers, 1972), 23.

114 Beaux, *Background with Figures*, 60.

115 Henderson, 215.

116 Beaux, *Background with Figures*, 63.

117 Ibid., 59.

118 Ibid.

119 Beaux, *Background with Figures*, 59.

120 Bowen, 150.

121 Knauff, Theodore C. *An Experiment in Training for the Useful and the Beautiful: A History* (Philadelphia: Philadelphia School of Design for Women, 1922), 55.

122 Tappert, 46.

123 Beaux, *Background with Figures*, 65.

124 Ibid.

125 Pitz, Henry C. *Howard Pyle: Writer, Illustrator, Founder of the Brandywine School* (New York: Clarkson N. Potter, Inc., 1975), 17.

126 Huber, 12.

127 Beaux, *Background with Figures*, 69.

128 Ibid., 70.

129 Ibid.

130 Beaux diary, November 27, 1875. Cecilia Beaux Papers. Archives of American Art.

131 Ibid., November 25, 1875.

132 Scharf, 838.

133 Walther, Rudolph *J. Happenings in Ye Olde Philadelphia 1680–1900* (Philadelphia: Walther Printing House, 1925), 43.

134 Scharf, 838.

135 Draft of speech delivered at Simmons College, April 20, 1907, "The Public and Modern Art." Cecilia Beaux Papers, Archives of American Art.

136 Ibid.

137 Beaux, *Background with Figures*, 70.

138 Ibid., 71.

139 Ibid.

140 Letter from Aimée Ernesta Drinker to Mrs. Bedford, April 10, 1902. Cecilia Beaux Papers. Archives of American Art.

141 Ibid.

142 Hellerson, Erna, Hume, Leslie Parker, and Offen, Karen M., eds. *Victorian Women* (Stanford, California: Stanford University Press, 1981), 134.

143 Thompson, Eleanor Wolf. *Education for Ladies 1830–1860* (New York: Kings Crown Press, 1947), 32.

144 Ibid.

145 Schlereth, Thomas J. *Victorian America: Transformations in Everyday Life, 1876–1915* (New York: HarperCollins, 1991), 249.

146 Thompson, 45, 46. Reprinted from *Godey's Lady's Book*, vol. LVI, no. 4, April 1858, 373.

147 Letter from Aimée Ernesta Drinker to Mrs. Bedford, April 10, 1902. Cecilia Beaux Papers. Archives of American Art.

148 Bowen, 144.

149 Ibid.

150 Beaux, *Background with Figures*, 73.

151 Ibid.

152 Beaux diary, December 11, 1875. Cecilia Beaux Papers. Archives of American Art. "L. [Lila] Redfield a lesson at 9 o'ck [sic] this A.M." "She began a pretty fine shading piece. Is enlarging it. Read her extracts from 'In a Studio' from Littell." Within two months there was further improvement. "Lila is doing her picture beautifully and I am very careful and particular."

153 Ibid., 84.

154 Ibid., 76.

155 "Philadelphia Lithographers: Thomas Sinclair (ca. 1805–1881)." The University of Pennsylvania Library. Online at http://www.library .upenn.edu/collections/rbm/keffer/sinclair.html

156 Beaux, *Background with Figures*, 75.

157 Ibid., 76.

158 Michaelis, David. *N. C. Wyeth: A Biography*. (New York: Alfred A. Knopf, 1998), 35.

159 Pitz, 20, 21.

160 Stacy, J. C. "The Brighton Cats." *St. Nicholas*, December 1873,. vol.1, no. 2. 51. According to the article in *St. Nicolas* magazine, the cats Leilie drew belonged to a man in Brighton, England, who had trained them to perform a variety of unlikely tricks, such as painting at an easel, moving chessmen on a board, dancing, and drinking the foam from a bottle of ale. The scene Leilie depicted is one in which the animals were instructed to "do penance" for disobedience by hanging from their paws on the back of a chair. "They never think of such a thing as escaping the punishment," the author of the article gaily assured his readers. "No indeed; they jump upon the chair at once, and, shutting their eyes, stand as you see them in the picture, two images of misery."

161 Bowen, 165.

162 Janvier, Thomas. "'The Brighton Cats' Lithograph by Miss E. C. Beaux." *The Press*, December 1, 1874. Cecilia Beaux Papers. Archives of American Art.

163 Letter from Aimée Ernesta Drinker to Mrs. Bedford, April 10, 1902. Cecilia Beaux Papers. Archives of American Art.

164 Ibid.

165 Wallace, David Rains. *The Bonehunter's Revenge* (Boston and New York: Houghton Mifflin, 1999), 81.

166 Ibid., 43.

167 Beaux, *Background with Figures*, 81, 82.

168 Beaux diary, October 10, 1875. Cecilia Beaux Papers. Archives of American Art.

169 Ibid.

170 Ibid., November 22, 1875.

171 Beaux, *Background with Figures*, 80.

172 Ibid.

173 Bowen, 161.

174 Beaux, *Background with Figures*, 83.

175 Beaux diary, November 7, 1875. Cecilia Beaux Papers. Archives of American Art.

176 Beaux, *Background with Figures*, 86.

177 Bowen, 135.

178 Beaux diary, November 26, 1875. Cecilia Beaux Papers. Archives of American Art.

179 Beaux, *Background with Figures*, 86.

180 Beaux diary, November 16. Cecilia Beaux Papers. Archives of American Art.

181 Ibid., November 8.

182 Ibid., December 10.

183 Beaux, *Background with Figures*, 86.

184 Ibid.

185 Ibid.

186 "Old Maids," *Littell's Living Age*. no. 1469. August 3, 1872.

187 "American Institute of Mining Engineers Monthly Bulletin," no. 46, October 1910.

188 Beaux, *Background with Figures*, 89.

189 Beaux diary, November 20, 1875. Cecilia Beaux Papers. Archives of American Art.

190 Philadelphia Free Library, Centennial Digital Collection. libwww.library.phila.gov/CenCol/tours-memorialhall.htm

191 Strahan, Edward. *The Masterpieces of the International Exhibition* (Philadelphia: Gebbie & Barrie, 1876). This illustrated catalogue contains descriptions of many of the paintings in the exhibition.

192 Ibid., 96.

193 Olson, Stanley. *John Singer Sargent: His Portrait* (New York: St. Martin's Griffin, 1986), 50.

194 Sartain, John. *The Reminiscences of a Very Old Man* (New York: D. Appleton and Company, 1899), 53.

195 Beaux, *Background with Figures*, 86.

196 Lucas, E. V. *Edwin Austin Abbey: Royal Academician* (New York: Charles Scribner's Sons, 1921), 13, 14. Edwin Austin Abbey wrote the following account of his student days with Christian Schussele in a letter to Academy President E. H. Coates, dated February 2, 1908: "I have seen a great deal since then—and heard artistic theories propounded without number—but the science of constructive drawing as taught by Mr. Schussele remains clearly with me, and is, in my opinion, as thorough and right as a method can be."

197 Goodrich, Lloyd. *Thomas Eakins* (Cambridge, Massachusetts and London: Harvard University Press. 1982), 169.

198 Pennell, Joseph. *The Adventures of an Illustrator* (Boston: Little, Brown, and Company. 1925), 50.

199 Ibid.

200 Goodrich, 173.

201 Tappert, 89. In her Doctoral Thesis, Tara Tappert sets the date of Beaux's one life class as January 30, 1877.

202 Beaux, *Background with Figures*, 87.

203 Goodrich, 283.

204 Huber, Christine Jones. *The Pennsylvania Academy and Its Women*, 21.

205 Ibid.

206 Ibid.

207 Pennell, 52.

208 Beaux, *Background with Figures*, 86.

209 Bowen, 136.

210 Beaux, *Background with Figures*, 86.

211 The Women's Centennial Committee, headed by Mrs. Elizabeth Duane Gillespie, great-granddaughter of Benjamin Franklin, was responsible for the selection of the exhibits in the Women's Pavilion.

212 Philadelphia Free Library Centennial Digital Collection: http://libwww.libraryphila.gov/CenCol/tours-womenspav.htm. Huber, 21. Martinez, Katherine and Talbott, Page, *Philadelphia's Cultural Landscape: The Sartain Family Legacy*, 153.

213 "Notices of New Books: The Art Amateur," *The New Englander*, No. CLVIII, January 1881, 835.

214 Critical reviews of Piton's treatise and an explanation of his methods are contained in "Recent Literature," *The Atlantic Monthly*, Vol. 43, Issue 256, February 1879, 268, and in Vol. 44, Issue 165, November 1879.

215 Beaux, *Background with Figures*, 84.

216 "A Veteran Philadelphia Photographer." *American Journal of Photography*, Vol. 13, No. 137, 125–28.

217 Beaux, *Background with Figures*, 84, 85.

218 Tappert, 68, 69.

219 Beaux, *Background with Figures*, 85.

220 Ibid.

221 *The Encyclopedia of Photography*, 1984.

222 Beaux, *Background with Figures*, 87.

223 Ibid.

224 Beaux, *Background with Figures*, 88.

225 Goodrich, 51.

226 Ibid.

227 Ibid.

228 Bowen, 209.

229 "A Judge at Paris," *Philadelphia Star*, October 24, 1899. Cecilia Beaux Papers. Archives of American Art.

230 Pennell, 69.

231 Ibid.

232 Ibid.

233 "Exposition Art Jury Accused of Injustice." *The Philadelphia Inquirer*, July 18, 1915. Cecilia Beaux Papers. Archives of American Art.

234 Beaux, *Background with Figures*, 91.

235 Ibid.

236 Beaux, *Background with Figures*, 92.

237 Bowen, 169.

238 Beaux, *Background with Figures*, 95.

239 Tappert, 111.

240 Cook, Clarence. "The Studio." Cecilia Beaux Papers, Archives of American Art.

241 Ibid., 136.

242 Beaux, *Background with Figures*, 94, 95.

243 Parrish, Anne. February 24, 1931. Cecilia Beaux Papers, Archives of American Art.

244 *Philadelphia Evening Telegraph*, February 24, 1886. Cecilia Beaux Papers. Archives of American Art.

245 Cook, Clarence. "The Studio," May 15, 1886. Cecilia Beaux Papers. Archives of American Art.

246 Beaux, *Background with Figures*, 98.

247 *The American*, June 19, 1886. Cecilia Beaux Papers. Archives of American Art.

248 Goodrich, 279. For Eakins's portrait of Mrs. William Shaw Ward, completed in 1884, the agreed price was $300. An 1885 likeness of Edwin M. Lewis earned Eakins $500.

249 Margaret Leslie married sculptor Henry Kirk Bush Brown and painted under her married name, Margaret Leslie Bush-Brown. Among her accomplishments as a painter was a large mural for the Women's Building of the 1893 World Exposition in New York.

250 Fink, Lois Marie. *American Art at the Nineteenth-Century Paris Salons* (Cambridge, Massachusetts: Cambridge University Press, 1990), 142.

251 Beaux, *Background with Figures*, 99.

252 Ibid., 205.

253 Ibid., 117, 118.

254 Letter from Eliza Leavitt to Cecilia Beaux. Sunday, 10:30 am, 1888. Cecilia Beaux Papers. Archives of American Art.

255 Letter from Eliza Leavitt to Cecilia Beaux, Friday, 7:30pm, 1888. Cecilia Beaux Papers. Archives of American Art.

256 Cecilia Beaux to Henry Thouron, January, 1888. Cecilia Beaux Papers. Archives of American Art.

257 Henry Thouron to Cecilia Beaux, January 13, 1888. Cecilia Beaux Papers. Archives of American Art.

258 Cecilia Beaux Papers. Archives of American Art.

259 Cecilia Beaux to the family at 4305 Spruce Street, January 14, 1888. Cecilia Beaux Papers. Archives of American Art.

260 Ibid.

261 Beaux, *Background with Figures*, 105.

262 Cecilia Beaux to her family, Friday eve, 1888, Hotel St. Antoine. Cecilia Beaux Papers. Archives of American Art.

263 Ibid.

264 Ibid.

265 Fehrer, Catherine. "New Light on the Academie Julian and its Founder (Rodolphe Julian)." *Gazette Des Beaux-Arts*, No 103, May, June, 1984, 207.

266 Tappert, 147.

267 Fink, 136.

268 Beaux, *Background with Figures*, 117, 118.

269 Wissman, Fronia E. *Bouguereau* (San Francisco: Pomegranate Artbooks, 1996), 111.

270 Cecilia Beaux to her family. Cecilia Beaux Papers. Archives of American Art.

271 Ibid. Translated, "Not bad, a lot of talent, I'm delighted to see."

272 Ibid.

273 William Foster Biddle to Cecilia Beaux. February 12, 1888. Cecilia Beaux Papers. Archives of American Art.

274 Beaux to 4305 Spruce Street, February 2, 1888. Cecilia Beaux Papers. Archives of American Art.

275 Ibid.

276 Ibid.

277 William Foster Biddle to Cecilia Beaux. February 12, 1888. Cecilia Beaux Papers. Archives of American Art.

278 Beaux, *Background with Figures*, 118.

279 Cecilia Beaux to her family, undated. Cecilia Beaux Papers. Archives of American Art.

280 Ibid.

281 Ibid.

282 Anna Klumpke later became known for her biography of her lover, the painter Rosa Bonheur (1822–1899). Amélie Beaury-Saurel, the massière at The Passages, eventually married Julian.

283 Beaux to her family, 1888. Cecilia Beaux Papers. Archives of American Art.

284 Cecilia Beaux to Eliza Leavitt, May 17, 1888. Cecilia Beaux Papers. Archives of American Art.

285 Cecilia Beaux to Aimée Ernesta Drinker, March 18, 1888. Cecilia Beaux Papers. Archives of American Art.

286 Varnishing Day, or "Vernissage," was a tradition at nineteenth-century exhibitions where paintings were stacked together in great numbers on gallery walls in natural light. In the Paris Salons the event was customarily held the day before the exhibition opened. Vernissage gave exhibitors a chance to see their work before the public was admitted to the gallery and to touch up their canvas with varnish so that any glare from the vagaries of the light could be reduced or eliminated. Grayson had a painting accepted in the 1888 spring Salon and was entitled to two tickets to the event.

287 Cecilia Beaux to Aimée Ernesta Drinker, April 12, 1888. Cecilia Beaux Papers. Archives of American Art.

288 Eliza Leavitt to Cecilia Beaux, April 1, 1888. Cecilia Beaux Papers. Archives of American Art.

289 Beaux, *Background with Figures*, 125.

290 Ibid.

291 Ibid., 132.

292 Cecilia Beaux to Aimée Ernesta Drinker, May 27, 1888. Cecilia Beaux Papers. Archives of American Art.

293 Cecilia Beaux to Aimée Ernesta Drinker, June 10, 1888. Cecilia Beaux Papers. Archives of American Art.

294 William Foster Biddle to Cecilia Beaux, July 24, 1888. Cecilia Beaux Papers. Archives of American Art.

295 In 1888 Thomas Eakins painted a portrait of Letitia Wilson Jordan, the woman Bacon would marry in 1890. Letitia's brother was a student of Thomas Eakins, and Eakins, after admiring Letitia at a party, asked if he might paint her. According to the Bacon family, Letitia's brother presented the painting to Leonard and his new bride as a wedding present. Letitia's married life was not particularly happy. Bacon had very little money, and his didactic opinions and sometimes surly manner often alienated him from friends and family. In addition, two of Leticica's three children died within days of one another in a scarlet fever epidemic. After her husband's death, Letitia sold the Eakins painting and with the proceeds took her one remaining child to Switzerland. The portrait is now owned by the Brooklyn Museum of Art, New York.

296 Beaux, *Background with Figures*, 147.

297 Cecilia Beaux to her family, Undated. Cecilia Beaux Papers. Archives of American Art.

298 Cecilia Beaux to her family, July 15, 1888. Cecilia Beaux Papers. Archives of American Art.

299 Cecilia Beaux to William Foster Biddle, August 10, 1888. Cecilia Beaux Papers. Archives of American Art.

300 Cecilia Beaux to William Foster Biddle, September 9, 1888. Cecilia Beaux Papers. Archives of American Art.

301 Cecilia Beaux to her family, September 2, 1888. Cecilia Beaux Papers. Archives of American Art.

302 Balch, Edwin Swift. *Biography of Edwin Swift Balch*, 1928. Balch Family Papers, Albert and Shirley Small Special Collections Library, University of Virginia Library.

303 Ibid.

304 Biddle, Henry D. *The Drinker Family in America.* (Philadelphia: privately printed, 1893), 27. John Drinker and Ruth Balch were married in Beverly, Massachusetts, in the late 1670s and were the first generation of the Drinker family to reside in Philadelphia.

305 Cecilia Beaux to William Foster Biddle, September 30, 1888. Cecilia Beaux Papers. Archives of American Art.

306 William Foster Biddle to Cecilia Beaux, October 6, 1888. Cecilia Beaux Papers. Archives of American Art.

307 Balch was the author of three books on art: *Comparative Art* (1906), *Art and Man* (1918), and *Arts of the World* (1920).

308 Cecilia Beaux to William Foster Biddle, September 9, 1888. Cecilia Beaux Papers. Archives of American Art.

309 Cecilia Beaux to her family, September 30, 1888. Cecilia Beaux Papers. Archives of American Art.

310 Eliza Leavitt to Cecilia Beaux, December 10, 1888. Archives of American Art.

311 Charles Lasar's book, *Practical Hints for Art Students*, was published in 1910. His "hints" ranged from the practical and apparent, such as, "The presentation of sunlight without shadow is impossible," to the more obscure, "Pink is the charmer, yellow the localizer, and purple the enveloper." His advice on portraiture likewise fluctuated between the sensible and the arcane. On the practical side he advised, "Look out for a few hairs on the top surfaces, they give depth to a beard." More subjectively he suggested, "Keep more shadows around women than around men. Women are surrounded by mystery, which can only be expressed by shadow. Keep men in light."

312 Cecilia Beaux to her family, 1888. Cecilia Beaux Papers. Archives of American Art.

313 Cecilia Beaux to Aimée Ernesta Drinker, February 4, 1889. Cecilia Beaux Papers. Archives of American Art.

314 Letter from Aimée Ernesta Drinker to Mrs. Bedford, April 10, 1902. Cecilia Beaux Papers. Archives of American Art.

315 Cecilia Beaux to her family. November 2, 1888. Cecilia Beaux Papers. Archives of American Art.

316 Beaux, *Background with Figures*, 165.

317 Cecilia Beaux to William Foster Biddle, October 6, 1888. Cecilia Beaux Papers. Archives of American Art.

318 Ibid., 169.

319 Ibid., 170.

320 Cecilia Beaux to William Foster Biddle, September 10, 1888. Cecilia Beaux Papers. Archives of American Art.

321 Cecilia Beaux to Aimée Ernesta Drinker, December 23, 1888. Cecilia Beaux Papers. Archives of American Art. In her letter to her sister, Beaux lists the studio address as 34 Notre Dame de Champs. In her autobiography the address given is 15 Notre Dame de Champs.

322 Cecila Beaux to Aimée Ernesta Drinker, March 3, 1889. Cecilia Beaux Papers. Archives of American Art.

323 Cecilia Beaux to her family, February 11, 1889. Cecilia Beaux Papers. Archives of American Art.

324 Perlman, Bernard B. *The Immortal Eight* (Westport, Connecticut: North Light Publishers. 1979), 33.

325 "Art Schools for Girls," *New York Literary Digest*, May 8, 1913. Cecilia Beaux Papers. Archives of American Art.

326 Wissman, 115–17.

327 Cecilia Beaux to her family, January 13, 1889. Cecilia Beaux Papers. Archives of American Art.

328 Ibid.

329 Cecilia Beaux to Eliza Leavitt, March 11, 1889. Cecilia Beaux Papers. Archives of American Art.

330 Ibid.

331 Cecilia Beaux to her family, March 28, 1889. Cecilia Beaux Papers. Archives of American Art.

332 Ibid.

333 Ibid.

334 Cecilia Beaux to William Foster Biddle, April 8, 1889. Cecilia Beaux Papers. Archives of American Art.

335 Cecilia Beaux to Aimée Ernesta Drinker, April 28, 1989. Cecilia Beaux Papers. Archives of American Art.

336 Ibid.

337 Cecila Beaux to Aimée Ernesta Drinker, February 4, 1889. Cecilia Beaux Papers. Archives of American Art.

338 Cecila Beaux to William Foster Biddle, May 1, 1889. Cecilia Beaux Papers. Archives of American Art.

339 Beaux, 178.

340 Cecilia Beaux to her family. January 13, 1889. Cecilia Beaux Papers. Archives of American Art.

341 Raverat, Gwen. *Period Piece* (New York: W.W. Norton & Company, 1952), 20. Maud DuPuy and her family (of French Huguenot extraction) were neighbors of the Leavitts in West Philadelphia. In the spring of 1883, Maud went to Cambridge to stay with her aunt Caroline who was married to Richard Jebb, a professor of Greek at the university. Aunt "Cara" introduced her young niece to the eligible bachelors in Cambridge. Among them was George Darwin. The couple married in 1884. When Beaux visited the family in 1889, the Darwins were busy with the first two of their four children, Gwen (1885) and Charles (1887).

342 Beaux, *Background with Figures*, 180.

343 Cecilia Beaux to May Whitlock, undated. Cecilia Beaux Papers. Archives of American Art.

344 Ibid., 185.

345 Cecilia Beaux to Cecilia Kent Leavitt, July 22, 1889. Cecilia Beaux Papers. Archives of American Art.

346 Oakley, 7.

347 Bowen, 208.

348 Beaux, *Background with Figures*, 193, 194.

349 Ibid., 205.

350 Bowen, 144.

351 Beaux, *Background with Figures*, 204.

352 "A Successful Woman Artist." *New York Journal*. undated. Cecilia Beaux Papers. Archives of American Art.

353 Beaux, *Background with Figures*, 203, 204.

354 Ibid., 196, 197.

355 Ingersoll, Sturgis R. *Henry McCarter* (Cambridge, Massachusetts: privately printed, 1944), 48.

356 Oakley, 7.

357 "Cecilia Beaux Gets Chi Omega Tribute Today." *New York Times*, 1933. Cecilia Beaux Papers. Archives of American Art.

358 Beaux, *Background with Figures*, 206.

359 Ibid.

360 "The Academy of Design: Some of the Paintings in the Sixty-Seventh Annual Exhibition." 1892. Unidentified newspaper clipping. Cecilia Beaux Papers. Archives of American Art.

361 Bowen, 224.

362 Ibid., 118.

363 Bowen, Ezra. *Henry and Other Heroes: An Informal Memoir of High Dreams and Vanished Seasons* (Boston and Toronto: Little Brown and Company, 1968), 135.

364 Ibid., 12.

365 "The Fine Arts: Cecilia Beaux's Paintings at the St. Botolph Club." December 1, 1897. Author and publication unknown. Cecilia Beaux Papers. Archives of American Art.

366 Aimée Ernesta Drinker to Mrs. Bedford, April 10, 1902. Cecilia Beaux Papers. Archives of American Art.

367 "Cecilia Beaux: Philadelphia's Talented Portrait Painter." Cecilia Beaux Papers. Archives of American Art.

368 "Honor to an Artist: Miss Beaux's Election as Instructor at the Academy of the Fine Arts." Unidentified Newspaper Article, 1995. Cecilia Beaux Papers. Archives of American Art.

369 Cecilia Beaux Papers. Archives of American Art. This was a note from a student dated February 26 (no year) and signed: One of your students.

370 Sherwood, Rosina Emmet. Diary entry, 1894. Emmet Family Papers. Archives of American Art.

371 Henry McCarter to Cecilia Beaux, April 20, 1896. Cecilia Beaux Papers. Archives of American Art.

372 The Palais des Beaux-Arts on the Champ-de-Mars was completed in 1889 for the Exposition Universelle. At the first Champ-de-Mars Salon held in 1890, Beaux's friend Alexander Harrison served on the jury.

373 Fink, 122, 123.

374 Hooper, Nettie. "Gossip From the French Capital." Unidentified newspaper article, May 13, 1896. Cecilia Beaux Papers. Archives of American Art.

375 Rochefort, Henri M. "Salon in the Champ de Mars." *New York Herald Tribune*, April 24, 1896. Cecilia Beaux Papers. Archives of American Art.

376 Henry McCarter to Fanny Warton, undated. R. Sturgis Ingersoll Papers. Archives of American Art.

377 Beaux, *Background with Figures*, 202.

378 Ibid.

379 Smith, Herbert F. *Richard Watson Gilder* (New York: Twayne Publishers, Inc., 1970), 151.

380 Ibid.

381 Beaux, *Background with Figures*, 208.

382 Ibid., 210.

383 Ibid., 218.

384 "A Judge at Paris." *Philadelphia Star*. October 24, 1899. Cecilia Beaux Papers. Archives of American Art.

385 Taft, Lorado. "Work of Cecilia Beaux." *Chicago Record*. December 21, 1899. Although Taft's article was published in 1899, his interview with Cecilia Beaux took place in 1898.

386 In her autobiography, Beaux claimed that the problem with her hand caused her no pain. However, in her letters she often discussed how she managed her discomfort.

387 "Art Jury Awards Miss Cecilia Beaux First Prize." *Philadelphia Public Ledger*. November 3, 1899. Cecilia Beaux Papers. Archives of American Art; Dorothea Gilder Papers. Archives of American Art.

388 Cecilia Beaux to Dorothea Gilder, Sunday, July 1, 1900. Dorothea Gilder Papers. Archives of American Art.

389 Ibid.

390 Cecilia Beaux to Dorothea Gilder, January 4, 1901. Dorothea Gilder Papers. Archives of American Art.

391 Cecilia Beaux to Dorothea Gilder, February 18, 1900. Dorothea Gilder Papers. Archives of American Art. Cecilia writes to Dorothea, "Before starting for school for which you are late and hurrying will you please ask Isaac to be sure to go over (taking the keys) and begin to clean the studio and get water."

392 Cecilia Beaux to Dorothea Gilder, March 5, 1902. Dorothea Gilder Papers. Archives of American Art.

393 Dorothea Gilder to Cecilia Beaux, April 4, 1902. Dorothea Gilder Papers. Archives of American Art.

394 Dorothea Gilder to Cecilia Beaux, June 3, 1902. Dorothea Gilder Papers. Archives of American Art.

395 Cecilia Beaux to Dorothea Gilder, June 25, 1902. Dorothea Gilder Papers. Archives of American Art.

396 Cecilia Beaux to Dorothea Gilder, September 22, 1902. Dorothea Gilder Papers. Archives of American Art.

397 Cecilia Beaux to Dorothea Gilder, October 14, 1902. Dorothea Gilder Papers. Archives of American Art.

398 Cecilia Beaux to Dorothea Gilder, Sunday, July 1, 1900. Dorothea Gilder Papers. Archives of American Art.

399 Cecilia Beaux to Dorothea Gilder, October 20, 1902. Dorothea Gilder Papers. Archives of American Art.

400 Cecilia Beaux to Dorothea Gilder, March 27, 1902. Dorothea Gilder Papers. Archives of American Art.

401 Beaux, *Background with Figures*, 228.

402 Ibid., 231.

403 Ibid.

404 Sculptor Augustus St. Gaudens told Helena Gilder that Beaux's portrait of Mrs. Roosevelt was "a painting for artists and that others would not like it."

405 "Art: Portraits by Miss Cecilia Beaux at the Durand-Ruel Galleries. An Impressive and Handsome Exhibition." *The Mail and Express*. March 3, 1903. Cecilia Beaux Papers. Archives of American Art.

406 "Miss Cecilia Beaux and Mr. W. M. Chase." *New York Evening Sun*. March 6, 1903. Cecilia Beaux Papers. Archives of American Art.

407 Beaux, *Background with Figures*, 348. Translation, Samantha Mach.

408 Bowen, 76.

409 Drinker, Henry S. *History of the Drinker Family*. (Philadelphia: privately printed, 1961), 82.

410 Ibid.

411 Ibid., 81, 85.

412 Cecilia Beaux to Dorothea Gilder, January 24, 1904. Dorothea Gilder Papers. Archives of American Art.

413 Beaux diary, December 24, 1911. Cecilia Beaux Papers. Archives of American Art.

414 Ibid.

415 Beaux, *Background with Figures*, 388.

416 Beaux was not the first artist to set up a summer studio in Cape Ann. American painters who proceeded her included Gloucester native Fitz Hugh Lane (1804–1865), Winslow Homer (1836–1910), who first painted in Cape Ann in the 1870s, and her friend Stephen Parrish (1846–1938), who rented studio space in the same building where Beaux painted *Les Derniers Jours d'Enfance*.

417 Hayden, Parker E., and Gray, Andrew L. Beauport. *Chronicle: The Intimate Letters of Henry Davis Sleeper to Abram Piatt Andrew, Jr. 1906–1915* (Boston: Society for the Preservation of New England Antiquities, 1991), 112.

418 Tappert, 403.

419 Harris, Géné. *Thornton Oakley* (Chadds Ford, PA: The Brandywine River Museum of the Brandywine Conservancy, 1983), 13.

420 Oakley, 1.

421 Henry McCarter to Fanny Warton, undated. R. Sturgis Ingersoll Papers. Archives of American Art.

422 Cecilia Beaux to Dorothea Gilder, January 24, 1904. Dorothea Gilder Papers. Archives of American Art.

423 Oakley, 3.

424 Beaux, *Background with Figures*, 341.

425 Ibid.

426 Ibid., 339.

427 Beaux diary, August 11, 12, 1912. Cecilia Beaux Papers. Archives of American Art.

428 "Le Beau Port" was the original name given to the area by French explorer Samuel de Champlain when he sailed into the harbor in 1604.

429 "Cecilia Beaux, Her Work and Ideals." *Boston Herald.* September 25, 1910. Cecilia Beaux Papers. Archives of American Art.

430 Bowen, 205.

431 Drinker, Henry S., 82.

432 Anna Murphy also worked in the studio and often helped Beaux stretch her canvases.

433 *Boston Herald.* September 25, 1910. Cecilia Beaux Papers. Archives of American Art.

434 Beaux diary, Saturday, August 28, 1909. Cecilia Beaux Papers. Archives of American Art.

435 Hayden, 12.

436 Beaux diary, Wednesday, March 15, 1912. Cecilia Beaux Papers. Archives of American Art.

437 Hayden, 30.

438 Henri, Robert. *The Art Spirit* (New York: Harper & Row, Publishers, 1984), 26.

439 Perlman, 90.

440 Gertrude Vanderbilt Whitney's collection of American art formed the nucleus of the Whitney Museum, which she founded in 1930.

441 Perlman, 154.

442 Ibid., 180.

443 Beaux diary, Friday, January 20, 1912. Cecilia Beaux Papers. Archives of American Art.

444 "Corcoran Exhibit," *New York Evening Post.* December 28, 1912. Archives of American Art.

445 Mathews, Nancy Mowll. "The Greatest Woman Painter: Cecilia Beaux, Mary Cassatt, and Issues of Female Fame." *The Pennsylvania Magazine of History and Biography*, Vol CCXXIV, No.3 (Philadelphia: The Historical Society of Pennsylvania, 2000.), 296.

446 Beaux diary, January 18, 1912. Cecilia Beaux Papers. Archives of American Art.

447 Oakley. 3.

448 Cecilia Beaux to Thornton Oakley, February 3, 1909. Thornton Oakley Papers. Archives of American Art.

449 Beaux diary, Friday, March 3, 1911. Cecilia Beaux Papers. Archives of American Art.

450 Faderman, Lillian. *Odd Girls and Twilight Lovers: A History of Lesbian Life in Twentieth Century America.* (New York: Penguin Books, 1991), 32.

451 Beaux diary, April 12, 1911. Cecilia Beaux Papers. Archives of American Art.

452 Ibid.

453 At a New Year's Day party in 1912, Beaux was surrounded by admiring men and noted in her diary, "I felt almost too free among admiring eyes and bending over heads. This should not happen often. I should deceive myself and think I could have it and that it was not too late for EYES." Beaux diary, April 12, 1911. Cecilia Beaux Papers. Archives of American Art.

454 Beaux diary, May 20, 1911. Cecilia Beaux Papers. Archives of American Art.

455 Cecilia Beaux to Dorothea Gilder, May 20, 1911. Dorothea Gilder Papers. Archives of American Art.

456 Cecilia Beaux to Thornton Oakley, February 15, 1925. Thornton Oakley Papers. Archives of American Art.

457 Cecilia Beaux to Dorothea Gilder, July 27, 1910. Dorothea Gilder Papers. Archives of American Art.

458 Cortissoz, Royal. "The Post-Impressionist Illusion," *Century*, 85, April 1913, 805–810, 812, 814, 815. Reprinted in Roderick Nash, ed. *The Call of the Wild (1900–1916)* (New York: George Braziller, 1970).

459 Cecilia Beaux to Henry Sandwith Drinker, June 9, no year indicated. Henry Sandwith Drinker Papers. Archives of American Art.

460 Cecilia Beaux to Dorothea Gilder, May, 1916. Dorothea Gilder Papers. Archives of American Art.

461 Gray, Allison. "The Extraordinary Career of Cecilia Beaux." *American Magazine*, ca. 1922. Cecilia Beaux Papers. Archives of American Art.

462 Rough draft of an address delivered by Cecilia Beaux at the Contemporary Club, "Opening According to First Speaker." January 11, 1926. Cecilia Beaux Papers. Archives of American Art.

463 *Friends of France 1914–1917 Told by Its Members* (Boston and New York: Houghton Mifflin Co., 1920).

464 Ibid.

465 Oakley, 16.

466 Cecilia Beaux to Aimée Ernesta Drinker, May 29, 1919. Cecilia Beaux Papers. Archives of American Art.

467 Beaux, *Background with Figures*, 238.

468 Cecilia Beaux to Aimée Ernesta Drinker, July 7, 1919. Cecilia Beaux Papers. Archives of American Art.

469 Beaux, *Background with Figures*, 248.

470 Cecilia Beaux to Aimée Ernesta Drinker, July 7, 1919. Cecilia Beaux Papers. Archives of American Art.

471 Beaux, *Background with Figures*, 243. "Madame, you are at home."

472 Ibid., 252. "Et vouz continuez encore!"

473 Ibid., 271.

474 Ibid., 273.

475 Ibid., 303.

476 Ibid., 325.

477 Ibid., 331.

478 Ibid., 328.

479 Cecilia Beaux to Aimée Ernesta Drinker, April 27, 1920. Cecilia Beaux Papers. Archives of American Art.

480 Beaux, *Background with Figures*, 285.

481 Gray, Allison. "The Extraordinary Career of Cecilia Beaux," *American Magazine*, c. 1922. Cecilia Beaux Papers. Archives of American Art.

482 Beaux, *Background with Figures*, 295.

483 Ibid.

484 Ibid., 299.

485 Ibid., 236.

486 Cecilia Beaux to Thornton Oakley, July 16, 1923. Thornton Oakley Papers. Archives of American Art.

487 Cecilia Beaux to Thornton Oakley, July 1924. Thornton Oakley Papers. Archives of American Art.

488 Oakley, 20.

489 Beaux, *Background with Figures*, 316.

490 Ibid.

491 Mechlin, Leila. "Notes of Art and Artists." *Sunday Star*, January 26, 1921. Cecilia Beaux Papers. Archives of American Art.

492 Mrs. Sydney L. Wright, Jr., to Thornton Oakley, October 30, 1943. Thornton Oakley Papers. Archives of American Art.

493 Mathews, Nancy Mowll. *Mary Cassatt: A Life* (New Haven and London: Yale University Press, 1998), 322.

494 Oakley, 24.

495 Lowengrund, Margaret. "Life Always Flowed Serenely for Cecilia Beaux and Her Art." *New York Telegram*, undated clipping. Cecilia Beaux Papers. Archives of American Art.

496 "A Victorian Canvas." *Chicago Journal of Commerce*. December 27, 1930. Cecilia Beaux Papers. Archives of American Art.

497 "Background with Figures." *The New Republic*, undated clipping. Cecilia Beaux Papers. Archives of American Art.

498 "Spirituelle." *California Art and Architecture*, undated clipping. Cecilia Beaux Papers. Archives of American Art.

499 Beaux, *Background with Figures*, 219.

500 Oakley, 22.

501 Bowen, 204.

502 Ibid., 210.

503 Gilder Palmer, telephone interview, August 18, 2004.

504 Henry McCarter to Fanny Warton, October 6, 1942. R. Sturgis Ingersoll Papers. Archives of American Art

505 Oakley, 28.

Bibliography

Baigell, Matthew. *A Concise History of American Painting and Sculpture*. New York: Harper and Row, 1984.

Baltzell, Digby E. *Philadelphia Gentlemen: The Making of a National Upper Class*. New Brunswick, NJ, and London: Transaction Publishers, 1989.

Beaux, Cecilia. *Background with Figures*. Boston and New York: Houghton Mifflin Company, 1930.

Bennett, Arnold. *Your United States: Impressions of a First Visit*. New York and London: Harper & Brothers, 1912.

Biddle, Henry D. *The Drinker Family in America: To and Including the Eighth Generation*. Philadelphia, PA: J. B. Lippincott Company, 1893.

Blair, William and William Pencak, eds. *Pennsylvania's Civil War*. University Park, PA: The Pennsylvania State University Press, 2001.

Bowen, Catherine Drinker. *Family Portrait*. Boston and Toronto: Little, Brown and Company, 1970.

Bowen, Ezra. *Henry and Other Heroes: An Informal History of High Dreams and Vanished Seasons*. Boston and Toronto: Little, Brown and Company, 1968.

Brown, Ann Barton. *Alice Barber Stephens: A Pioneer Women Illustrator*. Brandywine River Museum, 1984.

Burns, Sarah. *Inventing the Modern Artist: Art and Culture in Gilded Age America*. New Haven and London: Yale University Press, 1996.

Cable, Mary. *Top Drawer: American High Society From the Gilded Age to the Roaring Twenties*. New York: Atheneum, 1984.

Centennial Souvenir: 1876, Philadelphia. Philadelphia: Ostheimer Bros., 1876.

Clark, Judith Freeman. *America's Gilded Age: An Eyewitness History*. New York and Oxford: Facts on File, 1992.

Contosta, David R. *A Philadelphia Family: The Houstons and Woodwards of Chestnut Hill*. Philadelphia: University of Pennsylvania Press, 1988.

Contosta, David R. *Suburb in the City: Chestnut Hill, Philadelphia, 1859–1990*. Columbus: University of Ohio Press, 1992.

Corn, Wanda M. *The Great American Thing: Modern Art and National Identity, 1915–1935*. Berkeley, Los Angeles, London: University of California Press, 1999.

Cullen, Anthea. *Angel in the Studio: Women in the Arts and Crafts Movement 1870–1914*. London: Astragal Books, 1979.

Davies, Kristian. *Artists of Cape Ann: A 150 Year Tradition*. Rockport, MA: Twin Lights Publishers, 2001.

Drinker, Henry S. *The Paintings and Drawings of Cecilia Beaux*. Philadelphia: The Pennsylvania Academy of the Fine Arts, 1955.

Dusinberre, William. *Civil War Issues in Philadelphia 1856–1865*. Philadelphia: University of Pennsylvania Press, 1965.

Dastlake, Charles L. *Hints on Household Taste*. New York: Dover, 1969.

Faderman, Lillian. *Odd Girls and Twilight Lovers: A History of Lesbian Life in Twentieth-Century America*. New York: Penguin Books, 1991.

Falk, Peter Hastings, ed. *The Annual Exhibition Record of the Pennsylvania Academy of the Fine Arts, 1876–1913*. Madison, CT: Sound View Press, 1989.

Fink, Leon, ed. *Major Problems in the Gilded Age and the Progressive Era*. Lexington, MA and Toronto: DC Heath and Company, 1993.

Fink, Lois Marie. *American Art at the Nineteenth-Century Paris Salons*. Cambridge: Cambridge University Press, 1990.

Foster, Kathleen A. and Cheryl Leibold. *Writing About Eakins*. Philadelphia: University of Pennsylvania Press, 1989.

Frankfort, Roberta. *Collegiate Women: Domesticity and Career in Turn-of-the-Century America*. New York: New York University Press, 1977.

Gibbs-Smith, Charles. *The Fashionable Lady in the 19th Century*. London: Her Majesty's Stationary Office, 1960.

Goodrich, Lloyd. *Thomas Eakins*. Cambridge, MA and London: Harvard University Press, 1982.

Hamerton, Philip Gilbert. *Thoughts About Art*. Boston: Roberts Brothers, 1871.

Harding, J. D. *Lessons on Art*. London: W Kent & Co, 1866.

Harris, Géné E. *Thornton Oakley*. Chadds Ford, PA: Brandywine River Museum of the Brandywine Conservancy, 1983.

Hayden, E. Parker Jr. and Andrew L. Gray. *Beauport Chronicle: The Intimate Letters of Henry Davis Sleeper to Abram Piatt Andrew, Jr. 1906–1915*. Boston: Society for the Preservation of New England Antiquities, 1991.

Hellerstein, Erna Olafson, Leslie Parker Hume, and Karen M Offen, eds. *Victorian Women: A Documentary Account of Women's Lives in Nineteenth-Century England, France, and the United States*. Stanford, CA: Stanford University Press, 1981.

Henderson, Helen. *The Pennsylvania Academy of the Fine Arts and Other Collections of Philadelphia*. Boston: L. C. Page & Company, 1911.

Henri, Robert. *The Art Spirit*. Reprint. 1923. New York: Harper & Row, 1984.

Hershberg, Theodore, ed. Philadelphia: *Work, Space, Family, and Group Experience in the Nineteenth Century*. New York and Oxford: Oxford University Press, 1981.

Horowitz, Helen Lefkowitz. *Alma Mater: Design and Experience in the Women's Colleges From Their Nineteenth-Century Beginnings to the 1930s*. New York: Alfred A. Knopf, 1984.

Huddleston, Sisley. *Paris Salons, Cafés, Studios: Being Social, Artistic and Literary Memories*. New York: Blue Ribbon Books, 1928.

Huneker, James. *Chopin: The Man and His Music*. 1900. Reprint. New York: Dover Publications, Inc. 1966.

Ingersoll, R. Sturgis. *Henry McCarter*. Cambridge, MA: Riverside Press, 1944.

Lane, Roger. *Violent Death in the City: Suicide, Accident and Murder in Nineteenth-Century Philadelphia*. Columbus: Ohio State University Press, 1979.

Leibold, Cheryl. and Tara Leigh Tappert, eds. "Cecilia Beaux: Philadelphia Artist." *The Pennsylvania Magazine of History and Biography* 124, no. 3 (July 2000), 246–418.

Letheve, Jaques. *The Daily Life of French Artists*. New York and Washington: Praeger Publishers, 1968.

Levy, Florence N. *The National Art Committee Exhibition of War Portraits*. The National Art Committee, 1921.

Lister, Raymond. *Victorian Narrative Paintings*. New York: Clarkson N. Potter, Inc., 1966.

Lucas, E. V. *Edwin Austin Abbey: Royal Academician*. New York and London: Charles Scribner's Sons and Methuen and Company Limited, 1921

Maddow, Ben. *A Sunday Between Wars: The Course of American Life from 1865 to 1917*. New York and London: W. W. Norton and Company, 1979.

Martinez, Katherine, and Page Talbott, eds. *Philadelphia's Cultural Landscape: The Sartain Family Legacy*. Philadelphia: Temple University Press, 2000.

Mather, Frank Jewett Jr., Charles Rufus Morey, and William James Henderson. *The Pageant of America: The American Spirit in Art*. New Haven, CT: Yale University Press, 1927.

Mathews, Nancy Mowll. *Mary Cassatt: A Life*. New Haven and London: Yale University Press, 1998.

McHenry, Margaret. *Thomas Eakins Who Painted*. Oreland, PA: privately printed, 1946.

Melendy, Mary Ries. *Vivilore: The Pathway to Mental and Physical Perfection*. W. R. Vansani, 1904.

Michaelis, David. *N. C. Wyeth: A Biography*. New York: Alfred A. Knopf, 1998.

Morgan, Wayne H. ed. *The Gilded Age: A Reappraisal.* Syracuse, NY: Syracuse University Press, 1963.

Oakley, Thornton. *Cecilia Beaux*. Philadelphia: Howard Biddle Printing Company, 1943.

O'Gorman, James F., Jeffrey A. Cohen, George E. Thomas, and G. Holmes Perkins. *Drawing Toward Building: Philadelphia Architectural Graphics, 1732–1986*. Philadelphia: University of Pennsylvania Press, 1986.

Olson, Stanley. *John Singer Sargent: His Portrait*. New York: St. Martin's Griffin, 1986.

Pennell, Joseph. *The Adventures of an Illustrator*. Boston: Little, Brown and Company, 1925.

Perlman, Bennard B. *The Immortal Eight*. Westport, CT: North Light Publishers, 1979.

Philadelphia: Three Centuries of American Art. Philadelphia: Philadelphia Museum of Art, 1976.

Pitz, Henry C. *Howard Pyle: Writer, Illustrator, Founder of the Brandywine School*. New York: Clarkson N. Potter, Inc., 1975.

Pollock Griselda. *Mary Cassatt: Painter of Modern Women.* London: Thames and Hudson, 1998.

Repplier, Agnes. *Philadelphia: The Place and the People*. New York: The Macmillan Company, 1898.

Reverat, Gwen. *Period Piece*. New York: W. W. Norton & Company, 1952.

Rommell, John and E. M. Berlin. *Aims and Ideas of Representative American Painters*. Buffalo, NY: E. M. Berlin, 1901.

Sandhurst, Phillip T. *The Great Centennial Exhibition Critically Described and Illustrated*. Philadelphia and Chicago: P. W. Zeigler & Co, 1876.

Sartain, John. *The Reminiscences of a Very Old Man*. New York: D. Appleton and Company, 1899.

Smith, Herbert F. *Richard Watson Gilder*. New York: Twain Publishers Inc., 1970.

Sproat, John G. *The Best Men: Liberal Reformers in the Gilded Age*. New York: Oxford University Press, 1968.

Tappert, Tara Leigh. *Cecilia Beaux and the Art of Portraiture*. Washington and London: Smithsonian Institution Press, 1995.

______. *Choices—The Life and Career of Cecilia Beaux: A Professional Biography*. PhD diss., George Washington University, 1990.

Taylor, Frank H., ed. *The City of Philadelphia as It Appears in 1893*. Philadelphia: George S. Harris and Sons for the Trade Leagues of Philadelphia, 1893.

Tharp, Louise Hall. *Saint-Gaudens and the Gilded Era.* Boston and Toronto: Little, Brown and Company, 1969.

Thompson, Eleanor Wolf. *Education for Ladies 1830–1860*. New York: Kings Crown Press, 1947.

Visitors Guide to the Centennial Exhibition and Philadelphia: May 10 to November 10, 1876. Philadelphia: J. B. Lippincott & Co., 1876.

Wallace, David Rains. *The Bonehunters' Revenge: Dinosaurs, Greed, and the Greatest Scientific Feud of the Gilded Age*. Boston and New York: Houghton Mifflin Company, 1999.

Watson, John F. *Annals of Philadelphia and Pennsylvania in the Olden Time*. Philadelphia: J. M. Stoddart & Company, 1881.

Weisberg, Gabriel P. and Jane R. Becker, eds. *Overcoming All Obstacles: The Women of the Académie Julian*. New York. New Brunswick, NJ and London: The Dahesh Museum and Rutgers University Press, 1999.

Wilmerding, John. *American Views: Essays on American Art*. Princeton, NJ: Princeton University Press, 1991.

Wilson, Lisa. *Life After Death: Widows in Pennsylvania 1750–1850*. Philadelphia: Temple University Press, 1992.

Wissman, Fronia E. *Bouguereau*. San Francisco: Pomegranate Artbooks, 1996.

Acknowledgments

Cecilia Beaux proved to be an enigmatic, complex individual, and several years passed before I was able to understand her either as a woman or as an artist. I was sustained throughout a longer journey than I had anticipated by the support of many people. Chief among them are Cheryl Leibold and Barbara Katus at the Pennsylvania Academy of the Fine Arts, whose generosity made this project possible. Also pivotal were the contributions of friends and relatives of Cecilia Beaux and her contemporaries, whose recollections introduced me to the woman herself. I am indebted to Cecilia Saltonstall, Ernesta Ballard, Sarah Chapman, Gilder Palmer, Barbara Palmer, Nini Gilder, Mrs. Landsdale Humphreys, Jack B. Bacon, and Frederick D. Hill for sharing information, artwork, and memories.

Jane Glover at the Fine Arts Museums of San Francisco, Margaret Downs Hrabe at the University of Virginia Library, Margaret Kimball at Stanford University Library, James Craig at the Cape Ann Historical Association, Ilhan Citak at Lehigh University, Tamara Johnston at Bryn Mawr College, Laura Libert at the Masonic Museum of Pennsylvania, and the staff at the Pennsylvania Historical Society were also supportive during the research phase of this undertaking. Philippe Chapelin provided genealogical research on the Beaux family, Samantha Mach contributed graceful French-to-English translations, and Hawk Krall worked on photography and research in Philadelphia.

Museums and private collections around the world house Beaux's paintings, and assembling a representative sample required the cooperation of many people. Kristin Smith at the National Portrait Gallery and Sylvia Yount at the High Museum in Atlanta were especially helpful. During a long search for photographs of Beaux's student days in Paris, Christophe Emmanuel Del Debbio and Frank Verpoorten were patient and accommodating. Fellow author and publisher John Fleskes was more than obliging, taking time out of his own schedule to scan several of the images that appear in this book.

My agent, John Campbell, was the first person to imagine that a biography of Cecilia Beaux was a good idea—and he continued to support the project through every possible discouragement. Marlene Strauss and Linda Paulson were the first readers of the manuscript. Their expertise facilitated revisions in California so that by the time the text reached Ellen Cohen and Eva Prinz, my capable editors at Rizzoli, everything was in good order. The splendid design of this book is the work of Eric Mueller, whose exquisite taste and restrained aesthetic are the perfect foil for Beaux's lavish paintings.

I would like to acknowledge my students and colleagues at San Jose State University and my friends and family for their patience and assistance. I am grateful to J. Courtney Granner for sharing the journey to Les Baux with good grace and forbearance. My father, Ben Eisenstat, a great supporter of this project, did not live to see it completed, but my mother, Jane Sperry Eisenstat, helped enough for two. The LeNay family and Theodore and Elizabeth Carter were also steadfast in their encouragement. Finally, I would be remiss not to express my appreciation and admiration for my youngest son, Robert Thurston Carter, who, after putting up with his mother's late nights and early mornings for most of his life, is still determined to become a writer.

—Alice Carter

Index

Note: Page numbers in *italic* indicate art works and photographs.

Cecilia B